W9-DDI-175

MODERN PHILOSOPHY

MODERN PHILOSOPHY

BY

GUIDO DE RUGGIERO

Translated by
A. HOWARD HANNAY, B.A.
AND
R. G. COLLINGWOOD, M.A., F.S.A.
FELLOW AND LECTURER OF PEMBROKE COLLEGE, OXFORD

GREENWOOD PRESS, PUBLISHERS
WESTPORT, CONNECTICUT

Originally published in 1921
by George Allen & Unwin Ltd., London

First Greenwood Reprinting 1969

SBN 8371-2823-4

PRINTED IN UNITED STATES OF AMERICA

TRANSLATORS' PREFACE

FOR several years attention in England has been increasingly directed to the new developments of Italian idealism. The works of Benedetto Croce, the founder of the new school, have nowhere, perhaps, been more welcomed and discussed than here; and his chief books are all now accessible to English readers. But Croce represents the first stage only of the new movement; his position is by no means the last word of the school: it may indeed be said to point out new paths for thought rather than to lay down a final and complete system. The new paths have been followed with very striking results by Giovanni Gentile and Guido de Ruggiero. Gentile has been closely studied by specialists in England for some years, but his works have never been translated, and his name is little known except to professed philosophers; De Ruggiero is even less known, and the present volume represents his first appearance in English.

The interest of this volume is twofold. In the first place, it presents—in outline, it is true, and without detailed discussion—a positive philosophical position of great interest, avowedly in continuation of Croce and in close agreement with Gentile, which sums up the progress of Italian idealism down to the writing of this book, and is the only account so far accessible in English of the recent progress of the school. In the second place, it is a remarkable piece of historical work, and for that reason alone will, we hope, find a welcome from all who are interested in the recent history of thought.

It is perhaps not always realized by readers of Croce that beneath his lucid and easy style, his singularly fresh and spontaneous point of view, lies a very considerable mass of first-class historical scholarship. But on closer inspection it becomes plain that the primary characteristic, the very backbone of Italian idealism, is a historical training of the most thoroughgoing kind. Idealism for these Italians, as it was for Hegel, is a philosophy deeply rooted in history, and claims to show its superiority to other philosophies in nothing more than in its penetrating study and exposition of history.

The volume now offered to English readers is a striking example of this tendency and this strength. Its subject, the development of European philosophy in the last half of the nineteenth century and the beginning of the twentieth, has not, so far as we are aware, been comprehensively handled by any other writer ; and this fact alone is a tribute to the historical enterprise of Italian philosophy. Of the manner in which it is here handled we need not speak : its merits are sufficiently obvious, and its defect—if trenchant and outspoken criticism is a defect—not less so. Considered merely as a textbook of an exceedingly intricate subject, it is a work which no student of modern thought can afford to ignore ; and, according to the principle which its author shares with Croce and Gentile, if the history is sound the philosophy which inspires it finds in that fact its strongest advocate.

Modern Philosophy was first published in 1912, and it was only the war which prevented this translation from appearing several years ago. For this reason there are certain recent developments which find no place in these pages : the reader will recall among others Dr. Bosanquet's

Gifford Lectures and the rise of Anglo-American realism. But a history cannot remain up to date for ever, and it seemed better to publish the book as it stands, with the very definite unity which it possesses, than to ask the author to insert a paragraph here and there, which would impair the unity for the sake of very slight additions.

Finally, it ought to be said that in translating we have, with the author's full consent, from time to time expanded or paraphrased a passage which in its original form, though doubtless plain to an Italian, might have been obscure to an English reader. We venture to hope that a comparison of these passages with the original will show that we have faithfully represented the author's meaning.

A. H. H.
R. G. C.

March 1920.

CONTENTS

PART I

GERMAN PHILOSOPHY

CHAPTER I

CHAPTER II

CHAPTER III

PART II

FRENCH PHILOSOPHY

CHAPTER I

CHAPTER II

CHAPTER III

CONTENTS

CHAPTER IV

CHAPTER V

CHAPTER VI

PART III

ANGLO-AMERICAN PHILOSOPHY

CHAPTER I

INTRODUCTION

THE metaphysic which towards the beginning of the nineteenth century grew out of the Kantian idealism was a radical
criticism of the philosophy which underlay the Enlightenment and the Revolution. Oblivious of its own true character,
thought had, as it were, materialized itself into a barren
universalism, a tissue of abstract humanitarian ideals : it
now sprang into new life with the rediscovery of its own
historical nature and of the concrete and individual character
of its development. Among the greatest achievements of
this metaphysic was the recognition of the national character
of thought. This was no mere acquiescence in a narrowly
parochial outlook ; it was something much deeper, namely
the realization that humanity in general only exists in
individuals, and that only in the acquisition of concrete
individual form can the mind achieve its true universality.

This constituted a great step in advance : indeed, it was
premature, appearing as it did only a few years after the
declaration of the Rights of Man. Even its authors were
blind to its full significance, and very soon obscured it
altogether—Hegel with a misdirected spirit of patriotism
which made Germany the centre of the world : the historical
school of jurisprudence by relapsing into a kind of Platonism
and losing itself in a world of vague and sentimental ideals.

The subsequent development of philosophy was not in
keeping with this starting-point : although it maintained
the absolutely concrete and historical character of thought,
it nevertheless sullied its stream by carrying with it the
undissolved residue of the old abstract philosophies. The
naturalism which reasserted itself after the speculative
movement of Kant and Hegel is a sure symptom of that

internal conflict in which thought is involved when confronted
by unsolved problems ; but the peculiar thing about naturalism is that it expresses the conflict in the form of a dogma,
and offers as a definite solution what is really the incipient
doubt, which becomes more definite as the problem takes
shape.

The beginnings of naturalism are to be traced back to
the Hegelian philosophy itself, in which the merely mechanical
development of the dialectic in many parts of the system
and the introduction of the *caput mortuum* of the philosophy
of nature simply concealed the unsolved problems of which
they claimed to be the solutions.   But we can observe this
still better in the philosophy immediately following Hegel,
as we shall very soon see.   The completest form of modern
naturalism is the product of the empirical sciences, and
especially of biology.   The reason for this is clear.   Post-
Kantian idealism was a metaphysic of knowledge which sought
to resolve the object of thought into the act of thinking.
The naturalism which followed and contradicted it was an
anthropological naturalism which tried to disprove the originality and spontaneity of thought by deducing it from the
biological and organic conditions of the human individual.

This naturalistic movement destroyed all sense of the
historical character of thought.   Absolutely anti-historical
and impersonal, it introduced a new abstract philosophy,
a philosophy of ideal forms outside the process of history.
The keynote of its method was the conception of " laws
of nature," understood as a system of realities existing
objectively *ab æterno* ; and its political correlative was that
latest form of socialism which, having renounced all association with its own earlier phase as uncomfortably reminiscent
of the historical interpretation of the world, entered into
an alliance with positivism.

In its very beginnings we see reflected the impersonal
and anti-historical character of this naturalistic philosophy.
It did not develop, in the proper sense of the word, but
merely increased in bulk by the sedimentary accretion of
elements from outside : it did not appear in the different
countries as the continuation of a spontaneous historical
movement, but spread like a flood from one country into

another, nowhere displaying any peculiar local characteristics, but maintaining everywhere the same level. We can see this already in the philosophy immediately following Hegel, which was rapidly transplanted into the various countries of Europe, even where the existing historical traditions of thought rendered assimilation almost impossible. This is the surest sign of its naturalistic character, because a philosophy like the Hegelian, which was the culminating point of a very special historical development, could only have been transplanted into such different surroundings at the cost of losing all that was most characteristic and vital in it.

The naturalism which sprang from the empirical sciences spread in exactly the same way, but on a larger scale. The forms it assumed in each country were precisely similar. German naturalism differed in no respect from French, nor did French from English, and so on. Not one of them displayed any special peculiarity of its own except in so far as it was the thought of a particular subject, that is to say a process of individualization. But the object, being an abstract universal, was incapable of displaying any correlative uniqueness. And so we see this philosophy growing in every country during the whole of the nineteenth century, by the mere aggregation of ideas, each exponent of it influencing all the others. Mill, Spencer, Comte, Fechner and Haeckel were all successfully acclimatized to every environment, and everywhere they found successors and disciples.

But while in its attempt to abjure history naturalism did nothing more than erect into a final conclusion what was in fact only a conflict of ideas, this conflict was finding a solution in another field. The criticism of the Revolutionary philosophy which had been outlined by the great German idealists was born before its time and never completed ; but the problem was attacked once more, and this time successfully, in the sphere of practical politics.

The organization of nationalities is the true criticism of the abstract universalism which dominated the eighteenth century. This historical process, which is still going on to-day, was just beginning at the moment when Hegel thought it had already reached its close and its culmination

in Germany. And thus Hegel, who compared philosophy
to the owl of Minerva which spreads its wings at dusk—
when a historical movement is concluded—really heralded
with his own philosophy the dawn of the whole historical
development of the nineteenth century. This is explained
when we reflect that his philosophy was the outcome of that
ferment of ideas which marked the political redemption of
Germany, and that his all-absorbing patriotism led him to
mistake a mere premonitory upheaval for the consummation
of the entire process.

The self-assertion of nationalities and their achievement
of political unity was thus the work of the whole nineteenth
century. The process admirably exemplifies the real nature
of individuality ; which implies, not that the universal,
human nature, is frittered away into a number of independent
and atomistic fragments, but that, on the contrary, the universal attains concrete existence for the first time in the life
of the nation ; since it is only through the differences between
peoples and the unique historical development of each that
their profound human identity is truly demonstrated.

The philosophy of this new era in history is thus a national
philosophy. Criticizing the anti-historical and impersonal
tendency of naturalism, it springs from the traditional
thought of each separate people, and thus represents in the
spontaneity and originality of its growth the theoretical or
self-conscious aspect of this historical movement towards
the differentiation of nationalities. German, French, English
and Italian philosophy each reasserts its continuity with
its past, and from this continuity each derives its power.
It strikes one at first sight as an extraordinary thing, but
on reflection it becomes comprehensible enough, that these
philosophies have grown up in almost entire mutual isolation
and mutual ignorance. The idealism of Ravaisson and
Lachelier, on which the whole of modern French philosophy
is based, remained for years unknown outside France ; and
when it became known it had no real influence. J. H. Stirling
and T. H. Green are unknown in Germany and France, Italian
philosophy is a dead letter outside Italy. These are merely
a few examples, but anyone with the slightest knowledge
of the subject can verify the truth of my statement. In

the last few years there have been signs of a more lively exchange of thought, but it does not go beyond a superficial acquaintance, nor offer scope for anything like a real cross-fertilization. The attempt to acclimatize systems such as pragmatism, intuitionism and their like in foreign soil results in the production of deformities which are very quickly thrown aside by the movement of thought. That alone can maintain itself as a living philosophy whose life is bound up with the history of its own past, a past verified by the creative thought of the present. In complete contrast with the anti-historical naturalism, which, as a mere abstract universal devoid of any spiritual inwardness, was easily spread abroad as if by a mechanical force, these new growths of thought have sprung up, each the expression of a new-born national soul, and each with its own unique rhythm of development. Thus the task which lies before us begins to take form. We must trace each stream back to its source, follow its movement and disclose the immanent criticism which determines its direction and ultimate goal.

We have spoken of the nationality of thought, but we do not want this phrase to be misunderstood. It is not a question of the naturalistic idea of the race, but of the idealistic concept of the spirit. Inasmuch as it is concrete universality, the spirit lives by individualizing itself in history : and in creating its own history as a process of individualization it creates itself. The spirit, then, is not pure static and motionless thought outside history ; it is its own history. The modern spirit is therefore that process of individualization, which we call modern nationality, in which each nation sums up the whole of its own past in the individualized life of the present.

But our recognition of this element of difference, in virtue of which contemporary thought develops on divergent lines, must not blind us to the spiritual identity underlying the various tendencies. It is one and the same thought which is developing in different directions, and it is this fact that constitutes its indissoluble unity, a far profounder unity than any resulting from the superficial exchange of ideas and influences. From this point of view the history of thought appears in a new light. We shall see that although each philosophy develops on its own special lines, the philosophies of the different countries are all stating the same problems and endeavouring to satisfy the same needs. Widely though they differ in speculative ability, the central points round which they severally revolve are, we shall find, in the last resort identical. They are simply the various ways in which this or that national consciousness envisages one and the same group of fundamental problems—whether we call them theoretical or practical problems makes no difference—and upon these problems the apparently isolated lines of thought which we are to analyse are in reality converging.

Of course, every nation does not contribute in equal measure to the life of thought. We shall see that Germany has lagged behind, while France, England and Italy advance more abreast. But thought is not quantitatively measurable. Tested by its contribution to the development of constructive doctrine, German philosophy is of little account : but its main effort has been directed to the criticism of its own inadequate constructions and to clearing the way for new and higher truths. From this point of view its contribution, though negative, is directed to the same end as that of other national schools, and is of no less value. The identity of thought does not eliminate diversity ; it necessitates it ; and at the same time it assigns to each nation its part in the concert of civilization. This apportionment is not deterministic or mechanical ; it is not the decree of an external force, but the work of thought itself, unfolding its universality in the individuality of its forms.

In conclusion, it may be of some aid to the reader if we summarize briefly the course we propose to follow, the justification of which must be found in the actual development of contemporary thought. We shall begin by describing the decay of classical idealism and the rise of the naturalistic philosophy, and we shall try to discover the cause and the meaning of this double process. We shall then deal with the revival of idealistic speculation which followed upon the dissolution of naturalism, but brought with it new exigencies which proved that naturalism had not existed in vain. We shall follow the individual development of each of these movements of thought, tracing them back to the earliest stages of their existence ; and finally, we shall try to indicate the profound identity which underlies this variety, and to locate the centres of force towards which all these thrusts are directed. Such is our task ; it is no light one, but the attempt is worth making.

PART I

GERMAN PHILOSOPHY

CHAPTER I

ANTIMETAPHYSIC AND NATURALISM

§ 1. The Decay of Idealism.

THE interval between Kant and Hegel was as brief as that between Plato and Aristotle. When we reflect how many centuries of philosophical thought had to elapse before the gulf was bridged between the doctrine of the Idea and that of the Pure Act, we shall not be astonished that post-Hegelian philosophers without exception failed not only to understand the Hegelian system, but even to regain the road towards it which Fichte and Schelling had traced out. Those who derived their inspiration most directly from Hegel either confined themselves to the function of interpreters and commentators, in which they did not display any great insight, or, once having mastered the simple mechanism of the dialectic, gave themselves up to fantastic and irresponsible system-building.

It would be too naïve an error to suppose that these harmless system-builders and literal commentators deserve either the praise or the blame of having discredited idealism and caused the naturalistic and positivist reaction. The truth is that the philosophy of these " epigoni " was itself an expression of that very naturalism and positivism which seemed to rise up threateningly against it. Those who employed the dialectic upon ready-made concepts, and whose chief interest lay in rearranging, with as much aid as they were capable of deriving from Hegel, the mass of heterogeneous material which they took over from the empirical sciences, were much nearer than they believed to the new world-builders who were appearing, armed with the weapons of induction and generalization. There was little to choose between the intoxication of facts and the intoxication of formulæ, once the facts had themselves, under the clumsy hand of an unskilful operator, turned into formulæ, promising truth yet pregnant with mystery.

And, on the other hand, both tendencies were equally far removed from that idealism, the object of which was to analyse the inmost nature of fact by resolving it into the actual process of thinking. Whether the network in which they enclosed fact was that of induction or that of the dialectic, in either case it was a mere network, a mere classification ; the thought travelled round the facts instead of penetrating them. The title of naturalism thus belongs to both schools.

For a short time in Germany the illusion that the Hegelians and the anti-Hegelians represented two diametrically opposed tendencies of thought was allowed to last. And it is true that those Hegelians who devoted themselves to the history of philosophy, like Rosenkranz, Michelet, Lasson and Fischer, did all preserve, in however attenuated a form, the traditions of the school. But it is not to these that we must turn for the first signs of the influence of Hegelism on German thought : feeble echoes of a powerful voice, these historians were very soon driven from the highroads of philosophy. In order to see the immediate and direct effect of Hegelism, and at the same time the palpable proof of its radical transformation, we must rather study cases in which the doctrine was first drawn, so to speak, from its sheath and brought into contact with the problems and interests which were occupying men's minds.

Foremost came the religious problem, which was brought to a head by the very fact of the progress made in the empirical sciences and by new discoveries which seemed to jeopardize the existence of the supernatural. This problem, as everyone knows, divided the Hegelians into two wings, the right and the left. The latter was by far the most important, and included men of such different talents and tendencies as Ruge, Bauer, Strauss and Feuerbach ; but all its members agreed in taking up an attitude of hostility towards the supernatural and towards institutional religion. Although they recognized no other dress but the Hegelian, yet inside this dress there moved the new naturalism. The fact that they identified the dialectical negation of religion with the materialistic negation of the supernatural shows how completely Hegelism had been turned upside down by contact with the new doctrines derived from natural science.

Such inversions of Hegelian doctrines are common in the history of this period, and always betray the same fundamental tendency of thought. Haym, for instance, denied that the dialectic was the foundation of all life, physical and mental, and asserted that, on the contrary, physical and mental life was the foundation of the dialectic. A familiar instance is the trajectory described by Feuerbach, whose thought passed from God to reason and finally to man. But the most remarkable example of this inversion is provided by the authors of what is known as historical materialism, Marx and Engels, who, after accepting the dialectic, proceeded to maintain that consciousness does not explain the being of man, but that the being of man explains consciousness.

The same change was taking place outside the Hegelian school. Herbartianism, for instance, originally a speculative doctrine, was gradually losing all its philosophical character under the chilling influence of mathematical and psychological methods. The Aristotelian Trendelenburg, again, tried to effect a compromise between spirit and nature in the form of the concept of movement, and failed to perceive that his mediator was no mediator at all, being itself merely nature : so that, while he believed that he was building a bridge between nature and spirit, he was really reducing spirit to nature. Similarly the historian Ueberweg, after struggling for years to maintain an eclectic position between idealism and realism, finally lapsed into pure and simple materialism.

The students of the special sciences, history, jurisprudence and sociology, were the least liable to lapses of this kind. Living as they did on intimate terms with concrete realities, it was easier for them to preserve the idealistic attitude with which they had started, and they were less inclined to shackle themselves within the *schemata* of naturalism. It would be interesting to follow up these offshoots of idealism in the works of great historians like Mommsen, Ranke and

Ihering. Their thought always transcends the formulæ in which they profess to confine it ; and even when they declare themselves positivists and naturalists, they are very far from accepting the doctrines of the philosophical schools so entitled. A vein of idealism, again, however much attenuated and inclined to evaporate into a certain abstractness, is discernible in the two founders of the so-called psychology of peoples, Lazarus and Steinthal. But their theories, born out of due time and suffocated by the dominant naturalism against which they were unable to struggle, had little influence in their day, and have only lately been taken up again owing to the revival of the historical attitude of mind.

It must not be imagined that the transition in German philosophy from idealism to naturalism, which we have sketched above, was effected by a sudden change ; it came about rather by a gradual transformation. It would be a serious error to overlook the gulf that separated a man like Strauss or Marx from one like Büchner or Dühring. The former passed their lives in an intellectual environment in which the sense for history was deeply rooted ; and their conversion to naturalism had a unique character which marks them out from others and renders the process interesting to the historian. We shall therefore examine a few of the instances of this transformation which have most significance for the development of German thought.

§ 2. THE TÜBINGEN SCHOOL.

The founder of the theological school of Tübingen, F. C. Baur, derived his original inspiration from Hegel and Schleiermacher. From the former he got the idea of the history of religion, from the latter the foundations of dogmatic theology. Like Hegel, he was convinced that without speculation historical research cannot go beyond the superficial aspect of things, and that the more the historical subject belongs to the domain of the spirit, the more important it becomes not merely to reproduce what individuals have done and thought, but to re-think in oneself the eternal thoughts of the eternal spirit whose working is history.[1]

[1] E. Zeller, *C. Bauer et l'Ecole de Tubingue*, French tr., Patel, 1883, p. 52.

This at any rate was his programme, but it was never carried out. The deeper Baur penetrated in his historical studies, the farther did his analytical tendency of thought take him from anything like a synthesis, and the more inclined did he become to break up the reality of the religious experience of the ages into its component parts. Most painstaking in the search after facts and proofs, most punctilious in the distinction of historical truth from legend, he ended by losing sight of the significance of religious development and undermining with his criticism the entire structure of Christology. He believed that he could vindicate the element of human reality and historical fact in religion without in any way prejudicing the element of divine truth and the transcendental significance of the facts ; for his own work, he believed, was purely historical and independent of any theological presuppositions. The truth was exactly the opposite. For the very desire to distinguish the historical fact from its transcendental significance implied a theological presupposition ; and on the other hand the naturalistic procedure of historical research, issuing as it did in the reduction of a divine history to a merely human history, was bound to destroy the meaning of the divine history simultaneously with its truth. If no glimpse of the divine shines through historical fact, there is no hope of our being able to detect it elsewhere. In history there cannot be both a kernel and a shell : history is either all kernel or all shell. In vain do those who can only see in it the latter imagine something existing beyond it, perceptible by other means.

But Baur adhered firmly to this naïve dualism, incompatible though it was with his own philosophy ; and though he always promised himself he would make a historical synthesis, he never made it and was incapable of doing so. The fruit of his methods was very soon manifest in Strauss. Less prudent than his master, and of a still more analytical disposition, in his *Life of Jesus* he simply heaped negation on negation respecting the historical reality of Christ, and ended by reducing it to an empty shadow. Once the shell was removed, could even the tiniest kernel remain ? Baur deceived himself into thinking it could, as though there could be such

a thing as pure inner spirit, entirely divorced from all outward
form : but Strauss was more consistent. On reviewing his
religious beliefs he admitted, in his reply to the first of the
four celebrated questions, that he could no longer call himself
a Christian.   The concept of the personality of God appeared
to him incompatible with the conclusions of modern natural
science.   Nevertheless he continued to believe that the
ruins of Christianity still preserved the fundamental element
of every religion :   the feeling of dependence.   But what,
according to him, was the character of the new God ?   He
was the God of science : not the inexorable Jehovah, but
the universe, rational throughout.   The essence of the new
creed was the consciousness of the intimate relation between
the individual and the whole, a very different thing from
the external relation of which positive religion speaks.
But what exactly is this intimate relation of which Strauss
speaks ?   Man, in his real being, is a personality and can
only have intimate relations with a personality, while the
God of Strauss is impersonal—is nature.   Thus the intimacy
which religion claims for its own is really something quite
different from what religion supposes it to be.   It is the
intimacy experienced by the spirit when it goes outside
itself and communes with the entire reality in which it
lives and has its being : in a word, it is art.   This explains
his invocation to Goethe and the great artists with which
his book on the *Old Faith and the New* concludes.   In Strauss,
naturalism breaks its own bounds and enters the domain
of poetry.

§ 3. Historical Materialism.

The two great personalities of German socialism, Marx
and Engels, effected the same transition from idealism to
naturalism, but in a more drastic and thorough manner.
Taking as their starting-point Hegel's conception of history,
they enunciated a doctrine which was at once the antithesis
and the complement of the visionary communism of St.
Simon, Fourier and Owen.   Their study of the great historical
revolutions of the eighteenth century which had raised to
power the " Third Estate " had warned them against the

facile Utopianism of supposing that the preaching of humanitarian ideals could put an end to the new capitalist organization of society. Their study of Hegel suggested to them that
historical movements do not arise from external and superficial causes, but originate altogether from within ; and that
the true criticism of a social and political order consists
not in the schemes of a theorist, entangled in the net of
his own abstract concepts, but in the practical activity of
the society itself, when it destroys this order and substitutes
another. Every order, through the internal logic of its
development, arrives at a point when it renders its own
continuation impossible, and thus generates the antithetical
conditions by which it will be negated and its transformation
determined into a new form, into a new order which will
contain in itself a solution of the problems raised by the
two superseded moments. Thus in the history of political
economy we are presented first of all with communal ownership of land ; but the development of agriculture itself
renders this communal ownership more and more incompatible with the exigencies of production. It is finally
negated.; and after some intermediate phases private property
is instituted, which satisfactorily meets the new exigencies.

The principles involved in this view of economic history
were applied no less by Marx and Engels to social and
political institutions ; but they did not refine these down
into the mere manifestation and reflection of economic
conditions : this separation of kernel from shell was to be
the work of their degenerate followers, and was incompatible
with their own very delicate historical sense. On the
contrary, far from refining down what they called by the
rather unhappy and ambiguous term of a " superstructure,"
their constant desire was to consolidate it and incorporate
it into the economic structure. In short, they did not
degrade the state and society to the rank of a mere reflection
of economics, but raised economics so as to include in itself
the entire fabric of social and political life. History is in
the eyes of the creators of historical materialism all of a
piece : the divorce found in their immediate successors
between content (economic) and form (juridical, social) has
not yet arisen. The content is not to them lifeless matter ;

on the contrary, it is already form ; it is not the abstraction
of economic science, indifferent to any form, but concrete
economy historically conditioned, which is therefore identical
with the legal and political organization of a particular
historical moment. This is so far true that when a conflict
arises between content and form, and new exigencies of
production expose the inadequacy of the old forms, even then
there is no dualism. The new economic content is not pure
matter which is blindly hurled into new legal and political
forms created out of nothing ; it is matter already organized,
already containing in itself the new form : and it is solely
due to this fact that it can engage in a struggle with the
old form, now ossified and crystallized. This is the reason
for the idealistic character of the so-called materialism of
Marx, a character which eludes those who are themselves
entangled in dualism and are therefore incapable of conceiving the unity of the process of history.

If Marx and Engels had explored this idealistic aspect
of their doctrine further, they would have become convinced
that dialectic is reality in the making, and they would have
protected themselves from the error of anticipating in their
thought the future phases of history, and of thus falsifying
the dialectic by treating as already existent in thought that
which is only coming into existence. But the introduction
of the new naturalistic interest into the fundamentally
idealistic inspiration of their doctrine caused an ambiguity
in their conception of the dialectic. A law of nature is a
" seeing in order to foresee," a continual anticipation of
fact, for even becoming is present to it as a fact ; and under
the influence of the prevalent naturalism Marx began to
model his dialectic unconsciously on the plan of the natural
law. This gave rise to a serious confusion. The conception
of natural law does treat the future as if it already existed :
it presupposes everything to be given ; but precisely on
that account it renounces for ever the claim to conceive
what is actually taking place, the process of history. On
the other hand, a dialectical law which had effected a compromise with naturalism could easily prefer claims in both
fields, conceive the process and anticipate the event, be
both a history of the past and a forecast of the future. This

equivocation explains Marx's generalizations. It was with the penetrating eye of the historian that he traced the rise of the capitalist organizations out of the negation of primitive communism : but it was with the squint of one who would be at the same time both historian and naturalistic philosopher that he foresaw the further negation of capitalism and the birth of the new communism out of this negation of a negation.

Their lively historical sense always saved Marx and Engels from falling into Utopianism, but their successors, as we shall see, very soon did so. No longer sustained by that historical sense, they were more liable to mistake for an immutable doctrine what was merely a transitory position of thought which happened to be peculiarly interesting because it was the expression of two great personalities.

§ 4. The Psychology of Peoples.

This flood of naturalism, which, as we have seen, produced such interesting phenomena when it hurled itself against the old idealistic framework, left none of the ancient movements of thought unaffected ; and where it did not directly molest, it succeeded in damping and discouraging, as it were by its very proximity, all speculative thinking.

This consideration helps to characterize that last off-shoot of the Herbartian philosophy, Lazarus and Steinthal's " psychology of peoples," which of all the philosophical theories in vogue between 1840 and 1860 appeared to be least directly influenced by the new naturalism.   These two men founded in 1860 a review called *Zeitschrift für Völker-psychologie und Sprachwissenschaft*, which, after a few years of bare existence, came to an end amid general indifference. Yet their philosophy was very much superior, at least in originality, to that which has succeeded it and is so immensely popular in Germany to-day : I mean the philosophy of culture propounded by Rickert and his admirers.

In protest against the futile subjectivism of the individualistic and atomistic psychology of the stricter Herbartians, Lazarus and Steinthal attempted to maintain the autonomy and originality of the collective mind or spirit, of the

Volksgeist. Irreducible to single minds, which are not its creators but only its moments,[1] the objective spirit moves in history, develops with it, and is embodied in social orders and institutions. These have their life in history, and history in them. They are not eternal contents of thought, like art and science, but progressive acts of the spirit : and thus they sum up in themselves the whole of human life, in the different moments of its development.[2]

Nevertheless, even for its creators the collective spirit did not represent anything very well defined : it was rather a vague and fluctuating entity which embodied, so to speak, the demand that the human world should be rescued from the tyranny of the natural sciences, but it had no real theoretical basis of its own. It gave a sense of direction to the study, promoted by Lazarus and Steinthal, of religion, mythology, language and social institutions ; and it gave unity and internal coherence to the multiplicity of their phenomena. This conception of the collective spirit, understood as an irreducible historical unity, was made the basis for the distinction between two fundamental types of science : mental sciences, which conceive their object under the form of historical development, and natural sciences, which do not recognize the idea of development.[3] In the latter logical abstraction is predominant, in the former psychological intuition : the latter use general concepts in which the particular appears as an abstract example, the former concrete representations which grasp the particular in the individuality of its being and its becoming.

Such a distinction was possibly sufficient for students of the special sciences, who were thereby enabled in their historical researches on popular mythology, religion and customs to liberate the human reality with which they were dealing from the absurd travesties which the invasion of naturalism had thrust upon it. The recognition of the originality of the creations of the spirit enabled Steinthal to criticize in the field of philology the current fallacies about

[1] M. Lazarus, *Einige syntetische Gedanken zur Völkerpsychologie, Zeitschrift cit.*, 1865, p. 56.

[2] M. Lazarus, *Ueber die Ideen in der Geschichte, ibid.* p. 463.

[3] Lazarus and Steinthal, *Einleitende Gedanken über Völkerpsychologie, Zeitschr. cit.*, 1860, p. 7.

language as a storehouse of wisdom or a copy of thought (as though there were any meaning in " copying thought with the voice "),[1] and many others, and thus to understand the principles on which language organizes itself from within. But although these small achievements and most laudable aims stood for something far higher than mere naturalism, they were not calculated to carry any strong conviction. At bottom the distinction between the natural and mental sciences was purely empirical, and was not the result of genuine research in both fields : it represented rather an attempt on the part of a few serious-minded specialists to escape into a privileged domain, far removed from that of the natural sciences. Materialism and positivism, on the other hand, came forward as comprehensive theories of reality. They did not limit themselves to setting on one side every spiritual element ; they aimed at destroying it. And so, because of their inferiority in this respect, the few dissentient voices were overwhelmed amid the general chorus of naturalism, and were unable to make themselves heard again until much later, when their theories were reintroduced as part of a new general conception of the world.

§ 5. NATURALISM.

To recapitulate. We have witnessed the convergence towards naturalism of the decadent German philosophy. But while it is interesting to follow the curve described by some of the chief personalities belonging to that period of transition, it would be useless to analyse the thought of those who were from the beginning immersed in the turbid waters of naturalism. An essentially impersonal doctrine, naturalism has always absorbed the personalities of its supporters : so that to-day it is with the greatest difficulty that one succeeds in unearthing any particular name, and then it is connected rather with some extravagant or commonplace phrase than with any originality of thought. Nevertheless, in its very impersonal character naturalism is of importance, since it represents a somewhat extensive period

[1] H. Steinthal, *Ueber Charakteristik der Sprachen, Zeitschr. cit.*, 1862, p. 236.

in the history of thought, and one that is complicated by all the preoccupations and the crises which followed upon the period of the great scientific developments.

Just as the materialism of the eighteenth century was the product of the great astronomical discoveries, so the materialism of the nineteenth century proceeded from the development of biological theory, and particularly from the doctrine of evolution and the advances made in the physiology of the nervous system. This fact is of great importance in helping us to understand the reason of the new concentration of thought which followed materialism. The inability of the latter to explain satisfactorily the doctrine about which it was most emphatic, that of the derivative character of sensation, threw its mental character into emphatic relief. This was the sheet-anchor of the new idealism.

Starting from a position which was essentially anti-historical, German naturalism proceeded to display the most unblushing historical ignorance. It would have shown itself more cautious if it had been aware that its pompous and bombastic dogmatism was a mere revival of the position maintained by the philosophy of the Enlightenment, a hundred years before. And this applies not only to the positive doctrines of men like Vogt, Czolbe and Büchner, but also to th negative doctrines of men like Du Bois-Reymond, the author of the famous phrase *Ignoramus, Ignorabimus*. In all these alike, the spirit of the Enlightenment was reincarnate.

But the same ignorance and self-assurance prevailed among thinkers who were not, properly speaking, materialists. The positivist Laas summed up his whole historical experience in the principle that all idealism was at bottom nothing but Platonism : " Was even the Kantian principle of pure apperception so very different from the Platonic *Unum Bonum* ? " [1] Having thus compressed twenty centuries of philosophical speculation into one sentence, he had no difficulty in dismissing the lot with a gesture. No wonder that amid this general ignorance Dühring could so easily succeed in misrepresenting the historical position of his " Philosophy of Reality," an insignificant positivist monism, resembling in all essentials the current materialism. Dühring's

[1] E. Laas, *Idealismus und Positivismus*, Berlin, 1879–84, vol. i., p. 72.

philosophy was bitterly attacked by Engels, who even accused Dühring, amongst other things, of having plagiarized Hegel, by lifting bodily from the *Logic* the framework of his system. As a matter of historical truth this was about the only charge Dühring did not deserve.

Products of a reign of mediocrity, the German materialism and positivism of this period did not occasion any of those great religious crises in which great personalities are revealed. In general, hatred was expressed for the supernatural as being incompatible with the truths of science, and for religious worship and other similar restrictions upon the so-called freedom of thought. Only a few thinkers (Czolbe, for instance) embraced materialism as a moral conviction independently of these irrelevant preoccupations. To compensate for the abolition of religion, the rhetoric of materialism induced a sort of counterfeit piety, an adoration of the new idols of the laboratory or of the telescope. But for religious temperaments of this kind it was a matter of indifference, or, as Lange [1] puts it, a matter of taste, whether they worshipped the masculine " God," or the feminine " Nature " or the neuter " All " : a mere question of grammar.

On the other hand, naturalism led to the most extravagant conclusions in the hands of Fechner, the founder of psychophysics. Long consideration of both aspects of his formula convinced him that reality also had two aspects, a physical and a psychical : and as his metaphysical system only recognized the latter, he maintained that animals, plants, and even stars have souls.[2] This, he admitted, was merely a hypothesis ; but equally hypothetical is our belief in the souls of other men, for these too we neither touch nor see, but only imagine. It was on this irrefragable proof that Fechner founded his pan-psychism.

Although Edouard von Hartmann did not really display any greater understanding or depth of thought, popular opinion has, with an unconscious and cruel irony, raised him to the position of the last representative of German

[1] Lange originally said this, with very much less appropriateness, about Strauss. Cf. *History of Materialism*, Engl. tr., 1881, vol. iii., p. 340.
[2] Th. Fechner, *Zend-Avesta*, Leipzig, 1851, vol. i., p. 1.

metaphysics. Hartmann honestly believed that he had said the last word in metaphysics, summing up in a single thought on the one hand the Idea of Hegel and the Will of Schopenhauer, and on the other all philosophy and science. This single thought was the Unconscious, or perhaps, with greater truth, Unconsciousness. It failed to satisfy either the philosopher or the scientist. On the one hand, to a fine scientific instinct such as Lange's, Hartmann's attitude towards science seemed to resemble that of the Australian native who could only see in the action of a Leyden jar the work of a devil ; on the other hand, the philosopher is repelled by Hartmann's coarse handling of the concepts of will and thought, which he treats like things. He conceived a blind will, which required the light of the idea, and an inert idea which required the support of the will : in fact, a relation rather like that in the fable of the blind man and the lame man. But it possessed one great disadvantage compared with the fable, namely, that while in the fable the blind man and the lame man were connected by a good strong wheelbarrow, the point of union in Hartmann's philosophy was the unconscious, that is to say a principle in which the idea becomes clouded and the will paralysed.

The *Doctrine of the Categories* is freer from fallacies than the *Philosophy of the Unconscious* : but the improvement is very slight. There is the usual conflict between the logical and the illogical, and the usual application of the dialectic to ready-made and inflexible concepts. These speculations won for Hartmann great renown ; he was eagerly read both in Germany and abroad : nevertheless, he was never taken quite seriously, he never created a school. I only know a single follower of his, called Drews, and he was unable to derive anything better from his study of Hartmann than the following doctrine : that modern philosophy has taken a wrong direction in starting from the *Cogito* of Descartes, and that consciousness, far from being something primary, is the product of the friction of unconscious will against matter. Exactly like striking a match.[1]

But we must not take these instances of degeneracy as

[1] A. Drews, *Das Ich als Grundproblem der Metaphysik*, Freiburg, 1897, p. 213.

our criterion of the influence exerted on thought by naturalism, which was really very important ; indeed, it provoked by reaction a new phase of philosophical speculation. We must rather look to that new vision of the world which, even when not explicitly formulated, rose above any single department of scientific research and found its unity and co-ordination in the universal standpoint of the natural sciences. In face of the ever-increasing pressure of causal mechanism the old indeterminism (which the Babel-philosophy of the age, forgetting Kant, had revived as the last bulwark of idealism) was definitely compromised ; the repugnance to resolve spiritual life with its richness of content into the inert world of matter diminished in proportion as evolutionary science demonstrated that this richness of content had been built up out of a state of original poverty by means of slow changes and accumulations extending over long periods of time : in this way the passage from nature to spirit was being by degrees facilitated.   Those who succeeded, by rapid mental syntheses, in bridging the abyss which this passage concealed, settled down comfortably to the new conception : others stopped in perplexity : others with greater perspicacity perceived that, however far they penetrated with their thought, they were always left with an irreducible residuum of this spiritual reality. One of the most characteristic examples of this state of perplexity and doubt is provided in Hermann Lotze.

§ 6. LOTZE.

In his uncertain and contradictory compromise between naturalism and idealism, and in the general insecurity of his position, Lotze represents a new transitional period. It is no longer a case of thought being turned into nature, but of naturalism beginning to feel its own inadequacy and desiring to negate itself and be transformed anew into thought. This negation, however, was rather an expression of Lotze's moral convictions than an integral part of his philosophy. His thought was still divided between the contradictory claims of idealism and naturalism, which were not really mediated and were therefore continually at conflict. He figured knowledge and reality as set over against one another, and their unity as falling outside them in the personality of the philosopher.

This unity was a moral one. Having passed through a period of naturalism and assimilated from it all it could give, Lotze had become convinced that science ought not to touch the profounder life of the spirit. " We cannot," he said, " look on indifferently when we see cognition undermine the foundations of faith " ; and in conformity with this fundamental principle he maintained from the beginning that while the task of observing the mechanical order of the universe was unlimited in its scope, it was at the same time of absolutely secondary importance.¹ This new criterion of importance or value is the clue to Lotze's whole philosophical attitude. It implies that between the two worlds of nature and of spirit, of knowing and of reality, there must be some mediation, and that beyond the dualism there must exist a profounder unity, once thought, while yet confined within its subjectivity, is allowed to penetrate with its judgments of value and its demands this world of nature which is apparently alien to it. But the mediation itself is a mere demand : it is the immediate and unreflective apprehension of a moral unity in the world lying beyond the terms requiring unification. Lotze is in fact twice a dogmatist : first in accepting the unreflective dualism of nature and spirit, and again in postulating their ultimate unification.

The result of this is a logic of thought *quâ* thought and a metaphysic of being *quâ* being. Thought is the immediate certainty of itself as thought. Lotze quite failed to grasp the true significance of the idealistic attempt to resolve the object of thought into the act of thought and nature into spirit. The fact revealed in his insistent and short-sighted criticism of that idealism is merely his determination to avoid resolving the reality of nature into the abstract subjectivity of thought. He never realized that this sub-jectivity had long been superseded and that the new idealistic conception of subjectivity was something very different from what he imagined. Thus his ostensible attack on Kant and Hegel was really an attack on himself for failing to grasp

¹ H. Lotze, *Microcosmus*, preface, English tr., p. xi.

their conception of thought, and a refutation of his own abstract immediate subjectivism—a view which can never account for the existence of knowledge.

In fact, he missed the essential point of Kant's discovery, namely, the principle that so far as thought attains complete consciousness of itself it finds, included in this self-consciousness, consciousness of the other, of nature : herein lies the significance of the categories. According to Lotze the categories were simply another way of expressing the immediate certainty of thought ; they were mere duplicates, or at most a mere development of the truth already given in the immediate experience of the subject. Hence the problem of the reality of nature was quite independent of, and unaffected by, the logical inquiry into the problem of knowledge ; this latter being confined to an abstract and formal manipulation of concepts. But in reality it was only to Lotze's imagination that this problem appeared to remain unprejudiced. For it was very definitely prejudiced by his dogmatic assumption that natural reality was already given, and that he was only trying to establish a new proof of its extra-mental reality. A prey to the common illusion of all dogmatism, Lotze believed that he was thereby safeguarding natural reality from the arbitrary caprice of thought, whereas he was actually compromising it : for, by shutting the door to all reflective thought upon reality, he was handing it over to immediate and empirical thought, which means, in an ultimate analysis, to that very arbitrary subjectivity of thought from which he believed he was saving it. The metaphysic of nature was the product of this confusion.

We have seen that in Lotze's philosophy natural reality is not endowed with any greater consistency than the immediate reality of thought : both are creations of the same arbitrary subjectivity and stand on a par with each other. It is on this arbitrary foundation that Lotze builds up his metaphysic, borrowing on the one hand from natural science the concept of atoms, and on the other hand from psychology that of psychic units, and creating out of the fusion of the two the concept of the " reals," which are akin to the monads of Leibniz. But there is one great difference. Leibniz recognized the ideal character of the monads, attributing to each individual monad an existence as an idea in the consciousness of the others and conceiving the reality of all as the supreme idea of all entertained by God, the monad of monads. Lotze, on the contrary, pushed this idealistic conception into the background, and made the " reals " approximate to the atoms of matter. By his doctrine that " the monads have no windows," Leibniz effectively precluded all dogmatism, and at the same time cleared the way for an idealism which should regard the monad as containing the whole world within itself, and for a true view of the relations between realities as products in the monad and of the monad, that is to say, as concrete acts of thought. Lotze, on the other hand, sought to fling open every window into the monads, and thereby admitted the whole of the pre-Kantian dogmatism, with all its blind belief in infra-monadic activities and ambiguous relations between nature and spirit. He believed that in framing the hypothesis of an intercommunication of " reals " by means of reciprocal interaction, and the transference of activity and force from one to another, he was establishing the substantial unity of the elements of the universe and avoiding the discontinuity of scientific atomism. But this external and dogmatic unification was, in reality, so far as its entire lack of internal cohesion was concerned, indistinguishable from the discontinuity of atomism.

Lotze never overcame the contradiction arising out of these two conflicting claims of naturalism and idealism. However much he emphasized the idealistic significance of his doctrine and tried to embrace the whole of reality in a teleological and ethical view, his attempt was always frustrated by the very solid residuum of naturalism which would not be absorbed in an idealistic vision of reality. But it was impossible that an age which was strongly biased towards science should fail to notice the existence of this residuum, which betrayed the inadequacy of idealism and the shallow foundations of its highest syntheses. Lotze had relegated to the mysteries of faith the ultimate unity of thought and being : but what significance could be attached to this supreme synthesis when the principles of his philosophy were unable to solve the most elementary problems concerning the reality of space or of sensation ?   Lotze made the objective basis of spatial appearance spring from the incomprehensible interaction of the " reals," but owing to the dualism between thought and reality, this interaction was insufficient for the creation of the idea of space in the subject, and required to be supplemented by an appeal to the principle of psycho-physical activity.[1] Interest in problems of this kind was at that time intensified by the study of physiology, which introduced questions concerning the subjectivity of space and of sensations and the possibility of thought reproducing in itself an external reality.   Lotze's attempted solution was consequently regarded as merely evasive ; and in general, based as it was on the equivocation between naturalism and idealism, his philosophy was hardly calculated to inspire conviction.   This explains why its immediate influence in Germany was so slight when compared with that in other countries.   It was only later, when the confusion was cleared up, that Lotze's idealism was able to run its full course, and that one of his followers, Caspari, could point to a theological and ethical conception of reality as the foundation of the new German philosophy.

§ 7. THE NEW TENDENCIES.

The problem of immediate experience was the most urgent : is sensation really immediate reality or does it involve a physical and physiological mediation ?   Physiology and psychology were inclined towards the theory of the subjectivity of sensations and spatial intuitions : philosophy developed the theory and concluded that the so-called physical external reality is purely phenomenal.   It was believed that idealism depended on some such presupposition, a fallacy which illustrates well the ignorance of the times. For idealism (Kant and Hegel) had long ago realized that just as the purely abstract objective world of naturalism does not give an explanation of knowledge, so the purely phenomenal world within consciousness (Locke and Hume) cannot create science, which cannot be explained as a merely subjective product.   It had, further, discovered the abso-

[1] Cf. H. Schoen, *La Métaphysique de H. Lotze*, Paris, 1902, p. 152.

lutely primary act of pure apperception, a relation creative
of its own terms, which forms at once the conscious subject
and the object known.   The double abstraction of a mere
consciousness and a mere object was thus overcome, and
these two terms were shown, far from being the absolutely
primary reality, to be derivative and secondary, and to bear
all the marks of a subsequent analysis of an original
synthesis.

Nevertheless, the recognition of the unique and spontaneous character of sensations as products of the mind
represented an advance upon naturalism, and led to the
discovery that far from being a *prius* to the spirit and standing
as the mediator of sensible reality, the external world is
a *posterius*, a product of consciousness, the result of a mediation.   Thus contemporary thought has repossessed itself of
the discovery of the immediate and irreducible reality of
consciousness which was effected by English empiricism
almost two centuries ago.

This rediscovery was not confined to any single school :
it constitutes the true starting-point for the whole of contemporary German philosophy, which branches out from it
in different directions.   Schuppe and Mach, Lange, Brentano,
and Wundt, the founders respectively of the empiricist,
neo-Kantian, psychological and metaphysical schools, all
start from this principle of immediate experience.   Before
we can proceed to review in a single rapid synthetic survey
the manner in which they and their followers have developed
this principle, some preliminary considerations are necessary.

The principle affirms that the reality of the world is
identical with the reality of the immediate experience of
the subject :   the certainty of things is identical with the
certainty of sensations and the ideas of sensations.   It is
not a question of two certainties, but of one.   But after
the whole object has in this way been resolved in the subject, what basis is left for knowledge, which is essentially
objective ?   Kant, as we have seen, met the problem with
a bold denial of the principle of immediate certainty.
Contemporary German philosophy, on the other hand,
holds firmly to this principle ; and accordingly the problem
of the objectivity of knowledge, of science, which is becoming

more and more insistent, confronts it as a perpetually unsatisfied claim, and continually goads it on to elaborate and twist into a thousand different forms its principle of immediate experience, in the attempt to extract from it that which really lies outside it and which it therefore cannot yield.

We shall see that the exponents of the different schools of empiricism, Kantianism and the metaphysic of experience are becoming increasingly sensitive to the urgency of this problem, and that any attempt at a complete formulation of their doctrines always betrays, in spite of the calm and confident exterior, obvious signs of internal uneasiness. We shall, moreover, discover that outside the central nuclei of their systems lie vague nebulous regions to which they relegate the problems which, owing to the inherent weaknesses of their method, they have left unsolved.

The modern problem of the objectivity of knowledge and of the reality of nature is the complete reverse and the most pronounced antithesis of the problem presented by naturalism. There the presupposition was nature, the object ; and the difficulty consisted in conceiving the passage to the spirit, to the subject. Here the presupposition is the immediate subjective experience ; and the difficulty consists in conceiving how this experience is objectified. There is, moreover, this great superiority in the position of the modern problems, that while the old problems were concerned with two worlds which were considered absolutely disparate, with being as being and thought as thought, and therefore belonged to dogmatic metaphysics, the present problems are only concerned with the single sphere of knowledge— with the subject as conscious and the object as known— and therefore belong to the critical theory of knowledge. Nevertheless a profound identity of method is noticeable in both ; indeed, it is often barely concealed. For just as naturalism affirmed being as an immediate reality, so the new theory considers consciousness as an immediate datum ; and the result is that the new position of consciousness is converted into that of naturalism, in spite of the fact that it arose in antithesis to it : consciousness is transformed into a natural object and is treated as such.

The outlines of our historical sketch are now clear. It will cover German empiricism, Kantianism, psychology and the metaphysic of experience, and will trace their development from their original sources in answer to the continuous demands of new problems arising out of the actual solutions that have been reached on the way.

CHAPTER II

EMPIRICISM

§ 1. THE PHILOSOPHY OF THE GIVEN.

FIRST among the doctrines which accept unreservedly the principle of immediate experience comes positivism. In so far as its object is to conform to what is given in fact without transcending it, positivism is loath to admit the existence beyond sensation of a reality of a different kind which should determine or produce it. But before sensation is exalted to the position of an autonomous reality it must, so to speak, become impersonal. Sensations must cease to be regarded as mere changing attributes of a permanent, substantial self, a self standing motionless amid the flux of sensuous experience. Such a substantial self must be annihilated, resolved into the flux, and conceived as simply consisting of successive groups of sensations, just as material objects are resolved by Berkeleian idealism into variously organized groups of sensations. This doctrine, which indeed in its essential features is the same as that of Mill and Taine and others, has been expounded by Laas in Germany under the name of correlativism. The title is due to the fact that once a fixed centre of reference (the subject) is removed, the ego becomes relative to the world and the world to the ego, both being constituted, as they are, of the same stuff.

But the peculiarity of Laas is that, although his general theory is founded on the purest psychological empiricism, he nevertheless attempts to distinguish between a psychological and an epistemological point of view. Psychologically, there is no difference between truth and error, knowledge and opinion : each alike is a psychological fact, nothing more and nothing less. But Laas sees that the distinction between knowledge and opinion must somehow be made, and makes it by appealing to the conception of value. There are, he says, some psychological facts that are important, and others that are not. Regarded merely as psychological facts, both classes merit the same respect : but from the logical point of view, the one class has value and the other not.[1]

Very true. But Laas has here fallen into the trap of mistaking the statement of a problem for its solution. The conception of " logical value " has no business in his theory of knowledge at all ; for it contradicts the psychological empiricism with which he began. The question which he ought to answer is how, if his psychological method is correct, " logical value " can exist. John Stuart Mill, starting from the same position, did at least attempt to answer this question when he undertook the task of sticking sensations together by means of the inductive methods, in order to create a truth distinguishable from mere opinion. Laas shirked the whole problem, and contented himself with inventing the idea of a " Consciousness in general," lying beyond and above the shifting consciousness of individuals, to act as depository for these logical values.

The so-called " Philosophy of the Given," or " Philosophy of Immanence," of Laas's contemporary, Wilhelm Schuppe, represented a much more penetrating attempt to work out the conclusions of psychological empiricism. For Schuppe the fundamental axiom of philosophy is the conscious ego ; this is the primary standard by which the whole of reality is measured.[2] Everything that exists, exists for consciousness : and in consciousness subject and object, sentient person and objects sensated, are all one. The theory of consciousness which imagines it to be a kind of empty subjectivity which appropriates for itself in some unexplained way an objectivity extraneous to it, is a mistake : this subjectivity is simply the product of a subsequent reflection which abstracts from the concrete content of consciousness an empty form and sets it over against a formless content which is itself the product of the same abstraction. Consciousness is the immediate unity of subject and object, and as such it is the absolutely primary and concrete datum.

[1] E. Laas, *Idealismus und Positivismus*, Berlin, 1879–84, vol. iii., p. 675.
[2] W. Schuppe, *Erkenntnistheoretische Logik*, Bonn, 1878, p. 63.

But this unity is not in Schuppe's view at the same time unity and distinction, consciousness and self-consciousness. The unity of subject and object consists rather in the undifferentiated state of both in the simple fact of consciousness : it is not the act of self-distinction, but the undistinguished fact which only subsequent reflection distinguishes into abstract elements, subject and object, percipient and perceived. Thus Schuppe repeatedly insists that the immediate unity of the ego and the non-ego in the primitive fact of consciousness is the totally inexplicable miracle, the *Urtatsache* which must be accepted as given, without any attempt at explanation.[1] But the real miracle according to Schuppe's theory lies elsewhere. In its moments of complete unreflectiveness the ego lives its objects in itself and feels itself at one with the world without distinguishing itself from it : in this undifferentiated state there is no miracle. We only speak of miracles when something strange happens which requires an explanation : that is to say, when a differentiation has arisen. But Schuppe's conception of the undistinguished primitive consciousness contains no differentiation, nothing to explain. The miracle rather consists in the appearance of the reflection which abstracts and distinguishes an ego from a non-ego : for how is this possible ? How, from this gelatinous mass of consciousness which is neither matter nor spirit, but an undifferentiated state of both, can there appear reflection, distinction, abstraction ? To abstract is to extract : if the moment of distinction is not already in the alleged undifferentiated whole, it can never be got out of it. In short, without self-consciousness, consciousness is inexplicable, and knowing is a mystery. Thus the real miracle for Schuppe is precisely knowing.

By implication he accepts this miracle, and renounces any explanation of knowledge ; and so reflection becomes for him a datum among data, a fact among facts : not a principle of explanation, but a thing to be explained and analysed. Schuppe therefore states the problem of knowledge in the following terms : It is a fact that I know : what, then, are the ingredients of this fact ? When the problem

[1] W. Schuppe, *Grundriss der Erkenntnistheorie und Logik*, Berlin, 1910, 2nd ed., p. 7. *Erk. Logik cit.*, p. 145.

is stated in this way the nature of the solution is already determined. Schuppe completely loses sight of the real character of the synthesis of knowledge ; he regards this synthesis as a mere given fact to be analysed, and science or knowledge as a crystallized fact whose composition is to be studied from outside.

We must explain this rather more fully. All knowledge, consisting as it does of judgments, is a relation between terms. Now, unless there was a real distinction between the terms there would be no relation and no knowledge : it is thus precisely the apparent limitation of knowledge—its relativity, its ideal or formal character—that alone guarantees its concrete actuality. This conception of knowledge depends on so conceiving the unity of the moments of thought (form and content) as not to deny their real and absolute distinctness. It is here that Schuppe breaks down. In considering knowledge as a fact, a mere known, he can indeed distinguish in it a content and a form, but in their solidified union, not in a union that is at the same time distinction. In other words, it follows from Schuppe's identification of reality with the immediate object of consciousness that categories or relations cannot have any other reality than that of the given : the concept is embedded in the sensation. Hence thinking is not the production of knowledge but the finding of it : [1] science is not invention, discovery, creation, but the mere disintegration of the structure of the given and the excavation from it of what is already solidified in it, i.e. the concept. Thus Schuppe solidifies thought and reality into matter. His immanence of the universal in the particular, of the concept in the sensation, has often been considered as the concrete embodiment of thought in reality : but it is really the falsest type of immanence imaginable : thought, for Schuppe, is immanent in reality only in the sense in which matter is immanent in the fragments of matter. He solidifies the relations of thought into matter, and thereby degrades his system to the lowest level of empiricism, where it borders on materialism. And so the concept of " consciousness in general " which, according to Schuppe, gathers up into a single all-embracing unity

[1] Schuppe, *Grundriss cit.*, p. 37.

the whole of reality, is not substantially different from the general concept of matter in the materialistic systems. The only difference is that the matter of Schuppe is less solid and hard : being the mere undifferentiated state of nature and spirit, it is neither wood nor iron, but jelly.

The school of the " Philosophy of Immanence " has developed this fundamental thesis to the point of absurdity. In order to explain the formation of empirical objects and empirical subjects out of the amorphous matter of which the substance of the world consists, Schuppe was compelled to postulate a kind of agglutination of this substance into spheres and fragments. This theory is developed by Rehmke. According to him there exist things and subjects, both resulting from the mutual interaction or compenetration of a number of facts of consciousness : the first, however, are conditioned by space, the second not. One would think that in his individual being and knowing man would embody in himself both these categories ; yet it is not so : Rehmke has solidified things and subjects to such an extent that he cannot in any way reduce the one to the other, and is therefore compelled to deny that man constitutes in any way an individual being. Then what is man ? A merely neutral field of interaction between the two categories of reals.[1] It is clear that with two pieces of matter like these, however much he may shift them about at pleasure and pit them against one another, he will never succeed in showing how the one can become conscious of the other. Rehmke dimly sees this difficulty, but he believes that he can avoid it by drawing a distinction. He accordingly distinguishes between a strictly philosophical point of view and a psychological one. The philosophical point of view is satisfied by recognizing it as a fact that minds and things do somehow come together into an actual unity ; this, of course, simply amounts to a statement of the problem. But from the psychological point of view we must say that the mind knows things through the medium of the body :[2] a statement which, given Rehmke's premises, is contradictory, because the mind, being non-spatial, is no more contiguous with the

[1] J. Rehmke, *Philosophie als Grundwissenschaft*, Leipzig, 1910, p. 391.
[2] *Ibid.*, pp. 618, 655.

body than it is with external things : and so the suggested mediator is no mediator at all.

§ 2. THE THEORY OF OBJECTS.

Another consequence of Schuppe's theory of immediate consciousness is to be seen in the question : Is the immediate datum, the object of this consciousness, real ? Clearly it cannot be. The experience of the subject certainly includes perceptions of real facts, but it also includes imaginations and hallucinations. Therefore, Rehmke concludes, since the immediate datum is the ultimate fact, out of which everything is constructed, this ultimate is not reality ; behind reality there is a still more elementary region forming the source from which spring alike reality and unreality. Anyone who has some acquaintance, even if only by hearsay, with the history of Aristotelianism will immediately perceive the fallacy of this argument. For how can reality proceed out of unreality, the more from the less, the actual from the potential ? This is a fallacy which to-day seems very obvious (although it required whole centuries of philosophical speculation to expose it) : yet all those who stop short at the conception of fact, or the immediate object of consciousness, fall a prey to it. Fact can never escape from its own shadow.

But before Rehmke, Meinong had already fallen a prey to the same fallacy in his " Theory of Objects." Beyond the " objective," which is the object *quâ* existing or real, lies the pure object, freed from existence.[1] How we can ever pass from the latter to the former, extract reality out of unreality, is a profound mystery. But Meinong brushes this problem aside with the utmost nonchalance and proceeds to lay it down that the knowledge of the " objective," concerned as it is with a reality given solely in empirical experience, is *a posteriori* : while the knowledge of the " object," being devoid of presuppositions, is *a priori*. Meinong accordingly attempts to evolve a logic of the object in close alliance with mathematics, since this science also has nothing

[1] A. Meinong, *Ueber die Stellung der Gegenstandtheorie im System der Wissenschaften, Zeitschrift für Phil. u. Phil. Kritik* (1906–7), p. 66.

to do with empirical realities. This theory, which, we shall see, is held in England by Bertrand Russell and in France by Couturat, shows that the aim of Meinong and his followers (Höfler, for instance) is to construct a logic free from psychological matter, and yet resting on a purely psychological basis. At bottom they have done nothing but change Schuppe's position for the worse. Schuppe only asked for one miracle—the existence of the immediate object ; Meinong and his school, not content with this, demand a second— not only the object as existing, but the object as object. This comes of neglecting Leibniz' sage caution, that " miracles are not to be multiplied beyond necessity."

§ 3. CRITICAL EMPIRICISM.

Passing over these minor ventures in philosophy, we will try to follow the main development of German empiricism. We have seen that when Schuppe imprisoned himself within the undifferentiated unity of immediate consciousness, he thereby congealed thought into a kind of material substance. Unless we recognize the ideality of thought-relations and the distinction between object and subject in consciousness, knowledge cannot be explained : science is something embodied from eternity in the lifeless given, from which it is simply excavated by the act of an abstract reflection, itself inexplicable.

But is Schuppe's " given " the real object of immediate consciousness ? Critical empiricism replies in the negative. The really immediate is simply sensation : thought is not incorporated in the given, but is something ideal, subjective, abstract, superimposed on the given, which breaks it up and mutilates it in order to grasp it. Thought is the method by which the subject appropriates the given for its own purposes.

This distinction which critical empiricism draws between the immediately given and thought appears to me to represent a great advance upon Schuppe. Both agree in identifying reality with the immediately given : but while Schuppe solidifies thought in the given, Avenarius and Mach detach it, and assert the existence of a principle of reflection, of mediation. True, they maintain that reality is presented ready-made in sensation, and that the mediation of thought must therefore be a falsification, an arbitrary manipulation justified only by its utility ; the ideality of thought is thus reduced to an abstract and merely subjective ideality. But this has at least the merit of destroying dogmatism. According to this view science is not a " given," a ready-made whole : it is a process of production, of creation, and even though the creation is an arbitrary act of the scientist, yet there is wisdom in its arbitrariness. And we shall see that the conception of this latent wisdom has developed in the hands of Cornelius, an empiricist of real insight, into an idealistic motive through which critical empiricism transcends itself.

Even in his earliest published work Richard Avenarius regarded philosophy as an examination of the world according to the principle of least resistance. His *Critique of Pure Experience*, the fruit of maturer age, started with this assumption as a hypothesis which it undertook to prove in the course of its development, thus resolving in its proof its own presupposition. In so far as it is a simple description of the given, philosophy does not explain, but confines itself to observing. Now, the given consists of one complex of facts which we can sum up in a convenient phrase as physical, and another complex of facts which we can call psychical. Observation shows us that the latter vary with the variations of the former. There must therefore be a relation between the two ; and one that is not altogether immediate, because some psychical facts (hallucinations, for instance) occur without a physical stimulus. The relation is therefore mediate, and the mediator is to be found in the brain. The brain has for Avenarius a kind of symbolical, or more correctly a mythological significance. It does not merely re-direct forces ; it has specific autonomous characteristics and functions of its own. It works for its own conservation, and therefore is no merely passive recipient of stimuli, but reacts upon its own actions, in the effort to regain the equilibrium destroyed by these actions, and so to preserve its stability.[1] And thus, as Wundt has acutely observed, there

[1] R. Avenarius, *Kritik der reinen Erfahrung*, Leipzig, 1888-90, vol. i., p. 1.

exists a kind of dialectic of the brain, through which any disturbance that arises is in a subsequent moment negated, and equilibrium restored. In the psychological series this function of the brain is represented by the function of the concept. Psychical facts (sensations) are determined by the law of contrasts [1] in conformity with the oscillations of the central nervous system. The concept mediates between these contrasts ; it is the principle of equilibrium in psychic life, and therefore fulfils a function of vital economy in dependence on the nervous system. [2] But it must not be imagined that Avenarius maintains a psycho-physical parallelism : psychical and physical facts are not two different things, nor are they two different aspects of some third thing, but, and herein lies the characteristic part of his theory, they are themselves this third thing. This is neither more nor less than the undifferentiated psychophysical unity which we have already pointed out in Schuppe.

This theory provides its own criticism in the course of its development. We have seen that the concept acts as the mediator of sensible reality. But on the other hand it is itself mediated, inasmuch as it is a function of the economy of the brain. The confusion caused by this double mediation, which in fact amounts to a duplication of reality, is exemplified in the development of the theory by Avenarius's pupil Petzoldt. Petzoldt views the concept as an economic means, and science therefore as a schematic expression of reality which reduces the multiplicity of the senses to an ever greater simplicity. But the concept is at the same time a function of the brain, and the economy of the brain is not a principle of spiritual economy, rich with varied and inexhaustible applications, but simply a natural tendency toward equilibrium and stability. The equivocal position resulting from this twofold mediation leads Petzoldt to the most extravagant conclusions. No doubt, says he, science is developing to-day ; and it will continue to develop for some time. But there will come a time when the equilibrium

---

[1] *Op. cit.*, vol. ii., p. 74.
[2] Sensations and concepts, in Avenarius's abstruse and complicated terminology, are designated as " elements " and " characters."

of the problems will be re-established ; and then, stability
having been attained, science will of necessity come to an
end.[1] Art is in the same position as science ; the object
of æsthetic valuation must reach a state of stability or the
elimination of a state of ferment.[2] Let us pause a moment
to admire this truly poetic flight of imagination. Further,
art must represent the repetitions, the typical and essential
elements in phenomena.[3] How then does it differ from
statistics ? The result is still worse when Petzoldt tries
to apply his miserable formula to social problems. The
ethical tendency of humanity is towards harmony, a state
of permanence without any change : when this is attained,
the possibility of wars will be done away with, social differences will be abolished, and there will no longer be any
differences of birth, ownership or income.[4] This is what
comes of the conscientious effort to push a theory to the
point of absurdity.

But Avenarius himself (without being aware of it) has
supplied the most effective criticism of his own doctrine.
In the analysis of *The Human Conception of the World*,
which forms his latest work, he shows how this conception
has been developed by thought starting from immediate
experience and insinuating into it its own metaphysical
and transcendental point of view ; and how this fallacious
point of view is finally eliminated, and the conception
of pure experience reinstated. The essence of this fallacy,
detected by Avenarius's criticism and by him called "introjection," is that whereas experience gives us only one single
world of reality, we are led to duplicate this reality and
to imagine that it is given twice over, once in sensation,
and again outside sensation. If I had existed alone in the
world, the fallacy would never have arisen : it arises when
over against me *you* intervene. The consequence is that
I attribute to you an experience of your own and at the
same time I allow mine to continue to exist in addition
to yours : thus the one becomes your internal experience
(the world of sensations), while the other is externalized

---

[1] J. Petzoldt, *Einführung in die Philosophie der reinen Erfahrung*,
Leipzig, 1900–4, vol. ii., p. 156.
  [2] *Ibid.*, p. 265.   [3] *Ibid.*, p. 250.   [4] *Ibid.*, pp. 202, 204.

over against it and appears as the world of reality, of things. The same illusion takes place with regard to myself. Reality is as a matter of fact presented to me in immediate experience ; but when I reflect on the experience of others, and allow this experience to stand over against my own, I am led to describe it, quite illegitimately, as a world of reality lying outside my sensations.[1] Now let us examine the bearing of this on the theory of Avenarius which we were describing above. Granted this theory of immediate experience, what becomes of the brain, conceived as the mediator between physical and psychical facts ? The objective reality of the brain must be described simply as an illusion, an introjection. Sensation is the only reality of which I am immediately conscious ; hence the brain also is one of my sensations. But when I see a physiologist engaged in examining the brain, I imagine the immediate experience of the physiologist, which is itself only another sensation, to be a reality existing outside myself and previous to my sensation.

The discovery of the contradiction in Avenarius's theory vindicates the absolute immediacy of sensation : the equivocal double mediation of the brain and the concept is removed, and it becomes clear that the reality of the brain is not an immediate reality, but is mediated—is, in fact, a mere expression, abbreviated for convenience' sake, for psychological experience—and the concept remains as the only mediator over against sensation. Mach therefore, and not Avenarius, represents the genuine attitude of critical empiricism.

Philosophy is in Mach's doctrine the analysis of sensations. Everything, in fact, is resolved into this primary element : for what else do bodies contain except what is felt ? I am aware of things only so far as I see them, touch them, perceive them : if there does seem to me to be something else in them, it is because I involuntarily assume that the elements, the sensations, out of which objects are constructed, are objectively connected together in a thing-in-itself. But the body, matter, is in reality nothing else except this connection of elements : of sounds, colours, tones, etc. We must not, however, imagine that reality evaporates in this

[1] R. Avenarius, *Der Menschliche Weltbegriff*, Leipzig, 1905, 2nd ed., pp. 23–8.

way into thin air. Mach himself points out that what he
calls psychical is the same thing as what from another point
of view is called physical, material. The gulf between the
physical and the psychical only exists in the ordinary stereo-
typed way of viewing things ; in actual fact, a colour is a
physical object when we are investigating how it originates
from a luminous source and a psychical object when we
consider it in our immediate experience. It is not a question,
then, of a different content, but of a different way of viewing
the same content.[1] These premises also enable Mach to
assert that he accepts psycho-physical parallelism because
he does not attribute to it any dogmatic meaning : the
elements are the same throughout, and are only distinguished
according to the procedure of the thought which places
them in different relations.[2]

Thus we have really determined two questions, though
Mach thinks we have determined only one. First, that there
are elements or sensations ; secondly, that there are relations
between them. The latter cannot be of the same nature
as the former, since it is by reference to them that (in the
procedure of thought) the single and identical reality is
differentiated into physical and psychical facts. But this
double point of view cannot arise within sensation itself :
it can only be due to thought, which contemplates sensation
in two different aspects. Mach perceives the distinction,
but he misunderstands its true significance ; and the result
is curious. We have seen that he holds reality to lie in
the element, the sensation ; how then does he explain the
connections between the elements, the relations of thought ?
Their purpose, he says, is not to create a new kind of reality,
since the whole of reality is already created in the senses ;
but to give a shorthand version of this same reality. These
connections, in fact, represent as a unity in thought what
in sensation is a manifold ; and since the unity cannot express
anything that was not in the manifold, a simple mathematical
calculation (rendered possible by the homogeneity of the
terms) shows us that thought contains less than sensation,
and that the world of thought is simply the world of the
senses in shorthand.

[1] E. Mach, *Die Analyse der Empfindungen*, Jena, 1903, 4th ed., p. 14.
[2] *Ibid.*, p. 51.

This is the origin of the theory that science is an economic treatment of the given, a convenient caprice of thought designed in order to enable us to grasp more easily the inexhaustible variety of the senses. This theory, which is so simple, lucid and frankly naïve, has been echoed throughout the whole of Europe. It has found strenuous supporters and keen opponents, the former particularly among scientists, the latter among philosophers. And the reason for this is, if I may so call it, an economic one.

Provided that his experiment succeeds, and his law brings the facts within a system, the scientist does not trouble himself much about the subtle question as to whether the one, which in the shape of the law takes the place of the many, is the mere product of subtraction (a single fact left when the others have been removed) or whether it represents something radically new. He confines himself to a statement of the diminution in the number of facts to be handled, the economy ; absorbed in the facts, he only understands the purely external character of his procedure. But ask him whether without the law of gravitation (the one) there could be bodies with weight (the many) and he will laugh in your face. This means that he did not really think that the one is what remains after the rest of the many have been subtracted ; it is the actual condition of the many. But such an opinion is the precise contrary of the principle of economy. It indicates not that the one is selected out of the many, but that the many proceed out of the one : it is not thought that gravitates round things or sensations, but (as Kant pointed out) things that gravitate round thought.

We find the beginnings of this inversion in the present-day school of critical empiricism, in Mach and Cornelius. Mach is an excellent historian of science. In his history of mechanics and of the theory of heat, he tries to show how the principle of economy has continued to be actualized in a progressive simplification of concepts through which the scientific structure, reduced to a few firm lines, has gained both in elegance and solidity. The significance and value of the historical process as thus described far transcend the formula of critical empiricism, and are not unworthy of Kant himself. And the progressive achievement of truth which Mach describes as taking place in science is at the same moment asserting itself, though less decisively, in Mach's own philosophy.

Mach holds reality to lie in sensation : this is his starting-point. But on developing this premiss he realized that he would end by resolving the world into a mere permanent possibility of sensations, as Mill did. This is repugnant to him, and so he finally admits that there is something more real than the sensation in its isolated singularity ; namely, the *order* of the sensations, the functional relation of the elements.[1] In this theory critical empiricism is definitely superseded : the real is no longer sensation, immediacy, but relation, *ordo*, that is to say thought. This conclusion is certainly beyond the range of Mach, but he is on the road towards it. It is true he does not reach Kant, but he does not stop at Hume : with the conception of *ordo*, of relation, he attains to the position of Spinoza : and Hume and Spinoza are the two premisses of Kant.

But with all its ambiguity and instability, Mach's position is immensely superior to a pure empiricism like that of John Stuart Mill. The very premisses of his critical empiricism suggest that thought cannot be merely a copy of the given, but must be an elaboration of it, a continuous process of transformation. Hence Mach will have nothing to do with inductive and deductive logic : these classify ready-made thoughts, they do not explain science in the process of creation. We hear nothing of the scientist who collects the facts one by one, abstracts their general characteristics, formulates *axiomata media,* and thence proceeds to the conception of a law. A single experiment, says Mach, is often sufficient to create a law ; and the experiment generally takes place not in the laboratory, but in the mind of the scientist. These and other equally acute observations (although tinged with arbitrariness, because the mediation of thought is not yet understood as a true mediation) are evidences of the formation of an entirely new philosophical attitude, vastly superior to the barren poverty of empiricism. Similar observations are also to be found in the works of

[1] *Op. cit.,* pp. 283 and 287.

Helmholz, Kirchoff, Hertz, scientist-philosophers who have divined by a kind of happy intuition, rather than really understood, the living concrete character of scientific procedure, which, even though it does create *schemata* and abstractions, is not itself an abstract *schema*, as formal logic would have us believe.

This inversion of critical empiricism, whose true explanation we have already attempted to state, is still better exemplified in the work of Cornelius, the pupil of Mach and Kirchhoff. Mach's criticism of the empirical psychological subject had already pointed the way towards the new position. The Copernican point of view in philosophy can never be attained so long as the idea of the empirical ego persists as the self round which the world must be made to revolve. But once the empirical ego, like the empirical object, is resolved into a complex of sensations (as Mach had resolved it), it ought to be easier to understand the universal and unifying character of the mediation of thought, and to resolve the principle of economy into the principle of the transcendental unity of pure apperception.

Cornelius takes his stand on the road towards this transformation. He understands that in the flux of sensation, in the appearance and disappearance of sensible reality, there is something that does not change : the content changes, but the object remains the same.[1] What, then, is this identity ? It cannot be a mere " economy of thought " ; for how can the permanent be regarded as a shorthand expression of the changing ? Cornelius therefore considers this identity to be an identity of consciousness : without the identity of consciousness there can be no harmonious variety of phenomena, such as constitutes experience, but only chaos ;[2] moreover, a variety that is intelligible in itself is inconceivable : variety is only intelligible in the identity of the consciousness to which the variations are related. So the unity of thought is not an economy, but something entirely different. The whole point of a unity reached by economizing is that it suppresses all variety, and there only remains the one which is merely one, whereas the unity of

[1] H. Cornelius, *Einleitung in die Philosophie*, Leipzig, 1903, p. 265.
[2] *Op. cit.*, p. 208.

thought not only does not suppress the variety of sensation, but contains it, and in fact renders it possible. Now, it is a mystery to me how, after he had come so far on the right road, Cornelius can have persisted in confusing the identity of thought with economy of thought, and have remained satisfied with an incoherent and hybrid conception. Yet we must account it as a great merit to have broken down the premisses of critical empiricism and to have caught a glimpse, beyond them, of Kantian idealism. Cornelius, then, marks the point at which critical empiricism passes into Kantianism.

§ 4. The Philosophy of Illusion.

We have followed up to this point the clear and unmistakable outline of the development of German empiricism. Passing from Schuppe to Mach and Cornelius, we have seen the presentment of the problems slowly change from that of a dogmatic naturalistic view of consciousness towards an increasingly intensified critical attitude, through which empiricism finally supersedes itself by stating a demand which its own assumptions fail to satisfy, and which therefore remains an aspiration that cannot be transformed into an achievement.

So long as we adhere to the theory of the immediately given, the ideal nature of thought will continue to be something merely abstract ; and even though the need of realizing it as concrete is felt, the realization can never be effected : there will always remain the divorce between sense and understanding to bear witness to the primary error of procedure.

A typical and one might almost say morbid example of this discrepancy is provided by a theory which we may call illusionism ; I mean the philosophy expounded by Afrikan Spir. Spir considers sensation to be the source of immediate certainty : nothing else except our own sensations is given us in experience.[1] But at the same time he has immediate consciousness of another kind of certainty, a logical one, founded on the principle of identity, in the fullest meaning of the term, which includes in it every kind of *a priori*

[1] A. Spir, *Pensée et Réalité*, French tr., Lille, 1896, p. 38.

relation. These two types of certainty confront him in their irreconcilable dualism : sensible experience does not satisfy in any way the demands of logic, which in its turn is never in any way actualized in experience. What is to be done ? The empiricist would discredit logic ; Spir discredits experience. Because experience does not conform to the standard of our thought, it is false, devoid of any standard. Moreover, his identification of the logical with the ethical norm leads him to double the dose : nature (the phenomenon as given in experience) is not only illogical but immoral ; [1] it does not know the distinction between good and bad, but confounds everything in a monstrous indifferentiation.

In this state of affairs, what place is there for knowledge ? I see, feel and think, and believe I see, feel and think real objects. Herein, says Spir, lies the illusion. But it is not my illusion or yours : it belongs to the very nature of knowledge itself, which is a systematically organized fraud. The bodies which are given us in experience are not real objects, existing independently of us ; but our experience is organized as if the bodies which we perceive had an existence independent of any perception.[2] Our ego is a similar illusion : our internal experience is organized as if all our internal acts and happenings proceeded from a single, simple and identical ego. And so on. The relation between sensible experience and logical thought is thus finally reduced to a mere " as if." This being so, we can but complete Spir's argument by pointing out that on the one hand logical thought claims to be a standard but has no reality, because there are no means for applying it, and on the other hand sensible experience, simply as such, is unreal, because it does not correspond with the demands of thought ; and so the terms of reality, as well as the relation between them, are reduced to a miserable " as if."

And this is just what has happened ; a champion has now arisen in Vaihinger [3] to erect the " as if " into a philosophical method !

---

[1] A. Spir, *Esquisses de Philosophie critique*, Paris, 1887, p. 17.
[2] *Esquisses cit.*, p. 32.
[3] H. Vaihinger, *Die Philosophie des Als Ob*, Berlin, 1911.

CHAPTER III

NEO-KANTIANISM

§ 1. LANGE.

THE beginnings of neo-Kantianism in Germany can be traced back to about 1860, when in their different ways Lange, Liebmann and Zeller began to preach the return to Kant. Nor must we forget the lucid exposition of the philosophy of Kant given by Kuno Fischer, which subsequently proved of considerable influence in helping to familiarize people with his philosophy.

Yet the return to Kant does not bring into the field any substantially new problems. So great is the intellectual sterility of the first Kantians (with the exception of Lange) that no further definition of it is necessary than the bare monotonous refrain with which Otto Liebmann invoked this return, repeating at the end of every chapter in his book on *Kant and His Successors* : " We must then return to Kant."

Neo-Kantianism, in fact, begins by propounding exactly the same problem as empiricism, the problem of immediate experience : and it solves it in an analogous fashion. Reality is given immediately in representation ; the world is the phenomenon of consciousness. But while the empiricists only committed a philosophical error, and did not put forward their theory as anything but the expression of their own thought, the neo-Kantians added to this philosophical error a historical misrepresentation : for they claim to be merely interpreters of Kant's philosophy. They seem to have been unable to distinguish Kant from Reinhold or Schopenhauer.

The character and tendency of Kant's inquiry were very

different from this sort of thing. He did not start from the phenomenon as fact, but from the pure act of thought (the category), which is the self-creation of reality in the form of consciousness, the self-manifestation of the real (knowledge). Only in the indissoluble unity of the act of knowing are knowledge and consciousness (object and subject) really one : but if the unity is severed, then the synthesis is disintegrated in analysis ; and on one side consciousness decomposes into a mass of subjective facts, while on the other, knowledge crystallizes into a solid and opaque " Nature." Neo-Kantianism fails to comprehend this act, this *a priori* synthesis, and remains confined within the " fact " of consciousness. But yet it feels that there is something else beyond : that beyond the subjective phenomena there exists an objective reality that is free from all arbitrary interference. And so the problem arises : how can we pass from consciousness to knowledge ? We cannot : there is no bridge, and there never can be. Consequently neo-Kantianism either remains confined within consciousness and considers the problem of knowledge a mere ought-to-be, an abstract ideal, or else it imagines that it has achieved the passage, and losing sight of consciousness asserts the existence of knowledge without realizing that knowledge has thereby become opaque nature : and it accordingly finishes by externalizing the forms of sensation and the categories and treating them merely as natural laws. In short, the German neo-Kantians are like that kind of sportsman who can never attend simultaneously to his sights and to the game, so that whenever he looks at one he takes his eye off the other, and never hits anything at all. Thus the various oscillations whose history we shall sketch result in nothing but the shifting of the error from one side to the other.

Albrecht Lange may be regarded as the founder of neo-Kantianism. He arrived at the Kantian conception through a critical reflection on the materialistic philosophy of which he is the most accurate and profound historian. Lange does not conceal his sympathy with materialism, as the most complete and comprehensive conception of physical reality. At the same time he perceives that a criticism of materialism

does not mean the insertion here and there into its lacunæ
of an incomprehensible spiritual, or rather animistic, activity:
we must conceive materialism in its completest form as
though these lacunæ were non-existent, and then refute it
en bloc. Otherwise we should merely be criticizing one
actually existing type of materialism, whereas we ought to
be criticizing every possible type. He therefore makes it
the aim of science to explain even the most complex acts
and the most highly significant movements of human life,
by bringing them under the law of the conservation of energy
and reducing them to the effect of tensions set free in the
brain through the influence of nervous excitations.

But even if science achieves her aim in full, even if she
succeeds in explaining all this, she is for ever precluded
from bridging the gulf between the simplest sound, regarded
as the sensation of a subject, and the cerebral changes which
she must assume in order to explain this same sensation
of sound regarded as a fact in the material world.[1] But
this is not all. What other reality can a material fact have
except that of being the representation of a subject? The
reality which appears to us to be physical is such for us
in so far as the constructions of our minds make it appear
in this way. If the brain is of such and such a kind, if in
the encounter of bodies determinate phenomena are produced, this depends on the fact that our whole experience
is conditioned by an intellectual organization which compels
us to feel as we do feel, to think as we do think, while to
another organization the very same objects may appear
quite different and the thing in itself cannot be comprehended
by any finite being.[2]

But Lange is himself dissatisfied with this pseudo-Kantian
solution. At bottom he does not see any real reason why
the world should be considered to be more real when it is
resolved into the fact of consciousness than when it is expressed in physical terms. And he finally turns the tables
by ascribing to science as its future task the interpreting
of the Kantian philosophy in terms of physiology. " Perhaps," he says,[3] " the basis of the idea of cause may be

[1] A. Lange, *History of Materialism*, Eng. tr., vol. i., p. 23.
[2] *Op. cit.*, vol. iii., p. 158.   [3] *Ibid.*, vol. ii., p. 211.

found in the mechanism of reflex action and sympathetic excitation. We should then have translated Kant's pure reason into physiology and so made it more easily conceivable." But even in this way we shall not have advanced a step further towards an internal knowledge of things ; for supposing the task of science to be realized, we shall none the less be able to continue interpreting the physiological fact in terms of consciousness : the one interpretation will not be any more valid than the other. The deeper truth does not lie in either, but in a hidden third series, whose true nature remains incognizable by us.[1] Now this conclusion which Lange puts forward as a mere problem is exactly what Kant actually attained as a solid conclusion in his *Critique*, which is an attempt not to set up the psychical in place of the physical, but to conceive the absolute creative act of the spirit as the reality behind both.

Lange fails to grasp this ; he ingenuously believes that this problem was beyond Kant, whose sole object he has already defined as being the establishment of the mere subjectivity of consciousness. And so the truth, which he had glimpsed, evaporates into thin air. When he comes to define it, the *tertium quid* which transcends the two series, the psychical and the physical, and ought to be the concrete unity of both, is not an object of science, but of poetry. " Kant would not understand what Plato before him would not understand, that the ' intelligible world ' is a world of poesy, and that precisely upon this fact rests its worth and nobleness. For poesy, in the high and comprehensive sense in which it must be taken, cannot be regarded as a capricious plaything of talent and fancy with empty imaginations for amusement, but it is a necessary offspring of the soul arising from the deepest life-roots of the race, and a complete counter-balance to the pessimism which springs from an exclusive acquaintance with reality." [2]

In this way the need for a more concrete grasp of Reality is dissipated in a world of phantoms : that which should be the most concrete—and herein lies the absurdity of the theory—has become in fact the most abstract and imaginary.

---

[1] *Op. cit.*, vol. ii., p. 72.
[2] *Ibid.*, vol. ii., p. 232.

For this reason the attainment falls very far short of the need. Nevertheless, to have felt such a need and to have combated in its name the scepticism which was making progress on account of the irreconcilable dualism between the physical and psychical worlds constitutes Lange's great merit. In the continual struggle between recognized needs and recalcitrant facts, in the triumphs and regrets, in the vigour and glow of a thought that is always alive and growing, now rising and now falling in order to rise again, lies the secret of the power and inspiration of the *History of Material- ism*, the most fascinating and attractive book that German philosophy has produced in the last fifty years.

§ 2. LIEBMANN AND RIEHL.

The opposition between consciousness, as the merely subjective state of the percipient, and science or knowledge, as representing the actual truth of the object perceived, has been already analysed in the case of Lange.   In Liebmann it reappears ; but there is nothing in Liebmann to take the place of Lange's gallant attempt to reconcile the contradiction by means of poetry ; and in fact Liebmann never offers us even a glimpse of a reality lying beyond the conflict.

He looks at the world from the standpoint of immediate consciousness, and sees in it a mere phenomenon, not geocentric but anthropocentric or even cephalocentric [1] in so far as physiology has demonstrated to him the subjectivity of the forms of time and space.   On the other hand, he is convinced that this empirical view of the world is not the view of science.   And so he tries to distinguish between a conception of space and time such as is given us in empirical intuition and a pure or transcendental conception.   But where is the new criterion to be found ?   We must not look to consciousness, which only provides this empirical intuition, but to science ; and we must see whether science justifies a pure concept of time, of space and of the categories.[2] Here we have a typical example of the neo-Kantian sportsman we were describing.   He fixes his eye on the game and forgets

[1] Liebmann, *Zur Analysis der Wirklichkeit*, Strassburg, 1879, p. 167.
[2] *Ibid.*, p. 45.

to observe his sights : he attains the point of view of science and loses that of consciousness. Consequently he believes he is making a Kantian transcendental analysis of the *a priori* principles of science, when he is really carrying on a purely naturalistic research, re-abstracting the already once abstracted products of science. Thus, for instance, in dealing with time, he abstracts from the Newtonian conception of science the ideal form of succession, and calls this form " pure time," believing that he has thus established the *a priori* character of time.[1] Similarly he adds to the forms of space and time a third form, movement, since this too is a fundamental principle of science.[2] And finally he has the temerity to state, by way of explaining his own method, that Kant undertook a critique of the understanding with the same criterion and procedure as are employed by the scientist in his investigation of the material universe, that is to say, with the conviction that the process he was examining was subjected in the same manner to ultimate and highly general laws.[3] Why anyone should attribute to Kant an opinion so startlingly different from anything he actually believed, it is difficult to guess. One can only suggest that our author is talking not about the historical Kant but about another, who was called Otto Liebmann. Not content with bad philosophy, he insists on giving us bad history as well.

Liebmann at least makes no secret of his naturalism For him thought (like sight and hearing) is a natural product : considered from what he calls the causal point of view, it is just like any other process of nature. But he believes that by merely shifting his point of view he can instantaneously arrive at a teleological conception of thought, and so pass from nature to " ethos," from the brutally necessary law (*müssen*) to the spiritual norm (*sollen*).[4] Teleology, however, is not mere science, mere nature : it is the science that is also consciousness—knowledge as an absolute creative act. But we have seen that Liebmann fails to understand this act ; consequently his passage back from science through the concept of teleology to consciousness simply results in

[1] *Op. cit.*, p. 95.
[2] *Ibid.*, p. 126.
[3] *Ibid.*, pp. 219–220.
[4] *Ibid.*, p. 491.

his losing sight of science.   His teleology is thus suspended
in the void between the two spheres : it is a pure ought-to-be,
a norm without any reality.   We shall see how this situation
develops when we come to consider the " Philosophy of
Value."

The philosophy of Riehl contains this same dualism in
an aggravated form, due to a still more complete misinterpretation of Kant.   For while Liebmann was so far faithful
to the Critical Philosophy as to keep the dualism within
the field of knowledge, Riehl, on the other hand, transfers
it to the field of being, that is to say, he harks back to the
pre-Kantian metaphysics, and attempts a transition, from
a ready-made reality outside thought, to consciousness, in
a manner which would bring a blush to the cheek of the
most ingenuous dogmatist.

In fact, he denies that thought, judgment, creates reality ;
taken by itself, the form in which thought is expressed is
(he maintains) purely problematical.   It only borrows whatever reality it has from sensation, which stands with one foot
in consciousness and the other in the hard solid things outside
consciousness.   In this way sensation has reality, because
it consists of a mixture of subjective and objective elements.
And it can also furnish thought with reality, because by
means of it thought is put into communication with things.
From the position of a mediator thought is thus reduced
to that of something itself requiring mediation, and the
mediator (it seems almost incredible) is sensation.   Now,
this is no longer either Kantianism or empiricism (because
the latter recognizes the immediate character of sensation
and the mediate character of thought) : it is simply (we
cannot help saying it) a series of errors and confusions, in
which it is distressing to see a writer involved who has
devoted many long years to the study of Kant.

These errors are due to the fact that Riehl is obsessed
with the idea of the existence of hard solid things outside
consciousness.   " The heroism of Giordano Bruno," he says,
" who died for a new theory of the world, must seem to us
now but folly if that idealistic wisdom were correct which
denies the existence of planets outside the mind of man." [1]

[1] A. Riehl, *Science and Metaphysics*, Eng. tr., pp. 123, 140.

Consequently he would accept the Cartesian *Cogito*, but with a qualification, and would say: *Cogito ergo sum et est.* Clearly the additional statement is simply a grammatical error.

§ 3. MATHEMATICAL AND PLATONIC TENDENCIES IN KANTIANISM.

We have seen the dilemma in which neo-Kantianism is placed. It either remains within consciousness and loses science, the objective aspect of knowledge, or it establishes science and loses all touch with consciousness as its centre of reference, and ends by re-abstracting the abstract in a naturalism run to seed. We have seen Liebmann take this latter road, without, however, being conscious of it and while still believing that he was grasping together science and consciousness in a single conception, the Kantian category. Hermann Cohen, on the other hand, cuts himself adrift from consciousness deliberately, and starts on this road fully conscious of what he is doing. For him consciousness is no longer the centre of reference for the real; it is rather the pure form of modal reflection, establishing simply the possibility of the objects of thought and not their reality.[1] Thought in its objective aspect, as knowledge of reality, thus lies for him altogether outside the centre of consciousness, and is therefore not the concrete act of thinking, the Kantian category, but thought as mere science, as mere object; it is in fact the Platonic idea, thought hypostatized into an objective reality, into nature. Cohen believes that he is still a Kantian and that he can call thought, as he conceives it, a category; but in point of fact he has entirely missed the spirit of Kantianism: he is a Platonist with reminiscences of Kant which are entirely irrelevant to his real doctrine.[2]

[1] H. Cohen, *Logik der reinen Erkenntniss*, Berlin, 1902, pp. 389, 507.

[2] I am well aware that this interpretation of Cohen's philosophy, no less than my previous discussion of the empiricist school, runs counter to that of all the most authoritative previous writers. But if on that account the reader is inclined to dismiss my views with a mere shrug of the shoulders, I would beg him first to reflect that the generally accepted interpretations of these philosophies—the view, for instance, that Cohen's philosophy is a form of Kantian rationalism with traces of Hegelian influence—are not unknown to me, and that where I have departed from them I have not done so without close study and protracted thought.

Since he has eliminated the problem of consciousness at the very beginning of his inquiry and therefore absolved himself from giving an account of immediate experience, that is to say of explaining what sensation is and how it is related to logical thought, he naturally considers thought to be a self-dependent production, a reality in itself, realized not in consciousness (and therefore in no real sense a process), but in the science of nature considered in its abstract impersonal character. When, therefore, he lays down the principle, " We start from thought "—the principle that thought is the absolute beginning (*Ursprung*) and has no contact with sensation and representation [1]—he is merely expressing the logical consequence of his premisses ; and those who object to his making thought spring up like a fungus, without any relation to sensation, show that they have entirely misunderstood the nature of the inquiry he has undertaken. Cohen's error, as we have pointed out, lies not in his conclusion, but in his premisses.

Thought, then, as pure objectivity, as reality in itself (in Hegel's words), is science itself : in the mathematical science of nature we have an instance of the self-dependent production of thought. The principle of the absolute beginning is realized in pure mathematics, whose quali-quantitative reality is spontaneously generated, starting from the infinitesimal calculus which resolves every lacuna created in the process by the old antithesis between the continuous and the discrete. The whole system of mathematics and of the mathematical science of nature is developed autonomously from the principle of the infinitesimal : and the integration of the first principle becomes the mediator of new categories, substance, cause, reciprocal action, etc. Cohen does not exactly hold that this development is a deduction of the categories from an original apperception (a problem that is non-existent for him) ; it is simply a demonstration of the way in which the categories are integrated according to the inherent teleology of the mathematical science of nature, which, in its totality immanent in the process, is, so to speak, a kind of *a priori* principle. The categories are in Cohen's view merely the presuppositions

[1] *Op. cit.*, pp. 4, 20, 32, 33.

of a construction; new problems bring with them new categories : the development of the natural sciences always involves new categories. The world of categories is in short a nature within nature (within science) ; it is not a self-conscious process of creation, but a product on which a new product is based ; thought is that which solves the problems of science, and is thereupon absorbed into the body of science. Thus thought is identified with science regarded as a ready-made objective reality, and has not yet become a problem to itself.

But this is Plato : Kant's problem has not yet been raised. Cohen is under the illusion that he is conceiving the true self-creation, the development of thought, because he speaks of an activity of judgment that produces the categories. He fails to realize that thought for him is thought conceived as an object ; not an agent, but something acted upon ; not genuinely creative, but continually created. The fact is that the fundamental need for this conception— the conception of thought as a self-creative process—is something quite beyond the ken of scientific naturalism, with its habit of regarding thought as a kind of objectively-existing reality. Naturalism considers reality to be complete at every moment : for reality consists of " laws of nature," and these laws have existed from eternity. Yet science develops : but naturalism, from its external stand-point, can only observe the fact of development and cannot really explain it. And the act of development eludes the mere external observation of it, which only succeeds in noting the successive phases or aspects assumed by the thought which is developing, the mere stratifications of the process. Naturalism is under the illusion that it understands the creative act while it really only understands the product, the changeless product, of this act. Cohen shares this illusion.

In his school the naturalistic aspect of his theory is progressively accentuated. Natorp, in his historical studies, misunderstands the relation of Plato's position to that of Kant : having lost the conception of the concrete actuality of thought, the fruit of centuries of speculation, from Aristotle to Descartes and culminating in Kant, he bridges the gulf between Plato and Kant with a *fiat*. His theory, which is a mere re-elaboration and simplification of Cohen's theory, tends more and more to solidify thought into nature. And what right has he to criticize Mach for having made the given absolute, so that thought could no longer be justified, when on his own theory thought is no more justified ? [1] For thought, as he conceives it, is mere knowledge as distinct from self-knowledge ; the pure science of the other (of the object) which is revealed as something completely ignorant of itself ; the eye which sees everything except itself : in short, it is not thought at all, but nature.

This can be observed still more clearly in Cassirer. According to him the mathematical concept reveals itself as the absolute *a priori* element in knowledge, which expresses the rules of any possible scientific experience ; he thus claims that it supplants Kant's principle of pure apperception. It is accordingly necessary to find a mathematical concept of such a kind as to provide a regulative unity for the multiplicity given in experience. This need is satisfied by the concept of function or series, which resolves into itself those of quantity and substance. By means of this concept, mathematics becomes the universal science of form, containing in itself the rule of all possible experience. The whole body of knowledge which constitutes the natural sciences thus gravitates round number, understood in this way as an *a priori* form. Concepts such as substance, cause, etc., are simply constructions determined by the *a priori* demands of number,[2] and in number they find their connection and their unity. And so all reference to the facts of empirical experience gives place to the determination of the intrinsic nature of scientific constructions. For instance, in analysing the concept of the atom we must not inquire whether or not it satisfies the demands of the bodies around us ; we must simply refer to the universal laws and principles of mechanics. We cannot possibly decide, says Cassirer, whether absolutely rigid bodies in collision would or would

[1] P. Natorp, *Die logischen Grundlagen der exakten Naturwissenschaften*, Leipzig, 1910, p. 336.
[2] E. Cassirer, *Substanzbegriff und Funktionsbegriff*, Berlin, 1910, pp. 119, 185.

not obey the law of the conservation of energy : on the
contrary, we assert the validity of this law on the basis of
the *a priori* principles of science ; and we are bound to accept
it in the theoretical construction of the atoms and their
movements.[1]

It is obvious that by now Kantianism has been altogether
lost to view : the *a priori* element in knowledge has become
simply the basis of a construction, a fact, a premiss, according
to which another fact which is its consequence is regulated.
The *a priori* and the scientific construction differ only in
their degree of generality, in so far as the first is the more
general law that includes in it the other, which is simply
one of its applications. This is pure naturalism.

§ 4. The Philosophy of Value.

The aim of the philosophy to which we now turn our
attention is to effect through the concept of value a mediation
of the dualism, which we have hitherto been considering,
between abstract subjectivity and the objectivity of naturalism, between thought and being. Value, according to this
philosophy, represents not a theoretical but a practical
attitude of a subject towards a given object, an attitude,
that is to say, in which it neither affirms nor denies the
object, but simply determines its importance. Presupposing
as it does the existence of an objective reality, the given,
this philosophy begins by assuming a dualism. In order
to see how it attempts to resolve it, we must reconstruct
the whole genesis of its argument.[2]

We have indicated that there are, according to this
philosophy, two methods of considering reality : first, the
theoretical (scientific) method, which invests things with
the predicate of existence and constructs the forms of
naturalistic experience ; secondly, the method of valuation,
which considers the position of the subject towards an object
already presupposed as existing and pronounces a judgment

---

[1] *Op. cit.*, p. 210.
[2] I may refer here to my paper on the subject, *La filosofia dei valori in
Germania*, published in *Critica*, 1911–12, of which a few passages are here
reproduced.

of approval or disapproval. A judgment of the latter kind
is eminently practical, because it always expresses in each
case a sentiment of approval or disapproval, an acceptance
or a rejection : hence value is the practical activity of the
subject. This gives rise to two kinds of logic, the one formal,
investigating the mechanism of the concepts which affirm
the characters of things ; the other philosophical, having
as its object the forms of valuation.

This dualism is the starting-point of the philosophy of
value. Historically it represents a compromise between
formal logic and philosophical logic : the theoretical conditions of the thinkability of things are epitomized in the
external mechanism by which we form concepts : but besides
being thinkable in concepts, things admit of judgment,
valuation : and hence, superimposed on the logic of concepts,
we have the logic of judgments, which claims to be freed
from merely formal presuppositions and to consider the
conditions of the subjective valuation of the object. This
compromise is illustrated by the logical doctrines of Sigwart,
Lotze and Bergmann. But it is impossible to pass from
formalism to philosophy without taking a leap. The logic
of judgments does not resolve in itself that of concepts :
the subject remains dogmatically set over against the object.
Some important inferences may be drawn from this fact.

The valuations with which philosophy is concerned are
those which have a universal character ; they are not the
valuations of the individual as such, but those which transcend it. But if it is already decided that the object is
irreducible to the subject, then the universality that the
subject can establish is not concrete but abstract ; value
is a pure abstract idea, empty, devoid of reality. Being
and value are at the two antipodes, and no contact between
them is possible. Hence the union of formalism and logical
philosophy is only apparent : value is not the *a priori*
condition of being, but presupposes it. And finally the
formal logic of the concept absorbs into itself even the
philosophical logic of the judgment : for universal value
is itself nothing more than a pure abstract idea, a pallid
subjective reflection of an empirical objectivity. This
philosophy results in a debilitated naturalism.

There is no contact between the two worlds, because the very way in which the problem is stated precludes it, even though the intention of this statement is to create one. Value is said to be the universal idea, the good ; as such it is imposed on consciousness as a duty, a norm : value is the ideal norm of being. But by a norm is meant either this same abstract idea of value, in which case the gulf remains unbridged, or else the expression of an attitude adopted by empirical individuals towards the transcendent idea of value ; and in this case the idea remains equally incapable of realization. If we start from a dualism there is no means of arriving at a monism.

The philosophy of value starts from the subjectivity of consciousness and attempts to establish the objectivity of science through the concept of value, failing to perceive that the view taken of the object has already presupposed it. And so, instead of creating a true objectivity, it merely spreads the concept of value over the objective fact already presupposed, like a veil of mist, a pure ought-to-be hanging over that which actually is. The motive of this philosophy is idealistic, since it aims at resolving the concept of being into that of spiritual value ; but it fails to push its analysis home and to grasp the conception of the concrete actuality of thought, in which being is truly resolved ; and so, in its turn, value ends by being crystallized into a kind of being different from empirical being, an ideal abstract being, that is to say a pallid reflection of natural reality.

In this argument we have the kernel of the philosophy of Windelband and Rickert.

Windelband starts from Kant and Lotze, and interprets the Kantian category by the concept of value. He accepts the psychological tripartition of thought, will and feeling, and attempts to make this the basis for a theory of values, logical, ethical and æsthetic, which are all united together by the fact that value is understood in each case as a moral exigency : as the ethical attitude of consciousness towards the three spheres. This, according to Windelband, is the true account of the primacy of the practical reason ; the consciousness which supplies the criterion for the universal valuations of philosophy is the moral consciousness. Windelband's philosophical method thus consists in the appeal to the conception of duty, the " ought " discovered by Kant, which is set over against the empirical valuations of thought, feeling and will as the centre of absolute valuations. Logic thus becomes the science of the standards of thought, ethics of will and æsthetic of feeling.

Windelband imagines that once he has established these premisses he can assume that thought, will and feeling develop purely as natural products, and that he can explain these products as the application of value-standards. But if thought is already a mechanism of representations and associations,[1] the ideal standard of logic must fall outside it, and form a mere demand, a mere ought-to-be that need never actually be realized. Once thought is deprived of any internal criterion of truth, its standard, so far from being immanent, is stratified into a mere kind of being, abstract and ideal, that cannot contain the reasons for the development of thought, because it is outside thought.

The same thing happens in ethics, where the concept of freedom is not represented as something which resolves causal necessity, since it already presupposes that necessity, but is reduced to a mere way of looking at things independently and " in abstraction " from causality. The freedom of our moral judgments, says Windelband, answers to the attitude in which we consider simply the correspondence or non-correspondence of the actual will to the ideal standard of the moral consciousness, disregarding for the moment the causal relation of our volitions.[2] It is clear that freedom is in this way reduced to a mere point of view, that may well be an illusion on our part.

We find exactly the same process of thought in Rickert, only with a change of terms. Windelband's dualism between the ideal standard and empirical being reappears in him as a dualism between the immanent and the transcendent. Rickert accepts the doctrine of immediate experience, which maintains that being does not exist except as the content of consciousness : immediate reality is thus immanent in

---

[1] See the chapter *Denken und Nachdenken* in the *Präludien*, Freiburg, 1904, 3rd ed.

[2] W. Windelband, *Ueber Willensfreiheit*, Tübingen, 1905, 2nd ed.

consciousness as representation. It is not a question of any particular consciousness, but of consciousness in general, as an empirical concept. Hence the immanence of being in consciousness is nothing more than the immanence of the universal or concept of formal logic in its particular representation. On the other hand, Rickert insists that this does not provide a basis for the objectivity of knowledge, because a mere connection between representations cannot have a universal and necessary validity. And since, in his view, consciousness contains nothing whatever but the play of representations, he is compelled, in order to establish the objectivity of knowledge, to get away from consciousness and to devise a transcendent standard that has the required validity.[1] This leap to destruction is expressed, in logical terminology, as follows : the concept is immanent in representations, in the form of the consciousness of being : therefore there can be no such thing as the concept of transcendence. But does the concept exhaust the whole sphere of what is thinkable by generalization ? No : for over against the pure representative synthesis (the concept) there is the act that affirms or denies, that recognizes or does not recognize this synthesis, that is to say the judgment. Thus when the concept of the transcendent is denied, and precisely in that denial itself, there always remains the thought of the negation, and the concept of the transcendent is simply the thought of such a negation. The transcendent is not a content of consciousness, but the term of a judgment ; not a being, because to be is to be in consciousness, but an ought-to-be. In this way we arrive at the " ought," thought regarded as a standard, the criterion of logical valuations, which must save us from the empty immanence of consciousness that is unable to provide a basis for the objectivity of knowledge.

But we have not found a basis for it here either, for we are between two stools. On the one hand we have an abstract formalism, an empty idea of " ought " which encloses us in a circle : " What is truth ? "—what I ought to think ; " What ought I to think ? "—the truth. On the other hand, if I propose to myself to think as I ought, what is there

[1] H. Rickert, *Gegenstand der Erkenntniss*, 1904, pp. 16–17.

to assure me that I *have* thought as I ought ? The feeling of self-evidence, answers Rickert. To think what is true is to render immanent what was transcendent : self-evidence is the bridge from the one to the other. But this is more than we bargained for. If in the last resort it is self-evidence that tells us whether we have thought the truth or not, then self-evidence and not " what ought to be " is the criterion of truth, in which case the " ought " disappears : but if what ought to be is really the criterion, then self-evidence itself is also something that merely ought to be, and need never be realized. Either we abandon the criterion of " ought " and trust to self-evidence, and in that case we have to retrace the road followed by Descartes, or we hold firmly to the abstract " ought " and cannot ever get away from it.

But Rickert has himself realized the defective character of his theory, and he has recently condemned—as psychological—the abstract doctrine of " ought." His condemnation is, however, rather vague, because in the place of " ought " he substitutes " value," the ideal, and reduces the conception of " ought " to a mere stepping-stone from empirical knowledge to this ideal truth. The objectivity of knowledge becomes for him, in this second form of his theory of knowledge,[1] the ideal goal—absolute value—at which every particular knowledge is aiming in so far as whoever knows puts before himself the realization of this value as an ought, as an absolute need. The " ought to be," which before was a mysterious divinity, has now become the servant of another divinity. What exactly is the nature of this new divinity Rickert has not yet very clearly explained ; he has only roughly outlined his conception, which is simply a very diluted form of Platonism. Perhaps if he advances yet a little further he will realize that an abstract universality is entirely useless and he will pull down the new God as well.

Such an advance is possible in Rickert's case, for at bottom he is convinced that though truth as value is transcendent, a truth when it is attained becomes immanent. Since, however, he places thought on one side and truth on the other, he has perforce to create bridges between the

[1] H. Rickert, *Zwei Wege der Erkenntnisstheorie*, 1910.

two, and these naturally all collapse ; for when divorced from thought, truth becomes a shadow without substance, and the bridges end by being suspended in the void.

Of these bridges one of the most interesting examples, in the philosophy of Windelband and Rickert, is provided by the categories. The categories are not conceived by these authors in the Kantian manner, as categorizing activities of thought, but simply as ideal standards whose realization is a demand of thought. Hence arises the question—a question whose very existence betrays an ingenuously dogmatic attitude—where are these standards realized ? The sciences are divided into two great classes : the one natural, the other historical ; the question is : are the categories constituting the real those which preside over scientific research or historical research ?

Viewed from the genuine Kantian standpoint this question is meaningless. For if the category is understood as the actuality of thought, then the reality constituted by the category is simply actual thought : to say that Kant assigns the categories to the science of nature betrays a complete misunderstanding of his theory, because Kant, on the contrary, resolves the science of nature into thought, into the categorizing activity of the spirit. However, even Kant did not have an altogether clear conception of the true nature and import of his discovery, and so the misconception of his interpreters is to some extent justifiable.

The fact that in the conception of the categories advanced by Windelband and Rickert this misconception is rendered irremediable supplies an explanation both of the question whether science or history provides us with the constitutive forms of the real, and of Windelband's attempt at a compromise when he premises that natural science, with its abstract and general concepts, cannot claim to exhaust the whole of reality, and urges that a place ought to be left for the conception of phenomena in their individuality, that is to say, for history.[1] With this misapprehension of the nature of Kant's inquiry and the progressive identification of science with the *schemata* of formal logic, that is to say with the simple external mechanism of abstraction, Rickert's subse-

[1] Windelband, *Geschichte und Naturwissenschaft*, Strasburg, 1900, 2nd ed.

quent reductions become possible : the abstract concepts
of science forfeit their claim to all that reality which, in its
concreteness, is individuality, history. Hence the tendency
of the neo-Kantian philosophy to pass over into historicism.

§ 5. History.

The historical conception of reality which had culminated
in Hegel was absolutely lost in the period of naturalism,
a doctrine that is essentially anti-historical, and fixes reality
once and for all in the motionless forms of matter. Nevertheless, the historical sense which philosophy had lost was
not dead, but lived on in the works of the great German
historians. But if in their work it was realized in an actual
and concrete form, it did not attain to complete self-consciousness, and in its theoretical expressions it appeared
somewhat attenuated. We have already had occasion to
remark on this in Lazarus and Steinthal : the ambiguity
and lack of precise definition that characterized their work
gave an opening for the most disparate developments :
on the one hand, their conception of the collective spirit,
owing to its inherent vagueness and indefiniteness, was
liable to degenerate into the entities of the sociological
essayist : on the other hand, the theoretical side of their
distinction between naturalism and history could serve as
the basis of the new conception of the world, once the
naturalism that they had only put on one side was resolved
and negated.

And this is what actually happened. Passing over the
sociological treatises, which do not offer any interest for
philosophy, we shall follow the very slender thread of
philosophy that runs through the latter development.

Diltey adopts Lazarus's distinction between the natural
and historical sciences. The latter, however, are not in his
view pivoted on that vague entity, the collective spirit, a
reminiscence of the abhorred idealism, but—true to the
neo-Kantian principle of substituting one entity for another—
they are united in the concept of " Kultur." [1]   In the
world of " Kultur " the importance of social and ethical

[1] W. Diltey, *Einleitung in die Geisteswissenschaften*, Leipzig, 1883, pp. 7, 8.

influences preponderates ; the particular is of value in itself and not merely as an exponent and example of a group or class : hence the impossibility of its containing any repetitions, and the necessity of a unique form of thought in order to understand it, namely history.

But Diltey stops short at this purely methodological distinction, believing of course that he is employing the genuine methods of the critical philosophy and that he is in a position to judge and condemn metaphysics. But in reality his *Critique of Historical Reason* is of no very great importance, and its only positive contribution consists in some just criticisms of the attempt of sociology to treat historical individuality as nothing but raw material for its theoretical constructions.[1]

On the other hand, his narrow, almost atomistic interpretation of historical individuality provoked a reaction on the part of sociology. Barth, for instance, produced a work loaded with erudition but very slenderly equipped with ideas, in which he attempted to reclaim history for sociology. Barth contends that the purpose of history is not to describe the individual as such, but only in so far as the individual contains typical elements that are of significance for the life of the many. Hence he concludes that the philosophy of history is the investigation of that which all the branches of human history have in common ; it differs from history as being a science of a higher grade.[2]

Georg Simmel's theory of history is the work of a man of vastly superior mental equipment, but with a tendency towards a sociological point of view. The most interesting part of his theory is the attempt made to rise from a psychological and methodological starting-point to a philosophy of history. In his view history is not a mechanical play of forces, but a spiritual process, or, as he says, borrowing the idea from Lazarus, an applied psychology. Hence the possibility of undertaking for history an inquiry analogous to that undertaken by Kant for the natural sciences, that is to say, to see if there exist *a priori* conditions of the relations

[1] *Op. cit.*, p. 115.
[2] P. Barth, *Die Philosophie der Geschichte als Sociologie*, Leipzig, 1897, pp. 2, 9.

between the spiritual data that constitute the elements of history. Realism is out of the question here, for there is no ready-made reality to be copied ; the historian's data consist of relics and documents that are merely the external symbol of an internal process which only the historian can reconstruct : and the historian could never understand the personal element in history unless he were himself a personality. The whole problem is to discover how a subject (the historian) can endow his subjective construction with objectivity ; that is to say, how a particular psychological content that is evolved in the mind of the historian can be projected outside his individual consciousness and be attributed to a personality in the past.[1] We have seen already throughout the whole of the preceding analysis of Kantianism that there is no logical solution to this problem, because once the empirical subjectivity of the historian is premised, reality can no longer be attained. Still, it shows some penetration on Simmel's part that he should have felt a need which transcends his point of view. The solution which he offers is as follows : Objectivity is based on a feeling of the supersubjective truth of certain psychical constellations and connections, in virtue of the consciousness that these relations are independent of the fact of their being momentarily thought.[2] Unless I am mistaken, this is simply another way of stating the problem.

Although his general attitude from the very first page is mistaken, yet Simmel's philosophy of history is a work full of penetration and just observations. While he contends that history is the science of individualities, he nevertheless thinks that these contain an element of human universality, an essence that is to a certain extent outside time. This is a shrewd observation, but it remains a mere observation and is not worked out. His effort to arrive at a conception of progress is still better. The idea of historical development, he says,[3] is meaningless unless we assume as an *a priori* condition a permanent subject that endures and develops through the atomistic existence of its various moments :

[1] G. Simmel, *Die Probleme der Geschichtsphilosophie*, Leipzig, 1905, 2nd ed., pp. 4, 20, 31.
[2] *Ibid.*, p. 39.   [3] *Ibid.*, p. 150.

if there only exist isolated moments, it is futile to speak of any development. But this seems to him to be verging on metaphysics, and he halts on the threshold in alarm.

Rickert shows less insight, but he is more coherent and works with a more practised hand. We have already seen that Windelband conceives reality to be divided up by an amicable agreement between natural science and history. Simmel also is of this opinion. He regards science and history as antithetical, inasmuch as in the one law prevails and in the other it does not ; and these two categories comprise between them the whole of reality, which (through lack, he says, of a suitable faculty) we cannot grasp together in one conception.[1] Rickert, on the other hand, refuses to admit the existence of two faculties : according to him reality is all of a piece, and is wholly history. He regards science from a nominalistic point of view, as a system of abstractions. There are three stages in the scientist's procedure, constituting different phases in the progressive realization of his fundamental aim, which is to provide simplifications of reality. The first stage is constituted by the verbal expression, which already provides a primary simplification, by abstracting what is common to a group of representations and isolating it from the specific differences. But it is only in a few cases that the act of naming or verbal expression can fulfil completely the logical purpose of the concept. Its empirical universality lacks accuracy and precision : it is only the second stage, namely the class-concept, that can satisfactorily comprehend in a single term the qualitative multiplicity of sensation. The third and final stage of the concept completes the work already begun in the previous stages. This is achieved by the natural law, which renders possible not only a simplification of the infinite multiplicity of phenomena, but also the creation of order and connection in the world.

Thus the aim of natural science is the formation of systems of concepts, whose perfection varies in inverse proportion to the amount of empirical reality they contain. The scientific concept, therefore, has as its internal limit exactly these empirical individualities from which it makes its

[1] *Op. cit.*, p. 137,

abstraction. The uniqueness of the individual, of the particular as such, eludes the abstract concept ; and since this individual is what history takes as its object, historical procedure is shown to be autonomous and independent of scientific generalizations : it is the depository of that reality which eludes the simplifications of science.

On this merely empirical basis Rickert attempts to construct his philosophy of history, interpreting historical individualities as values, and explaining the antithesis between science and history as the antithesis between the realm of nature and the realm of the spirit. On the one side we have abstraction, on the other concreteness ; on the one side the rule of law, on the other individual causality ; on the one side lifeless mechanism, on the other autonomous values, immediate and in a wide sense human. Although historical interest is not restricted to humanity in the narrow sense, but is also extended to what we usually call nature, yet in the ultimate analysis historical interest is always human, because every true historical individuality has a universal value and every universal value is truly human.

Humanity is the true centre of history, for the very reason that history aims at a system of universal valuations. But since these are actualized in civil society, in the world of culture, historical values become social, cultural values.[1] This is the origin of the movement called the " Philosophy of Kultur," which is enjoying such popularity in Germany to-day and finds expression in a review called *Logos*.

Now I fail to see, in this whole theory of Rickert's, anything more than an empirical methodology, uselessly distorted in the attempt to extract from it a philosophy of history. Far from overcoming the intellectualism of Kant, as is usually claimed, it never touches Kant's problem : the creative act of history eludes it, as does the creative act of science (which is itself also history). Confined more than ever within the conception of fact, all he does is simply to substitute historical fact for natural fact, and he entirely fails to grasp the nature of the historical process. Hence he misses entirely the

[1] H. Rickert, *Die Grenzen der Naturwissenschaftlichen Begriffsbildung*, pp. 573, 577.

true spirituality of history, which is identity in development and through development; the true humanity of history, which is human unity in the variety of the experiences of the centuries; and the true immanence of the historical process, which is mentality, subjectivity, and therefore a continuous process of individualization or progress. And he remains confined within the discrete and atomic unity of the individual, of fact, without being able to do anything else except solidify value inside the individual so conceived.

The empirical character of Rickert's method is, moreover, even beginning to be recognized in the school of the philosophy of value. I will mention here Hessen, who interprets the master's doctrine as a transcendental empiricism. And, in fact, if we remove the superstructure that Rickert has erected upon the concept of individuality, this individuality is seen to be, in its initial form, the pure given fact, the immediate element that eludes the abstractions of scientific concepts—a result that shows the resemblance between Rickert's methodology and critical empiricism.

§ 6. NEO-KANTIAN VITALISM.

Rickert labours under the illusion that he can improve on Kantianism by substituting for the categories as expounded in the Analytic of Pure Reason the category of historical individuality; but in reality, so far from having transcended Kant's position, he had not even so much as reached it. His philosophical method, consisting as it does of "substituting" one category for another, shows that he regards the spirit as a kind of bag into which you can put anything you please and always be certain of finding it again. But Rickert's procedure has at least one merit: dissatisfied with Kant's doctrine of the categories, he does not merely mutilate it or patch it, but tries to turn the whole thing round and make it face in a new direction. This may be a mistake, but at any rate the point is arguable. The physiologist Driesch goes to work in a very different spirit. He is obsessed by the idea that Kant in his doctrine of the categories devoted the whole of his attention to the physicists; and Driesch wants

to reclaim a modest portion of it for himself. So, removing
the category of reciprocal causality, which comes third in
the categories of relation, he tries to substitute one that
serves his purpose, namely individuality, which will help
to advance the understanding of life. But had not Kant
himself supplied, in the *Critique of Judgment*, a method
for understanding the organism? Yes, replies Driesch, he
did, but it was not enough, it was a mere regulative form
of experience, and not constitutive. So he quietly goes
and plants out his own category, where it is likely to acquire
greater solidity, in the Analytic of Pure Reason. This is
really too ingenuous. The fact is, Driesch regards the
categories as so many bits of machinery, which one just
sets going from time to time as required. For example,
what is the category of causation? Simply this: I find
by means of introspection, in my psychological subjectivity,
a mode of reference of my psychical facts which I call
causality; and I then apply this by analogy to the external
world.[1] If that is what the categories are, there is of course
nothing in the world to prevent the category of individuality
from joining the company; but it simply comes to this,
that the categories are a name for our habit of sticking
labels on the matter of the physical sciences and the organism
of the biological sciences; matter and organism remain
merely matter and organism, and Kant's formula " I think "
is left out in the cold. But one wants to know what business
Driesch has to catalogue his merely scientific investigations
with the labels of the Kantian philosophy.

But let us leave Kant, the understanding of whom is
not Driesch's strong point, and approach directly the
philosophical problem of vitalism as a biological point of
view. Driesch is an able physiologist; and it is clear that
in a time like the present, when the philosophical discussion
of the problem of life is very active, this aspect of his inquiry
has an altogether different value. And first of all, is there
a philosophical problem of life in the sense of organic life?
Is life something which is autonomous in itself and by itself?
Driesch answers in the affirmative. According to him, there
exists in the organic body a vital principle, an " entelechy,"

[1] H. Driesch, *Vitalism*, Ital. tr., 354, 355, 357.

through which it is an individual. If this were so, if it were possible to revive the entelechy of Aristotle and Leibniz, giving it a strictly biological significance, the whole of Kant's philosophy, which developed the concept of entelechy into that of apperception and of the spirit, would be false (except for Driesch's private variety of Kantianism) and life as an autonomous principle would not presuppose thought, self-consciousness, but would itself be a presupposition of thought.

It seems to me that by means of his conception of the entelechy Driesch ends by shutting life up inside the body, and does not appreciate the fact that the reality of life consists in relation, creation, experience. Life is no doubt individuality, but an individuality that asserts itself in its relation to another, to bodies, to objects ; and this means it is not a ready-made individuality, but a process of individualization, the realization of itself through relation with another. It is not, then, merely life, but consciousness. The life which is imprisoned in the body is a concept of the laboratory, a mere fact, localized and materialized in the body, not the creative act of life, which is experience and consciousness. For what exactly is this individuality which is described as mere individuality ? I experience my body as an individual, but I can only do so in so far as I am in relation with what is other than me ; and it is only in this relation that I discover myself. My body is then in reality the act of my self-individualization : it is only by losing sight of the concreteness of this act that I can objectify my body to myself, and I then proceed to postulate the objective existence in this body (simply as organized body) of the mere possibility of relations, acts, etc., thus fabricating entirely imaginary entelechies, vital principles, in order to provide mere matter with an explanation of what, as mere matter, it does not contain, namely life. But in reality it is simply a question of an hypostatization, a materialization of life, a false intermediary between the experience of the physiologist and the concept of the philosopher. If I objectify my body to myself as a fact, a phenomenon, this fact simply consists of matter, constituted in this or that determinate way according as the physiologist decides :

there is no entelechy in it. But if I view my body as it really is, as my experience, that is to say as the experience which I affirm as mine in my relations with other bodies, then the truth, the absolutely *a priori*, must be this ego which is in relation to itself in so far as it is in relation to another, and in relation to another in so far as it is in relation to itself : it is self-consciousness, individuality that is at the same time universality (the act of individualization), and not the mere organized individual. Driesch's entelechy attempts to compromise between these two extremes : it attempts to discover the activity of life, which is experience and consciousness, in a fact, a phenomenon, consisting of the material body ; and being unable to find it in actuality, it alleges it to be there as a potentiality, as though the potentiality could precede the act and contain its reason. This entelechy is in fact a mere relic of scholasticism.

§ 7. The New Historical Materialism.

In studying the history of neo-Kantianism it would be profitable to examine two derivative offshoots which represent vividly the tendencies of that attitude of thought : the juridico-social theory of Stammler and the theology of Ritschl.

We have seen that Marx was divided between two conflicting interests, the one historical, the other naturalistic, and that the encroachment of the latter upon the former brought about a naturalistic interpretation of the dialectic which anticipated history by showing the advent of communism to be a fact towards which society was being impelled by a natural necessity. But the solution of this conflict is to be found in Marx's actual practical programme. For by inciting the working class to revolution he implicitly recognized that history is something human and is not mere crude nature, and he thus superseded his own theoretical formula.

On the other hand Stammler, who is an advocate of the materialistic theory of history, developing some suggestions thrown out by Lange and Cohen, contends that the Marxian ought only to revolutionize people's minds, that is to say inculcate the materialistic conception of history with all its consequences, in order that this by itself may produce the desired effect. In this way he revives the fruitless ideology that Marx had attempted to demolish. In fact, he is simply viewing *sub specie æterni* that formula of the future communism which still preserved in Marx a certain concrete aspect, inasmuch as it was put forward as the goal of the historical development of modern life : and even the formula became, in Marx's hands, invested with some of the reality and concreteness of this development.

Stammler, being a loyal neo-Kantian, makes a distinction between a form and a content in social relations : the law is the form, the economic element is the content. And he accordingly adapts Kant's famous principle and concludes that a juridical rule without a matter to be regulated is empty, an economic content without the idea of a determinate regulation is chaotic.[1]

He conceives the relation between form and content to be that of means to an end : law is a means towards economic production. Hence the obvious conclusion that the aim of legal regulation is to create a social life corresponding to economic ends. Hence also the reason for supplementing the idea of end with that of duty : a certain social system ought to be attained.[2]

Marx's crude materialism is thus laid on the soft bed of the idea of duty, the demands of morality ; but the bed is so soft that it verges on nothing. What is left of Marxianism ? That economic content which in Marx was solidified by union with its internal form, and so enabled to break up pre-existing crystallized forms and create itself as a new juridical and social form, has become here soft matter, at the mercy of pliant legislative norms or standards, which, with their gaze fixed on the highest ideals, mould it and remould it at their pleasure. Marxianism is inverted, and in its inversion has lost all its serious character.

But Stammler is thoroughly convinced of the soundness of his formula and claims to raise it to such a degree of

---

[1] R. Stammler, *Wirtschaft und Recht nach der materialistischen Geschichts-auffassung*, Leipzig, 1906, 2nd ed., p. 161.

[2] *Ibid.*, pp. 392, 394.

universality that it can include in itself the whole of Marxianism as simply a particular instance. In fact, if we assume
the relation between means and end, with all its consequences,
the search for the end of society becomes the search for a
unifying point of view for all the social tendencies, for a
final unconditioned goal of social life in general. Now this
end must be merely formal, so as to eschew all empirical
particularity ; it therefore consists in the free will. Hence
he concludes that a community of men enjoying freedom of
will is the unconditioned aim of social life. And the means
to attain it (always assuming that people's minds have
been revolutionized by the principles of historical materialism)
is a just system of law. But will the State in which this
end is realized be a communistic one, as Marx said ? Here
Stammler has an opportunity of treating Marx *de haut en bas*.
This communism, says he, is only an empirical concept ;
it is only one of the possible and particular applications of
this pure formal principle. Merely by way of a concession,
Stammler adds that the socialization of the means of production may be a means of satisfying the demands of the
social ideal ; but otherwise he leaves the question of a solution
unprejudiced because it is of an empirical nature.[1]

Thus scientific socialism, which was drawn down by
Marx's powerful personality into the world of history, has
been replaced by neo-Kantianism in the realm of Utopia.

§ 8. NEO-KANTIAN THEOLOGY.

Protestant theology is by nature inherently anti-historical.
Its basic principles remain as they were fixed by Luther,
the revealed word and the inner faith. Everything else is
excluded ; all dogma, all the religious experience of the
ages is rejected. The believer ought to approach the Gospel
alone with his faith. As Boutroux [2] acutely observes, the
Reformation is the history of the accidental conjunction of
two phenomena, the exaltation of inner faith and the return
to the ancient texts and monuments ; the problem how
to bring these two disparate principles together into one

[1] *Op. cit.*, pp. 619, 620.
[2] E. Boutroux, *Science et Religion*, Paris, 1908, p. 215.

doctrine has been the torment of the Protestant mind. It has never solved the problem, because it has never been able to fuse the letter and the spirit, the sources of evidence and its own inner life. It has arbitrarily forced the letter into the preconceived forms of the spirit by attempting to make a distinction in it between what is essential to history and what is superfluous ; and in its turn the letter thus understood has reacted on the spirit and imprisoned it in the abstract subjectivity of its faith, where it is only ostensibly preserved and in reality destroyed.

In consequence, the letter and the spirit, history and religion, are mutually destructive. We have already observed a similar phenomenon in Baur. With his method of reduction he resolved religion into a nullity, so much so that when Strauss tried to sum up his beliefs, he found that the whole of Christianity, with its idea of a divine personality, had vanished and there only remained an empty deification of naturalism. Ritschl protests against these consequences of the philosophy of the Tübingen school, although he accepts the same premises. He too rejects all ecclesiastical authority, all dogma, all institutional religion. Christ and the believer with his faith : these, he maintains, make up the whole of religion. He therefore tries to escape the conclusions of the Tübingen school by emphasizing the idea of faith, of spiritual value, and attempting by means of this idea to fill the void that has been created. The power of the Gospel lies no longer in the Church or the solid tradition of the ages, but in the consciousness of the individual : the Gospel is true because the individual attributes to it the value of truth. Ritschl believes that in the innermost recess of consciousness he can preserve that faith which the whole corporate witness of humanity is powerless to uphold. But, by force of its own logic, error awaits this faith in the very hiding-place in which he has sought to preserve it. For he is really applying to the religious consciousness exactly the same method of refinement and reduction which Strauss applied to history : he distinguishes in the individual between what is nature and what is spirit, denying categorically that natural knowledge has any relation with religious experience, and confining the latter to the higher sphere of pure spiritu-

ality.[1] He believes that in this way he is interpreting
the need, formulated by the Kantian philosophy, of super-
imposing on the world of nature a world of spiritual life ;
and he does not realize that this bloodless and attenuated
spirituality is a mere abstraction, a nullity.   Thus the reign
of God is restricted to the experience of the individual
consciousness, which is completely divorced from the concrete
life of the individual.   What kind of truth, then, can the
value-judgments of this consciousness produce ?   Ritschl
replies that if we are firmly convinced of its value for our
wellbeing, we can thereby know in its essence everything
in us that is divine, and even God himself ; and that the
divinity of Christ can be demonstrated, not indeed by an
act of disinterested knowledge, but solely within the religious
experience.[2]   But does the judgment of value really justify
this step ?   Or does it not rather conceal the impotence of
mere abstract subjectivity to rise to the concept of God ?
Have we not here another instance of the fallacy which
we have shown to run through the whole history of neo-
Kantianism ?

There is a great deal of talk nowadays about value :
Höffding actually places the essence of religion in judgments
of value ; it has become a word to conjure with.   But to
me it seems to be, especially in religious problems, a mere
evasion ; an ambiguous term midway between an affirmation
and a negation ; something, in fact, that betrays not merely
a conflict of theories but a profound inconsistency within
consciousness itself.

Harnack is another seeker after the essence of religion.
He too thinks that the substance of the Gospel ought to be
divested of the dress in which history has clothed it.   But
the result is exactly what he confidently declares will
never happen.   He is like a child who, after stripping a
bulb of its successive coats in order to get at the heart,
discovers that he has nothing left in his hand.[3]   And this
is not because the bulb simply consists of a number of coats,
not because religion is an external aggregate of religious

[1] A. Ritschl, *Die Christliche lehre von der Rechtfectigung und Versöhnung*,
Bonn, ed. 4, 1895, iii, p. 208.
[2] *Ibid.*, pp. 376, 377.
[3] A. Harnack, *What is Christianity ?* Eng. tr., p. 14.

facts, but because Harnack has dissected religion with the hands of a child. To what, in fact, does he finally reduce religion ? To the worship of God the Father. Not of the God made man in Christ, not of the God who lives in the history of humanity, not of him in whom we live and move and have our being, but of the abstract God of theism. What kind of faith can we have in such a God ? It can only be the exaltation of what is utterly inexplicable to the individual, an arbitrary and isolated fact in the life of humanity. The God of Harnack, like the God of Ritschl, cannot be worshipped, loved or feared, but only criticized as a logical error : he is the Thing-in-itself, the remnant of dogmatism that lingers in Kant's philosophy

CHAPTER IV

PSYCHOLOGY AND PHILOSOPHY

§ 1. PSYCHOLOGISM.

IN the medley of psychology and physiology that Fechner and, following him, Wundt have baptized with the name of psycho-physics, we have a survival of the old naturalism. The advocates of this new movement maintain that it has removed psychology from the sphere of philosophy proper and has erected it into an autonomous natural science. As such, we wish it all success. But this does not relieve us from the obligation to examine it briefly, to attempt to appraise it from a philosophical point of view. In so far as it obliterates the distinction between psychical and physical facts by applying to them the concepts of function and correlation, it is a philosophical conception of life and of thought, not a genuine natural science. There is no science except of the homogeneous, of fact, of the given : and psycho-physics arbitrarily forces into the *schemata* of the homogeneous what is not pure homogeneity, pure fact, in order to make this the foundation of a scientific construction. The psychical facts which it interprets as a parallel series to that of physical facts are not the actual facts of psychological experience, but the product of an elaboration that presupposes a whole naturalistic theory of the spirit. Psycho-physics is an attempt to found a science on a metaphysic. It is therefore neither genuine science nor genuine philosophy, but naturalism, that is to say, a false metaphysic.

We need not discuss it any further, but will rather try to follow a much more interesting movement of thought, starting from the same empirical and neo-Kantian basis and proceeding from the same desire to transcend immediate consciousness and to attain objective reality, though in other respects it has close affinities with descriptive psychology. We refer to what is known as psychologism, the doctrine which attempts to unite psychology and philosophy and rejects the twofold point of view dear to the neo-Kantian schools, which very often enables them to play a double game with thought. And in reality the whole of modern philosophy from Descartes onwards is psychologism, the affirmation of the real as the spirit, subjectivity. Only there is psychologism and psychologism; there is empirical psychology and there is philosophical psychology, and between the two lies an abyss. But the nature of the abyss is quite misconceived by those who play the double game, when they assume that once the psychological character of an investigation is recognized, philosophy ought to beat a retreat. It is not a gulf separating two classes of problems, psychological and philosophical, but one which separates two conceptions of reality, two philosophies, the one arrested and the other advanced, so that the second has every right to appraise and criticize the first. Incidentally one might point out that the idea entertained by Münsterberg, James and Hodgson that they could be naturalists, or even materialists, in psychology and idealists in metaphysics is a complete mistake : James the psychologist transfers the psychological conception of life to philosophy, and Münsterberg and Hodgson do the same.

This being the case, it is not the premisses of German psychologism that are at fault, as Husserl has attempted to demonstrate in a pedantic treatise, but its development of them, in so far as its conception of the psychological subject is, as we shall see, philosophically false.

Brentano is the founder of psychologism. Like Lange and Schuppe (and even before the latter) he started from the datum of immediate consciousness. According to him, psychical facts enjoy the prerogative over physical facts of immediate certainty. To deny their absolute certainty means to fall into the doubt that destroys itself, as Descartes showed. Physical facts, on the contrary, have no certainty except what is mediated by the psychical ; they are simply phenomena, the mere indications of something that is real. To attempt to argue that the certainty of physical facts is greater than that of psychical facts because they alone can be touched and seen, would mean to convert into a mark of superiority what is the characteristic mark of their inferiority ; what is truly real does not fall within the phenomenon, and the phenomenon is not truly real.[1] Hence Brentano's theory of the superiority of psychology to natural science, which he maintained, in a period of naturalism, with a vigour that was amazing. Lange had been far less energetic in his statement of the same principle ; for with his greater penetration he had an intuition of the problem which this solution concealed.

Brentano, like Lange, tries to use his point of view in order to establish the objectivity of knowledge. Only, as he feels more confident about the point of view than Lange, he regards the problem not merely as a vague need, but as a question to which he can give the answer. He believes that all psychical facts share the common characteristic of referring to an object ; by which we ought not to understand an objective reality, but a more general relation : in a representation something is represented, in a judgment something accepted or rejected, in love some one loved. All these facts have in common the reference to an object, but not to a reality.[2] This observation is precisely that which Meinong makes in his theory of objects, which we have already examined when dealing with empiricism. We saw there that the observation does not advance the problem of objective reality a single step ; the emphasis laid on the feature common to mere representations and to judgments of reality simply serves to hide the gulf that separates them. How does Brentano deal with this difficulty ? He believes that he has already bridged the gulf by establishing the general concept of reference to an object ; so he only goes on to distinguish between representations and judgments as two special cases of it, and never realizes that he has simply gone round the problem instead of solving it. He describes

[1] F. Brentano, *Psychologie vom empirischen Standpunkte*, 1874, pp. 11, 12, 24.
[2] *Ibid.*, p. 115.

the edges of the ditch and believes that he has therefore leapt it.

According to him, representation and judgment are specifically different things. The first is the simple act of presentation to consciousness, pure givenness, as Schuppe and Rehmke have defined it, quite independent of whether the given is affirmed or denied. Judgment, on the other hand, is the affirmation of the represented content as true or its rejection as false. In this Brentano is in agreement with Sigwart and Lotze ; and, as we have seen, Windelband and Rickert's philosophy of value takes its starting-point from all three.

In so far as it is affirmation or negation, judgment is always existential ; not because it adds the predicate of existence to a representative content, but because in the act of judgment content and existence are one and the same. This is very true : only from his static and descriptive point of view Brentano does no more than describe representation and judgment, without being able to conceive the transition from the one to the other.

Herein lies the inferiority of his psychologism to the neo-Kantian philosophy. For even though the latter fails to conceive the transition (a feat which is really impossible, since in order to understand the relation of the two terms we must invert them, and go not from representation to judgment but from judgment to representation), still it perceives that the point of view of pure subjectivity does not help it to attain objectivity, and accordingly does its best to escape from the subjective point of view.

But, on the other hand, Brentano rises far above the dualistic psychology that believes in a soul-substance. Like Lange, he explicitly denies such a substance : hence both their theories have earned the title of " psychology without a soul." The place of this idea is taken by the somewhat Kantian concept of the unity of consciousness. Without this unity, says Brentano, psychical life is impossible. We see a colour and hear a sound, and compare them, noticing their difference. How is this possible ? If a blind and a deaf man were to compare together their sensations of sight and sound respectively they would not arrive at anything :

comparison is only possible on the basis of the unity of consciousness. A person listening to a melody is aware that while one note represents itself to him as present, others are represented as past: or again, whoever knows how to see and to feel knows also how to do the two together.[1] Without apperception, as Kant would put it, there is no perception. In this concept Brentano rises to the level of neo-Kantianism; he is, in fact, a neo-Kantian without knowing it and without desiring it.

Lipps is the successor of Brentano. He feels more acutely the urgency of the problem concealed in Brentano's descriptions and definitions, and in consequence he has more explicitly revealed the weakness of the procedure common to both. He too starts from consciousness as "immediately given"; but he understands that the object is not explained by this point of view, and so he sets up the object over against the subject with a "demand," a claim to recognition. A concept of this kind conceals an element of naïve dogmatism, which has every opportunity of displaying itself in the course of his investigation. Just as Brentano distinguished between representation and judgment, so Lipps distinguishes between a "qualitative apperception," confined to observation and statement of the given, and an "empirical apperception," concerned not with the quality of the given as such, but with the right of a qualitative determination to exist.[2] It is by this recognition of "right to exist" that the demand or claim of the object for recognition in consciousness is satisfied. Consequently the principle of empirical apperception is expressed as follows: in so far as the object is the same object, its demand upon consciousness is the same demand; that is to say, the same predicates belong to it. We see here that the concept of the claim is simply a remote way of saying that there is a thing-in-itself with all its own wealth of determinations, which imposes on consciousness the manner in which it shall be recognized. The Kantian principle of apperception, to which even Brentano granted some right of citizenship in psychology, is here supplanted by the purest dogmatism, inasmuch as

[1] *Op. cit.*, pp. 209, 210.
[2] T. Lipps, *Leitfaden der Psychologie*, Leipzig, 1903, p. 61.

the identity of the real is not the identity of apperceptive consciousness, but that of the object outside and previous to apperception, which makes a demand upon consciousness for its own recognition. From this point onwards every new step that Lipps takes towards a more specific determination of the concept of this "identity of claim," which even extends to include the principle of natural causality, is a step towards a more and more absolute dogmatism that enriches the thing-in-itself with all the determinations of thought, in the belief that these can be brought back to thought by means of the ambiguous concept of "claim" or "demand."

This conclusion fails to satisfy even Lipps himself At bottom he is convinced that a reality thus understood is little better than a nonentity. "The subject as we conceive it," he says, "as consisting of psychical facts, is an empty shadow."[1] From a limited and finite point of view it is impossible to conceive the true unity of the real; but for this very reason psychology refers the question to metaphysics, which alone can furnish the solution of our ultimate problems. Is this double appeal possible? Unfortunately not; and in fact the metaphysic which Lipps proceeds to outline is simply his own psychology seen through a magnifying glass. In the first instance we were presented with a consciousness on a small scale; now we have a life that is conscious of everything, self-complete and self-organized, and regarded by Lipps as a transcendent entity. This transcendent entity cannot manifest its action except by demanding activity of us. "In all the demands felt by me," says Lipps, "there is expressed the consciousness of the world demanding to become my consciousness." But if this consciousness is transcendent, how can it ever become immanent? If it is self-complete and self-organized, if it is an eternal fulfilment of the demand, how can it require to be fulfilled in us? The truth is that this transcendent consciousness is the same thing-in-itself which was introduced incognito in the psychology. And it is revealed in the metaphysical version to be a mass of contradictions, indicating an entirely false statement of the problem.

[1] *Op. cit.*, p. 339.

This tendency towards a metaphysic of the transcendent is not uncommon, and we shall meet it again later. We shall see that all such attempts are due to the desire to escape from the empiricism of immediate consciousness, but that they fail to free themselves from the real fallacy of empiricism, namely, the attempt to grasp reality in an immediate vision ; the fallacy is merely transferred from the empirical self to the transcendent self. We shall encounter Lipps again. But for the moment we shall pause to examine some of the conclusions drawn by psychological philosophy.

§ 2. The Psychology of Value.

In distinguishing among the facts of consciousness, Brentano placed side by side with representation and judgment a third category, constituted by the facts of love and of hate. He thus reduced the phenomena of will and feeling to a single concept, and criticized the traditional division of psychology from the point of view that will and sentiment possessed a common characteristic : that of referring in one and the same way to a content of consciousness. Similarly Lipps adds to " qualitative " and " empirical " apperception an " evaluative " apperception which considers the object from the point of view of its value to the personality valuing it.

On the basis of this category of facts of feeling, of value, Meinong constructs a whole psychology. Considered empirically, value is defined as a fact which presupposes a valuing subject and a valued object. Hence the problem : are things of value because we desire them, or do we desire them because they are of value ? This problem is identical with that presented in the neo-Kantian theory of consciousness : do things exist because we know them, or do we know them because they exist ? Being incapable of grasping the *a priori* synthetic act, neo-Kantianism has never been able to stop labouring at this insoluble problem, now shutting itself up in the pure subject, now in the pure object. The same thing occurs in the psychology of value.

There is in point of fact a certain truth in saying both that we desire things because they are of value, and that

PSYCHOLOGY AND PHILOSOPHY 101

they are of value because we desire them. But this truth is changed to complete falsity unless we grasp the concrete act of valuation as the *a priori* condition of both value and desire. In the single and indivisible act of valuation there is no dualism; this dualism is the work of a subsequent reflection, which resolves the act into its elements and then sets itself the absurd task of reconstructing out of the elements the act which it has destroyed. All it can actually do is to repeat the refrain : Do we desire things because they are of value, or are they of value because we desire them. Meinong and Ehrenfels go round and round this vicious circle first in one direction and then in the other.

Meinong defines value as the subjective feeling accompanying the judgment by which we recognize the existence of a thing ; it is, in fact, the pleasure or pain with which we recognize this existence. Value is thus the subjective colouring, so to speak, of an objective condition of fact. It follows that things are of value because we find pleasure in their existence. But at this point the object enters a protest : would it not be truer to say that we find pleasure in the existence of things because they are in themselves of value ? And it is quite right to protest, because Meinong has denied that value lies in the act of valuation, an act which, he contends, does not create value but only recognizes it.

In a subsequent treatise we find Meinong modifying his definition : value, he now says, lies in the strength of motivation with which the object asserts itself in the struggle of motives.[1] In this way value is made to reside in the object, which possesses an intrinsic power of motivation : the subject is reduced to a pair of scales in which the motives are weighed against each other. It is still worse when this theory is carried into ethics, where egoism and altruism are made to play at seesaw. But even if we keep to this empirical point of view, the subject must have an innings too, and state its claims. Where, it will ask, is an object to be found that has a power of motivation ? Whatever power the object has is surely conferred on it by the subject,

[1] All these theories are reviewed by F. Orestano, *Valori umani*, Turin, 1907.

in so far as it accepts or rejects, loves or hates ; without this the object would be simply inert. And we can only repeat the old refrain : Which came first, the hen or the egg ?

Ehrenfels holds that things are of value because we desire them, and not vice versa. " We attribute value to those things which we either actually desire, or which we would desire if we were convinced of their existence. The value of a thing is its desirability." [1] And he tries with some acuteness to justify his subjectivist point of view by criticizing the objectivity of value, which he regards as an illusion. He shows that the illusion comes about by means of inference from the fact that we may desire a thing not for itself, but for the sake of something else with which it is connected in a causal or constitutive relation.[2] But the enemy is not conquered by bringing him into one's house ; the argument for objectivity is not resolved in this way, but is merely removed *ad infinitum.*

Krüger also, starting from Ehrenfels's premises, seeks to resolve objectivity into pure subjectivity. He understands objectivity not as an illusion but simply as a comparatively constant valuation, in contrast with merely subjective valuations. He believes that he has thus solved the problem ; he fails to realize that the criterion of constancy is only valid for cataloguing and classifying facts, the products of valuation, and not for understanding the act of valuation itself. But surely Kant's treatment of the subject has settled for ever the distinction between the formal analysis of the act itself and the mere classification of acts, and the absolute necessity of adopting the former point of view. The question is not one that ought to require discussion to-day.

[1] C. Ehrenfels, *System der Werttheorie*, Leipzig, 1897, i. p. 53.
[2] *Op. cit.* p. 51.

CHAPTER V

THE METAPHYSIC OF EMPIRICISM AND ITS SELF-ANNIHILATION

§ 1. THE METAPHYSIC OF EMPIRICISM.

WE have so far seen German philosophy, empirical, neo-Kantian and psychological, developing with varying success a single fundamental theme : immediate consciousness. But in doing so, it has almost always avoided a central group of problems which remind it too closely of the metaphysics it abhors, namely God, the soul, the world—in fact, the ultimate reality of things. Yet in its boycott of these problems we have a stronger proof of the radical insufficiency of its procedure than in its affected contempt of metaphysics. It is at times, indeed, tempted to lift the veil inscribed with the mystic words *keine Metaphysik mehr* ; and on these occasions we have indisputable proof that beyond the region to which it confines itself there lies a void which is barely concealed by some label designating it as the world of faith or of poetry.

The thinkers, on the other hand, whom we are now going to consider are far more courageous, and, armed with the same weapons, have tried to attack these " ultimate " problems. In studying their work we shall have the opportunity of observing how this empiricism which moved with such certainty in the field of immediate consciousness, but yet was unable to attain to the point of view of science as defined by the Analytic of Pure Reason, finally arrived, in a state of absolute exhaustion and collapse, in sight of the problems that we are wont to call metaphysical.

Wundt, the most distinguished exponent of this move-ment, starts from the general assumption of empiricism, the identity of subject and object in immediate consciousness. Our representations are, in the first instance, the objects themselves. Space and time, far from being *a priori* forms, belong to the data of perception and are, so to speak, embedded in it.[1] The distinction between a form and a content of consciousness only comes later : after a time, out of the homogeneous mass of the life of representation, some elements detach themselves and disappear, while others are found to be more permanent ; and thus gradually arises the distinction between a variable and transient matter (sensation) and a permanent form (space and time). Any further elaboration of the given, by which it is systematized and fixed in conceptual forms, is the work of thought. The organon of thought is abstraction ; its incentive to action is the contradiction latent in the given. This contradiction, becoming manifest, necessitates a co-ordination through which the given frees itself and enters again into a harmonious and coherent system.

This work of thought is effected through grades of generalization. The various moments of it are not the creating of reality, of truth, for reality is already completely made in sense, in the immediate given : it is therefore simply a question of impoverishing reality in order to render it more coherent. The first grade of generalization is constituted by the empirical individual concepts : the value of these concepts is of the highest kind, inasmuch as they adhere most closely to the given. Then come general concepts, such as number, abstract space, matter, form, etc. : these are not empirical, because needs of thought are realized in them which are not given in any real experience.[2] Yet Wundt still attributes to them a scientific value. Why ? Here the *naïveté* of the empiricist is revealed in all its completeness. He believes he is trying, like Kant, to determine the limits of scientific experience, while all the time he is really presupposing a science ready made and complete, which he employs as a standard whereby to determine the validity of its own concepts. In reality Wundt has no criterion of valuation : his criterion is that of a mere classi-

[1] W. Wundt, *System der Philosophie*, Leipzig, 1889, pp. 92, 129.
[2] *Op. cit.*, pp. 226, 227.

fication. Thought has for him no other object than a progressive emptying of the given, and it is only by an arbitrary act that Wundt himself is able to note the stages of this work, that is to say in so far as he has his eye fixed on a perfect and complete science.

The third grade is constituted by the most general concepts, which are absolutely devoid of representative content : the concepts that Wundt, in a phrase reminiscent of Kant, calls concepts of reason, as opposed to those of the understanding : namely God, the soul, the world. Given his premises, God becomes for Wundt a *flatus vocis*, a concept without content. How, then, is it that on Him rests the supreme unification of the real ? In this confusion lies the whole of the colossal illusion of empiricism. Reality is first refined away, evaporated to almost nothing, and it is pretended that this residuum, this nonentity, is the supreme ruler of the world. But, says the empiricist, it is only the human concept of God which is thus empty ; God in Himself is a highly concrete reality. The truth is that, having reached the goal of his philosophy and found it a cipher, he is now merely trying to fill the void by packing into it his own preconceptions and endowing it with a reflection of his own logic's impotence : but the cipher remains the cipher it was proved to be. What a gulf there is between the modern scientist's attempts at a logic and the massive logic of the old monk who worked out the ontological proof of the existence of God !

After these logical preliminaries let us prepare ourselves to hear Wundt's metaphysic. The author himself has taken care, before producing it, to discredit it by considering it implicitly as a vacuum, the last relic of abstractions, devoid of any truth because devoid of any controlling power : a futile play of concepts.

And indeed Wundt's metaphysic is a very emasculated thing : it has the strength neither of truth nor of error. The concepts with which it is concerned are those of the world, the soul and God. The first problem, that of the world as a whole, involves Kant's cosmological antinomies. Is the world finite or infinite ? We can maintain both propositions with equal justice. But, as Kant also pointed out, the thesis and antithesis may both be false : a profound truth, though obscured by the shadow of the thing-in-itself, which prevented Kant from grasping the positive side of the negation. The world as a physical totality, which forms the centre of the Kantian antinomy, is nothing but the thing-in-itself, the empty projection of thought, which anticipates the whole at once, as though what is continually being given in the progressive synthesis of knowledge were already given as a whole. Once the absolute character of this synthesis is recognized, the true world is seen to be not this empty shadow, but the synthesis, concrete thought itself : not the mere infinite, nor the mere finite, but the infinite coming into being as finite, the infinite becoming definite in the single act of knowledge, and, in so far as it is infinite, transcending this single act once the act is complete and advancing to a new synthesis, creating new experiences.

This is the true solution of the Kantian antinomy. Wundt, on the other hand, simply evades the question and asserts that the antinomy does not exist : the limited and unlimited can, according to him, coexist, because they do not refer to the same object. We arrive at the idea of the finite when we think of the world as a quantitative unity ; at that of the infinite when we think of it as a qualitative system of many substantial and causal elements. Thus the world implies a totality of things limited in itself, which, however, we never think of as confined within determinate limits.[1] Where, then, has all Wundt's empiricism gone ? Surely to admit that the world is a totality limited in itself is to revive the thing-in-itself of intellectualist dogmatism that is so repugnant to the empiricist view, according to which the world in its reality is psycho-physical identity created in sensation and perception. This empty idea is nothing else than the shadow of his whole procedure, whose very emptiness prevents him from escaping it.

Equally mistaken in our opinion is the reasoning of Wundt's Rational Psychology, whereby he believes he can free himself at a single stroke from the conception of the soul-substance and substitute an " activist " doctrine which regards the soul as the pure act of volition. But an act

[1] *Op. cit.*, p. 368.

which is defined as the greatest of abstractions and not as absolute concreteness is a *flatus vocis*, a nothing, a mere misplaced reminiscence of a profound truth of idealism. Indeed, very soon afterwards Wundt treats this apperceptive act as a thing, sets over against it the cosmological idea, viewing it also as a thing, and then tries to find a compromise between the two. Hence arises a compound of psychology and cosmology, in which beings are considered as so many volitional centres which are interconnected and co-ordinated into a series by means of the representative activity.[1] And finally, as the ultimate unity of reality, we have God, the will of the world ; and this abstraction is presented as a proof that the development of the world is no less than the development of the divine volition and activity.[2] This is the metaphysical system which is held up to admiration as the highest achievement of German thought, the thought that boasts the names of Kant and Hegel !

Paulsen reproduces the faults of Wundt's argument in an exaggerated form. He considers everything as being of a psycho-physical nature : the psychical and volitional world is coextensive with the physical world. Hence we can say that in the physical world mechanical causality dominates, but in the corresponding psychical world purposiveness, teleology, is all-powerful. Materialism is right when it says that all natural processes, even vital processes, may be explained purely physically : there is no interference by an intelligent cause. But Spinoza and Schopenhauer are also right when they say that all physical processes point to concomitant inner processes, and that we can not only find between them an external causal connection, but also an internal one which we can call teleological.[3]

These profound conceptions of a double-faced reality are not uncommon. Fechner, among others, advanced a similar doctrine : he regards the world as a bowl, on one side concave, on the other convex ; on this side psychic, on that physical. It is the illusion of the child who sees the sky over his head as concave, and imagines that on the other side it would look convex : and it never occurs to him that

[1] *Op. cit.*, p. 421.   [2] *Op. cit.*, p. 442.
[3] F. Paulsen, *Introduction to Philosophy*, Eng. tr., p. 227.

this convexity is a creation of his own imagination, that he
has objectified into a thing in itself what is only a phenomenon
of his vision.   Paulsen's whole theory of pan-psychism, of the
All-beseelung, is just as childish.   He takes a piece of iron
and alleges that it has an inside and an outside. He never
reflects that this inside is just as physical as the outside—
the whole thing is iron all through—and tries to see in it
the " other side " of reality, the psychical side, while the
outside has already been shown to be physical ; and then
he concludes : This internal aspect cannot be the Idea, which
is too flimsy and nebulous : it is the will, which is more
solid—so solid that it can petrify itself until it attains the
hardness of the piece of iron in question.   And he claims
that he has hereby surmounted the so-called intellectualism
of Kant and Hegel, which give too much to thought and too
little to will.   But Kant and Hegel were not such children
as Paulsen imagines, and never had the least intention of
enclosing the Idea in a piece of iron.

Here then, according to Paulsen, we arrive at the idea
of the universal will which penetrates all beings and, uniting
in varying degrees with intelligence, ranges them on a scale
from the lowest to the highest.   But how do we arrive at
it ?   By analogy : we feel that our intimate being is will,
and we ought to be courageous enough to extend this
principle by analogy to the whole scale of beings.   He fails
to perceive (what Kant had already pointed out) that analogy
cannot give an identity of terms, but only an identity of
relations : it can say that will is for man what perhaps
instinct is for dogs, but not that will and instinct are of
the same stuff.

But Paulsen continues to elaborate his thesis and concludes with a conscious absurdity, euphemistically described
as a paradox.   If the procedure by which we extend the
will to inferior beings is analogy, then obviously the farther
we get away from ourselves and descend to the inferior
grades in the scale of beings the more problematical does
the analogy become, and the more incomprehensible the
internal aspect : we can admit that the dog has something
that resembles the will, but that the piece of iron has something similar, no !   It requires a person of Paulsen's fertile

imagination to do that. But, then, how does it come about that the brute matter that is so incomprehensible is known by us so well and so much more clearly than organic life, which, being near to us, is more comprehensible ? So far from being baffled by a difficulty of this kind, Paulsen makes it into a principle : the better we conceive things the less we understand them, he says, and conversely.[1] Knowledge is the opposite of understanding, thought the opposite of comprehension. In Paulsen's case this may be true.

The effect of all this is to transform idealism into the most florid kind of dogmatism, to materialize the idea and the will into the thing-in-itself of the dogmatic and naturalistic philosophy. An idea and will of this kind are merely the forces and energies of physics which have been evaporated into metaphysical abstractions. It has been completely forgotten that the philosophy of Kant and the post-Kantians was a metaphysic of knowledge and not of being, and that its ideas were not tenuous beings, flitting about in the world of physics, but the world of physics itself, in so far as it is created in the absolute act of knowledge.

In a book which bears a very promising title, whose connotation, however, is completely deceptive, *A System of Objective Idealism*, Bergmann puts forward very similar views. He starts from the concept of the identity of thought and being in consciousness, and claims to be a direct successor of Fichte. But he adds, as a corollary : " In my experience I do not recognize myself as a subject, but as an objectively identical being. This is to me a fact. I appear to myself as persistent and lasting, therefore in order to appear as such I must already be such." [2] Here is our disciple of Fichte : he has not attained even to Descartes' view of subjectivity, since he places being before appearing ; and yet he believes that he is navigating the waters of the post-Kantian philosophy ! Firmly established in this position of being, he recognizes himself in psychological experience as a conscious being, and armed with the lantern of analogy goes in search of conscious beings along the whole scale of being from the highest to the lowest, and where he cannot see them he

[1] *Op. cit.*, p. 373.
[2] J. Bergmann, *System des objectiven Idealismus*, Marburg, 1903, p. 46.

imagines he can, so dazzled is he by his lantern.   Such are the foundations of pan-psychism.

§ 2. THE REMNANTS OF NATURALISM.

This is the type of metaphysics which German philosophy has produced ;   the best it was able to produce with its empirical premisses.   Just as a small mountain torrent running between shattered walls of rock presents at times the appearance of a deep stream, but when it reaches the plain loses its energy and direction, and reveals itself for the mere rivulet that it is, so German philosophy appeared teeming with thought while pent within the narrow walls of empirical consciousness, but no sooner did it emerge from them and confront first science and then metaphysics than it, too, was exposed in all its poverty ;   by the time it reached metaphysics it was already exhausted and was only able to skim the surface of the problems without ever penetrating them.

Thus it has never succeeded in overcoming the naturalism which it believed it had definitely refuted, at the very start, by resolving the natural fact into immediate consciousness. This naturalism dogs its every movement, haunts it like the ghost of an unburied man.

The latest reappearances of naturalism, in the work of Ostwald and Haeckel, are of no philosophical importance, and are in themselves not worth noticing : their popularity is explained by the fact that naturalism is the expression of a mood which recurs whenever a problem presents itself in vain for solution.   Ostwald and Haeckel have simply reproduced in a new dress the old fantastic ideas of Fechner. Haeckel preaches in the name of the Darwinian theory an evolutionistic monism, and proceeds to deify and worship a series of puppets created by his own imagination.   Ostwald, a physicist, discovers in the concept of energy an aspect that escaped the notice of Robert Mayer, namely the psychical :   and he accordingly sees in that concept the principle of a philosophy based entirely on pan-psychism.[1]

[1] W. Ostwald, *Vorlesungen über Naturphilosophie*, Leipzig, 1905, 3rd ed., pp. 373, 374.

But fortunately his sense of scientific decency prevents him from working out this idea, and he lingers on the threshold without daring to cross it.

These are old theories. But their revival and their popularity are significant ; they signalize the feeling of dissatisfaction which is provoked by the hesitating conclusions of contemporary German philosophy. Even where the latter has attempted to drive its conclusions home, it has not really justified its claim to have achieved a higher position. The so-called idealistic metaphysic of Paulsen certainly cannot claim to be on a higher level than the philosophy of an Ostwald.

With its naïve theory of a two-sided reality, naturalism has at least steered clear of the hybrid theories of the physical interaction of soul and body : while we see an alleged idealism actually attempting to vitalize an abortion of this kind. Here may be mentioned Busse, a pupil of Lotze, who has advanced a doctrine, rejoicing in the name of interactionism and propounding a reciprocal interaction of soul and body, which would have appeared a piece of utter idiocy to a seventeenth-century philosopher. What does it avail that the names have changed, that instead of matter as conceived in the time of Descartes the new concepts of energy have been introduced ? The old fallacies of the ambiguous relation remain : there remains the absurdity of trying to make spiritual life spring up like a fungus, at a certain moment in the organic process : [1] all fallacies which carry us back to an age anterior to Cartesianism. Contrasted with this pseudo-idealism, Ostwald's type of conception appears incomparably superior.

But though the dogmatism inherent in naturalism betray its radical inadequacy, yet viewed as a negative moment in the development of thought it is of great significance. It marks, in fact, the point at which thought, till now suppressed and absorbed in things, feels the need, by way of antithesis, for turning back upon itself and so becoming thought again. We shall observe the forms in which this phenomenon is manifested in contemporary German philosophy. We shall see how from the heart of naturalism

[1] L. Busse, *Geist und Körper, Seele und Leib*, Leipzig, 1903, pp. 462, 476.

there rises a tendency which is opposed to it and attempts to suppress and destroy it, but which nevertheless carries in itself the germs of the very corruption from which it is trying to escape.

§ 3. NIETZSCHE.

In a dramatic but ultimately morbid form this tendency is personified in Friedrich Nietzsche. In him the struggles of the man and the thinker are identified, and the crisis of thought becomes a profound moral crisis.

The moral philosophy of naturalism is a crude egoism. The only initiative in life is the interest of individuals; the only check is the interest of the many. Nietzsche called the resultant morality a morality for slaves and opposed it with all his might. And yet his own morality, the morality of his superman, springs from this same soil. He learnt from Darwin and Spencer that life is a continual struggle for existence, that everywhere the weaker is suppressed by the stronger and that it is an inexorable law of nature that life only perpetuates itself through death. It is this law, raised to a higher power, that is embodied in Nietzsche's superman; he is not mere nature, and he therefore transcends nature, but living as he does by dominating and trampling down, simply in order to realize his sovereign will to live and to dominate, he acts according to the same law. The real superman for whom nature cries aloud is he that will conquer nature and her slave-morality, and will overturn her whole table of values with its petty virtues and petty human vices.

But is the freedom of Nietzsche's superman really freedom from slave-morality? Is it not rather the extreme expression of it? Does not his life presuppose this same morality and in its turn consolidate it? Herein lies Nietzsche's whole illusion: he wishes to destroy the life of the little and vulgar interests, the life of the little men; and yet his great man cannot live except among these little men and only among them can he realize his power. The superman does not represent the purging element of Nietzsche's thought, but its very malady. He sums up in his imposing grandeur all the disgust of Nietzsche's great and noble mind (that dwelt in the world of the Greek heroes, like his kindred spirits, Hölderlin and Novalis before him) in contact with a little bourgeois and industrial world that ignored all that was great and levelled everything down to its own standard. If Nietzsche had lived in the time of Novalis and Hölderlin, his superman would have been a pure contemplator of beauty ; at most, he might have cast a scornful glance at the vulgar philosophy of the Enlightenment, which was disappearing at the beginning of the century. But Nietzsche lived in a time of dominant naturalism, and his romantic hero found himself face to face with the doctrines of Spencer and Darwin. Hence an acute crisis that convulsed Nietzsche's mind and finally brought about the illusion that he had drawn from nature itself the means of conquering nature. In reality it was he who was conquered : and the superman was just the expression of his own internal confusion amid a world that was not his.

This struggle and collapse of Nietzsche's thought has a symbolical significance for the whole of the remaining development of German philosophy that we have to consider. Only here the drama, enacted by Nietzsche in all the earnestness of his soul, merely ruffles the surface of thought. Just as the great romantic had tried to transcend human morality by means of his superman, so this metaphysic tries to transcend the theoretical position of the ego by means of the superego, to appeal as against naturalism from the natural to the transcendent. But just as Nietzsche superimposed nature upon nature, and was accordingly unable to overcome the one with the other, so this metaphysic superimposes an immediate upon an immediate, a revelation of super-consciousness upon a revelation of consciousness, and hence fails to overcome a fallacy that it has not really dissipated but only repressed. Like Nietzsche, it plays upon a romantic *motif*, but in a very much lower key.

§ 4. THE METAPHYSIC OF THE TRANSCENDENT.

Rudolph Eucken leads the new metaphysical movement. He feels that a philosophy which is not metaphysical is

8

a very poor thing, yet he carries with him into his speculation a whole half-century of hostility to metaphysics. Hence there is something impalpable in his theories : demands continually make themselves felt which remain unsatisfied, truths are divined and not grasped, suggestions are made and not developed : and over everything there hangs a certain vague and nebulous atmosphere which very often betrays an internal void. Such is Eucken's metaphysic ; it expresses a state of aspiration, not of attainment.

He understands that the theory of the immediate subjectivity of consciousness leads to naturalistic subjectivism, and that it must therefore be surmounted. Now, Kant did actually surmount it. But Eucken misunderstands Kant's discovery. He says : " The impression made by this displacement from the objective to the subjective standpoint is of necessity disturbing and disheartening. For it was clearly the consideration of truths as entirely independent of us which gave them their significance and value. From truth in the old sense of the term we are now completely shut out, and shut out for ever." [1] Fortunately, we would add: except that Kant has established a far more solid objectivity which escapes Eucken, confounding Kant as he does with English subjectivism. But if he misunderstands Kant, he does not therefore misunderstand the German philosophy amid which he lives, whose capital vice consists in this very subjectivism. How is it to be remedied ? Eucken has not understood Kant, and therefore cannot follow the path indicated by him ; and he accordingly imagines that in order to rescue it from subjectivism we must elevate the life of the spirit to a sphere above subjectivity.[2] As though such a thing were possible ! Hence this life of the spirit which develops outside the subject must necessarily appear to him as something vague and nebulous. It contains nothing definite : it transcends the sphere of knowledge and is therefore not constituted by knowledge ; the life of the spirit is something supratemporal which yet lives in the

[1] R. Eucken, *The Problems of Human Life* as viewed by the Great Thinkers from Plato to the Present Time. Eng. tr. by Williston S. Hough and W. R. Boyce Gibson, London, 1910, pp. 441-2.
[2] R. Eucken, *Geistige Stromungen der Gegenwart*, Leipzig, 1904, p. 24.

historical process, something superhuman which is nevertheless actualized in the life of man. The spirit is the highest grade of reality ; it is above nature, and yet it is ineradicably bound up with the immediate life of the soul. This exactly expresses the need which the whole of contemporary German philosophy provokes without satisfying. And Eucken does not satisfy it either. He simply renders explicit all the defects of this philosophy without having the power genuinely to overcome any single one of them.

His intense appreciation of great historical figures, and his temperamental inclination towards history, induce in him a feeling of repugnance to naturalism, which he incisively describes as " essentially anti-historical. It is not only in opposition to particular theories of history but would make of history itself one great error." And on the other hand he describes with great subtlety of analysis that painful feeling of vanity and emptiness which rises in the very fullness of life and is characteristic of our age. A philosophy which believes it has discovered in sense all the richness of life is unawares exposing the void within itself : this alleged richness is in actual fact the direst poverty.

But these are observations, not philosophy. And really apart from them nothing is left of Eucken except a stirring invocation to something which lies beyond the German philosophy of to-day and is summed up in these words : " Back to Kant is an excellent motto when it means that from our manifold confusions we must climb with him into the clearer air of a world historic movement and gain direction from him as to our task. But if we are bidden to cleave to all the cumbersome machinery and learned scholasticism of the Kantian system, if we are bidden to deny that the rich and versatile nineteenth century has made any contribution to the ultimate questions of truth, if we are told to rivet on our own age with its seething ferment and unrest the forms and formulas of the past— and whether the past be nearer or more remote does not alter the impropriety—then we say No ! and again No ! and to the challenge Back to Kant insistently reply, Away from Kant ! Beyond Kant ! " [1] Yes, but how ?

[1] *The Problem of Human Life cit.*, p. 457.

This tendency towards a philosophy of transcendence also appears in the Kantian school, just as it did in so-called psychologism. In a work entitled *Experience and Thought,* Volkelt starts from the position of immediate subjectivity, but realizes the difficulties that result from remaining in it. However much we redistribute and rearrange the facts of consciousness, they can never succeed in getting outside themselves. Objectivity is either something trans-subjective or it is nothing. But yet, since I cannot emerge from my states of consciousness, there must be actually in them an indication, a premonition of the trans-subjective. Volkelt finds this indication in the principle of causation. A century of Kantian philosophy ought to have sufficiently exposed the sophism concealed in this lapse into the thing-in-itself. But Volkelt himself is convinced that an indication is not sufficient to establish a certainty, and that the trans-subjective remains for empirical thought a faith, a belief. Only if we cease to consider thought in its empirical character and turn to its metaphysical aspect shall we recognize its unity with the trans-subjective, and thus this metaphysical unity is revealed to be the sole condition which can render intelligible the certainty of empirical thought itself. But, as we have already seen, these reminiscences of Lotze only state the problem to be solved, and do not solve it.

And to crown matters, the trans-subjective which Volkelt advances as being above and beyond mere thought really conceals the actual dogmatic and naturalistic preconception that it is trying to surmount. In fact, the trans-subjective is regarded as one thing and thought as another ; and the categories are simply the acts of passing from the one to the other. What can this mean except that reality is conceived as ready-made outside thought ? Volkelt calls it by the deceptive title of the trans-subjective. With greater frankness, but at the same time without being stirred by philosophical doubts, the naturalist calls it nature, matter. The Kantian, it is true, is more philosophical about it, and the very vagueness of the title by which he designates what he is unable to grasp shows that he feels the difficulty, but nevertheless he does not surmount the dogmatism of the naturalist.

In an essay on the philosophy of nature, Lipps, a psychologist with whom we are already acquainted, develops the idea of the superego. He contends that nature as it is conceived in science is a construction of the scientist, of thought understood as pure subjectivity. Hence he regards science as something analogous to a work of art : its language is figurative, metaphorical. The concepts of natural science, such as energy or " work," are the products of art ; they do not belong to reality, but are due to the spiritual, organizing and creative hand of man.[1] Hence a certain mystery about science : how is it that the construction of the spirit is valid in reality ? The mystery, says Lipps, cannot be solved unless nature, reality, is itself shown to be spirit.

But he has already placed an insuperable obstacle in the way of our understanding it as such. Once we are shut within abstract subjectivity there is no way out of it. He accordingly tries to escape from it by a supralogical act and attains in an immediate vision to the superego, the transcendent in which the demand which the ego makes, but does not resolve, is satisfied.

As we have previously seen, Rickert also has recourse to the transcendent ; but he regards it as something unreal that merely ought to be. Lipps, on the other hand, perceives that if this transcendent is not a reality, it does not solve the problem ; if reality is not truly one, then the work of thought cannot be explained. And he therefore has recourse to immediate vision, to *Erlebnis*, in order to attain to the superego in which nature and thought are wholly one.

But what is the relation of the superego to the ego ? That of the whole to the part : as an area of space is in the immensity of space, so is the ego in the ocean of the superego.[2] But to describe the transcendent in terms of whole and part is to relapse into naturalism ; and thus the naturalism which the doctrine of the transcendent did not truly surmount but only violently repressed, reappears with its unsatisfied claims from the very summit of the transcendent.

[1] Th. Lipps, *Naturphilosophie*. In *Die Philosophie im Beginn des zwanzigsten Jahrhundert*, ed. Windelband, Heidelberg, 1907, pp. 72, 113.
[2] *Op. cit.*, p. 175.

Cohn has learnt from Rickert that the reality expressed in scientific judgments is irrational. This irrationality he treats as a conclusion and not as a problem, and yet he is discontented with it and wishes to go beyond it. If he had understood that irrationality is always a problem, and never a conclusion in which one can rest content, he would have surmounted Rickert's position and have resolved this irrational moment into a higher rationality. But, as I have said, he regards it as a conclusion ; and so in trying to advance beyond it, instead of making progress he only loses his way and abandons himself to a new revelation. Thus there rises up in him the idea of a reality that is not thought, but lived, of an unreflective moment of the spirit in which it feels itself at one with the world. This unreflective moment is the world of poetry. Art thus becomes the fulfilment of a supralogical end which logical knowledge itself imposes as a continual stimulus that it can never of itself satisfy. The unconditioned, the absolute end of knowledge, has become an attainment that is above and beyond all knowledge. This explains, he says, why the great poets who have attempted to embrace the world and humanity in their mental grasp have had such immense significance for philosophers. " I shall be understood now," he adds, " if I answer the question as to the way in which I represent to myself a concrete vision of the world, with a name, with the name of Goethe." [1]

Münsterberg expounds a similar " immediate vision " theory with regard to ultimate reality. He, too, advances it in opposition to the intellectualism of science, but in a form that fails to overcome this intellectualism and is only affirmed to lie beyond it, as the purely immediate vision of the spirit. The sciences of nature, he says, mutilate life as we live it, and scatter its fragments to the winds. These fragments the scientist presents as created nature, while we feel ourselves as free creators. The scientist falsifies our human relations by setting them over against one another as subject and object, while in reality the other, with whom I agree or disagree, is not for me an object of perception but a subject for recognition, not a thing that

[1] J. Cohn, *Voraussetzungen und Ziele des Erkennens*, Leipzig, 1908, p. 505.

I find but a volition that I approve or combat : in short, a fraction of reality which, as such, does not belong to nature. Likewise with things : the distinction between the percipient and the perceived does not belong to the reality that we live, but is a scientific construction.[1] Thus if philosophy would conceive reality in the fullness of its values it should eschew the scientific method which only produces a crystallized nature, devoid of value.

But the only substitute that Münsterberg has to offer for the method of science is an irrational act of will, an incomprehensible revelation. There is, says Münsterberg, a fundamental act of will from which we do not attempt to abstract, and which is independent of our empirical subjectivity : the will, namely, that a world should exist, that the content of our immediate life should not be compelled to justify itself in the form of mere life, but should assert itself by itself, independently of our personality. This ought to make everything clear. We have here the primary act which gives an eternal meaning to our life and without which life would be a mere dream, a chaos, a nothing.[2]

But is not this act rather a surrender of self than an act which puts us in possession of ourself ? Is not this eternal significance which it is attempted to remove from the sphere of life, as transcendent, in point of fact an integral and immanent part of life itself ? And instead of conferring reality upon life, does not the assertion of this transcendent reality intensify its discords ?

This path leads Münsterberg into a cloud of mysticism. The ultimate reality of things is not possessed in thought, but in belief. Metaphysic is the philosophy of belief. By its means we are raised from the empirical world of the ego to the superego, to the transcendent ; and we recreate in ourselves the creative process of reality. We thus repudiate every conception of reality as fact, and attain to the conception of the pure act. Reality is act : only in act is complete freedom attained, since here what is willed and the consequence are all one. As something that is merely willed the end of the volition is a " not yet," a future ; as a consequence, the volition is a " no more," a past : only if the

[1] H. Münsterberg, *Phil. der Werte*, Leipzig, 1908, pp. 18, 19.　[2] *Ibid.* p. 74.

two become completely one and coincide do we have an act : in the act, past and future are all one, and this alone is the meaning of eternity. The act of the world is eternal in time, just as the circle is infinite in space. In time there is never an end nor a beginning : in the eternal the act of the world is completed ; for the universal will, there is no past that is not a future, nor a future that is not a past.[1] The world then is will, act, realization of itself, hence progress. But this does not mean that the new achievement is of greater value than the preceding one : value does not lie in the moments but in the process.

There is a good deal of profound insight in these statements, as in all the effusions of lyricism and mysticism. But a principle that is merely invoked and not reached is not a truth ; and the attainment of truth is not a revelation, but a process. It is a transcending of every position that has been taken up, but also a possessing of it even while it is transcended. The physics of the transcendent on the other hand fails to grasp the principle of this process, and abandons the positions it has taken up merely by leaping out of them. And although it may be true that this leap represents the forcible solution of its fundamental contradiction by a thought which has chosen a wrong path and shut itself in a circle from which it cannot escape ; although it may represent therefore the utmost that this thought could achieve, still it recalls the dog of the fable, who forsakes the substance for the shadow

§ 5. SUMMARY.

We have reached the point from which we can survey at a glance the path we have traversed and sum up the whole development of German philosophy. We have watched in the decay of classical idealism the foundations of the new naturalism being laid, and the expansion of this into a materialistic conception of life which culminates in its own apotheosis. From this point there begins a period of reconcentration which finds its first representative in Lotze. This philosopher combines in his theory, in a contradiction

[1] H. Münsterberg, *Phil. der Werte*, Leipzig, 1908, p. 474.

that he fails to resolve, the two antagonistic moments of being as nature and of consciousness as immediate subjectivity. But in a gradual process represented by Lange, Schuppe, Brentano and Wundt the naturalistic position resolves itself into that of immediate consciousness. The same impetus gives rise to the various currents of thought which, in spite of their diverse cultural backgrounds, develop the same idea and satisfy the same demand.

In empiricism reality is the " given " of consciousness. Schuppe incorporates thought as well in the given ; hence reality is created *ab æterno* and science is merely the reflection upon the given and the extraction from it of what it already contains. But if science is really a reflection, thought cannot be endowed with the immediate character of the given, but must be other than the given. The school of empiricism thus effects a division in the given, the true given becomes sensation, and thought begins to assume a reflective character. The presupposition, however, that reality is constituted by the given causes the reflective and mediatory character of thought to appear a falsification, an arbitrary act of convenience (Mach). But the logic of empiricism itself evolves its own negation. In so far as the reflection of thought is not merely reproductive, but productive, reality is no longer the given but that which gives : no longer the mere sensation, but the order of sensations, and sensation itself is not intelligible apart from this order.

The principle of economy is thus reversed : the true *a priori* becomes the reflection of thought, the act of economy which for this very reason is not mere economy but also order, identity of consciousness, principle of apperception (Cornelius and Mach again). Empiricism thus verges upon Kantianism.

We have observed an analogous process in the neo-Kantian philosophy, which starts from the position of immediate consciousness and then attempts to attain to the objectivity of knowledge. In Lange, the passage is no more than an unsatisfied demand, and he remains confined within abstract subjectivity : Liebmann, and still more Cohen, believe that they have effected the passage, but they have lost the position from which they started and have lapsed into naturalism. The philosophy of value attempts to mediate between the two extremes ; but since it presupposes both the terms of the problem to be given, it only succeeds in crystallizing into an abstract idea the concept of value which was to have effected the mediation. The neo-Kantian philosophy is thus the outcome of the same attempt as empiricism, and, like empiricism, it fails even to reach the position of Kant.

With Brentano psychology propounds the same problem, but instead of attempting the passage, it contents itself with describing the terms ; with Lipps it regards objectivity as a mere demand ; with the school of Meinong it imprisons itself within the empty formalism of the two abstract positions, continually reappearing because they are never resolved.

We have seen this same tendency of thought, which, although it is expressed in different forms, always labours under the same fundamental contradiction, finally brought face to face with the problems of metaphysics in the philosophy of Wundt, Paulsen and their followers, and forced to make a public exhibition of its inadequacy. This failure opens the door to a reassertion of naturalism, which German philosophy has never succeeded in overcoming. This defect is cloaked by most of its exponents, who believe that they can exclude ultimate problems and fail to perceive that such a course only emphasizes the defect. Finally, by way of expressing at once the inadequacy of its own position and the unsatisfied need to transcend it, German philosophy seeks to annihilate itself and to attain by an immediate revelation that unity of the real which it has never been able to reach, and which never could have been reached, by the logical development of its own doctrines.

PART II

FRENCH PHILOSOPHY

CHAPTER I

FROM ECLECTICISM TO THE PHILOSOPHY OF LIBERTY

§ 1. THE COLLAPSE OF ECLECTICISM.

THE impression left by French philosophy is one of a much greater richness and variety as compared with German. Although it only now and then, in some culminating point, actually attains a higher level, yet where it develops the same favourite theme—the immediate life of the spirit—it carries into its inquiry a much greater vitality and exuberance, and so lively a sense of concrete reality that the life of the senses is transfigured and becomes the symbol of a more profound truth. It is this sense of concreteness that is characteristic of French philosophy. It views immediate life not as something entirely on the surface as the German and English empiricists do, but as a symbol of what lies beneath.

French philosophy is a young philosophy. While German thought has a glorious past in comparison with which the present appears decadent, French philosophy is just rising ; its sense of the concrete is not a heritage, but an attainment, a reaction against an empty past.

If one recalls the condition of philosophy in France about 1840, one can hardly believe it possible that so many changes should have taken place in so short a time. At that period eclecticism held a monopoly of academic thought and reigned unopposed. Eclecticism was not a philosophy but a creed. Out of a few reminiscences of German idealism and numerous extracts from the Scottish psychologists, its high-priest, Cousin, had built up a system whose cardinal points were psychology and metaphysics. His philosophical formula is first, by means of accurate introspection, to extract from our own minds a number of fundamental general ideas, and then

125

to elaborate them into a metaphysical theory. But we must ban Kant, because he is a sceptic ; and we must eschew the theological errors of Schelling and Hegel (Cousin had himself given way to them earlier in his career), and above all we must observe religious and philosophical orthodoxy. For more than half a century this programme paralysed thought : with the result that creative thinkers, like Vacherot and Renouvier, were impelled to react against eclecticism, as though to shake off this insidious paralysis.

But Cousin's school proved itself incapable of carrying out the whole of the master's programme : it perceived that the way of metaphysics was somewhat slippery, and so, following the example of Jouffroy, it confined itself to psychology. Hence the appearance of numerous theories of the faculties of the mind, of which that of Garnier, which has achieved celebrity as a model of inconclusiveness, is typical.

But it would be unjust to deny that eclecticism had very definite merits. Its presupposition that philosophy was already created and only had to be extricated piecemeal from the systems in which truth was mingled with error was an incentive to historical studies. Cousin meritoriously led the way by commenting, translating and explaining ancient and modern philosophies ; and following his example a host of patient and laborious students devoted themselves to the most painstaking researches into the philosophical master-pieces of the past. If to-day France is philosophically the best educated nation in Europe, we must not forget that it is mainly due to the eclectic school, which first overcame the prejudice against history which had been deeply implanted by two schools, first by Cartesianism, secondly by sensationalism.

And in the second place, its tendency to fuse together psychology and metaphysics was not merely a personal whim on the part of Cousin. The same tendency had already shown itself in Maine de Biran, and is reappearing in the new French philosophy. All that Cousin did was to render it superficial ; but once purged of this superficiality it could be grafted upon the stock of that Leibnizian philosophy which has from the beginning constituted the basis of the whole of nineteenth-century French culture.

But eclecticism was quite unprepared to cope with the

problems of natural science. Between psychology and metaphysics there was no place for the natural sciences ; eclecticism had, in fact, always avoided them, and on the rare occasions when it did try to recognize their existence, it merely succeeded in reviving some old doctrine in physiology (for instance, vitalism or animism) or in physics (such as Rémusat's speculations on matter).

§ 2. POSITIVISM.

But nevertheless the natural sciences developed and flourished. They contained latent within them an absolutely new conception of life, which was in direct contradiction with eclecticism. Eclecticism preached introspection, while they distrusted it and demanded experiment : eclecticism adhered to the orthodox conception of the relations between body and soul, while they investigated the cerebral mechanism of sensation ; but the main difference was that eclecticism was based on a void and they analysed facts.

Auguste Comte's positivism, the complete antithesis of the empty speculations of the Cousinians, is symbolical of the new direction of thought. Its power lay not in itself but in what it represented : it was really nothing but a proclamation of the right of science to exist, and its authority was simply that of science, which it borrowed in support of its own doctrines. Comte's distinction of three stages in speculative thought, the theological, the metaphysical and the positive, shared the popularity of the science whose triumph it announced ; the classification of the sciences, according to their degree of abstractness and complexity, was welcomed as a new point of view calculated to check the fissiparous tendencies of scientific specialization ; and sociology, with which that classification finished, was hailed as the final jewel in the crown of science.

In point of fact sociology, the only new positive element in Comte's doctrine, wears but a counterfeit splendour, the mere reflection of the light of natural science. The classification of the sciences was only a provisional systematization, and merely concealed the fundamental disparity between the different sciences. And finally, the distinction of the three stages only revived in a new dress the old generalizations of Cousin, who had careered through the entire history of thought, riding the four philosophical systems which in his view summed up the whole of philosophy. Nor was the so-called positive religion, the final deification of the new sociological concepts, likely to add solidity to the positivist construction.

Nevertheless this construction was an undeniable advance upon the old eclecticism, from the very fact of its orientation towards a more modern conception of life, such as sprang from the natural sciences. The eclectics themselves admitted it, and deemed it necessary to modernize their outlook. This explains why positivism did not give rise in France to any directly antithetical doctrine, as it did, for example, in England and Italy. For since in France there was a real need for it, it was gradually absorbed and assimilated by subsequent philosophy ; which therefore did not feel called upon to oppose it, but only to deepen its superficial classifications, infusing into them that living thought which it seemed to have banished by its rigid *schemata* of scientific classes and types.

Positivism, then, did not find any genuine obstacles in its way because it was confronted not by the Kantian but by the eclectic philosophy. For in spite of the efforts of many thinkers the Kantian philosophy remained unknown in France until about 1860, at least in its inner significance. And even those who, on the decline of eclecticism and the rise of positivism, professed themselves followers of Kant, could only view Kant through the eyes of positivism, and were therefore not really Kantians but positivists. This is the case with Vacherot.

Although he accepts the Kantian metaphysic and the principle of criticism, he reduces both to a mere reflection of the natural sciences. For him, as for positivism, *a priori* principles cannot be anything but purely analytic : hence the *a priori* character of logic and of mathematics, which come thus to be placed at the very bottom of the scale of knowledge. Hence Vacherot shares the misconception of positivism with regard to logic, regarding it as the empty *a priori* schematism of thought ; whereas really such a schematism is a *posterius*, a crystallization of past thought. This error has been perpetuated throughout the whole of modern French philosophy. But once the Kantian significance of the *a priori* was lost, no other road lay open for Vacherot except to set over against the merely analytic *a priori* a merely synthetic *a posteriori*, that is, to set over against logic and mathematics the science of nature.[1] Hence science can only appear to be based on an absence of thought : the unreflective work of experience, it is built up by external super-imposition. And all that metaphysics does is to continue this unreflective work, carrying it to a higher degree of abstraction. This is exactly the " linear " development of thought which positivism advanced as its vision of reality. It does not reflect upon itself, but merely constructs ; and its constructions grow feebler in proportion to their abstractness. Just as when positivism reaches the supreme concept of God, which is for it the most empty of all, it is unable to recognize in this concept the concrete Being of historical religion, but must fashion for itself a *Grand-Etre*, Humanity, which sums up all the emptiness of its idea ; so Vacherot also finishes by depriving his concept of God of all reality and relegating it to the realm of abstract ideals. Certainly his metaphysic conceals better than that of the positivists the void which it has created : he asserts that the idea of God is absolutely perfect, and for that very reason incompatible with the imperfections of the world of things.[2] But is not such an idea of God rather reminiscent of the famous mare of Orlando, which had every perfection except the small defect of being dead ?

The dawn of positivism, as we have said, put an end to the old eclectic philosophy : its epitaph was written in 1857 by Taine's satirical pen. But although in its general outlines positivism presented a seductive appearance, its core was unsound. So long as it kept to generalities, to the field of pure classification, it enjoyed a reflection of the prestige of science ; but this was obviously not enough. There are problems which cannot be solved by mere classification, nor yet by proclamations of the right to exist. And it is

[1] E. Vacherot, *La Métaphysique et la Science*, Paris, 1858, vol. i., pp. 406, 407.
[2] *Op. cit.*, vol. ii., p. 537.

just when positivism attempts to deal with these problems,
such as that of the reality of the life of the mind, its relations
with the organism and with crude matter, that the ambiguity
latent in the appeal to " the simple facts " begins to appear :
for these " facts " already embody theories imbued with a
strong bias towards materialism. Thus, instead of just
ignoring the reality behind nature, in accordance with its
principles as stated, positivism destroys it by reducing it
to the " facts " of naturalism.

But on the other side a few positivists like Cournot,
who were averse to materialism, developed a very slender
vein of idealism, seeing in the very organization of knowledge,
as conceived by Comte, a harmony and order superior to
the mere facts and tending towards a theism of a wholly
common-sense and unspeculative character. Moreover, in
his laborious philosophical encyclopædias, Cournot indicated
from time to time lacunæ in the field of knowledge covered
by the natural sciences, and developed some " probabilist "
and " contingentist " ideas that were to bear fruit later.

But Cournot's work passed altogether unnoticed ; and
it is only to-day that, after a considerable struggle, it is
becoming the object of more general interest. It is Taine's
work which represents the completest development of the
positivist tendency, besides being more consonant with the
premisses of the school. His inspiration is derived from Mill,
the only real positivist, if, indeed, there ever was one, among
the positivists. Like his master and inspirer, Taine pro-
fesses an extreme nominalism. General ideas are for him
nothing more than names, and the belief that an idea has
any reality other than that of a name is an illusion. The
only immediate reality is sensation ; but Nature in her
benevolence has attempted to provide us, in cases where we
cannot use it, with a surrogate, imagination. Sensible
reality has two sides, a psychical and a physical : the latter
simply translates the former, which grows more and more
complicated in proportion as it rises in us to the higher
forms of consciousness ; but none the less " we have abund-
ance of evidence that it is still the same book and the same
language." [1]

[1] H. Taine, *On Intelligence*, Eng. tr., p. 199.

How do we pass from the immediate life of the senses to the idea of external reality, from sensation to perception ? If Taine had been a more penetrating nominalist he would have perceived that the sensation which he posited as an *a priori*, as something transcending the distinction between real and unreal, was simply an abstraction, a *flatus vocis ;* but his half-hearted nominalism landed him in the absurd problem of how to pass from the imaginary world of the senses to that of empirical reality ; and to meet this he invented the formula which has remained famous through its very paradoxical character, that perception is simply an accurate hallucination. But what gives it its truth ? Its relation with the other sensations, or, better, with the permanent possibilities of groups of sensations, in Mill's phraseology.[1] What else can this mean except that the relation conditions the sensation as such, and that therefore the word " hallucination " is a misnomer ? Just as he evaporates the outer world into a void, so Taine reduces the inner world to a nonentity ; the ego becomes a conglomeration of images. Reality is thus all surface, beneath which there is nothing at all. Such is the flimsy and insignificant shadow into which that positivism has dwindled whose birth was heralded with such pomp.

§ 3. THE NEW SPIRITUALISM.

Meanwhile, starting from the Leibnizian philosophy, there was growing up within this same French culture a new movement towards inner reflection. The Leibnizian philosophy, which was still influential and had indeed become naturalized in France, thanks to Maine de Biran's work, had never lost sight of the inner aspect of things, and had invested the same world that was governed by physical laws with spiritual principles, revealing moral demands within the very heart of nature. Developing certain tendencies of this philosophy, Biran had looked beneath the surface of consciousness and discovered the profound reality of the subject. He had thus conceived a voluntaristic and dynamist doctrine of reality. But Biran's philosophy was

[1] *Op. cit.*, p. 353.

completely overshadowed by the success of eclecticism
—notwithstanding that Cousin had attempted an exposition
of it, which, albeit, was, as usual, superficial—and it was
only later on that it was revived by the last thinkers of the
eclectic school : by Ravaisson and, with less penetration,
by Janet. These writers accepted Cousin's formula of
philosophy as psychology and metaphysics, but they supplied
it with a content drawn from Leibniz and Biran. At the
same time they sought to satisfy the demands of natural
science and positivism by finding room in their philosophy
for the problems of nature, which eclecticism had thrust
on one side.

The new system thus formed owes its structure to the
philosophy of Leibniz, which attempted to embrace spirit
and nature in a larger synthesis, but it owed something to
Biran, whose dynamism was an effort to correct the over-
mechanical and rigid character of Leibniz' synthesis. The
new philosophy thus achieved an intuition of the psychological subject which aimed at looking beyond the phenomenal self and penetrating into the very heart of personality,
to find in the inmost self the free cause of the facts of
consciousness and at the same time the informative principle of the life of the real. Hence also an argument based
on analogy which tries to rediscover that same principle
in the world of organisms and even finally of matter ; and
lastly, as the centre towards which all reality faces, the God
of the Leibnizian Theodicy. Here in its main outlines we
have the so-called new spiritualism.

It is an old doctrine, but nevertheless it strikes a new
note. It is developed in the sphere of the metaphysic of
being and not of knowing : its tendency is essentially
dogmatic. It affirms on one side the spirit, on the other
nature, yet with the demand that the latter shall be resolved
into the former. It shares with the pre-Kantian philosophy
the fallacy of attempting to spiritualize the already fixed
forms of matter ; hence the ideal forms which it conceives
remain discrete entities without any immanent unifying
principle, and require to be summed up and completed in a
transcendent Divine Being. In short, we have not yet got
beyond Leibniz.

FROM ECLECTICISM TO LIBERTY   133

Yet Ravaisson does stand for a new tendency. With
Leibniz he criticizes the conception of reality as a mechanism,
showing that in so far as mechanism resolves everything
into its elementary conditions, it renders impossible any
explanation of the fact of organization itself with its complex
variations. It reduces everything to an identity and passes
over all variety, spontaneity, creation ; qualities which are
to be found everywhere, not only in the kingdom of life
and of thought, but even in such an elementary fact as the
contact of two bodies.[1] He maintains also with Leibniz that
a complete conception of reality can only be given by a
synthesis of mechanism and teleology, and that therefore
the inner consciousness where reality and perfection coincide
is the only conceivable centre of orientation for a conception
of the world. In fact, an examination of consciousness
will show us that its action consists in determining by means
of thought the order and teleology by which the unknown
powers latent within our complex individuality are given
form and direction. We first discover this principle of
teleological unity in ourselves, but we afterwards detect it
everywhere by means of analogy. We understand other
organisms by ascribing to them this identical type of internal
organization. This permits us to arrange them in a hierarchy ;
and by working out the principle we can link up natural
reality through our own personality to God, the supreme
principle of order, harmony, and perfection in reality. This
is all Leibniz : but there is also something more, namely,
the growing emphasis laid upon the spontaneous creative
impulse of organization, which gradually destroys the
equilibrium between the world of teleology and the world of
causality. The parallelism of Leibniz is thus undermined.
Life is not only entelechy, organization : it is self-organization,
spirit. To live is not simply to change, but to triumph
over change ; it is to rise again at every moment from
death ; for the spirit, it means continually to find oneself
and know oneself again ; to remember oneself always and
eternally.[2] Here is already the whole of Bergson. But

[1] F. Ravaisson, *La Philosophie en France au XIX Siècle*, Paris, 1904,
5th ed., p. 264 (first published in 1867).
[2] *Ibid.*, p. 48.

although Ravaisson's conception of the principle of life contains a principle of spirituality, of inner reflection and mediation, yet just because his starting-point is the metaphysic of being, this principle cannot be fully developed. In so far as spirituality in its concreteness always falls outside beings as particulars, who are therefore ranged in a hierarchical scale whose order is not immanent within them, but transcends them, the development of life is not inwardly self-reflective, but unilinear ; and the progress of the forms of the real is not a genuine progress, because it only exists over against a transcendent principle. In other words, what we do not find is the unity and continuity of the subject, without which progress is unintelligible.

Ravaisson is accordingly unable to include in the kingdom of life that which is not living—for instance, the matter of physics, which no metaphysic of being, but only a metaphysic of knowledge like Kant's can resolve into spirit. If life is this unilinear development, this perpetual flux of things, how can we explain what is static, inert ? To meet this difficulty Ravaisson gives a symbolical picture, which betrays all the inadequacy of his position : namely, that God, in creating the world, had to destroy something of the fullness of His being in order to lead that which exists through a kind of reawakening.[1] Hence his explanation of progress presupposes a fall ; life must presuppose matter in order to be able to rise again from it. This involves a revival of the theory of matter as the thing-in-itself which Kant confuted ; and it remains in French spiritualism as a basic dogmatism from which not even Bergson has been able to free himself.

An attenuated version of Ravaisson's theory is offered by Janet, who is also an investigator of final causes in organic life. But with him the Leibnizian dogmatic tendency is uppermost : the idea of teleology which is understood as the preordained representation of ends[2] becomes more abstract and external, and consequently the God of intellectualism is in the ascendant, banishing the creative spontaneity of which Ravaisson had caught a glimpse. Moreover, the immense lacunæ of spiritualism, successfully concealed

[1] *Op. cit.*, p. 279.   [2] P. Janet, *Final Causes*, Eng. tr., p. 401.

by Ravaisson's broad treatment, leap to the eye in Janet. Spiritualism is by its very nature dualistic : it affirms the separation of body and soul. Hence Janet's vain struggle to demonstrate the independent reality of bodies by means of the feeling of tension, of effort, which reveals a reality outside consciousness. In this respect the new spiritualism is indistinguishable from the old.

We find an echo of these doctrines in Vacherot, who was converted to spiritualism towards the end of his life. His philosophical testament, as the book came to be called in which he gave final expression to his thought, is an attractive work, although it does not contain any new point of view. The old " freethinker," as he described himself, who used to deny the existence of God, is converted to theism, but a theism quite free from anything morbid or sentimental : his God remains at bottom nearer to the *ordo* of Spinoza than to the God of religious orthodoxy.[1]

As has already been indicated, the essential element in Ravaisson's philosophy, from the point of view of its subsequent development, is the emphasis it lays on the idea of the freedom, the creative spontaneity, of consciousness. This idea forms the starting-point of the new currents of thought. Before Ravaisson gave it prominence this idea, viewed somewhat differently, had already formed the central theme of Sécretan's work. We mention Sécretan here, out of his chronological place, because his work was for a long time absolutely unknown in France, and has only lately begun to be read and discussed as a result of an article by Janet. Sécretan's philosophy of freedom is connected with the last phase of Schelling's speculation. Although in its starting-point it is dogmatic, in so far as it attempts to determine in the manner of Spinoza an autonomous principle behind which it is impossible for thought to go, it nevertheless seeks to resolve, as it proceeds, its initial Spinozistic dogmatism. The simple idea either of substance, or of the efficient cause of existence, says Sécretan, does not fulfil this condition. On the contrary, substance must contain its cause in itself, and be produced by itself as an activity : in other words, it must be a life. But this is still inadequate ;

[1] E. Vacherot, *Le nouveau Spiritualisme*, Paris, 1888, p. 313.

because the law of life might come from elsewhere. We must therefore conceive life as giving itself its own laws ; that is to say, we must conceive it not only as life, but as spirit, as a free will.[1]

But Sécretan attempts to go still further, and lapses into arbitrariness. Just as though liberty conceived as spirit were not an absolute autonomy, he wants to make the first principle give itself freedom ; hence the arbitrary formula : I am what I will.[2] The reason for this is that Sécretan never really freed himself from the " substantialistic " point of view with which he started ; and the same arbitrary conception of liberty leads him to presuppose a being which posits itself as free, namely, the God of religion. From this principle, which Sécretan admits to be incomprehensible and supra-rational, he develops a fantastic theogony and cosmogony which reminds us of the visionary constructions of Boehme and Schelling, but lacks all their imaginative power.

Nevertheless the unconditional affirmation of the principle of liberty which we find in Sécretan is of great importance in the history of French thought : for it expresses a presentiment, however nebulous and fanciful, of subsequent developments.

§ 4. THE NEW TENDENCIES.

As presented in the new spiritualism, the concept of freedom was ill-qualified to resolve in itself that of causal necessity. The product of an inner revelation of consciousness, it found itself confronted with the causal mechanism of the external world in all its impalpable rigidity. Spiritualism was thus constrained to go out of its way to minimize the inner revelation, in order to reconcile freedom with the necessity of phenomena, which it could not resolve and therefore sought to include in the teleology of the spirit. This simply resulted in a repetition of the attempt already made by Leibniz.

The concept of freedom as genuine autonomy and as the resolution of causal necessity is a Kantian concept.

---

[1] Ch. Sécretan, *La Philosophie de la Liberté*, Paris, 1849, 1st ed., pp. 329–31.   [2] *Ibid.*, p. 321.

It was only in Kant's philosophy that nature was really brought within the sphere of the spirit and shown to follow its law. Ever since 1860 the French have gradually been acquiring a more accurate knowledge of Kant ; and this profounder conception has entered into the development of French philosophy and is leading it by degrees beyond the Leibnizian position.

Renouvier contributed a great deal by his example towards arousing interest in Kant ; but at bottom he failed to master Kant's point of view. In his first essays he kept to the plane of Hume ; a position which he afterwards deserted, rather because of an inner discontent than through the influence of Kant's doctrine. Jules Lachelier, on the other hand, an incomparably profounder thinker, both understood Kant and made others understand him. Unfortunately, we have only a few very brief essays of his, which cannot possibly give us any idea of the tremendous range of his work, which expressed itself for the most part in teaching. But from these essays, which, as we shall see, reveal a deep thinker, and from the continual allusions to his work which we find in the more recent French writers, we can understand that his influence on contemporary thought has been very great indeed.

Lachelier developed the concept of liberty from its Kantian presuppositions. It leads to a conception of the spirit as standing definitely on a higher plane than nature, and thus signs the death-warrant of the Leibnizian compromise between efficient and final causes. The world of creative spontaneity cannot be simply the other aspect of that of mechanical necessity. This is the conviction which is steadily gaining ground.

If this Kantian conception had been the only dominant one, the resolution of mechanism into creative spontaneity would soon have been an accomplished fact ; but this conception was only inserted into the Leibnizian background of a " pre-existing harmony." The result is that spiritualistic subjectivism is not giving place to Kantianism, but trying rather to adapt itself to meet the demands which Kantianism makes. Hence the immediate revelation of consciousness, the revelation of creative spontaneity in the depth of the spiritual life, remains intact ; hence objectivity, nature, is still to a certain extent set over against immediate consciousness, except that the denial of the Leibnizian compromise has diminished its importance and caused its " natural " character to be regarded as a falsification. This is the point at which arises the movement towards the criticism of science, the anti-intellectualistic movement which has enjoyed such popularity. It has a stronger foundation than the similar movement which we have observed in Germany, since the latter is not really anti-intellectualistic but merely empiricist. Its closest analogy is with that philosophy which we called the metaphysic of the transcendent, at least so far as regards its initial motive ; although it is developed very differently and in an incomparably more profound manner. We must, however, point out that, in France, too, the critical movement is connected, at least on its negative side, with empiricism ; and that sometimes, where the revelation of consciousness is less profound, a covert empiricism is actually visible in its conclusion. Conversely, in its more outstanding manifestations this movement is idealistic or rather spiritualistic, in the sense that it attempts to establish by means of its criticism of science and of naturalism the conception of creative spontaneity, the freedom of the spirit. In a later chapter we shall follow this movement, of which Bergson is the most eminent representative.

In antithesis to this movement stands a revival of the old naturalism, which assumes in Fouillée a Platonistic form, leading, in its ethical conception of life, to an æstheticism steeped in Utopianism.

Finally, from the idealistic concept of freedom and in opposition to the æsthetic view of life, there rises, in a great spiritual concentration, the Philosophy of Action, culminating in Blondel.

We shall therefore examine in turn Phenomenalism ; the philosophy which is inspired by Kant ; the Criticism of Science, with Intuitionism ; the Platonistic theories ; and finally the Philosophy of Action, with a brief reference to Modernism, properly so called, which presents in the work of Loisy a profoundly idealistic significance.

CHAPTER II

PHENOMENALISM

§ 1. RENOUVIER.

THE founder of the theory known as phenomenalism or neo-criticism is Charles Renouvier. His philosophy is not Kantian but empiricist, although it is based largely upon a study of Kant. It accepts the principle that reality is the fact of consciousness, of representation ; thus its starting-point is that of Berkeley. But in contrast with Berkeley's dogmatic idealism, which resolved the external object into the phenomenon but left the subject intact (and so necessitated an appeal to the idea of God in order to explain how the spiritual world externalizes itself into a world of appearances), neo-criticism remembers Hume, and resolves the subject also into phenomena, into representations.[1] Hence a general relativism, according to which every phenomenon is given in relation with others, and the whole of reality is resolved into functions and relations between facts of consciousness.

Kant had already surmounted this position, pointing out that while it describes the fact which we know it does not explain the fact that we know it. Knowing is not merely relation to another—the phenomenon—but relation to oneself in the other ; it is essentially, then, a knowing of oneself. Only in the transparency of self-consciousness is the other than oneself illuminated and spiritualized. In pure phenomenalism, on the other hand, in so far as reality is continual reference to another, in so far as it is a circumference whose centre is continually moving, the other becomes a thing-in-itself. In other words, Renouvier believes that

---

[1] Ch. Renouvier, *Essais de Critique générale. Premier essai*, Paris, 1875, 2nd ed., vol. i., p. 37.

139

he is freeing himself from the conception of the subject as the centre of reference of the real, and yet, since he must have some centre of reference, he treats the object as such a centre. And while he believes that with his idea of the phenomenon he is getting rid of the noumenon, he fails to realize that this very phenomenon of his is a noumenon, a thing-in-itself.

The result is a pure dogmatism masquerading as a version of the *Critique*. For Kant the categories represented the self-knowledge which was the condition of knowledge. Renouvier, on the other hand, having already presupposed the whole of reality as already there in the phenomenon, can only explain the categories as the most highly generalized relations between phenomena. Far from conditioning reality as the phenomenon, they are conditioned by it : and so the character and value of Renouvier's revised version of the Kantian table of the categories is merely that of an external description. For example, phenomenalism regards the category of number as nothing more than the relation of plurality to quantitative unity. But this is simply a description of a completed enumeration ; whereas, in the actual process of counting, numerical plurality is not understood as something in relation to a unity which is itself also numerical, but both together are conceived in relation to the unity of consciousness which effects the synthesis between them. And so on.

The purely naturalistic character of the categories in phenomenalism is emphasized still more in the school of Renouvier. Thus Dauriac, borrowing the idea of contingency from Boutroux and misunderstanding altogether the Kantian categories, comes to maintain the contingency of the categories. For him the alleged necessity of the categories is simply conditional. This results from the very nature of reality, which is a congeries of particular objects none of which can be derived from any other.[1] Here, obviously, all trace of Kant has disappeared.

The most noteworthy thing in Renouvier's work is his attempt to solve, according to his own principles, the Antinomies of Pure Reason. In reality he cannot even

[1] L. Dauriac, *Essai sur les Catégories* (in the *Année philosophique* of 1900), p. 47.

grasp that there is an antinomy. We will take a single
example : the antinomy of the finite and the infinite.
Starting from the concept that the actual infinite is impossible and absurd, he rejects the antithesis of the Kantian
antinomy and accepts the thesis. Hence for him the world
is internally finite, that is to say, it has a definite measurable
size, outside whose limits nothing exists. But on the other
hand, although of a definite size, this world cannot be actually
measured by the beings who form part of it ; for they can
only investigate, either by reasoning or by experiment,
relations which are subordinated to other relations.[1] This,
as is evident, is a return to the distinction between reality
in itself and reality for us,, but only a return to it within
the phenomenon ; that is to say, Renouvier enriches the
distinction by adding to it a contradiction which Kant had
at least avoided by distinguishing between the phenomenon
and the noumenon. And here again, as I remarked at the
outset, we can see that Renouvier erects the phenomenon
into a thing-in-itself. The German empiricists, such as
Petzoldt, are more consistent : for although they accept
the premisses of phenomenalism they nevertheless deny
that the world as a whole constitutes a problem at all, and
maintain that only particular relations can form true and
genuine problems.

But Renouvier was gradually led to abandon the conception of the phenomenon as absolutely disconnected, as
mere reference to another. Already in his first *Essay in
General Criticism* he recognizes that in the progress of
organic forms individualities are remoulded and characterized ;[2] and this implies that they are not mere aggregates.
Subsequently his study of the characteristics of human
personality impressed upon him with increasing clarity the
fact that the individual does possess that centralizing and
unifying power which he had denied to it. The intimate
connection between volitional acts and personality makes it
increasingly difficult to regard the unity of the self as that
of a mere aggregate of representations. " When freedom,"
he says, " makes its appearance in a given being, that being,
bound by a thousand relations to other beings, acquires an

[1] *Op. cit.*, vol. iii., p. 282.   [2] *Op. cit.*, vol. i., p. 158.

incomparably more individual existence : what was only distinguished is now separated ; what was a self becomes self-subsistent, an essence, or if you will a substance, in the meaning sometimes given to these words ; an individual and the most individual individual that is known ; the human individual, the human person." [1] Here Renouvier is beginning to abandon his relativism, which denied all substance and resolved everything into relations between phenomena. It is true that he has not yet relinquished that position in so far as he confines this distinction, between personality as a higher grade of existence and the pure phenomenon as a lower, to the field of practical beliefs. This shows that the position has begun to crumble, though not yet visibly : and one can trace the development of the process as time goes on. And finally, in Renouvier's last work, *The New Monadology*, the long-threatened collapse of phenomenalism takes place under our very eyes. The assertion of the monad as a centre of spontaneity means the negation of the phenomenon. The affirmation of the phenomenon implied the correlativity of subject and object ; and the subject itself was therefore the " mere other," the simple phenomenal object becoming a subject to itself. The monad, as a representative power, on the other hand (as Weber quite rightly points out), endowed as it is with the faculty of producing representations, is simply the subject isolated from the object and asserted as anterior to it.

Owing to his failure to understand the *a priori* synthesis, throughout the whole development of his thought Renouvier simply described a circle round it : he grasped in succession its limbs, but never its soul.

§ 2. GOURD AND BOIRAC.

The school immediately derived from Renouvier did not produce anything very remarkable ; but outside this school a similar criticism of pure phenomenalism was advanced by two thinkers of totally divergent characters, Gourd and

[1] Ch. Renouvier, *Essais de Critique générale : Deuxième Essai*, 1875, vol. ii., pp. 368-9.

Boirac. Gourd's criticism was merely negative ; he confined himself to showing that the conception of the phenomenon when developed was self-destructive. Boirac, more constructive, pointed out that that conception owed what power it possessed to an idealistic element.

For Gourd reality is all phenomenon : if there is something beyond what is immediately or mediately given to us, it must also be phenomenon. Gourd thus attempts to maintain a radical phenomenalism. But there are already determined in the phenomenon, according to his view, irreducible dualities which it is the task of philosophy to observe. The phenomenon has two aspects—identity and difference ; two moments, the psychic and the physical ; two elements of fact, being and not being. These are its ultimate differences, each pair, as Gourd says, being arranged in a progressive order, in the sense, for instance, that the psychic and the physical cannot be considered as two coexistent aspects of reality, but only as two successive moments which are therefore mutually exclusive.[1] If this is so, then the only kind of unity possible in the phenomenon which tolerates such internal contradictions is a verbal unity. And this conclusion is inevitable. Phenomenalism is by its very nature led to consider consciousness as a receptacle into which you can put whatever you wish ; it fails to realize that a genuine unity of consciousness cannot contain any radical diversity.

But if the contradiction is insurmountable, then philosophy, as the science of the co-ordination of phenomena, must give way to the science of that which cannot be coordinated. With science, says Gourd, we run the risk of remaining confined within a world of pure phenomena, that is to say, of objective representations, of successive states of consciousness from which all the inwardness, all the mystery of existence, has vanished, together with all real and genuine activity. And this is indeed the case : in phenomenalism everything lies on the surface of consciousness ; hence Gourd's transition to the doctrine of the " incoordinable " points, at least in negative terms, to the inadequacy of a philosophy which is ignorant of the inward-

[1] J.-J. Gourd, *Le Phénomène*, Paris, 1888, p. 357.

ness of life. And therefore alongside of science, which postulates a reality independent of thought and on this basis increases knowledge extensively, co-ordinating its objects, there rises a doctrine of the incoordinable, which attempts to increase reality intensively, revealing that which eludes natural laws and yet is not set over against them. Alongside of the morality which, on the basis of the postulate of a system of forces extended throughout the universe, increases our will extensively, co-ordinating our ends to social exigencies, there rises a morality of the incoordinable, of sacrifice, which transcends the social organization : alongside of the æsthetic of the beautiful, an æsthetic of the sublime.[1]

All these tendencies converge in the philosophy of religion, of the incoordinable *par excellence.* The peculiar contribution of Christianity is its history of the incoordinable, of the Absolute in the universe and in the spirit ; this is the good tidings of religion, the incomprehensible tidings of God in us and with us ; its " folly " of the Cross.[2]

Boirac's doctrine is more profound and better co-ordinated. Beyond the phenomenon no existence is conceivable, either of an unknowable or of a noumenon : we do not find reality divided between the two opposite poles of the phenomenon and the noumenon, but wholly contained in one of the two poles : the other, far from engendering a superior reality, simply represents for thought the possible negation of the real.

But, Boirac adds, if we would banish the shadow of the thing-in-itself, we must understand thoroughly the nature of the phenomenon. Phenomena are only given in relation with other phenomena : together they form a complex and continuous unity in which only our thought makes distinctions. From the point of view of distinction the phenomenon is simply one of the aspects from which we conceive every existence : the aspect of succession, difference, multiplicity ; but for this very reason it implies the correlative aspect of permanence, identity, unity. If this second aspect is called being, we may say that the phenomenon

[1] J.-J. Gourd, *Philosophie de la Religion,* Paris, 1911, pp. 227–9.
[2] *Ibid.*, p. 273 : " To the Greeks foolishness."

is inconceivable without being ; but it is equally true that being is nothing apart from the phenomenon : it is within it and consubstantial with it : it is the phenomenon itself considered in its undivided and continuous unity, a character which it possesses no less than the opposite one of infinite differentiation.[1] So far this is Leibniz ; but Boirac attempts to take yet a further step and to reach Kant's position, yet without abandoning his own. In so far as every phenomenon is within consciousness, the relation being-phenomenon can be expressed as subject-object. This distinction is effected within the phenomenon without its inner unity being severed. The first aspect of the phenomenon, in so far, that is, as it appears to us and is thought, felt, or represented, is the objective or passive aspect : the phenomenon in this aspect is the object. In the other aspect, in so far as it appears to itself and feels, represents, or thinks itself, it is the subject. Thus, although remaining one, it is reduplicated ; it is set, so to speak, over against itself ; it is polarized, yet without being divided. The existence of the phenomenon is not separated by a single instant of time from its representation : consciousness is not an act which is superimposed upon the fact of sensation, the idea. The inner phenomenon does not, so to speak, issue out of itself by a kind of repulsion, after having placed itself within its unrelated unity, in order to return to itself by a kind of attraction : it is, doubt-less, equivalent to such a series of successive moments, but does not traverse any such series : it is their instantaneous and indivisible synthesis. Being and phenomenon, subject and object, are thus an indivisible synthesis of opposites.[2]

Yet this is a false step : we cannot pass in this way by a single jump from Leibniz to Kant. Boirac's aim is to show that the phenomenon is thought in the making, which is inconceivable because the phenomenon is, by definition, thought ready-made. In the affirmation of the phenomenon can be discovered being, the substance of the phenomenon, but a fact can never by duplicating itself extract from itself something that it does not contain. Very soon after-wards, in fact, Boirac relapses into the Leibnizian point of

[1] Boirac, *L'Idée du Phénomène*, Paris, 1894, pp. 243–5.
[2] *Ibid.*, pp. 95, 96, 125.

view from which he started, showing thereby that he has
not understood the profoundly new concept of self-consciousness, which is the negation of the metaphysic of being.   He
confuses consciousness and self-consciousness, and transforms
the latter into the former.   Hence he figures reality as a
system of numberless self-conscious beings, of subject-object
unities, which are simply the monads of Leibniz.   He is
evidently returning to the metaphysic of being from which
he derived his original inspiration.   It is true that he
attempts subsequently to free himself from the presupposition
of substance by considering it as an act, but he does not even
thus escape from the Leibnizian philosophy, because the
act in the metaphysic of being is simply the entelechy.
As he himself recognizes, his conception of act is the
Aristotelian one : [1] but for that very reason it is not the
Kantian.

So for Boirac reality consists of monads, of entelechies :
their unity is thought in so far as it is relation to inner
being.   But his thought is not thought as it is conceived
in the metaphysic of knowledge ; it is not a human thought.
" Every phenomenon brings with it and contains in itself
its conscious subject, but it does not belong to a consciousness organized like our own.   Thus the universe is extended
indefinitely in space and time beyond our thought and every
human thought." [2]   Boirac has not given this non-human
thought, which penetrates reality, its true name (he could
not do so, because he believed that he was very far removed
from Leibniz) : it is the Pre-established Harmony.

Hence arises Boirac's final doubt, which he expresses in
the following terms.   We have said that reality seems
divided and concentrated into a number of distinct and
reciprocally impenetrable spheres :   these spheres are the
different spirits, in the image of which we conceive the
other substances, atoms and monads.   Is this multitude
of partial thoughts an appearance and an illusion ?   Or, on
the other hand, is the unity of the total thought a fiction ?
Or, finally, is it possible to reconcile this multiplicity of
individual subjects with the unity of the universal subject ?
And he prophesies that this problem which he has left

[1] *Op. cit.*, p. 329.   [2] *Ibid.*, p. 344.

unanswered will be solved by the metaphysic of the future. But while this would have been a legitimate prophecy for Leibniz to have made two hundred years ago, it is not so for a thinker who has lived since Kant and Hegel. The concept of entelechy has broken down ; and with it has collapsed the vision of a thought which traverses the world of beings in so far as they are beings. The rise of the concept of self-consciousness as the unity of a world no longer conceived as physical, as a world of beings, but as a spiritual world, a world of Knowing, has made impossible the disintegration of reality ; and the human conception of the world has established itself.

Thus we have seen phenomenalism start with Renouvier from the position of Berkeley and Hume and reach that of Leibniz : its limit is the monadology ; of Kantianism it has only skimmed the surface.

CHAPTER III

FROM KANT TO ABSOLUTE POSITIVISM

§ 1. LACHELIER.

THE most distinguished representative of the Kantian movement in France is Jules Lachelier, who stands out as the most profoundly speculative mind of modern French Philosophy. As a pupil of Ravaisson he took from him the idea of fusing psychology and metaphysics, but he understood it in an altogether different sense. Already in his thesis for the doctorate, in 1871, on *The Basis of Induction*, he interpreted the distinction between the two orders of efficient and final causes, which in Ravaisson was largely a reminiscence of Leibniz, in the light of the two *Critiques* of Pure Reason and of the Judgment. He deduced efficient causes from the formal law of pure thought, as the determinative unity of the spatial and temporal multiplicity of phenomena ; final causes he deduced from the principle of reflective judgment, the judgment of totality as productive of its parts. This latter point of view provides the basis for a more truly internal connection between the elements of reality than is possible with the former ; it envisages reality as the organic unity of a variety in which every constituent expresses and contains in its own way all the rest.[1] It is on the principle of final causes, on the existence of a rational order of things, that Lachelier founds induction : to found it on the empirical regularity of phenomena—the " uniformity of nature "—would be to found it on itself.

But the uncertainties latent in this theory of induction, the difficulty of the mere coexistence of the two principles of mechanism and teleology which the example of Kant

[1] J. Lachelier, *Du Fondement de l'Induction*, Paris, 4th ed., pp. 1902, 55, 79.

had already shown to be insurmountable, the necessity of resolving mechanism into the teleological activity of the spirit, determined an alteration in Lachelier's position, culminating in the essay *Psychology and Metaphysics*.

Psychology is here an abbreviated Phenomenology of the Spirit, and Metaphysics something analogous to Hegel's logic, also in an abbreviated form. Psychological analysis, Lachelier says, simply gives us the data of consciousness, namely sensation, emotion, will. But there is also something else, which adds nothing to the content of sensation or perception, but stamps the sense-consciousness with the mark of objectivity. If the sense-world appears to all men as a reality independent of their perception, this is not because it is a thing-in-itself external to all consciousness ; but, on the contrary, because it is the object of an intelligent consciousness which, by making it an object of thought, frees it from the subjectivity of the sense-consciousness. If all men believe that their states of consciousness are something in themselves, and not only in the present, but also in the past and in the future, it is not because these states have their seat in a chimerical entity whose existence, if it had any existence, would itself also be limited to the present : it is because they are the object of a thought which, raised above all temporal limitation, sees them equally in their present, past and future reality. If thought is an illusion, we must suppress all science.[1]

Analysis, therefore, leads to the conception of thought as the basis of the truth of the world. But how is it that thought, the idea, on which the sense-world is modelled, exists in us ? Can it be, like the innate ideas of popular spiritualism, a " fact of reason," an inexplicable datum of the intellectual consciousness ? If this were so, the idea would only be another kind of thing ; it would be the primary object of thought, but not the subject ; and it would have to justify its truth over against an even more primary idea before it could be made the criterion of the truth of things. If it is to enable us to judge all that is given us, the idea cannot itself be given : and the only

---

[1] The article *Psychologie et Métaphysique* is reprinted in the volume *Du Fondement de l'Induction*, q.v., pp. 150, 151.

alternative, Lachelier concludes, is that it produces itself in
us and that both it and we are a living dialectic.   Thus to
a certain extent we suspend thought in the void : and we do
not shrink from so doing : for it can only rest upon itself,
while everything else can rest upon it : the ultimate *point
d'appui* of all truth and of all existence is the absolute
spontaneity of the spirit.[1]

Analysis had up till then considered thought as a given
fact : to consider it as a self-creative process is to pass from
analysis to synthesis, from psychology to metaphysics.
In psychology thought was a created fact which Lachelier
resolved into its elements : the last of these elements, pure
thought, is an idea which produces itself from itself, and
which we can only know by producing it in ourselves by a
process of *a priori* construction or synthesis.[2]

This is the great conception of the post-Kantian
philosophy ; and to have understood it is Lachelier's merit.
From this he deduces by a synthetic process pure consciousness, pure volition and self-consciousness.   This last form
is the truth of the other two, and is also the ultimate truth :
the progress of thought comes to an end when, after having
been sought first in the necessity of mere consciousness—
as it were in its own shadow—and then in the will—as it
were in its own body—it has finally found itself in the
consciousness of itself, which is absolute Liberty.   But
surely this is not so much a finality as in the real sense a
progress ?   Lachelier's whole argument implies an affirmative
answer : it is the end of mere " seeking," but not of that
" seeking " which is an eternal self-discovery.   He does not
say this, but he leaves one to suppose it.   In his view the
three moments of being do not succeed one another tem-
porally in the Hegelian manner.   " Being "—as he understands it—" is not first a blind necessity, then a will which
must always be imprisoned in that necessity, and finally
a freedom which would simply have to recognize the existence
of both.   It is freedom through and through, in so far as

[1] *Op. cit.*, p. 157.
[2] This distinction between phenomenology and philosophy gives rise
to serious difficulties, which we shall analyse later on when we come to deal
with Italian Hegelianism.

it is produced by itself ; will through and through, in so far as it is produced as something concrete and real ; necessity through and through, in so far as this production is intelligent and gives an account of itself. In the same way each of us is not first a mechanism of internal states, then a character, which can only be the expression of this mechanism, then a reflection or an ego, the useless and irresponsible observer of our inner life. On the contrary, the act by which we affirm our own being constitutes it wholly, since it is this same act which realizes and fixes itself in our character, and manifests and develops itself in our history. We must not, therefore, say that we affirm ourselves to be what we are, but that we are what we affirm ourselves to be. Above all, we must not say that our present depends on our past, which is itself no longer in our power ; for we really create all the moments of our life in one and the same act, which is both present to each moment and above them all."

Such is Lachelier's philosophy, sketched, as he himself says, in a few lines, in an article for a review. Such a concentration of thought has never been attained in France since the time of Descartes' *Meditations*.

§ 2. The Kantians.

The speculative value of Lachelier's philosophy has met with scant appreciation in France. The transition from Leibniz to Hegel was too abrupt for people to follow it at once. In Lachelier's time the necessary foundation of Hegelian scholarship was lacking, and it is only of late years that this gap has begun to be filled. I will mention here two important studies upon Hegel. The first is by Noel, a keen-witted exponent of the *Logic*, who I believe attained to Hegelianism by grasping the essential principle of Lachelier's teaching. I infer this from an article in the *Revue de Métaphysique*. He understands Hegel's close connection with Kant, and shows how absurd is the pretence of attempting to stop at Kant, as though Kant's philosophy were not a point of transition to that of Hegel. And he has given his fellow-countrymen a warning which they seem so far to have failed to appreciate. Hegelianism, he says, is neglected but not confuted ; it is abandoned to the empty declamations and facile burlesques of superficial minds, but it still demands from thinkers its right to a serious consideration and so to speak to actual existence. Of all philosophies it is the only one whose foundations have not been undermined by criticism, and which among the ruins of earlier systems still stands upright in its imposing integrity.[1]

The other important study upon Hegel is that of Berthelot,[2] which clears away many of the misconceptions that have collected round the Hegelian philosophy, such as that of Absolute Determinism, of wholesale Optimism and of Panlogism. Berthelot's study has given rise to an interesting discussion in which Boutroux has also taken part, and which shows how the French are gradually acquiring a more thorough knowledge of Hegelianism. We shall see this still better subsequently, when studying Weber's work.

But Lachelier's earlier school interprets his doctrine too much in the sense of a dualism, considering the world of causes and that of ends as products of two separate demands which are not really unified. In this it has based itself upon the uncertainty in which Lachelier's own thought was involved in his first essay on induction, but which was cleared away by its later development.

In Liard, for instance, subject and object are found over against one another. In the object are actualized the so-called categories of science, from which universal causal mechanism is derived. But the world of science, of phenomenal relativity, does not suppress the Absolute, towards which all the categories really converge, without, however, attaining to it.[3] The science of the object thus refers back to the metaphysic of the subject. Here we pass beyond the mechanism of nature and enter into the kingdom of ends. Every idea affirmed by human activity as an end evokes and disposes the means of its own realization. And since the final cause is an effect which precedes the efficient cause

[1] G. Noel, *La Logique de Hegel*, Paris, 1897, pp. 183–4.

[2] It has been reprinted in Berthelot's volume, *Évolutionnisme et Platonisme*, Paris, 1908.

[3] L. Liard, *La Science positive et la Métaphysique*, Paris, 1879, pp. 306, 326, 352.

and determines it, we find in the human world a reversal of the order of natural causes. Man sets before himself the good before experiencing it, and realizes it because he wills it ; thus the will has an effective, determinative function. This constitutes our moral personality, which is unfolded in the struggle of ideas and triumphs in the freedom of conscience. In the field of science the categories, unless they have some extraneous content, remain in the sphere of pure possibility ; in the practical sphere, on the other hand, ideas contain in themselves the principle of their own realization : the free will is that by which pure possibilities are made to enter into action on the stage of consciousness. And so in this case the maxim of Epictetus holds good : to perfect what depends on us and to take other things as they come. To perfect our ideas, so Liard comments, means to harmonize them with that which is our perfection, that is to say, to substitute the moral ideal for the sense ideal.[1]

In the moral certainty of the Absolute lies the value of metaphysic, which scientifically would have no value. Science and consciousness : it is the old dualism over again, the dualism which we analysed at length in our discussion of German philosophy. To which of the two terms do we give the prize ? *La conscience prime la science*, says Liard. But the mere negation or suppression of science by consciousness does not solve the difficulty. Liard interprets the Kantian primacy of the Practical Reason only in its most superficial sense, as a mere renunciation of thought, an abandonment to the revelation of consciousness.

Like Vacherot and Renouvier, the French neo-Kantians have been very much concerned with the problem of the solution of the antinomies. But in maintaining one term to be true in preference to the others, or in reduplicating each antinomy and considering both terms to be true from two different points of view, they have done nothing except reveal their own dogmatism. Another Kantian, Evellin, recently has devoted his attention to the same problem, and has attempted to provide a solution somewhat after the manner of Leibniz. For instance, he accepts the thesis

[1] *Op. cit.*, pp. 417, 419.

of the first two antinomies, but argues from this not to
an atomism but to a monadism. This shows his incipient
realization of the fact that the solution of the antinomies
can only be a dialectical one : the monad, in fact, is not the
mere finite, but the immediate unity of the finite and infinite.
Yet his conception is very rudimentary : for he does
not understand the deeper meaning of the negative term,
which for him is " as sterile as it is empty." [1] Hence his
dialectic always ends by failing to extract its real significance.
This is thrown into very strong relief by his treatment of
the third antinomy : that of necessity and freedom. According to Evellin, freedom is real because it is self-sufficient,
while necessity is merely phenomenal. Free action, in fact,
is affirmed by itself ; but we must reflect, he adds, that at
the very moment in which we state that the action is affirmed,
it has been affirmed, and that, as such, it falls into an
irrevocable past. The creative moment instantaneously
becomes the created fact ; a tendency completed is a work ;
an effort is no sooner made than it is transformed into a
result. [2] If Evellin had deepened the genuinely dialectical
significance of this principle, if he had understood the value
of the negative moment, the moment of necessity, he would
have realized that the spirit is not abstract freedom, but
the continual conversion of freedom into necessity and
the continual rising again from the negation of necessity.
Instead of this he regards the negative moment as irrelevant ;
hence he finishes by crystallizing act and fact, freedom and
necessity, into a within and a without, reality and appearance : forgetting that a fact cannot contain within itself
something different from itself.

Brunschvicg, a writer who is well known for a fine book
on Spinoza, also moves in the sphere of Kantianism, but
with great difficulty, and he finally lapses into an ill-concealed
empiricism. His starting-point is Kantian : judgment should
be considered as the beginning and the end of the spirit,
indeed, absolutely speaking, as the spirit itself. A doctrine
of judgment is thus a philosophy of the spirit, at the same
time a logic and a metaphysic. To distinguish logic from

[1] F. Evellin, *La Raison pure et les Antinomies*, Paris, 1907, p. 312.
[2] *Op. cit.*, p. 166.

metaphysic would be to create a logic without authority and a metaphysic without a basis.

But Brunschvicg considers that the philosophy of judgment can be reduced to a yet simpler form, to a doctrine of the modality of judgment : the logical problem of modality implies the metaphysical problem of the right which the spirit has to affirm being.[1] Hence Brunschvicg's philosophy is summed up in the problem of the necessity, reality and possibility of the judgment.

But although his starting-point is Kantian, his development of it is not : it is a lapse into the most complete dogmatism. Brunschvicg, in fact, presupposes that reality is a given, that it is the impact of the external world which is revealed to us in sensation. The spirit, on the other hand, in so far as it is pure inwardness, appears to him as a necessary being, not dependent on anything other than itself. Hence knowledge, as the relation of the spirit with things, is expressed merely in the form of possibility, and hence the absurd result that the possible is the concrete. It is strange that a thinker like Brunschvicg, whose essay on Spinoza displays such acuteness, should not have perceived that he was begging the question by presupposing all the terms of his problem : a reality in itself, a necessity in itself and a possibility which is the shadow cast by both. It is a threefold dogmatism in a single formula !

Expressed in scientific terms, that formula runs as follows : between the two poles of mathematical judgment (a form of pure thought, and hence necessary) and perception (a form of reality) lies the true concrete judgment, that of probability, the judgment of scientific empiricism which represents the progressive advancement of thought and of the real. But how can this harmony result from the union of two such blocks of granite as a reality in itself and a thought in itself ?

§ 3. Weber and Absolute Positivism.

Louis Weber is absolutely unknown in Italy, and in France he does not appear to have won the recognition which he

[1] L. Brunschvicg, *La Modalité du Jugement*, Paris, 1897, p. 41.

deserves. He sums up in himself, while he supersedes, the whole of contemporary French philosophy, and represents a tendency which is at the same time advancing in Italy and to a certain extent in England, towards a philosophy of Absolute Immanence, which in the opinion of the present writer is the highest fruit of Hegelianism.

Weber's doctrine is Absolute Idealism, but since it presents itself as the negation of all transcendence, he calls it Absolute Positivism. It may be outlined as follows. There is nothing which is not reducible to thought. The object, in the sense of ordinary realism, does not exist ; it is no more than a dialectical appearance, the symbolical expression of the fact that since the progress of knowledge is unlimited, the arrest of thought before a finite determination of being leaves before it a still unexplored space which thought fills with its own self-negation.[1]

The problem of Absolute Positivism is stated thus : on one side we have the experience of the physical, which is expressed in a particular language ; on the other, that of the psychical, expressed in another language : experience, regarded as a mere fact, is incapable of deciding which of the two beliefs is the true one, and for this reason neither the realism of the physicist nor the idealism of the psychologist are explanations of experience, but simply the statement of it. Dialectic alone can provide a solution to the problem.

And, in fact, Weber adds, psychological knowledge is a mediate knowledge ; it is a negation of the immediacy of reality as given us by the physicist. But the philosophical point of view, which classes psychology and physics together as special sciences, reaffirms physical reality, but with quite a different significance. It is no longer the reality of the thing in opposition to the spirit, nor of the thing as identified with the spirit ; it is simply the reality of the physical science itself, which exists no less than psychological science and alongside of it. Thus above Being and Not-Being (the physical and the psychical) philosophy places knowledge as Becoming, as an expansion of the system of science, as an extension of its domain by means of an inner stimulus, a

[1] L. Weber, *Vers le Positivisme absolu par l'Idéalisme*, Paris, 1903, p. 220.

kind of self-moving impulse, which is simply the tendency of the system to affirm its Being, to persevere in Being.[1]

This third moment, which is that of reflection, of the philosophical judgment that judges the physical and psychological judgments, is the concreteness of knowledge, the unique synthesis of the past and present of science, the adding of the new to the old by means of a Becoming whose laws, inherent in the structure of the system, are only explicable by the internal reasons of the system itself.

From this point of view reality, far from being the negation of thought, is on the contrary the affirmation of thought itself by itself : it is the empty form which gives itself its content, the bare skeleton which animates itself with concrete life ; in a word, it is science in all its fruitful diversity and all its regulative unity. " Thus science seeks the real, and in seeking it finds only itself. *Tad twam asi*, this art thou, even this, the infinite search for which is thy essential reason, thy generative reason, and the possession of which, if it were ever possible, would be thy final negation. . . . The positive significance of Absolute Idealism can be summed up in these words : the search for reality is reality itself. Thought includes and constitutes the universality of Being. Since it is impossible that thought should deny itself absolutely, its relative negation, in a search that is orientated towards externality and objectivity, is simply an instrument of variety and progress, and is sooner or later reconciled with a higher grade of reflection than that in which it originated ; with an affirmation confirming the unity of Being and its identity with the unity of knowledge."[2] To supersede positive science is therefore not to deny it, but on the contrary to affirm it more compréhensively and to give it the sanction of reflection.

To define reality by reference to the becoming of its idea, and to identify it with this same becoming, means to widen correlatively the significance of the idea, to emerge from the narrow confines of the determinations in which psychology imprisons it. The idea is itself and its other : regarded as given existence, it is the concept, the product of thought ; regarded as inexhaustible existence, as progress,

---

[1] *Op. cit.*, pp. 306, 307.   [2] *Ibid.*, pp. 327, 328.

it is mental activity, the irresolvable function in which all the relations of subject and object are summed up. The duality of Being and Becoming, of past and future in all progress, falls within the idea, just as the distinction between idea and object is simply a moment of the idea in so far as it is reflection. This distinction between idea and object is therefore never absolute : it simply expresses the dialectical moment in which knowledge takes the shape of fact, of the " known," and the union of idea and object is the formation of the new synthesis, of the new knowledge. Herein lies the eternity of the progress of science.

Thus Absolute Idealism transforms the static concept of truth into a dynamic and fluid concept. " To define truth by reference to the object is to place truth in the object, that is to say, to assert the reality of the object in itself ; and this, in a word, is to deny the principle which gives birth to the very idea of truth. For this principle, in fact, affirms at the same time the idea of error ; and, in affirming the freedom of the judgment, proclaims thereby the most profound aspect of the idea of truth : search, struggle, effort." [1]

Such, in its broad and simple outlines, is Weber's philosophy. On particular points I disagree with it strongly (for instance, with his view that the physicist's reality is immediate and the psychologist's mediate : the truth is precisely the opposite : a fact whose consequences are very important) ; but this is not the proper place to discuss Weber's doctrine in its details. A survey of contemporary philosophical movements ought not to pass judgment upon questions which are still throbbing with life and which we are still struggling to elucidate, but only upon what is already superseded, in order by this means to bring into focus the new thought which is in the act of shaping itself. Weber's view of the problem of science stands on the very crest of modern thought and represents a demand which Kantianism and Hegelianism leave unsatisfied.

[1] *Op. cit.*, p. 340.

CHAPTER IV

SCIENCE AND METAPHYSICS

§ I. The Philosophy of Contingency.

WE have seen the neo-Hegelian manner of stating the problem of science. With Weber every remnant of transcendence in the conception of the object, of nature, is resolved and science itself becomes concrete reality in so far as it is pure thought, including within itself that objectivity which seemed to confront it as something irreducibly outside it.

But the problem of science had already occupied the attention of a number of thinkers more closely connected than Weber with French spiritualism, from whom it had accordingly received a very different solution. We saw that Ravaisson's spiritualism, inspired by Leibniz, had asserted two types of cause, efficient and final, thus trying to satisfy the demands both of science and of metaphysics. But the moment of creative spontaneity, of the living teleology of the spirit, did not run well in double harness with scientific mechanism ; nor could it be explained as the same thing seen from the opposite point of view. Hence even Ravaisson had insensibly destroyed the unstable equilibrium by emphasizing the significance and value of spontaneity.

The thinkers whom we are now going to consider have worked out this tendency by adding a negative criticism calculated to dissolve that mechanistic conception of the world which Ravaisson's work attenuated but did not overcome. The final result of this criticism has been the rise of a new spiritualism which, freed from the shackles of science, has developed with very much greater force the idea of the spontaneity of the spirit. But we shall see that this movement has perpetuated the initial error of a dualistic spiritualism ; and that, instead of being genuinely resolved in a metaphysic of knowing, the problem of science has only been revived in an accentuated form in a new metaphysic of being.

At the head of the new school stands Émile Boutroux. The criticism of scientific mechanism has constituted the principal theme of his work. Ravaisson had already shown that the forms of the real are disposed in a hierarchy according to the principle of final causes, from crude matter through the organism right up to the human spirit. The aim of this hierarchy is to elude the mechanistic conception which resolves the different forms into their elementary conditions, and accordingly fails to conceive progress, since its only principle is the casual regress which reduces the superior to the inferior, the organism to the chemical compound, the physical world to the mechanical *schema*. Having stated the problem in these terms, Boutroux proceeds to examine the mechanistic conception and to ask whether it does not really fail to grasp the essence of that which it analyses. In resolving the organism into the chemical compound do we not thereby lose exactly that which constitutes the novelty and originality of organic life as compared with chemical combination ? The appearance that nothing is lost is due to the fact that we start our analysis from the point of view of the highest and unconsciously forget that which constitutes its originality. Thus in investigating the life of the organism we take for granted that which really constitutes its life, and therefore we think that we really can resolve the organism into chemical elements. But invert the point of view, and the illusion is no longer possible. If we start from the lowest, from the inferior forms of reality and knowledge, can we out of these elements reconstruct the highest ? The negative answer to this question constitutes the Philosophy of Contingency.

Boutroux shows that the lowest and most general form of necessity is logical necessity : A is A. But being so general, this form presents a minimum of objectivity. It governs the surface of things and does not determine their nature.[1] In fact, even in the field of logic itself every form

[1] E. Boutroux, *Natural Law in Science and Philosophy*, Eng. tr., p. 32.

that contains a greater degree of objectivity, such as the concept and the syllogism, implies something new over against the mere judgment of identity   for example, the many contained in the one, the relation of the implicit to the explicit, etc. Beyond logic lies mathematics, which is not merely a further stage of logical intelligibility, but implies a new principle of synthesis, the recourse to intuition. Mathematics creates relations of composition ; with the aid of intuition, it introduces diversity into the identical. Nor do the passages from mathematics to mechanics and from that to physics and biology take place without a leap : mechanical causality is something new superadded to the mathematical function, and so is organic reciprocity in respect to causality. In short, if you wish to reason *a priori* you cannot do it by deducing the higher forms from the lower by way of analysis, because the first contain elements which cannot be reduced to the latter. The first find in the second only their matter, not their form   The link which constitutes the two seems to be a radically synthetic one.[1]

So far his argument is obvious : from the less we cannot extract the greater, from the empty the full. But although this very obvious premiss may enable us to draw some sort of negative conclusion against materialism and, in general, against scientific dogmatism, it is of little assistance in providing a positive explanation. In fact, the contingency of the higher forms of the real with respect to the lower is simply one more mystery added to the mysteries of science, and does not by itself provide the means of solving any mystery.

Yet Boutroux does not stop at the statement of this contingency, but offers an explanation which betrays all the inadequacy of his doctrine. For he believes that the function of the spirit is limited to propounding general *a priori* analytical *schemata* such as those of logic, in order to attain to a ready-made reality which exists in itself outside thought. Hence his empiricism. If the principle of logical *a priori* necessity is the analytical law of identity, then the basis of mathematics is already wholly outside the spirit, or, rather,

[1] E. Boutroux, *The Contingency of the Laws of Nature*, Eng. tr. by Fred Rothwell, Chicago and London, 1916, p. 152.

11

it represents the work of the spirit which, incited by things to exert itself, creates a mass of symbols in order to subject these things to necessity and thus make them capable of being assimilated by itself.[1] Kant, no doubt, spoke of synthetic *a priori* principles. Boutroux denies that there are such principles : for him the *a priori* is merely analytical and is not the basis of any reality. But further he misunderstands Kant, believing that the Kantian synthetic *a priori* is something " previous to " and " beyond " experience.[2] If he had understood Kant he would not have described logical necessity as the lowest form of reality ; and he would have perceived at the same time that the empty schematism of the laws of identity and contradiction, in which he sums up the whole of the *a priori* element in thought, is really the negation of thought. He dogmatically makes the whole of reality fall outside thought, and does not realize that he thereby makes the whole of thought fall outside itself.

Hence he does not attain to a level of thought at which the problem of the critique of science can even be formulated : for if thought is not the basis of reality, and if reality is a thing-in-itself, then science is reduced to a mere compromise between the spirit and an unknowable : an absurd compromise, because one of its terms is unknown. Scientific laws, says Boutroux, result from the collaboration of the spirit with things they are the products of the activity of the spirit when applied to extraneous matter : they represent the effort which the spirit makes to establish a meeting-point between things and itself.[3] But how is a meeting-point possible when thought does not know the thing which it is to meet ? The whole doctrine is mere empiricism. In short, Boutroux criticizes one kind of dogmatism only to fall into another. He rightly says that it is not possible to resolve the higher forms of reality into the lower ; but he then goes on to resolve thought itself into these lower forms—thought, which alone can make intelligible the progress from the lower to the higher. The consequence is that progress is swallowed up in the gulf of contingency, and all

[1] *Natural Law, etc.*, p. 47.
[2] *The Contingency, etc.*, pp. 152 and 153.
[3] *Natural Law, etc.*, p. 61.

the forms of the real become things-in-themselves, which
thought merely adumbrates in its concepts and can never
represent to itself completely.

Herein lies the dogmatically empiricist basis of Boutroux's
philosophy. Yet it contains an idealistic motive. For
reality is regarded by Boutroux as a progress, although
this progress is defined by the nebulous idea of contingency.
But it is a progress without a soul. Thought has become
mechanical, not the immanent spirit of the whole process,
but something introduced from without at a certain stage.
This is not progress as it is conceived by the idealistic or
human view of the world   it implies a transcendence, a
divinity outside the world, to make good by its own absolute
continuity the discontinuity of the world-process, so that
the course of evolution is controlled by a teleology beyond
our comprehension. And so the positive side of Boutroux's
criticism is simply a repetition of Ravaisson's spiritualism.

As we have seen, Boutroux believes he is criticizing
science while he is really criticizing a puppet of formal logic,
as though the logical power of thought were exhausted in
the principle of identity, A is A. And conversely he introduces a worse form of dogmatism (since it is philosophical)
by his empiricist view of the whole of reality as given *a
posteriori* in experience. We find this view repeated by
Milhaud, who also attacks the windmills of formal logic in
the belief that he is undermining the position of scientific
thought. He, too, thinks that the whole *a priori* faculty of
thought is limited to applying the principle A is A. Hence
an analysis of any proposition, even of the most absurd,
suffices for him to show that this principle can never be
adequate to serve as the basis of any objective truth.[1]
I fully agree : but for centuries past philosophy has abandoned the idea of attempting to base certainty upon the
principle that A is A ; with Descartes it discovered the
criterion of self-evidence, with Leibniz of sufficient reason,
with Kant of apperception, with Hegel of the dialectic ;
in other words, it has not stopped at merely rejecting the
law of identity. Milhaud, on the other hand, simply denies

[1] Milhaud, *Essai sur les Conditions et les Limites de la Certitude logique,*
Paris, 1898, 2nd ed., pp. 25, 35, 36.

the objectivity of the laws of identity and contradiction, and rests quite content with this bare negation. Very well, he concludes ; if logical certainty does not exist we are adrift on the open sea of empiricism (no, we are worse off than that, for even empiricism has its criterion, the " association of ideas ") ; further, the logical rigour of science is simply a matter of subjective arbitrary choice, a mere definition, a mere hypothesis, or something like that. This is tilting at windmills with a vengeance.

But Milhaud does not stop at this point, as so many of his successors have done. His negative criticism leads him to the conclusion that logical certainty cannot apply to the facts of experience, none of which fit in with it exactly. What, then, of science, which tries everywhere to determine its propositions with logical rigour ? Obviously, if the problem is stated thus, science cannot be a copy of things, since if it would copy things, it must forgo certainty. This consideration, as in the case of Mach, leads to a view with idealistic tendencies, regarding the work of the scientist not as the copy of a logical certainty existing in things (a veritable absurdity), but as the creation of certainty and truth. The dogmatic presupposition, however, that outside the process of science there exist complete and ready-made things, causes this creation of certainty to be understood as something arbitrary, and the ideal character of thought as equivalent to useful falsification of reality. But even so, it is a great advance to have grasped the ideal character of thought at all. Thus, for example, Milhaud says that the understanding of the scientist leaves its mark on his work not only by giving an orientation to his research, in fixing its directive idea, but also in determining the ' coefficient of certainty " of the logical construction of thought—in fact, in creating scientific truth. Here we have an idealistic principle ; but its abstract subjectivism and its false and purely empirical manner of viewing the activity of the subject make it impossible for us to consider this vein of idealism as anything more than a mere presentiment of a profounder truth.

Outside the process of science (which, nevertheless, is not a copy of reality) there remains, according to Milhaud, a reality ready-made and complete. As for the relation between pure speculation and reality, he says, we must not demand that the one should penetrate directly the other, but we must be content to affirm between them a kind of parallelism and correspondence.[1]

But in this case, how are we to regard that part of science which is due to the active intervention of the spirit ? If we suppose a reality completely created outside thought, it must be an arbitrary intervention, a falsification. This way leads directly to the negation of science. On the other hand science can only be ratified if that ideal factor which Milhaud has glimpsed is developed to its extreme point, without stopping half-way, without leaving " a something " beyond the process of science.

Those who cry out against the scandalous assaults made against the truth of science by these modern critics and recoil in horror from their scepticism should realize that we must not beat a retreat, but on the contrary press the argument home with all our might. These criticisms look paradoxical because they are only half-truths ; we must carry them much further (and by a very different process) in order to obtain the complete truth. If Kant had recoiled in horror from Hume's " scandalous " criticism he would never have emerged from dogmatism and established the Critical Philosophy. But he only established it by driving the argument home, by passing from Hume's negation to a very much profounder negation. Only from this could he have risen to that powerful affirmation of science, the *Critique of Pure Reason*, while Hume's negation, arrested as it was midway, could only produce scepticism.

§ 2. THE CRITICISM OF SCIENCE.

In the transition from Boutroux to Milhaud we notice an accentuation of the empiricist character of their theory of science. The later members of the school emphasize it yet further. Being no longer sustained by a spiritualistic inspiration, these arrive at an absolute negation of the certainty of knowledge. Their criticism has no longer an

[1] G. Milhaud, *Le Rationel*, Paris, 1898, p. 106.

idealistic significance ; that is to say, it does not combat
the encroachments of naturalism upon the life of the spirit,
but only aims at showing that knowledge pertains to the
sphere of the probable, that every criterion of certainty
is equally arbitrary, and that in the last analysis the sciences
are only languages *bien faites*, as Condillac said. All this
is, in fact, simply the old French empiricism and sensationalism over again, brought up to date and seasoned with a
relish of paradox, an art in which certain scientists are well
practised. Yet its influence on modern philosophy is
certainly important, for it has helped to dispel the dogmatic
slumber induced either by the uncritical acceptance of
science pure and simple or by that Kantianism which has
perverted the critical philosophy into a new scholasticism
and re-established under the protection of a Kantian
terminology the completest dogmatism.

As regards its actual philosophical content, the new
criticism of science represents a long superseded stage of
thought. It is a mere methodology raised to the rank of
a philosophical conception   it deals only with a superficial
aspect of thought, from which every inner impulse of development—every spontaneous and creative act of the mind
which takes up a reality, already created in a superseded
thought, and transforms it into a new reality—is banished,
and everything is reduced to an arbitrary act of convenience,
the provisional equivalent of a reality in itself, created
ab æterno. Unable to grasp the actuality of scientific
thought in which subject and object coincide, it lets everyone
follow his own bent, only claiming that to a certain extent
and for some mysterious reason everyone does actually
agree with everyone else. Hence its favourite idea, which
betrays all the inadequacy of its conception, is the idea that
the concept " works." If thought merely interprets itself
and its symbols, then any act of thought which also " holds
good " of reality is a successful act, a good guess. But
this is not an explanation : it is just an admission of ignorance.
Such is the boasted criticism of science which has deceived
us all in our time, and has been acclaimed as the last
word in philosophy.

But before we glance at the philosophy of some of the

purer representatives of this movement we must say something about a group of writers who, though still working
on the lines of Boutroux and Milhaud display the same
tendency towards empiricism.

Among these is Hannequin. In an essay on the atomic
theory he maintains that physical atomism is not imposed
upon science by reality, but by our method and by the very
nature of our knowledge. We are wrong in considering
that it necessarily implies the actual discontinuity of matter,
for it really only implies that we render matter discontinuous
by holding it together in thought. In a word, atomism
has its origin in the universal use of number, which stamps
with its imprint everything it touches.[1]

This is a half-truth and for that very reason it gives
rise to two mysteries. Science in its dogmatism, introduces
only one mystery, the atom. Here, on the other hand,
reality in itself, which is not a collection of atoms but something else, is one mystery ; and the other is that the atom,
a concept constructed purely to meet the exigencies of
thought, holds good of and can be applied to this non-atomic
reality. But these compromises only attenuate the problem :
they give a superficial appearance of a well co-ordinated
system, but beneath the surface yawn abysses. Hannequin
perceives the difficulty, and tries to show that reality in
itself, although it does not consist of atoms, yet necessitates
atomism, which thus becomes a *phenomenon bene fundatum*.
Acuter than the other critics of science, he does not rest
content with merely stating the compromise, but understands
that in order to speak of a compromise we must suppose
that not only thought but also reality should be such as to
make the compromise possible ; and once on this road he
ends by inclining towards the Leibnizian philosophy and
considering reality as constituted by monads.[2] This is
obviously an inadequate solution nevertheless it shows
that he has perceived behind the plausible screen of empiricism the metaphysical problem which demands a solution.

In Payot we have an instance of an empiricist who has

[1] A. Hannequin, *Essai critique sur l'Hypothèse des Atomes*, Paris, 1899,
2nd ed., p. 26.
[2] *Op. cit.*, p. 381.

arrived at the criticism of science through a doctrine of belief. He maintains that reality is for us simply the sum of our sense-impressions, tactile, auditory, visual, etc., woven upon a solid woof of muscular sensations which endow our knowledge with objectivity.[1] Biran's conception of " effort," upon which spiritualism attempts to base the reality of the external world outside consciousness, is thus reinterpreted in the interests of a doctrine of immediate consciousness, and serves to prove the impossibility of our ever freeing ourselves from our subjective world and grasping a reality in itself. The conclusion is a theoretical scepticism, supplemented by a philosophy of belief which shows us how this world suffices for the ends of our conduct, whether scientific or practical.

Payot surprisingly believes that he has thus arrived at the conclusions of the *Critique of Pure Reason*. Muscular effort is for him a form, an *a priori*. There is no such thing as a pure isolated sensation, just as there is no such thing as the atom of mechanics. Sensation only exists in perception, which consists of the sensations themselves projected upon a network of muscular data. And since on the one hand sensations cannot reveal to us anything of reality in itself, and on the other hand our muscles have simply an offensive and defensive function, it follows that to perceive does not mean to know absolutely, but only to organize a world of appearances and to subject them to our domination.[2] Ordinary knowledge, like scientific knowledge, is an impoverishment of sense-reality : a fixation of those aspects which are practically more important. Its goal is therefore not the true, but the useful.

But if there is such a thing as reality in itself, why should it be so docile as to let us dominate it by, so to speak, burning it in effigy ? This is the flaw in this pragmatism, and in all the other pragmatisms which flourish to-day : they believe that they can confine themselves to the field of the mere subject and at the same time control at their pleasure an ever-present unknown reality in itself : they do not see that they are presupposing a definite metaphysic, and that one of the falsest and crudest imaginable.

[1] J. Payot, *La Croyance*, Paris, 1896, p. 32.   [2] *Op. cit.*, p. 51.

But the culminating point of French critical empiricism is to be found in the work of a number of well-known scientists, such as Poincaré and Duhem, who have carried out extensive investigations into the procedure of their science and yet have never risen above an intelligent empiricism.

According to Poincaré, scientific fact is simply the crude fact of ordinary experience translated into a convenient language.[1] From among the tissue of relations between empirical facts, science selects such as prove most useful for the purpose of its research ; and this selection is a convention, an arbitrary practical act of the scientist. As for the scientific conceptions of space and time, it is not Nature who imposes them upon us, but we who impose them upon Nature because we find them convenient. This is a totally different matter from the legislation of which Kant spoke : for we only exercise our legislation upon ourselves, upon the symbol which we have created and which we call nature. The real nature, which suggests to us that symbol, lies outside our categories.

But if science simply translates from one language into another, this presupposes that there is an invariable element in both : if there were no identity of language it would be futile to make any claim of translating. What is this invariable element ? According to Poincaré, it is constituted by relations between crude facts whose objectivity is not questioned, while science, being of a conventional and arbitrary character, is limited to the mere elaboration and translation of these relations.[2]

From this it can be seen that Poincaré's criticism is limited to that restricted field of scientific inquiry where the selection of the most convenient instances of a given phenomenon is entrusted to the skilful but arbitrary choice of the scientist, and that it leaves absolutely untouched the philosophical problem of science : that is to say, the problem of the significance and validity of the relations between facts, whether in ordinary or in scientific experience. In fact, it presupposes this problem, it presupposes that the relations we experience are intelligible : for this pre-

[1] H. Poincaré, *La Valeur de la Science*, Paris, 1909, p. 231.
[2] *Op. cit.*, p. 247.

supposition alone can justify not only the manifold ways in
which science expresses the phenomena of experience, but
also their translation into any scientific language at all.
Poincaré consequently does not give us a doctrine of science,
but presupposes one : what he does give is a mere empirical
methodology founded on a dogmatic basis.

What is the character of the relations ? Are they facts
of the same type as sensations of sight, sound, etc. ; or
are they on the other hand acts of thought ? All these
questions are beyond the scope of Poincaré's inquiry. But
nevertheless, like Mach, he has a delicate scientific sense,
and he consequently has an intuition that the true criterion
of the objectivity of knowledge is to be sought in relations,
and not in the changeable qualities of things ; and he even
ends by perceiving that these same relations presuppose a
primary identity without which they would be unintelligible.[1]
But this is all. In the main he is still a dogmatist. Beyond
the relations he still sees a nature composed of things which
remain inaccessible to us ; and he fails to understand that
this " Nature in itself " is exactly the same crude fact whose
inconsistency has driven him to seek for the objectivity of
knowledge in relations. He fails to understand this because
he has not attained to the philosophical problem of science,
but has assumed it as solved in a prescientific stage of thought ;
and has thus ended by crystallizing into crude facts those
relations whose ideality, if he had ever discovered it, would
have helped him to eliminate both the naturalistic residuum
in his theory and also the superficial interpretation which
he gives of the arbitrary act by which science elaborates
its premisses and defines its own status.

Duhem is another critic of science, standing in closer
relation to Mach. His view is that a physical theory is not
an explanation, but a system of mathematical propositions,
deduced from a small number of principles, whose aim is
to represent as simply and as exactly as possible a collection
of empirical laws. These latter are in their turn economized
sense-data : hence by condensing the empirical laws into
theories, the human spirit redoubles the economy already
effected by the substitution of laws for concrete facts.[2]

[1] *Op. cit.*, p. 265.   [2] P. Duhem, *La Théorie Physique*, Paris, 1906, p. 31.

The purpose of this economy is to facilitate the firm grasp of laws and facts, by grouping them together and systematizing them ; at the same time it produces a certain beauty and harmony of construction, which satisfies our æsthetic sense. Yet although it cannot lay claim to truth, because it is impossible to speak of truth where the question is purely and simply one of economy, the act of theorizing is very far from being merely arbitrary. In proportion as it advances in perfection the theory of physics assumes the character of a natural classification of facts, and the groupings which it effects provide an insight into the real affinities of things.[1]

The work of Duhem shows a sane and balanced mind, absolutely untouched by the hankering after paradox. His observations upon his particular science are often very shrewd ; but his purely external and classificatory point of view prevents him from grasping any genuinely philosophical problem. He looks at science from the outside, as a completed building, and describes its more obvious features ; but the mind of the architect, because it does not appear visibly in the building, is altogether banished from his view.

Following this course, the theory of science ends by merely taking us behind the scenes in the laboratory, by merely retailing the technicalities of research. It does not even elucidate the psychology of the scientist. For just because it is impossible to be a scientist without using one's own technical devices and making one's own definitions, the scientist is believed to be a collector of abstractions, who does not search for truth or fight for an idea, but takes as true whatever happens to be convenient for the purposes of his experiment, and mutilates and falsifies according to this standard the reality given him. If this is a true account of the psychology of modern scientists—a question which cannot be decided here—one can only say that there has been a considerable falling-off since the days of Galileo.

§ 3. THE PHILOSOPHY OF INTUITION : BERGSON.

We have seen the theory of science, no longer sustained by an idealistic inspiration, decline into a barren and merely

[1] *Op. cit.*, p. 43.

destructive scepticism, tempered here and there by some
constructive ethical doctrine.   We will now turn our attention to another school of thinkers by whom this same
destructive attitude is carried to its extreme point, yet is
made to assume a very different significance because it
is considered as the means to a more far-reaching reconstruction.   This school depreciates science not simply in
itself, but by comparison with philosophy ; a fact which
implies a profound belief that truth exists and is attain-
able.

We have already pointed out that Boutroux exhibits
an idealistic tendency derived from the philosophy of
Ravaisson.   The school of which we are now speaking
simply develops this tendency without accepting Ravaisson's
compromise between science and metaphysics, between
efficient and final causes, which the Philosophy of Contingency had shown to be futile.   At the same time it rejects
the long-established belief in final causes as conceived by
Leibniz : for if reality is the creation of the new, of the
unpredictable, it cannot bow to the dictates of preordained
purpose any more than to those of scientific law.   The new
conception is thus neither finalism nor mechanism, but
something which transcends both.   And its method of
demonstration is psychological analysis as understood in the
spiritualistic school of Ravaisson, but employed with greater
penetration.

The founder of French Intuitionism is Henri Bergson.[1]

The development of Bergson's thought is marked by
three distinct phases, which we can indicate provisionally
by the titles of psychology, epistemology and metaphysics.
They coincide with the publication of his three greatest
works: the *Essai sur les Données immédiates de la Conscience :*[2]
Matter and Memory : and *Creative Evolution.*   These three
phases correspond with the development of one and the same
problem in Bergson's mind : a problem which by the very
fact of its self-expansion outgrows the limits first of psycho-

---

[1] The following pages on Bergson have been taken from an essay of
mine which appeared in *La Cultura* of February 15, 1912.

[2] Translated into English under the title of *Time and Free Will* by F. L.
Pogson, Swan Sonnenschein & Co., 1910.

logy and then of epistemology, and finally reveals its true metaphysical character.

Bergson begins, as I have said, with psychology. He begins by raising the question, How do we intuite directly ? The succession of emotions, of thoughts, in general of states of mind, has a quite unique character. It is not a superimposition of facts on facts, but an interpenetration of moments, the one within the other, a combination in a progressive and irreversible series in which every element is fused with the preceding one and enriches with its absolutely original tonality the state of mind with which it is fused. This organization of the facts of consciousness is the work of time, nay, it is time itself. Time is the form which the succession of our states of consciousness assumes when our ego lets itself *live*, when it refrains from separating its present state from its former state, when on remembering these states it does not set them alongside its present state as one point alongside another, but unites them organically with it, as happens when we recall the notes of a melody, fused, so to speak, into one another.

Thus the analysis of our innermost ego reveals a qualitative series of heterogeneous moments, none of which has fixed and clear-cut outlines, but each of which merges, as it were, into the other, and permeates it : their succession is not a quantitative accumulation, but a qualitative progression.

If at this point we turn from the internal to the external, and observe the manner in which the products of consciousness are organized, no longer in their spiritual actuality, but as the content and matter of knowledge, the spectacle changes completely. We no longer have the fusion of heterogeneous states in a unique whole, but the superimposition of homogeneous inert elements : the character of the whole is produced simply and solely by the addition of the parts. The material elements are not fused, but are essentially impenetrable : they are not continuous, they do not succeed one another in time, but coexist in space ; that is to say, within the limits of geometrically fixed outlines : matter is intrinsically " ballasted with geometry." Here we see Bergson's dualism taking shape : internality and externality, time and space, soul and matter.

Bergson gradually becomes conscious of the "long and terrible decline down which he is slipping" : but having once begun by identifying reality with the immediacy of life lived, so far from resolving the dualism he is driven merely to intensify and "exasperate" it. Yet it must be resolved if knowledge is to be possible. Is not knowledge, in fact, a resolution of the other into the ego, of nature into the spirit ? Now, there is a so-called empirical science which attempts a compromise, a mediation between the terms of the dualism : it solidifies the forms of qualitative becoming into the *schemata* of quantity, and temporal progress into coexistence in space. May not this be the means of surmounting pure psychological immediacy ? Does not this offer at any rate a provisional point of contact between spirit and nature ? The 1eal solution of the problem does no doubt lie here ; but we have seen that Bergson has already identified reality with the immediate experience of the subject : hence any compromise between subject and object, spirit and nature, must necessarily appear to him unreal, a falsification of pure experience. But how, then, does he explain the transition from duration to extension, from reality as it is lived to his solidified *schema* in space ? There must be such a transition, or how explain the fact of knowledge, the existence of science ? The ground of this transition, Bergson proceeds, is not to be found in the innermost self ; the self, if left to itself, would let itself live eternally, without ever passing over into something different from itself : being absolutely irreflective, immediate, it rejects all reflection and denounces it as false. The impulse must come from elsewhere. And thus, without any previous warning, we suddenly come upon an intruder into the realm of the innermost self, in the shape of the will, of action. We have to construct a nature in the forms of space because our action wills that it should be so, because action can only move among solids, among things with clear and definite outlines upon which it can take a hold. Natural science is thus our means of possessing ourselves of the real : in it we mutilate the real, divide it up, destroy it as reality in order that we may conquer it, get the mastery of just that part of it which will serve our purpose, control it better according to the needs of our active life.

This scientific pragmatism, however, has the grave defect that, while explaining everything, it fails in the most important thing of all, to explain itself. For is it conceivable that an external reality, an unknown x, should adapt itself so complacently to the needs of our actions ; that if our whole system of scientific concepts is the mere product of an arbitrary subjectivity, it should nevertheless " work " when applied to nature ? And so we see Bergson, conscious of the difficulty, beginning to make concessions : perhaps, he says, there is a kind of compromise between spirit and nature.[1] But this is just the difficulty : granted the premisses, how can nature adapt herself to the laws of the spirit ?

Then, from the other point of view, when we consider the external world we are in the habit of saying that things exhibit duration, development, motion : in other words, we affirm that the terminology of psychical life can be used in describing the material world. Is this usage a mere figure of speech ? Strictly speaking, given Bergson's presuppositions, it must be. Yet Bergson is constrained to admit that, although we ought not to say that external things endure, yet there must be in them some inexpressible reason in virtue of which we cannot consider them at successive moments of our own duration without observing that they have changed.[2] But what else is this indefinable reason except an implicit confession that the psychology of the subject has failed to resolve the object into itself ? In short : without the identity of subject and object, of spirit and nature, it is not possible to explain how the order created by the spirit " works " when applied to nature, how science holds good of reality. The ostensible pragmatism conceals, therefore, a metaphysical problem : what is nature, the object ? The *Données de la Conscience* leave this problem open ; the work *Matter and Memory* will attempt to solve it.

In this second phase of his thought Bergson places himself at a point of view diametrically opposed to his first : there he starts from the subject, here from the object. What is matter, external nature ? According to a widespread superstition it is a mysterious x, outside us, which we attempt

<hr>

[1] H. Bergson, *Time and Free Will*, p. 223.   [2] *Ibid.*, p. 226.

patiently to copy with our concepts. Nothing is farther from the truth. Matter is exactly that which we see and touch or, better, perceive. Must we, then, in order to fashion the external world, project outside ourselves the web of our perceptions ? Not at all ; this is the illusion of Berkeleianism. This illusion is the result of our method of first positing dogmatically the subject and then introducing into it—by an error which Avenarius calls introjection—the external world. The truth is the exact opposite. In the process of knowledge we do not start from the ego and proceed first to our body and then to the external world, but from the very beginning we place ourselves in the external world, and then, little by little, we detach from its firm structure our bodies and ourselves.[1] Here we see Berkeleianism reversed, and in this reversal, for the first time, becoming coherent. Matter, then, is a complex of images, of mental facts. This mentality is exhausted in the act of perception itself : it is, as Leibniz would say, a *mens momentanea*. Here is the point of contact between spirit and matter : but it is also the only point. For, starting from here, the two terms separate along divergent lines : matter tending more and more to become merely a succession of infinitely brief moments which can be deduced the one from the other and are therefore equivalent : while spirit, on the contrary, tends to compress perceptions, to fuse the past with the present and to conceive the continuity of its own states, their progress. The spirit is essentially memory.

Matter and memory : this is the new dualism : a dualism affecting the theory of knowledge only and not metaphysics, Bergson might maintain, because matter is revealed in its spiritual character. Yet the metaphysical dualism is concealed and not resolved. In fact, this matter, reduced to a complex of images which are compressed within and limited to conscious perception, is only the appearance and counterfeit of mentality. It is rather a crystallization of mental fact, as much purely passive as the matter of atomism. It is the pure phenomenon as fact, not the phenomenon in the

[1] H. Bergson, *Matter and Memory*, Eng. tr. by Nancy Margaret Paul and W. Scott Palmer, London, 1911, pp. 44–5.

making. It is, in short, crude fact, not experience; and therefore it is truly matter and not mentality. Bergson's statement of the problem renders the passage from matter to memory, from nature to spirit, as impossible as does the current materialistic statement of it.

He does certainly take the great step of conceiving the subject as a potentiality which, escaping from matter, rediscovers itself in the dynamic process of memory as a free creator; but this is only a reminiscence of the subjectivism of the *Données de la Conscience*. Logically developed, the thought in *Matter and Memory* ought to end by denying the metaphysic of the subject and resolving the latter into a mere aggregate of images, as Mach does. Bergson, on the contrary, labouring to save both the goat and the cabbage, the idealism of the subject and the empiricism of the object, ends by finding himself once more involved in the metaphysical dualism which he thought he had transcended. Matter does not lose its opacity from the mere fact of ceasing to be an assemblage of atoms and becoming an assemblage of images: in either case it is crude fact, and nothing but crude fact. To conceive matter spiritually can only mean repudiating the concept of " fact " in all its senses and replacing it with that of " act ": that is to say, including matter in the process of the spirit. It is not a question of conceiving it as a mental fact, but as a mental creation. Instead of starting from the object, which is a fact and not a becoming, we must start from the subject and conceive a phenomenology of the spirit, which will also be the creative process of nature, of matter.

Creative Evolution faces this problem resolutely and in its true light, no longer distorting it from metaphysics into psychology. *Creative Evolution* is a return to the subjectivism of the *Données*, but with the great difference that the aim is now to conceive the dynamics not of the psychological subject, but of reality as the subject. It is a return, in fact, to the data of consciousness through the mediation of *Matter and Memory*, that is to say, with the new demand that nature must be resolved in the process of the spirit.

The new subject is Life as creation, as impulse which

12

is asserted and realized in its development in time, creating beings and forms, never repeating itself in its infinite productions, always original and progressive. It is not in the power of the abstract intellect to understand life. For the intellect solidifies life in its concepts and thereby loses all that is vital in life, the very principle of organization in the organism. To understand life means to live it again : not to observe it from above, but to accompany it in its creative course ; not to catalogue the organized products, but to watch the act of organization. What characterizes life is the unity of the impulse, of the impetus constituting it. This unity disintegrates itself, life branches out in a thousand different directions ; but the basic identity of the various currents remains always an identity of impulse, not of end or of result. To speak of a single goal to life, to define its aim, is to think of a pre-existing model which has only to be realized. It amounts to supposing that everything is given, that the future can be read in the present. Life, on the contrary, does not presuppose anything as given, and is absolutely original in its creations.

Here we see how the Leibnizian monadism, breaking down its internal barriers, is swept through and through by a vast flood of vital energy and at the same time profoundly modified by the contingentism of Boutroux. The vital unity is the unity of impulse : once set in movement, the enormous torrent advances forward without any prearranged plan, but plans gradually as it advances.

Now this vital impetus, which presupposes nothing to sustain it, but incomprehensibly arises and grows and expands and disintegrates, explains, or ought to explain, the development of all the forms which life assumes right up to the reflection of thought, in which life reviews and recreates itself, and to the matter in which life is solidified and externalized. Bergson's programme is a very ambitious one ; for he would explain at the same time the evolution of life and of the intuitive thought which contemplates it ; the creation of matter and of the intellect which imprisons it in its *schemata* and adapts it to itself. And at this point, in the revelation of the identity of thought and the object of thought, of intellect and matter, Bergson's scientific

pragmatism would find its true and proper justification.
Yet it is just here that the Bergsonian theory comes to
grief and reveals its radical insufficiency. For is this *élan
vital*, this creator of forms and beings, indeed absolute
creator ? Bergson is at pains to show how life in the course
of its progress ramifies. But why does it ramify ? Is it
itself the sole cause of its diremption ? The reason why a
waterfall or a river bifurcates at a certain point in its course
is that it meets an obstacle. It is the same with life as
conceived by Bergson. This life is not the sufficient reason
for its own action ; it must have an obstacle, a μὴ ὄν
which opposes it and introduces variety into its course.
This is because it is not self-reflective ; it does not produce and
mediate its own moments, but is a unilinear development,
immediate, unreflective, which needs an obstacle to make it
turn back on itself ; in short, it is not consciousness, but
nature.

   This conclusion is brought out still more clearly by the
way in which Bergson attempts to explain the genesis of
matter. Matter is an interruption of the vital current, a
negation inserted into the continuity of evolution, a solidification of life.[1] But how is this arrest of the vital current,
this lapse into stagnation, explicable ? Life, as Bergson
conceives it, if left, so to speak, to itself, ought to progress
eternally : if it bends back and is deflected, it does so because
something obstructs it. Thus life, which in its movement
ought to create matter, itself presupposes an obstacle in
the shape of matter. This is the enormous vicious circle
in which the Bergsonian metaphysic revolves.[2] We have
already indicated the ground of this vicious circle. It is
because he regards life as nature, not as consciousness,
reflection, dialectic. In short, for lack of the true circle,
which is that of thought, Bergson is compelled to traverse
a false one. If we try for a moment to think what a vital
impulse involves, we shall see that an impetus which does
not start from *terra firma* is inconceivable. Think again of

---

[1] *Creative Evolution*, translated by A. Mitchell, London, 1911, p. 261.
[2] This vicious circle has already been pointed out by Aliotta in his book
The Idealistic Reaction against Science, Engl. tr. by Agnes McCaskill, London,
1914, p. 136.

a stream, a river : it needs some medium through which it can flow. In his conception of life Bergson indeed makes a brave attempt to get rid of this presupposition, but the attempt fails, because of the very inadequacy of the concept.

But there is a further difficulty. Why should life, when it breaks against an obstacle, at one moment become consciousness, at another become matter ? [1] Life as such does not contain the reasons for the variations which arise in its course : these must therefore depend upon the nature of the obstacle. And so mere passivity, the pure $\mu\grave{\eta}$ $\check{o}\nu$, has to be enriched with different determinations to explain its different effects. Matter, which Bergson has persecuted without ever dematerializing it, revenges itself finally on his system by drawing it over unconsciously towards naturalism.

I will not stay here to discuss other consequences ; but I want to point out what seems to me to be the fundamental vice of Bergson's philosophy, and to bring inevitable ruin upon his system. Bergson begins and ends his career with the praises of immediate life, of intuition. Now, intuition presupposes its object and does not create it : hence thought is for Bergson a mere observing, as in a metaphysic of being, instead of an absolute creating, as in a metaphysic of knowledge. Thought, according to him, accompanies creation but does not create : it watches the evolution of life, but is not itself life ; in short, it presupposes its whole object, as does every form of dogmatism. Hence its immediacy and unreflectiveness, far from being a sign of superiority, is on the contrary a sign of its very inferiority. And the result is that all the forms of reflection, of distinction, or in general of science, remain outside (or better, above) the reality within which Bergson is confined. Therefore in vain does he attempt to destroy the web of the concepts ; he does not and cannot solve the problem of knowledge, he only " exasperates " it, to use one of his own expressions. The problem of science cannot be solved, if we insist upon remaining below science, in a beatific region of intuition, as this Rousseau of epistemology proposes to do—great men though they are, both the old Rousseau and the new.

[1] *Creative Evolution*, p. 151.

It can only be solved by entering the domain of science and marching boldly through it till we rise above its dogmatism. By the latter process the validity of science is established ; by the former it is destroyed.

In vain do we seek in a stage preceding that of science, of knowledge, for a reality that shall be rich, complete, harmonious, sufficient in itself ; such embellishments are the work of phantasy. The new Rousseau does not view the state of nature directly, but imagines it through the medium of the state of civilization in which he lives.

§ 4. THE BERGSONIAN SCHOOL.

In the wake of Bergson, we have the philosophy of the primitives, the men of nature. Among these is Le Roy, who outlines the programme of the philosopher as follows : to be freed from time, from number and from space, to break the obsolete limits of a barbaric language, to rise above the discursive thinking whose aim is to define and to judge ; to rediscover in the depths of spiritual life the living sources of the logical mechanism.[1] Philosophy thus defined is simply a reflective and conscious return to the data of intuition. If we would understand the truth of the Bergsonian philosophy we must abandon clear thought, he says, for thought that is lived : but how can the thought that is lived ever agree with reflective thought ? The truth is that Le Roy is a man of such primitive *naïveté* that in his eagerness to cast aside the sophistications of the civilized life of thought he has also cast aside his knowledge of the history of philosophy, and does not realize that he is on the point of falling into the arms of Condillac and John Stuart Mill. Matter, according to him, is a possibility of images linked one with another in an inevitable order, a source of discursive thought, individual and social.[2] This is authentic John Stuart Mill. But neither Le Roy nor his master, with all their exaltation of the life of the spirit, is able to overcome the ancient Aristotelian dualism of

---

[1] E. le Roy, *Science et Philosophie* (*Revue de Métaphysique et de Morale*, 1899, p. 719).
[2] *Ibid.* (1900), pp. 58, 66.

potentiality and act, and explain how a mere possibility can be the source of an actuality. Then, again, his explanation of the connection between space and sensation is that " the appearance space has of being applied to the given arises from the fact that it is itself a residual image of the given." [1] This is still John Stuart Mill. But in his view of science he follows Condillac. He considers science to be a falsification of given truth for the purposes of discursive thinking and social life. And so forth.

But this primitive man does not realize that these are the words of irresponsible reaction, leading not to the primitive life of his desire, but to a life of barbarism, the repetition of old long-abandoned themes. As I have said, he is fundamentally naïve, and if in his thought he cannot rise to the heights of speculation, yet inwardly he lives that spiritual life into which Bergson has given him insight. Le Roy is an enthusiast ; and his very criticism of science ends by being a misplaced glorification of it. This might appear paradoxical to anyone who has not appreciated the radical transformation whichi the terms " practical " and " action " have undergone with Le Roy in the course of assimilation of the elements of the Blondelian philosophy. We have no longer the " practical " in the sense of Mach and Duhem, but a mysticism of action.

Le Roy's criticism of science (and the same is true of the other Bergsonians) really concerns rather an obsolete conception of the logic of science than science itself. They start with the preconception that, in order to be true, science must be a copy of a reality already given. They are then struck by the progressively active and spontaneous intervention of the spirit in the creation of real truth ; and so they infer that they have good reason to discredit science, while in reality they are only discrediting an ancient logic which has been superseded for centuries. And the very development of this anti-intellectualism has finally resulted in an overvaluation of the " practical," of " action," by means of which Le Roy has arrived, as I said, at a misplaced glorification of science. We will return to Le Roy's mysticism later on in our discussion of the philosophy of religion.

[1] *Ibid.* (1899), p. 406.

To conclude : we have seen the theory of science pass from contingentism to critical empiricism and fade into a colourless nominalism, while on the other side the idealistic motives of the philosophy of Ravaisson and Boutroux have found a new concentration in Bergson. Bergson sums up in his personality an age-long tendency of French thought, and carries dualistic spiritualism to the highest perfection of which it admits. But a criticism of the Bergsonian philosophy has convinced us that an idealistic conception of matter and life cannot be given by a metaphysic of being, which Bergson's metaphysic really is, just as much as Ravaisson's, in spite of all appearances to the contrary. Hence, for a metaphysic of knowledge it is only valuable as a negative moment. For in such a metaphysic matter and life taken separately are viewed not as things in themselves to be vivified with a current of psychical life, but as abstract moments of that knowledge which is self-conscious reflection of thought upon itself.

Under the influence of Bergson psychological investigation has flourished, and often reached a high level. I will instance here Rémacle, who bases psychology on the principle that in order to know ourselves we must create ourselves. Every act of reflection has this character of being a creation of ourselves for ourselves.[1] Since, therefore, psychology is an attempt to realize the mind, it follows that the mind is not the object but the final cause of psychology. And since the mind is a process of creation, a becoming, a synthesis of being and not-being, every real psychology must be considered as the consciousness of the stage which that development has attained at the moment, thanks to this very act by which it has become conscious of itself and thanks to the mental effort which the construction of this psychology requires. Following out this theory, which is a Bergsonism with a vein of Kant, Rémacle concludes by exalting the practical reason, not in the sense that the practical is different from the theoretical reason, but in the sense that reason is essentially practical, moral. Rauh, too, under the influence of Boutroux, inclines towards moral voluntarism.

[1] Rémacle, *La Valeur positive de la Psychologie* (*Revue de Métaphysique et de Morale*, 1894, p. 154).

The interesting feature of these speculations, as also of Bergson's inquiries from which they are derived, is their orientation towards an actualistic conception of the spirit, which repudiates fact, substance, and attempts to figure reality as activity, progress. From this arise the fine and sometimes even magnificent passages which are to be found in their writings (especially in those of Bergson himself) proclaiming the creative spontaneity and the living reality of the spirit, passages instinct with life and pervaded with a feeling of concreteness, of reality. This is what Le Roy means when he speaks of a new positivism, far truer than the old, a positivism which instead of moving within empty *schemata* of fact, investigates the genetic creative process. Yet because of its very presuppositions this philosophy fails to supersede the naturalistic conception of fact, and fails therefore to understand completely the nature of that reality which it grasps. For it does grasp reality; but rather by virtue of a kind of unerring insight, an immediate revelation, than by virtue of a real conquest; and for this reason it has never succeeded in establishing it as the only true reality.

CHAPTER V

POSITIVISM AND PLATONISM

§ 1. THE SOCIAL SCIENCES.

THE old positivism of Comte and Littré has been completely absorbed by the intellectual renaissance due to the master thinkers of whom we have been speaking ; and no trace of it remains, saving some harmless cosmogonies fabricated by wholesale dealers in science, and not calling for our attention. Comte's classification of the sciences—the main plank in the positivist platform—has been taken up and developed in a very different direction by the so-called New Spiritualism ; and Boutroux, with his more speculative mind, has carried it to its logical conclusion. As for the religion which Comte invented, the French have always regarded it as a farce ; and in fact it is simply the final effort of naturalism to counterfeit by an act of self-deification that spiritual inwardness which eludes its *schemata*.

The positivist tradition is much more recognizably preserved in the social sciences. Indeed, especially of late years, we have had a veritable harvest of sociological doctrines which, in spite of their unbroken level of mediocrity, have attracted a great deal of attention. We will glance at a few of these, in order to make our historical sketch complete.

Espinas was one of the first to apply the socio-biological method to the treatment of social questions. According to him the instinct of sociability is found in all grades of being, and is shared by animals and men alike : the difference between them is merely one of degree, and both are bound by the same biological laws.[1] But Espinas lost himself

[1] A. Espinas, *Les Sociétés animales*, Paris, 1878, 2nd ed., pp. 138–9.

185

among the ants and the various other swarms of animals, and failed to develop this idea very far ; in consequence, he did not distort and degrade human societies enough to satisfy the principles of positivism.

In this task Tarde has proved more successful. He has discovered the one and only formula of social life, namely imitation ; which indeed is supreme in biological life as well. And, since imitation presupposes anterior invention, everything can be reduced to these two great moving principles of human existence. From the social point of view everything is either an invention or an imitation : the imitations are the rivers, the inventions the mountains which rule their course. If we consider social science in the light of this truth we shall see that human sociology is related to animal sociology as the species to the genus : a unique species, no doubt, and one infinitely superior to the others, but yet a sister species.

This entirely mechanistic idea leads to a conception of society as " a collection of beings regarded as engaged in a continual process of mutual imitation, and as resembling one another even when they do not actually imitate, in which case their common traits are long-established copies of one and the same model." [1] The " social being " does not set its own organization before itself as an end ; this organization is simply the means of which imitation is the end. History is not a collection of remarkable things, but of the most successful things, that is to say of the inventions which have been most imitated.[2] Every imitation tends towards an indefinite progress ; but the interference of obstacles generates social struggles : the end of the process will come when the imitative power has permeated society from top to bottom, and everything will finally reach an equality : the barriers of castes, of classes, of nations will disappear and equilibrium will be established.[3] Imitation will then reign supreme.

Tarde complacently quotes the pronouncement of an " illustrious French historian," who called his law of imitation a key which would open all locks. To us, this was somewhat

[1] G. Tarde, *Les Lois de l'Imitation*, Paris, 1904, 4th ed., p. 73.
[2] *Ibid.*, p. 151.   [3] *Ibid.*, p. 399.

of a surprise. We had imagined that a key was designed to open only one lock—its own ; those which open all locks we were in the habit of calling by the significant, if depreciatory, name of skeleton keys.

A sociological theory based upon a more scientific criterion, and developed by means of less crude conceptions, is presented by Durkheim. According to this writer, social science should follow the same procedure as the natural sciences ; it should first observe the facts and then from these extract their laws. Hence it must do away with all search for the inner essence, and rest content with observing phenomena from the outside. Thus the biologist recognizes a biological fact by certain palpable marks, and does not require to create a philosophical concept. In the same way the sociologist should not see in the facts of morality any inner spiritual meaning, but only their external characteristic, namely obligatoriness.

Now, no one can deny the legitimacy of such a procedure : the only question is what results it can give. It is quite permissible to abstract from certain characteristics of human action, especially those which are least dependent on the personality of the individual and therefore common to many people. But it is obvious that once we have divorced ourselves from the inner spiritual meaning of the moral act, this meaning must remain absolutely unprejudiced by our inquiry. Yet with scientific sociology it is exactly the contrary ; and herein lies its sophism. For having once pronounced obligatoriness, for instance, to be the characteristic, the merely external definition, of the moral act, it then trespasses right into the domain of the inner life and ends by pronouncing on the morality of the act, while, given its presuppositions, it could only pronounce upon the class into which the act is to be put. In short, it desires to treat morals as a natural science, and in the process it converts morality into a natural product.

By playing on this equivocal position, Durkheim is able to maintain a theory of social determinism. He asserts progress to be a mechanical fact ; men change, in his view, because they must change, and the velocity of this change is determined by the greater or less pressure which men

exercise upon one another in proportion to their numbers.[1]
He is able to maintain several other things also, but they
are not a credit to his method. Here, as everywhere, the
positivist turns out to be a concealed materialist.

And finally, by means of a new equivocation, whose
significance he does not seem to grasp, he suddenly reverses
his position entirely, and after having stated once and for
all that social life is a product of crude mechanical forces,
he says : " Although it is the effect of necessary causes,
civilization can become an end, an object of desire ; in a
word, an ideal. At every period of its history, the collective
life of society has, in fact, a certain normal degree of intensity,
given the number and the distribution of the social units.
Of course, if everything happened in a normal manner, this
state would be realized of itself ; but in point of fact we have
the power of trying to bring it about that things should
happen in a normal manner." [2] Thus, that inner life which
was suppressed by one equivocation is reintroduced by another,
which extracts it out of a purely mechanical conception.

This seems to us to be the outstanding characteristic of
these sociologies : their play upon an equivocal position.
They start out with the modest claim of wishing to observe
facts and induce laws, failing to grasp that if they adhered
strictly to their principles the most they could do would be
to tabulate statistics of social facts. And yet that claim
of theirs contains a whole philosophy of a very doubtful
nature, which very soon comes out of hiding to engage in
a war of extermination upon everything which lies outside
its narrow view.

§ 2. History.

For positivism, the passage from sociology to the
philosophy of history is a short one. According to Lacombe,
historical science is the recognition of resemblances and
connections : hence the material of history must be divided
into that which can be assimilated by scientific concepts
and that which proves recalcitrant to them. Hence he

---

[1] E. Durkheim, *De la Division du Travail social*, Paris, 1893, p. 376.
[2] *Ibid.*, p. 379.

considers the spirit as a stratification of various elements, of which some belong to all times and all places, others to particular periods of culture, and yet others to contingent historical moments ; but he at least understands that these elements are combined in a single element, in so far as each historical individual acts at the same time as a man and as a man belonging to a determinate civilization.[1]

Though his book contains a few just observations here and there, it yet contains a great deal more that is merely flippant. He defines religion, for instance, as "imaginary economics," which is witty, but hardly serious. Elsewhere he remarks that the phrase " civilization is a beautiful plant grown in manure " is literally true, because the progress in manuring has determined the progress of humanity. And what has determined progress in manuring ? Even a positivist can hardly suppose that a field manures itself.

The same problems of the methodology of history have been studied in a far more serious spirit by Xénopol. His inquiry has not, properly speaking, a philosophical significance, and I do not think that it was intended to have one ; yet it abounds in penetrating observations and accurate descriptions. Xénopol distinguishes between facts of repetition and of succession : the first belong to the natural sciences, the second to history. The latter, in the broad sense of the word, is not a special science, as it has been regarded up till now, but constitutes one of the two universal modes of conceiving the world, namely the mode of succession, as contrasted with that of repetition. Corresponding to these two different fields, there are two types of causality exemplified in the connection of related facts : scientific causality is short-winded because it at once reaches ultimate laws ; the historical type, on the other hand, leads back from link to link *ad infinitum* without ever stopping. This is an acute observation.

Since they cannot be repeated, historical facts constitute well-defined individualities ; they are not subjected to general laws, but are arranged in irreversible series whose connection manifests a certain character of fatality. But this fatality only attaches to the completed fact, inasmuch

[1] P. Lacombe, *De l'Histoire considerée comme Science*, Paris, 1894, p. 248.

as what has happened has happened and therefore must have happened. Yet Xénopol's view of historical development is inclined to be naturalistic, owing to a distinction which he draws between the constant and variable factors in evolution : a distinction connected with the positivist point of view.

But, as I have said, we must not look to this doctrine of history for anything more than an accurate methodology. Xénopol still follows Aristotle and Bacon, not Kant, in his science. He is afraid of Kant, thinking that to apply Kant's thesis to history would be to reduce it to a phantasmagoria : an illusion which is common to all amateurs in philosophy. He holds that the foundation of knowledge is constituted by impressions transmitted from the senses to the soul, through which knowledge of things such as they are in reality is produced.[1] In short, there is not the slightest trace of philosophy in him : but he does give an accurate description of historical procedure ; and it is this which makes his book useful and attractive.

§ 3. Positivism and Platonism.

This is all that the purer form of French positivism has produced lately ; and it is not very much. The tradition can still be traced outside sociology, but here it has failed to maintain its purity and has become fused with other conceptions into a sort of eclecticism. Platonism is one of them. This combination ought not to appear strange, because, when viewed apart from its process, as a system of laws crystallized *ab æterno* above a basis of contingent and changeable facts, science is Platonic, and the more its naturalism is emphasized, the more clearly is its Platonic character manifested. This is further shown in the manner in which scientific minds usually visualize moral problems. When they look back at the past they can descry in it nothing but miserable struggles of warring interests and passions ; but when they turn to the future they see a new Eden coming to be : scientific progress and invention will abolish social distinctions, wars, rapine : right will rule, egoism will dis-

[1] A. D. Xénopol, *La Théorie de l'Histoire*, Paris, 1908, 2nd ed., p. 459.

appear, and the millennium will arrive.[1] The reason for the Platonism of science is that in the scientific conception nature is an abstract idea materialized into an object ; it is an essence outside time. Hence science lacks the concept of progress immanent in history, and can only conceive instead archetypes or ideals that supply either by attraction or by *vis a tergo* the motive power of human history. Its union with Platonism is simply a manifestation of what science already contains.

Fouillée is a naturalist with Platonic tendencies who has exercised a certain influence on French philosophy. He sets out to reconcile scientific naturalism with idealism, facts with ideas ; and concocts for the purpose the concept of idea-force, which is a mechanical juxtaposition of the two elements. The method of science which reduces everything to its material conditions is for him only a partial truth : it passes over what is for us an unquestionable certainty, namely the inner experience of the subject. This is the true point from which metaphysics ought to start in order to embrace in a vast synthesis psychology and cosmology.

In so far as psychological experience reveals us to ourselves as will, as nature, we can interpret nature in psychological terms, but in so far as we are also thought, the idea " has also a right to consideration and to inclusion as an element in a complete conception of the world." Certainly it cannot be considered as predominant, but it cannot have absolutely no influence. Its function is to be one among the factors of universal evolution ; hence the theory of idea-forces.[2]

From these premisses a metaphysical theory is developed which is best described by an untranslatable French term, *plate.* It has its counterpart in von Hartmann's metaphysic, which we have already discussed, without Hartmann's

---

[1] It may be worth remarking that the author is not implying that Plato's Republic is such a " new Eden " ; the Ideal State exists only in the World of Ideas, and can never be realized in history. The tendency to expect a new Golden Age is cited only as an example of that failure to understand " how history works " that is characteristic of Platonizing Realism.—Trs.

[2] A. Fouillée, *L'Avenir de la Métaphysique fondée sur l'Expérience,* Paris, 1889, p. 263.

" unconsciousness." It accepts the evolutionism of modern scientific theories and reduplicates it in an enfeebled form in its idea-forces ; it denies all teleology and reduces everything to the mechanism of mental matter ; and while it believes that it has spiritualized nature, it fails to see, as a French critic observes, that it has turned the idea into nature. Fouillée's philosophy is simply the echo of German naturalism ; and it has achieved that kind of reputation which very striking echoes often enjoy.

Berthelot, whom we already know as the author of a clever essay on Hegel, is also a Platonist. He attempts to reconcile Kantianism and Spencerian evolutionism in a higher synthesis. The inadequacy of Kantianism is due to its failure to relate to the eternal laws of thought the laws of the temporal development of the universe : but on the other hand Spencer has failed to understand the universal element in the evolutionary process.[1] Hence the need for a synthesis which takes account of ideas no less than of scientific mathematical theories. But is not Plato's doctrine, he asks himself, a critical rationalism, a dialectic, a mathematical philosophy ? Only Plato is no evolutionist ; and on the other hand his teleology is incompatible with modern science. And so Berthelot concludes by saying that " there is nothing to prevent us from preserving the directive ideas of Platonism while we reject this latter doctrine and admit that the order of the sense-world, which is always more precarious in proportion as we deal with more complicated groups of facts, can be explained without recourse to final causes. We can therefore define our doctrine as an evolutionistic Platonism." [2] But how can the leap from the Hegelian to the Platonic dialectic be explained ? Berthelot has forgotten that between the two there intervened the three *Critiques* of Kant.

Dunan is another Platonist, or rather he is an Aristotelian, who is fully conscious of his own position—a fact for which he deserves praise at a time when authors are so very ready to confuse the historical antecedents of their doctrines. According to him there are two kinds of idealism : the one

---

[1] R. Berthelot, *Evolutionnisme et Platonisme cit.*, pp. 272–4.
[2] *Op. cit.*, p. 280.

true, which ends with Aristotle, the other false, which begins with Descartes' *cogito*.

Nothing exists except through participation in ideas : the principle of that which exists is the idea, which is thought and does not exist. But this is a very different thing from a reassertion of Plato as against Cartesianism. The Platonic idea is like the eye which sees everything but itself : it is an intelligible principle which illuminates the sensible world while itself remaining shrouded in still greater obscurity. Dunan follows Plato in asserting the existence of a hierarchy of concepts representing the stages in the progress of thought towards an integral conception of reality ; hence an ever greater concreteness in concepts in proportion as they become more general. The concept of tree is more concrete than that of fir-tree, and the concept of fir-tree more concrete than that of the fir-trees of the forest, because there is in the act of thought which forms them a principle of intelligence. Now if I remove from the representation of fir-trees every intelligible element, there remains neither likeness nor difference between them, they no longer present any determinate character, they can no longer even have a position in space and time, but they flit across my vision like impalpable ghosts, equally strange to the domain of the senses and to that of the spirit.[1] But, on the contrary, the farther the intelligible is removed from the sense-world, the greater its consistency, and the ideas themselves take on the character of facts : the whole progress of our knowledge consists in conferring on new ideas a positive character. An idealism of this kind, Dunan adds, would be also the genuine positivism, which positivism has never succeeded in being ; for it would be a philosophy of the real that is given in experience, which is the true philosophical meaning of the term positivism.[2]

It is interesting to observe how the idea of a " genuine positivism " haunts the French mind. We have already seen it in Weber and Le Roy. It betokens a concrete way of looking at problems which is characteristic of modern French philosophy. But Dunan's positivism is a very

[1] C. Dunan, *Les deux Idéalismes*, Paris, 1911, p. 32.
[2] *Op. cit.*, p. 43.

different thing from Weber's ; it is the crystallization of the idea in the fact, not the absolute actuality of knowing ; Platonism lacks the conception of the subject, and its " idea " is simply the highest among the objects of the sensible world.

§ 4. The Ethics of Platonism.

On the basis of his theory of idea-forces Fouillée has founded a Platonistic system of ethics which, while accepting the sensationalism of English ethics, believes that it has superseded it by maintaining that evolution will lead to the substitution of altruistic ideals for the current egoism. Here, as everywhere in Fouillée's philosophy, the idea is a force ; hence, once it is begotten, it begets in its turn a belief in the possibility of its own realization, and this in turn gives rise to feelings and inclinations which ultimately lead us to actualize the means which will convert the idea into a reality.[1]

The ideals of to-day are thus the reality of to-morrow : to-day, sense motives prevail, but since we are understanding as well as sense, and the understanding is by its very nature impersonal, objective, the morality of to-morrow will be wholly altruistic and impersonal. This future morality does not recognize obligation ; it no longer says " I ought and therefore I can," but " I can and therefore I ought " ; and it looks to science and industry for the realization of the happy life of the future. The whole point of view is absolutely superficial and ignorant of the depths of spiritual life ; it thus looks for its goal to an impersonal consciousness, and for means of realizing it to something which is outside the life of consciousness altogether—namely, scientific progress, which is to lay down the new laws of morality.

All this is an apotheosis of ethical dilettantism. Morality is not one thing to-day and another to-morrow : the moral life does not mean sitting still and waiting for manna to fall, some fine day, from the sky of science, till when, we can go on indulging all our worst passions with a clear conscience.

[1] A. Fouillée, *Critique des Systèmes de Morale contemporaine*, Paris, 1887, 2nd ed., p. 25.

Our business is to create the moral life within ourselves :
if we cannot do that, it is no use our waiting for an ethical
millennium to accomplish in time something that is essentially
outside time. But an artistic temperament may find this
vision of the morality of the future, so different from that
of to-day, a very attractive idea. The sweeping formula
of a new morality, to be realized without trouble or pain on
anybody's part, is singularly welcome to one who is too
indolent to reach a higher life by the road of renunciation.
It justifies his indolence ; and he can afford a smile of puerile
scorn for those who toil panting along the rocky paths of
an unexplored world instead of flying with him through the
free air of imagination.

This is exactly the temperament we find in Guyau. He
is an overgrown child, who by some chance found in his
hands one day the works of Bentham and Spencer, and—
incredible to relate—extracted from them poetical inspiration.
The future of humanity—that gulf unplumbed by science
and unfilled by any tissue of naturalistic formulæ—becomes
peopled with the visions of his lyrical fancy.

Morality, he remarks, has sprung from life and ought
not to escape from life, but to advance it in all its fullness.
Now even in the life of the mere cell there is a principle of
expansion which makes it impossible for the individual to
be sufficient to itself ; and the richer life is, the more
prodigal of itself it becomes, the more inclined to communicate
itself to others. Hence it follows that the most perfect
organism is also the most sociable, and that the ideal of
individual life is the life in common. This is the ideal
towards which life is tending in the course of its natural
development as disclosed by science ; but science does not
give us a complete conception of it ; we must anticipate
science and see whither that movement is tending which
science only envisages in a fragmentary form. " We are as
it were on the *Leviathan*, from which a wave has torn the
rudder and a blast of wind carried away the mainmast.
It is lost in the ocean as our earth is lost in space. It floats
thus at random, driven by the tempest, like a huge derelict,
yet with men upon it ; and yet it reaches port. Perhaps our
earth, perhaps humanity, will also reach that unknown end

which they will have created for themselves. No hand
directs us ; the rudder has long been broken, or rather it
has never existed ; we must make it : it is a great task,
and it is our task." [1]

What, for Guyau, is the ideal of humanity ? A social
life without laws, without obligations, because morality will
have become natural ; a life in which men will no longer
feel within them the shock of conflicting passions : from
which every sanction will have disappeared and a bond of
brotherhood, of affection, will unite us all.

There is no harm in being lyrical ; but the fault of these
Utopias is that they transfer their formulæ into the field of
real life and embark upon irresponsible criticism of actual
institutions. Thus Guyau preaches the absolutely unlimited
freedom of the individual as the infallible means of attaining
his ideal ; he denounces religion as a most pernicious restriction,
only capable of obstructing the progress of humanity, once
it has reached a certain stage in its evolution ; and conversely,
with the decay of religion he hopes to see art arise and advance
the free play of life. Play—that is Guyau's real ideal. He
urges us to " take life as it comes," as the saying is, with the
cheerful şmile of a child when it wakes up and looks round ;
only caring to preserve our self-possession whatever happens,
in order to acquire possession of things.[2] And he plays with
everything, including philosophy : he believes that science
has destroyed the supernatural, that life and death are
merely correlative ideas, and that the human individual
is just a little eddy on the river of life.

But this is not the last word of his philosophy. Faced
with the problem of immortality, he stops perplexed. On
the one hand, science denies any eternal life ; on the other
hand, subjective feeling, the feeling of the artist, would affirm
it. " The poet who feels individuality everywhere, even in
a flower, even in the ray of light which colours it, even in
the drop of water which adorns it, would wish to immortalize
the whole of nature ; he would desire eternity for a jasper-
tinted drop of water, for the rainbows in a soap-bubble :

---

[1] M. Guyau, *Esquisse d'une Morale sans Obligation ni Sanction*, Paris, 1885,
pp. 251, 252.

[2] M. Guyau, *L'Irreligion de l'Avenir*, Paris, 1887, p. 176.

for how could nature ever contain two identical bubbles ? And while the poet would desire everything stayed, every- thing preserved, would not extinguish any of his dreams, would stop the ocean of life, the scientist replies that we must let the eternal sea flow on and the great tide rise, swollen with our tears and our blood, let Being and the World be free. To the scientist there is something more sacred than the love of the individual : the flux, the reflux, the progress of life." [1]

Here there is no such antinomy of thought as might arise in the mind of the philosopher ; it is an antinomy of the fancy, created and solved within the vision of the artist.

Thus scientific ethics ends in an æstheticism, a rather affected, rather frivolous 'pose, which is ignorant of any spiritual inwardness and resolves everything into a play of fancies. But this is not the genuine expression of that spiritual fervour which pervades the French philosophy of to-day. We shall see how in antithesis to this conception there has sprung up a philosophy inspired by the depth and seriousness of life. Life is not a game, it is a serious thing, said Ollé-Laprune. And this is not a platitude : it is the expression of an entirely fresh orientation of thought, which we shall see culminate in a thinker of profound genius, Maurice Blondel, the most attractive temperament in- modern philosophy.

[1] *Op. cit.*, pp. 463, 464.

CHAPTER VI

THE PHILOSOPHY OF ACTION AND MODERNISM

§ 1. THE PHILOSOPHY OF BELIEF.

IT was a favourite idea of eclecticism, and one which spiritualism adopted as its own, to place at the summit of its speculation the three concepts of the good, the beautiful and the true, unified and identified in God, the goal both of speculation and of the process of reality. Renouvier's theory of knowledge, with its identification of being with the phenomenon, had destroyed this synthesis and abolished the conception of deity; and it was only later, after abandoning his early intellectualism, that Renouvier restored the ideas of God and of moral spontaneity to a place in his philosophy. But this was not to re-establish the old synthesis in stable equilibrium; it merely introduced a new disturbing force which for the moment counteracted the old. Absorbed in the problems of pure speculation, Lachelier had neglected those of ethics; and when he found himself confronted with the problem of good and evil he was thrown into perplexity. Although it seemed to him that the dialectic ought to justify evil as well as good, he had forbidden himself such a solution, on the principle that speculation should not justify what morality condemns. Boutroux alone of the recent French philosophers, as the one who adhered most faithfully to the philosophical programme of spiritualism, presents us with a restoration of the old synthesis, reinstated by him in the final theistic interpretation of his contingentism.

But the problem of the relations between the good and the true arose as a necessary consequence of the criticism of knowledge. In proportion as the subjective view of consciousness sapped the objective foundations of knowledge, there grew up in the depth of the subject a new source of objectivity, the moral belief in the order of the world, which should compensate for the failure of thought to conceive the ultimate truth of being. The same anti-intellectualistic tendency which we have seen develop through the criticism of science into a metaphysic of intuition develops on the other side, on the same negative basis, into a philosophy of the supremacy of the practical reason.

This other branch of French philosophy is closely connected with religious movements ; indeed, it has itself furthered such a movement by its attempt to amalgamate the divine and the human, and to reinterpret Christian doctrine by substituting a philosophy of concrete life for the Platonism of orthodox theology. Yet the result has rather been an unstable compromise, whose instability becomes more and more evident as the activist conception of life is more clearly defined. On the one side we have a Platonistic intellectualism, an affirmation of transcendent being as the basis and ground of life ; on the other side a conception of action, of will, which denies the pre-eminence of intellectual motives and therefore tends to negate the *a priori* character of being and assert that of acting, doing. In some thinkers, in whom the orthodox religious sentiment and the speculative impulse are equally strong, this conflict becomes intensely dramatic, and issues in a struggle in which it is difficult to decide who is the conquered and who the conqueror. We shall observe this struggle in the case of Blondel.

The Platonistic standpoint is an essential element in traditional religion. It ·is present in the theology of all ages, but there was a marked development of it in France in the nineteenth century, in the religious philosophy which sprang from eclecticism and spiritualism. In some of the fathers of the Oratory, for instance Gratry, its exposition assumed a strongly emotional and fervent character. Gratry is particularly connected with the movement which we are considering ; but more in the enthusiasm and faith which he brought to bear upon theological problems, and the search for God in everything, than in the principles of his doctrine, which was a rather incoherent compound of sensationalism and intellectualism. Gratry's God moved too much amid the computations of the *mécanisme céleste*, and too little in the inwardness of the spirit. Hence the conflict, which is peculiar to religious Platonism, between the divine and the human. A theologian, who was also something of an artist, once remarked that we are, through our own fault, a bad pen for expressing the divine thought : we write down the good things which God says to us, but we write abominably ; our reality ill suits our ideal beauty. This dualism of the divine and the human, of the is and the ought to be, already looks towards a solution ; but the solution lies where Platonistic theology can never completely reach it, in the philosophy of immanence.

Ollé-Laprune is one of the pioneers of this movement ; he is, in fact, Blondel's master. The distinctive mark of his mind is an intense spiritual concentration, the direct antithesis of the æstheticism which we have just examined. A morality which tries to place itself beyond good and evil is a scepticism in disguise. To approach life purely as an amateur, as a dilettante, is to condemn oneself to sterility and egoism : it is to go against the laws of life itself. Life is neither a game nor a spectacle : he who, like Narcissus, only thinks of admiring himself in the transparent stream of things, will die as Narcissus died : for ceasing to act means ceasing to live, and the laws of life are not ignored with impunity. "By what right," said Ollé-Laprune to Guyau, "do you speak to me of a high exalted life, of a moral ideal ? It is impossible to speak like this with a purely naturalistic ethics : for merely to name these things implies that there is in life not only intensity but quality. You suppress duty because you can see in it only a falsely mystical view of life and of nature : and you do not understand that between duty and life there is a profound agreement ; you reduce duty to life, and in life itself you consider only its quantity and intensity, and regard as illusion everything that is of a different order from the physical natural order in which you imprison yourself."[1]

For Ollé-Laprune, life is not contemplation but action, creation. "There are things to be made," he says, "whose measure is not yet determined; there are things to be

[1] L. Ollé-Laprune, *Le Prix de la Vie*, Paris, 1895, 2nd ed. pp. 138-9.

discovered, to be invented, new forms of the good, ideas which have never yet been conceived, creations as it were of the spirit that loves the good." It is in this that the educational significance of Ollé-Laprune's doctrine lies. We must will, act : the will is not something ready-made, created ; it creates itself by the very act of willing.

His work also contains passages of great speculative insight—" To phenomenalism I oppose," he says, " what ? Not the idea, but that which everyone in his inner consciousness and apperception can point to as the deepest, the most permanent and most continuous principle of all diversity : the act. The act eliminates everything material ; it is the simple thing. The act eliminates all entity : it is the concrete thing. In it we are raised above the phenomenon. We possess Being, real Being. A dynamism, a realism—this is what we oppose to phenomenalism." [1] The concept of action is an irreducible concept. We cannot transform the act into a phantom abstracted from the activity and the agent. It is thus more than a concept : we no longer have to do with a spectacle and with a sort of abstract residuum, once the spectacle is finished. The act is only perceived when we are acting, only seen when we are producing : in the act we find true substantiality and true causality.

But over against this actualistic concept of life, and in complete contradiction to it, we find maintained in Laprune's philosophy an absolutely intellectualistic conception which reveals the inadequacy of his theory of knowledge. To the act he opposes the given. Thought takes place amid the given, which cannot be eliminated because we are to a certain extent given to ourselves. But do we contain in ourselves the ground of our existence ? It is only a being that exists in itself that has no need of the given. And once on this road Ollé-Laprune attempts to reconcile his doctrine of the given with that of the act. We do not, he says, only produce action ; we also undergo it. And even when we do produce something there is always something else which we have not willed. It is true that *esse est agere :* but at the same time we are limited, we are not pure action, but also negation,

[1] L. Ollé-Laprune, *La Raison et le Rationalisme,* Paris, 1906, pp. 158–9.

passion ; hence we are compelled to assert the existence of
pure act, God, exempt from our limitations. Hence the
curious result that the conception of God arises not because
of what we are but because of what we are not : He is the
justification of our weakness, not the source of our strength.
It follows that what strength we have is self-sufficient ;
and that, so far as we are active beings and not passive
nature, we are independent of God.   This is a result which
Ollé-Laprune neither desired nor suspected, but which
follows logically from his premises.

But at bottom he fails to understand the full import of
his doctrine of the act.   He certainly tells us that his conception implies the negation of being ; but at the same time
he asserts a Platonistic element in thought which can never
be eliminated.   These two positions are contradictory ; but
Ollé-Laprune does not even recognize their incompatibility.
He thinks he can reconcile them in a single act of faith.   For
faith is Ollé-Laprune's last word. On this he bases knowledge.
Starting from a conception of thought which does not go
beyond Descartes, he considers the truth of thought as an
act of faith, a moral adherence.   This does not mean, he
says, that thought is not luminous—on the contrary, it
possesses an intrinsic light ; but only that man, not being
self-existent, is a datum to himself ; that facts are imposed
on him from without, and that his spirit is for him a fact ;
that being dependent both in his thought and in his existence
on the *ens per se,* the Self-existent Being, he clings to this
Being which is the basis of his own being ; and therefore
our natural trust in the veracity of our intellectual faculties
is in a sense a trust in God.[1]   The doctrine of the act has
vanished, and we are face to face with pure Cartesian
intellectualism.

Brochard is another thinker connected with this movement who has attempted to base the truth of thought on
the moral criterion.   He starts with the presupposition that
thought is not the measure of being.   He accepts, indeed,
the Kantian doctrine that in its relations with things the
spirit is not a mere mirror, does not subject itself to the
laws of things, but imposes on them its own laws ; but he

[1] *Op. cit.,* p. 217.

falsifies this doctrine by a quite inadequate conception of thought. He believes that Kant's theory reduces thought to a mere play of ideas or representations, which cannot establish truth : hence the necessity of the marriage with action, with morality, in order to remove this deficiency. The fallacy is the same as that which we have already pointed out in Rickert. And, like Rickert, Brochard believes that the act of judgment does not attain its certainty in thought, but in action.

Certainty is always an act of belief. But belief, pre-supposing as it does an idea present to the spirit and a feeling which persuades us to adopt it, is an essentially volitional act : this act is free. Neither the logical clearness of the idea nor the intensity of the feeling is sufficient to deter-mine it wholly and infallibly. Certainty is never a forced adherence ; it is not the victory gained by reason over the will, but results from the harmonious, spontaneous, and in the last analysis moral union of the reason and the will. There is therefore a moral element even in the adherence we give to scientific truths, and still more in religious and philosophical truths, where the personal element is greater.[1]

The inadequacy of this doctrine is revealed most clearly when Brochard tries to base upon it a conception of error. Like truth, error is not given to the spirit, but the spirit, by applying *a priori* its forms to sensations and ideas, attempts combinations which may or may not conform to reality ; it must therefore adapt itself to reality by a series of experi-ments. Error would thus be the product of the same freedom which is the foundation of the certainty of truth.[2] But what has become of the doctrine that thought is not a copy of a ready-made reality, if error is an unsuccessful attempt to copy reality ? It is obvious that both Brochard's doctrine of truth and the correlative doctrine of error are only valid for truths already created, for that which is already known, and not for the explanation of the process of knowing, which remains untouched by the absolutely external criterion of moral adherence.

The complement of this doctrine is a theism which finds

[1] V. Brochard, *De l'Erreur*, Paris, 1897, p. 163.
[2] *Ibid.*, pp. 212, 237.

in the supreme good the ultimate foundation of moral certainty.

§ 2. THE PHILOSOPHY OF ACTION : BLONDEL.

Maurice Blondel is the thinker who has summed up all the scattered tendencies of the philosophy of action or volition and has developed them to a very high speculative level. His famous book *L'Action* has all the structure and method of Hegel's *Phenomenology of the Spirit*. Like Hegel's book, it is in many details confused, but at the same time, regarded as a whole, it shows the same great profundity and wonderful clearness.

The philosophy of action is the philosophy of life. Why do we set before ourselves the problem of life ? Because it is of supreme interest to know if human life has a meaning or not ; and it is a problem which is especially urgent to-day, when dilettantism—scientific and unscientific—amuses itself by playing with our destiny. But once the problem is put, it draws us inevitably forward. Might we perhaps desire to give it a negative solution ? This will not help us : to affirm nothing is at the same time to affirm being. " The symbolical representation of nothing always rises from a double synthesis : the subject is affirmed without the object and at the same time the object is affirmed without the subject. In this concept there is therefore an alternative union and opposition of the phenomenon and being, of sensible and invisible reality." [1]   Whenever we deny one of these two terms we are really turning our attention to the other : the will to nothing is necessarily a self-contradiction. But how clearly the analysis of these ambiguities reveals the secrets of the heart ! When we think we are aspiring towards nothing, we are really willing simultaneously the phenomenon in being and being in the phenomenon : we affirm, in fact, the problem we have denied. And so pessimism is overcome by the mere fact of asserting itself.

The problem of life must therefore have a positive solution ; and in solving the problem the criticism of life

[1] M. Blondel, *L'Action : Essai d'une Critique de la Vie et d'une Science de la Pratique*, Paris, 1893, p. 38.

must also solve the universal problem. Here lies the profound significance of Blondel's work ; he understands that the human problem is also a universal problem.

The method of his criticism is dialectic, which mediates the contradictions posited and overcome by action, life, in the determined connection of its moments and necessary steps. Every new moment to which action attains is an advance ; but at the same time, since in the course of its development action fails to raise itself to a level with its impulse, a continual contradiction is set up between the infinite power of will and what is willed, the will solidified into fact ; a contradiction which is the stimulus to a further advance. So it comes about that action passes through the stages of scientific determinism, the critical reflection on determinism, organic life, human life ; every new stage being a new synthesis, irreducible to the preceding one ; a necessary synthesis, because it is the determinism of action itself that leads us to it, but at the same time free because of the originality of the spiritual creation that it expresses.

The justification of the process lies in the process itself : stopping at an intermediate stage means dying to life, extinguishing in ourselves the expansive power of action ; in other words, allowing ourselves to be overwhelmed and swallowed up by the development of life itself. This development is outside time : time is simply a mode of representing the subjective unity of action in the multiplicity of subordinate phenomena ; and the necessity immanent in the linking together of these phenomena is simply the objective projection of the transcendent teleology from which action gains its inspiration.[1] This transcendence will be explained later : for the moment we would remark on the close analogy between Blondel's reasoning and Hegel's.

There is, however, one great difference between them : action is not the Idea. Blondel's concept of action is not very well defined : it is not pure will, because any conflict between will and thought is repugnant to Blondel, but, on the other hand, it is not the idea as act, as the reflection of thought on itself and through itself which overcomes in its mediation all alienation of the real from itself, all transi-

[1] *Op. cit.*, p. 120.

tion to externality, all transformation of thought into nature.
The Blondelian concept of action contains a profound contradiction.   In its struggle to raise itself to an equality with
its infinite power of expansion, and thus to overcome what
it has already affirmed with a new affirmation, it is reflection,
dialectic ; but, on the other hand, all action as such is a
transition into externality, and therefore a kind of self-
alienation of the spirit, a making itself other than itself.
In so far as it is dialectic, action is a continual resolution of
transcendence, of the reality in itself of the moments which
it traverses : a resolution of it, just because it transcends
these fixed moments and therefore conceives them in the
absolute immanence of its process : in so far as it is mere
action, the alienation of the spirit from itself, it is a continual
affirmation of transcendence—of a reality in itself that is
immediate and does not reflect upon its moments.   This is
the contradiction which Blondel fails to resolve, because it
is inherent in his fundamental principle.   As we shall see,
he simply oscillates between the two opposite demands of
his thought.

As we have observed, the beginning of the process of
action is affirmed by the very impossibility of giving the
problem of action a negative solution.   Something must be
affirmed.   The first " something " is mere sense-apprehension ;
but the affirmation of the given of sense already contains in
itself that which transcends and is the negation of the pure
given, namely, the empirical universal, empirical generality
(this is Hegel).   This leads to the doctrine of the universal,
i.e. science.   Science resolves the discontinuity of sense,
but the continuity that it establishes is simply a higher
discontinuity : the discontinuity of the natural synthesis
itself, which science presupposes but does not explain.   There
is in science an inner incoherence : on the one hand it cannot
exist unless everything is bound by universal determinism,
with the continuity of deduction ; on the other hand, it
cannot move a step forward unless intuition supplies it
with original products, syntheses which cannot be reduced
to one another.   Now, what are these new syntheses except
rudimentary affirmations of subjectivity ?   Without this
subjectivity, determinism itself would not exist.

Blondel proceeds, in a very subtle analysis, to demonstrate the formation of inwardness, of the subject. Inwardness only exists where, instead of the subjection of a part to the whole, we find one point victorious over the entire universe. Now, even in the inorganic world we find this inwardness foreshadowed in the peculiar manner in which one body reacts against the impact of others. Inwardness here is interpreted as the presence of the whole in the part and of the part in the whole, so that action and reaction are never merely correlative : thus arises the concept of force. Force implies, therefore, a peculiar kind of action which, arising out of universal mechanism, reacts upon it and requires to be considered apart from it. Even matter thus exhibits a kind of rudimentary synthesis. By an internal evolution, consciousness detaches itself from the surrounding universe, whence it obtains its nutriment, but from which it differentiates and frees itself. But this process is not a sequence in time, but a synthetic deduction. Far from being an epiphenomenon, the act of consciousness contains and concentrates in itself everything with which it nourishes itself : the facts which are the object of science would not exist without it. Thus fact exists simply through the act ; and without the subjective phenomenon there would be no other.[1]

The establishment of subjectivity brings us within the sphere of the science of action. Subjectivity presents itself in the form of reflection upon determinism, and therefore in the form of freedom, since the feeling of any definite state both presupposes and actually is a higher state. But freedom only exists through knowing itself, and yet, in knowing itself, it destroys its own inevitability. It puts itself before itself as an object, as an end : *de jure* the supreme motive, *de facto* one motive among many : it is mine, but is no longer myself. This explains why, when we set freedom before ourselves as an end, we feel a discrepancy between the will that is willing and the will that is willed. Now, this discrepancy must be removed. But what does such a demand imply ? " It means that we must give back to this apparent nothing of objective liberty the infinity of that

[1] *Op. cit.*, pp. 90, 92, 93, 102.

inner power of which reflection has given us a clear consciousness. That is to say, we must transport the life of
the subject into the object which it sets before itself as an
end. That is to say, all that we know of force and of freedom
is simply a means for attaining the fullness of that which
we will. That is to say, that so long as we are not identified
with that which we will, we stand in a relation of dependence
towards our true end." [1] This heteronomous moment is duty.

Thus is established the dialectic of action. Consciousness
as inwardness is reflection on and liberation from mechanism ;
but the inadequacy of pure inwardness over against the
infinite potentialities of action results in a discrepancy
within consciousness itself, and this leads it to negate itself
and to pass over into externality. Will alienates itself in
order to enrich itself : social life, the family, country,
humanity, are successive stages in this objectification of
action. To recoil before the danger of socialism is futile :
we must pass through a provisional socialism in order to
attain a higher individualism.

Action simply passes through these forms and does not
possess itself in any of them : it only really possesses itself
when it understands the full and true identity of what is
and what ought to be.[2] Hence the will that alienated itself
from itself is once more rehabilitated in the life of speculation :
metaphysics is a particular synthesis of universal reality,
which is incorporated in thought by means of action. But
although metaphysics is the manner in which action overcomes the natural order, it does not even so remove the
discrepancy in action. There still remains an unreconciled
residuum. Hence the attempt to bring human action up
to the level of human will has given rise to the many forms
of superstitious activity.

This attempt of Blondel's to interpret magic as an advance
on metaphysics is most extraordinary : but it can be explained
as due to the inner contradiction under which he is
labouring, and which is manifested even in the movement of
his dialectic, as has been indicated in the summary exposition
which we have just given. The discrepancy which he finds
in action really lies in his own theory : whenever he over-

[1] *Op. cit.*, pp. 129, 133.　　　　　[2] *Ibid.*, p. 283.

comes it for a moment it is renewed by the ever-present conflict between his two warring conceptions of action.

But on reaching this point he feels the need of asking once more the question : Is it possible to will oneself, and what is the true meaning of the inevitable impulse to do so ? " Divided between that which I do without willing it, and that which I will without doing it, I am always as it were excluded from myself. How can I penetrate into myself again and put into my action what is doubtless there, but without my knowing or grasping it ? In order to will myself fully it is necessary that I should will more than I have yet been able to find." [1]

The discrepancy of action with volition is thus ultimately removed only by appeal to the transcendent, the God of religion. The recourse to the transcendent is an act of choice, the alternative to which is that the will should go on asserting itself, always continuing to leave outside itself —as *ex hypothesi* it cannot help leaving—an unresolved residuum. And so here too, as in Ollé-Laprune, we see the transcendent based on a residuum left by the procedure of thought.

But, unlike Ollé-Laprune, Blondel does not stop at this point. The dialectic reasserts its authority over the residuum of transcendence which action has left, and the transcendent God becomes the immanent life of action itself. But this position is not arrived at without a struggle and continual hesitation.

At first, the thought of God seems to involve the annihilation of action ; but before long action reappears in order to claim for its own the God Who seemed to enshrine its supreme impotence. " The thought of God in us depends in two ways upon our action. On the one hand, since in our acting we find an infinite discrepancy in ourselves, we are compelled to seek *ad infinitum* for something to remove this discrepancy. On the other hand, since, although we affirm absolute perfection, we never succeed in raising ourselves to a level with our affirmation, it is to action that we must look in order to make good the defect of our attainment. The problem which action posits, action alone can solve." [2]

[1] *Op. cit.*, pp. 337-8.　　[2] *Ibid.*, p. 351.

What can this express except the exigency that the circle
of the real should be completed within the field of action ;
that action should itself resolve the transcendence which it
posits ?

This resolution of the transcendent proceeds with the
progress of the dialectic. " At the very moment in which
we seem to be grasping God by a stroke of thought," says
Blondel, " He eludes us unless we embody Him in action.
His immobility can only be viewed as a fixed end, if accompanied by a perpetual movement. Whenever we stand
still, He is not ; whenever we bestir ourselves, He exists.
It is a necessity that we should ever be moving on, because He
is always beyond."[1] This is the culmination and the limit
of Blondel's philosophy : he conceives being in the form of
act, and yet at the same moment he attempts to make
being anticipate the act. He says that God only exists in the
act, and yet he falsifies that existence by transforming it
into a transcendence. He affirms that God creates Himself
in us, but he adds : If He does not *exist*, how can He create
Himself in us ? Thus immanence attempts to include
transcendence, but at the same time to leave it existing in
itself and for itself at the very moment in which it absorbs
it—which is a pure contradiction. This is because immanence
as Blondel understands it is not true, absolute immanence.
It is the immanence of action, of the externality of the real
to itself, which contains its opposite in itself without mediation. Hence the arrest of the dialectic at its culminating
point.

But if Blondel does not attain to the resolution of the
transcendent—and he neither desires nor is able to attain
it—yet his dialectic is always urging him on towards this
goal. The ultimate phase of the dialectic of action is the
apotheosis of worship. Religious action is affirmed as the
synthesis of man and of God, and worship gains from this a
new significance. The necessity for visible symbolism does
not depend on the desire to express supernatural dogmas ;
it is due to the development of the practical activities and
the strivings of the will to rise to a level with its own impulse,
which demands something external corresponding to our

[1] *Op. cit.*, p. 352.

inner action, the necessary complement without which the external action would still fall short of the internal standard. It is not enough that dogmas should be the vehicle of the transcendent : they must be the immanent truth and contain the Real Presence ; the flesh becomes the Word. In the literal practice of religion the human act is identical with the divine.

And so the last teaching of the philosophy of action is that " true infinity lies not in the abstract universal, but in the concrete individual. This enables us to perceive in all its grandeur the function of what has been called 'the letter' or 'matter,' of all that constitutes the operation of the sense world, of that which forms action, the body of action. It is through this matter that each individual gains an intimate insight into the truth of the infinite that overwhelms him ; it is through it that each individual is protected from being overwhelmed (*accablé*) by the infinite truth. In order to reach man, God must traverse the whole of nature and present Himself to man there under the crudest material aspect ; in order to reach God, man must traverse the whole of nature and find Him there under the veil in which He only hides in order to be accessible. Thus the entire natural order lies between God and man as a bond and as an obstacle, as a necessary means of union and as a necessary means of distinction." [1] The whole order of nature with its twofold aspect thus fuses into a single centre of convergence. But is this centre of convergence the God of Platonistic theology ?

§ 3. Modernism.

Considered in its philosophical significance—and that is the only one which concerns us here—modernism is a conception of religion which embraces the whole problem of life. It is hostile to any kind of dualism. In psychology it does not admit a spirit separate from the flesh, but vivifies and spiritualizes the flesh with the spirit ; in theology it does not admit an abstract God outside the world, but its God is a God living in us and in the world ; in history it

[1] *Op. cit.*, p. 449.

does not admit a kernel and a shell, but it sees the historical process as all of a piece, and human reality in its progressive development as exalted finally to the divine ; in social life it does not admit purely contemplative ideals, but social reality is for it action, love, reform. But over this absolutely modern picture of life there has been stretched a veil of Platonism, that ineradicable Platonism, as Ollé-Laprune called it, which belongs to the old conception of life and dims to a certain extent the colours of the new.

Modernism is the final expression of the Catholic religion, that is to say, of that religion which introduced into the Roman world the idea of the subject, of metaphysical and moral personality, that was lacking in the Greek world. It is a genuine product of contemporary French culture (although it has antecedents in England and followers even in Italy) and marks the very striking contrast between French and German culture. Protestantism, in the latter, is the paralytic son of a great and glorious mother, the Reformation. The Reformation represented the transition to the modern conception of life ; its value was simply that of a transition. To-day, crystallized into a religious formula, it is the mere shadow of itself. It sees God and the believer ; nothing else. History is therefore the history of human aberrations ; the believer is pure subjectivity abstracted from the concrete human reality in which he lives, and which is the fruit of his whole past ; and God is the thing-in-itself outside the world. The God of modernism, on the other hand, is the Christ, the Word made flesh ; the Church is the continuity of human experience throughout the ages ; the subjective nature of the believer is unfolded in worship, in obedience to dogma, which sums up the whole religious life of humanity and which, revivified in the action of the individual spirit, brings to a head in the person of the believer its own past and that of all mankind, which only lives in him and through him, and he in it and through it.

This is the life of the Catholic Church ; but to have disclosed this life, to have resolved it into reflective thought, means to be already outside it : has not Blondel said that the consciousness of a definite state implies liberation from that state ? It is merely the veil of Platonism which still binds modernism to the Church.

The spiritual father of modernism, as must be evident to anyone who has understood the slight outline that I have sketched in a few lines, is Maurice Blondel. Following him have come forward many interpreters of his profound doctrine : interpreters more or less penetrating, but none who have really plumbed its depths. I must confine myself to mentioning merely a few names and indicating only a few doctrines, otherwise I should be exceeding the limits of my historical picture.

Father Laberthonnière is a zealous and fervent follower of Blondel. Being is understood by him as subject, in harmony with Christian realism and in antithesis to Greek idealism. The ideal of Greek philosophy is a static ideal, a merely beautiful object of contemplation. It gives the spectator an æsthetic pleasure, superior in its subtlety to the pleasures of the senses. It therefore exercises an attraction, but does not create any obligation, since it is merely to be contemplated and not to be realized. The ideal beckons man from outside, but does not stir in him any inner movement. Christian realism represents on the other hand an inward movement of the spirit : man feels his spiritual inwardness, and meditates upon his destiny ; his question is no longer : What are things ? but : What are we ? Whence do we come and whither are we going ? [1]

The conception of the concrete and active subjectivity of the believer is made the basis of what Laberthonnière calls moral dogmatism. Speculatively, this is the explanation of certainty by means of action : in order to know being and believe in it, we must co-operate in giving being to ourselves in our own life of free will. Practically, it is the putting into practice of the critical and ascetic method in order to free ourselves from all the relativity inherent in our own manner of being and thinking.[2] But freedom is not a suppression of the flesh, of the matter that is in us : the

---

[1] L. Laberthonnière, Le Réalisme chrétien et l'Idéalisme grec, Paris, 1904, 3rd ed., pp. 20, 38.

[2] L. Laberthonnière, Essais de Philosophie religieuse, Paris, 1903, 2nd ed., p. 108.

constant effort of modernism is to spiritualize matter, to
show that nature itself demands that which is above nature
This demand for the divine in nature does not mean its
transformation into nature; there is no question of pantheism,
as has erroneously been affirmed : it means the transformation
and elevation of nature, its irradiation with grace. We
could not seek unless we had already found, said Pascal ;
"Nature," says Laberthonnière, after Pascal, "would not
call for the supernatural if she were not already penetrated
with divine grace."

The influence of Pascal on modernism has been, indeed,
considerable : its anti-intellectualistic attitude, its method
of immanence and its touch of religious mysticism (a natural
ally of the philosophy of action, itself an ethical mysticism)
are all elements derived from Pascal's philosophy. And
following Pascal, Laberthonnière, like Blondel before him,
attempts to introduce into apologetics the method of
immanence. This method consists in beginning not with
the verification of the historical facts in which faith is
externally epitomized, but with the discovery of a meaning
for our existence, the explanation of what we are in living
reality : it is only by this method that we can interpret the
historical facts. We must not falsify them by preconceived
ideas, but seek their inner truth. From this point of view
dogmas appear as facts which explain what we are and what
we ought to become. They no longer bear an abstract
character, but express the life of God and of man in their
relationship. The fall of Adam becomes thus an event that
is above time and has lasted up till our day and will last
until the end of human history.[1] Christ is not presented to
us as a past fact in the past, of whose reality we must assure
ourselves as though He were an historical problem to be
solved, but as a present reality, which is for us the truth and
the life ; that is to say, as a problem which is set before us
in so far as we are living.

In this manner the absolute character of the divine is
only communicated to us by becoming human and entering
into our own relativity in order to help us in casting it off.
It is not an absolute which the spirit receives ready-made

[1] *Essais cit.*, p. 288.

and to which it has to submit : the motives to believe in the absolute do not become such until they become our motives. And on the other hand the supernatural is not something added to nature from outside, by juxtaposition or super-imposition, but it is in the very inner being of Nature. It is not an entity beside another entity, nor a force beside another force, but the very life of God Who penetrates to the heart of our life and informs us even to the inmost core of our being. To be a Christian does not, therefore, mean to add to natural thoughts and actions supernatural thoughts and actions, but to give a supernatural character to all our own thoughts and all our actions. It is, as it were, an elevation of our whole being to a higher power.

Such, in fact, is the life of Catholicism : in so far as it is life, concrete reality, it resolves in its process the Platonistic ideology which is its symbol ; but in so far as it is religion, the condition of its life is the very contradiction between what it does and what it says it is doing. To have disclosed this contradiction means to have denied the abstract moment of religion as such and to have given the religious life a place in philosophical thought, that is to say, to have raised religion itself to philosophy. But, like Blondel and all the modernists, Laberthonnière is not entirely conscious of the import of his doctrine and continues to distinguish between an ontological order and a vital or practical order, failing to perceive that he has already negated the ontological order.

An echo of the modernist movement has penetrated even into the mind of the Bergsonian Le Roy, the author of a theory of dogma which made a great stir in the Catholic world. Le Roy's thesis is that dogma is the formula of a rule of practical conduct. In this lies its essential character and eternal substance, while the intellectual vehicle is merely changeable and contingent. The dogma " God is personal " signifies " Conduct yourselves in your relations with God as in your relations with a human person." Similarly, " Jesus rose from the dead " means : " Be in your relation to Him as you would have been before His death, as you are towards a contemporary " ; and so on.[1] This view was attacked as atheistical, but Le Roy was able to defend it

[1] E. le Roy, *Dogme et Critique*, Paris, 1907, pp. 25–6.

successfully, because " action," " practice," is understood by him (as it is by the philosophy of immanence) no longer as mere conduct, but as the mysticism of conduct. Dogma is no longer the given, the created—a fact which Le Roy himself has shown he does not understand—but the interpretation of fact according to the principle of immanence. Hence a concealed vicious circle. On the one hand, the concrete character of action, its spiritual value, lies in its speculative function, and on the other hand, action is only genuinely religious in so far as it is stripped of every speculative element, since such elements are contingent and changeable.

The historical problem of religion stands in intimate connection with the religious problem. Modernism gives the spiritual significance of the fact precedence over the empirical reconstruction of the fact itself : but this priority should not be understood in a temporal sense, nor in any sense that implies dualism, but, so to speak, in a transcendental sense. The *a priori* character of the spirit with respect to the letter, the given, simply means that the letter, the given, is only revealed in the spirit that is immanent within it. As Laberthonnière says, " If the story of the Bible is secondary, it is certainly not so in the sense that the historical truth of its leading facts could be contested without hurt to its doctrine. On the contrary, if separated from this historical character the doctrine vanishes, since it is constituted by the dominant facts in which reality, so to speak, articulates itself. The facts thus become doctrinal. Tradition, from this point of view, is no longer a mere deposit to be handed on like a piece of stone in which any modification would be a diminution ; it is rather an organic whole, which in the essential unity of its germ goes on developing, unfolding itself throughout human history and utilizing every detail in order to illustrate itself. In order to prove that she exists, the Church walks ; in order to prove that she lives, she organizes herself. She integrates in herself successively the different aspects under which reality is presented. And remaining always the same, she is thus renewed in the minds which live her, as she is in the spirits which think her. Such is the point of view from which we must regard the religious problem in its historical aspect." [1]

This point of view is shared by Loisy. Just as Laberthonnière's religious conception is the most complete antithesis of a conception like that of Ritschl, so Loisy's view of history is the direct opposite of Harnack's. Harnack, in dealing with religious history, is so thorough in his removal of all surface matter that we can well ask if anything at all is left. Labouring under the illusion that if he removes all that is contingent he will find God, he finds a phantom ; and imagining that he is reviving the Gospel in its purest form, he solidifies the truth of the Gospel into an isolated inexplicable fact. Loisy, on the other hand, realizes that the truth of the Gospel is not a truth ready-made, but a truth creating itself in history. " The Gospel has not entered the world as an unconditioned absolute doctrine summed up in a unique and steadfast truth ; but as a living faith, concrete and complex, whose evolution proceeds without doubt from the internal force which has made it enduring, but none the less has been in everything and from the very beginning influenced by the surroundings wherein faith was born and has since developed." [2]

The Gospel is thus simply the germ of a religious development that has taken place by means of and through the Church. Far from finding a ready-made truth, the Church has created one by creating and affirming itself in the course of its own history. " Why not find the essence of Christianity," Loisy exclaims, " in the fullness and totality of its life, which shows movement and variety just because it is life, but, inasmuch as it is life proceeding from an obviously powerful principle, has grown according to a law which affirms at every step the initial force which may be called its physical essence, revealed in all its manifestations ? Why should the essence of the tree be held to be but a particle of the seed from which it has sprung ; why should it not be recognized as truly and fully in the complete tree as in the germ ? " [3]

[1] L. Laberthonnière, Le Réalisme, etc., cit., pp. 50, 78, 159.
[2] A. Loisy, The Gospel and the Church, Eng. tr. by Christopher Home, London, 1903, p. 87.   [3] Ibid., preface, p. 16.

This idea that truth is in the making is an essential characteristic of modern philosophy, and Loisy himself is conscious of it. " Truth," he says, " does not enter all ready-made into our brain ; it makes itself slowly, and we can never say that it is complete." [1] But he fails, like all the modernists, to go right through with it, and always ends in anticipating the process with the product and considering truth in itself as unchanging, and its necessarily inadequate expression in our minds as the only thing that changes.

But all the rest of his work is in contradiction with this residuum of Platonism. Loisy, in fact, attains not only to the conception of reality as a process of creation, as a development, but also to that of the rationality of the development, which is the absolute immanence of thought in its own history. " The Church can say that in order to be throughout the epochs what Jesus desired that the society of His friends should be, it had to be what it has been ; in fact, it has been what it needed to be in order to preserve the Gospel and itself." [2] The whole struggle of the Church to affirm itself in the world is thus justified and rendered comprehensible by the immanent rationality of its work. And further, the permanent mission of the Church finds in the same fact its justification and confirmation. " A permanent society, a church, alone can maintain the equilibrium between the traditions which our heritage of acquired truths preserves for us, and the unceasing labours of human reason to adapt the old truths to the new conditions of thought and science. It is inconceivable that each individual should begin over again by his own efforts the interpretation of the past, and reconstruct the whole of religion for his own use. Here, as everywhere else, each individual is helped by all and all by each." [3]

In conclusion, by way of indicating the social problems raised by modernism, we will glance at a book by Fonsegrive. This writer considers morality and society to be antithetical : when the former is allowed free sway it would seem that the latter is compromised, and *vice versa*. Hence the conflicts to which, more than any other, the Catholic Church has been

[1] A. Loisy, *Autour d'un petit Livre*, Paris, 1903, p. 191.
[2] *L'Evangile*, p. 172.   [3] *Ibid.*, p. 172.

exposed by its dual character as a system of social government
and as attempting to maintain the inner principle of a moral
life. A great many observers, says Fonsegrive, have been
so struck by this kind of opposition between the advance
of the Gospel and that of external ecclesiastical authority,
that they have been led to believe that the Gospel and the
Church are contradictory or hostile to one another.[1] The
conflict is aggravated when we consider the mutual relations
of the religious conscience and religious authority. If we
allow the latter to guide us, are we not authorized to act
against our own conscience and to be irreligious in soul ?
If we give to conscience the ascendancy, how are we to
remain Catholics, as the term is understood by the Church ?

This conflict would seem to be the theoretical formulation
of the real conflict which the threat of excommunication on
the part of the Church has created in the minds of the
modernists. And Fonsegrive's solution is no less uncertain
and wavering than the conduct of the modernists. He says
that whenever the conscience is found in conflict with
authority, with law, it should be ready to extinguish itself,
to yield before authority. But yet he adds that when the
oppression is too great the individual then has the right to
refuse to obey. This solution supplies absolutely no criterion
of conduct, because it is based on the empirical criterion of
" too great " and " less great," terms which vary according
to the individuals. And the action of the modernists has
demonstrated the inadequacy of such a solution.

Fonsegrive's problem, like that of the modernists, is
insoluble because wrongly stated. In its desire to keep at
an equal distance from the two banks of religion and
philosophy, modernism has been swept into the vortex of
the current and has capsized.

§ 4. Sorel's Syndicalism.

Blondel is the dreamer of religious action, Sorel of social
action : both are mystics, but their mysticism is the product
of a mentality very superior to that of the current flaccid
intellectualism.

[1] G. Fonsegrive, *Morale et Société*, Paris, 1907, pp. 30, 33.

Just as we have contrasted the French religious movement, the expression of the spiritual fervour of the France of late years, with the German, which is the offshoot of neo-Kantianism, so we would now contrast Sorel's syndicalism, which is derived from Bergson's philosophy, with the new historical materialism of Stammler, Staudinger and Vorländer. But just as Bergson's philosophy is rather a protest against intellectualism than a genuine victory over it, so Sorel's conception is a cry for rescue from the positivist culture, but a cry which meets with no echo, not even in Sorel's own soul. And so he remains a dreamer of Napoleonic victories—victories that annihilate—and at the same time a melancholy and pessimistic contemplator of the moral poverty of the present day.

Sorel's revolutionary attitude is shown in the distinction he makes between myths and Utopias. The myth is to him what action is to Blondel and intuition to Bergson. Revolutionary myths provide an insight into the activities, feelings and ideas of the masses who are preparing to enter upon a decisive struggle ; they are not descriptions of things, but expressions of will. Utopias, on the contrary, are products of the intellect, the work of theorists who, after having observed and discussed the facts, attempt to set up a model by which they can compare existing societies in order to measure the good and the evil that they contain.

The myth *par excellence* for the insurrection of the labouring classes is the strike. With the strike is introduced the idea of a catastrophic revolution, of the great Napoleonic battle which the proletariat will wage against the *bourgeoisie*. It repudiates socialist schemes with their ideological results ; its partisans consider that even the most democratic reforms have a *bourgeois* character, and should therefore be scorned : in their view nothing can abate the fundamental opposition of the class struggle.[1]

But yet (from Sorel's point of view, of course) this class struggle predicted by Marx will never be realized ; the *bourgeoisie* apparently tends to absorb the proletariat and to transform it into a *bourgeoisie*. Must we say, then, that Marx's foresight has proved wrong ? By no means ; for

[1] G. Sorel, *Reflections on Violence*, Eng. tr. T. E. Hulme, 1916, pp. 127–8.

proletarian violence comes upon the scene just when social peace seems to be settling the disagreements ; proletarian violence confines employers to their task as producers and tends to restore the structure of the classes in proportion as these seem to be becoming swallowed in a democratic fog.[1] The *bourgeoisie* has thus for Sorel a necessary negative function ; it is the matter, the μὴ ὄν, of proletarian action, which it must oppose in order to be overcome. And if it does not lend itself willingly to this thankless task and appears rather reluctant, the proletariat compels it to do so, in order to be able to triumph over it the more easily. Here Sorel would seem to be reckoning without his host, as the saying goes, and to be manipulating the unfortunate *bourgeoisie* too much to suit his own ends. For supposing it yielded, and in yielding absorbed the proletariat, where would this redeeming violence be exercised and who would exercise it, except in Sorel's imagination ? Does not the myth thus end by becoming a Utopia ?

But Sorel's theory cannot really be criticized, because it is not really a theory, but a noble and exalted state of mind ; it is the protest of a man of high moral ideals against modern democratic mediocrity. It is in his criticism of modern culture that Sorel is most effective : he points out its continuity with the eighteenth-century philosophy of the Enlightenment, with which it shares in common its superficiality and narrowness, and at the same time its immense arrogance of statement. The *bourgeoisie* of to-day regard science as a machine which produces solutions to all the problems that are put to it ; religion is treated in the most superficial manner ; morality is reduced to an education in docility for the purpose of securing order ; and the last utterance of philosophy is pragmatism, the doctrine which suits every Philistine who wishes to gain acceptance in a highly indulgent world.[2] It is against this current mediocrity that Sorel revolts with his concept of proletarian violence which will clear the atmosphere of fog and create a new environment. The fusion of the insurgent class with the old *bourgeoisie* is therefore hateful to him, and he would

[1] *Op. cit.*, p. 59.
[2] G. Sorel, *Les Illusions du Progrès*, Paris, 1908, p. 276.

have the struggle carried to extremes : the idea of the struggle lifts the proletariat from the depth to which it has fallen through contact with the *bourgeoisie* and gives it self-consciousness. The proletariat is called upon to do away with the ethics of philistinism and to realize the ethics of the sublime.

This is Sorel's great vision. Can his experience of syndicalism have convinced even him that his proletariat was very different from the real one, and was but the embodied visualization of his protest against the degradation of the times ?

§ 5. SUMMARY.

Now that we have outlined the most characteristic features of recent French philosophy we can gather up the threads of our long exposition. We have seen French philosophy as at once the continuation and the antithesis of French spiritualism, old and new. The continuity is manifested in its possessing the same philosophical programme of fusing psychology and metaphysics, and of finding in the life of the subject the basis of the reality of the universe ; the antithesis in the need for a concrete conception of life as against the abstract intellectualism of the old philosophy.

This progressively felt need supplies the internal impulse for the development of the various tendencies. Phenomenalism, as the affirmation of the superficial (representative) life of the subject, and therefore as the negation of true subjectivity, is dissolved in Renouvier's own thought and generates its antithesis, monadism : the real, which in phenomenalism was scattered broadcast, retires and is concentrated within itself, but the synthesis of the two moments is still not reached. And the same story is repeated in the phenomenalistic school, from Gourd to Boirac, which carries the conception of the phenomenon to its farthest logical point and to the greatest concreteness of which it will admit.

In the Kantian school, Lachelier, in a sudden blaze of thought, attains to the concrete Idea of the post-Kantian philosophy. His achievement is lost by the first Kantians, but revived in a richer form by Weber's positivism, which overcomes the two abstractions—pure psychological experience and naturalism—in the absolute concreteness of science as self-conscious knowledge which resolves continually in its procedure the nature which it itself affirms.

Boutroux's contingentism is more closely allied to Ravaisson's spiritualism, but already contains in itself the negation of the mechanical causality which the latter—following Leibniz—still left coexisting to a certain extent with spiritual teleology. But the spirit, in Boutroux's philosophy, is the obscure power that is always sought and never found (as an acute critic has remarked) : it is freedom only in the sense that it is contingency. The canker that is eating into it is empiricism : and this is seen more clearly in Boutroux's school and in the criticism of science, which finishes in a half-sceptical, half-dogmatic " probabilism." But, on the other hand, Boutroux's diffused and obscured spiritualism is focused and illuminated in Bergson's philosophy, which represents the most powerful attempt hitherto made by dualistic spiritualism to transcend its starting-point. The summit of Bergson's speculation is reached in the mysticism of intuition, the abandonment of the spirit to the immediate revelation of life.

In a period of such great spiritual concentration positivism has naturally been swept aside. It makes a last attempt at revival in a travesty of Platonism, which results in Fouillée's insipid and lifeless speculation and in Guyau's moral dilettantism, half scientific, half æsthetic, the symbol of a dire inner poverty. And finally, from the same negation of intellectualism, which has produced the philosophy of intuition, and from the opposition to ethical dilettantism there has arisen the philosophy of action, viewed as the primacy of moral faith in Ollé-Laprune, as the dialectic in Blondel, and in Modernism as the immanence in reality of the spirit, of the pure act. Yet the theory of action as process does not completely solve the problem ; and leaves a residuum which opens the door to the introduction of a Platonistic theory of transcendence which in many ways detracts from the significance of the immanentist philosophy.

The characteristic feature of contemporary French philosophy is its orientation, partly conscious, partly unconscious, towards the Hegelian idealism. Traces of Hegelianism are to be found in Boirac ; Lachelier is a Hegelian, and Weber has arrived at his absolute positivism through the Hegelian philosophy. The anti-intellectualistic motive of the philosophy of intuition and its conception of reality as act, as creation, are all Hegelian elements, while on the other hand the methods followed and the doctrine of intuition derive from quite other sources.

Blondel's Hegelianism is manifest ; and, indeed, the immanentism of the modernists (I allude to the leaders, not to the herd) and Loisy's conception of history also reveal the same origin.

I do not mean by this to imply anything as to historical sources : indeed, many of the authors I have quoted would marvel at the pedigree I have bestowed on them. I only mean to show that the problem of Hegel is alive wherever the criticism and negation of science is most acute. And France, standing as she does in this respect—and that means in every respect—in the forefront of modern thought, has felt also with the greatest intensity the Hegelian problem. The fact that she has not felt it as such is the strongest proof that it is alive ; it is not a reminiscence or a revival ; it is a new demand, arising out of the absolutely original development of French thought.

PART III
ANGLO-AMERICAN PHILOSOPHY

CHAPTER I

EMPIRICISM AND NATURALISM

§ 1. HAMILTON AND MANSEL.

THE empiricism which we have seen in Germany and France concealed with such varying degrees of success and under so many different disguises has in England maintained its genuine form and enjoyed full consciousness of its own true character. Attempts have certainly been made to disguise it ; but these have been both rare and unsuccessful, and have never concealed for long the real nature of the underlying thought.

England, of course, is the classical land of empiricism, the country of Bacon, Locke and Hume. From Hume a long succession of English empiricists carried on the tradition unchallenged and unopposed; but this very lack of opposition resulted in sterility and stagnation. The empiricist tradition progressed, so to speak, by mere *vis inertiæ*, or rather by the sedimentary stratification of new data on the old, of a new evolutionism deposited on the top of the old sensationalism. There is no true development of thought: in Hume the historical function of empiricism is completed and its highest point of originality attained.

In the person of this thinker, the greatest ever born on British soil, European philosophy burnt its boats. The hopes of ingenuous dogmatism were finally shattered and no other road remained for thought except that of idealism. Hume's critical analysis of knowledge has a purely negative value ; it simply emphasizes in unmistakable terms the necessity for a real solution of the problem. But once this pure negation is stiffened into a rigid and positive system, once the demand is mistaken for a conclusion, the value of empiricism is gone, and nothing remains but one of the many forms of naturalistic dogmatism which base themselves on an intellectual vacuum.

For this reason we cannot consider modern English empiricism as a continuation of classical empiricism. If we must call it a continuation, it is only in the sense in which night is the continuation of day : the light vanishes, and everything else remains. The true continuation of Bacon and Hume's empiricism is to be found in the idealism of Kant and Hegel. In the philosophy of Bentham and Mill and Spencer, thought fails to maintain its circular movement, the true movement which follows the orbit of reality through the grades of perfection ; it continues to move, so to speak, along the tangent, in a monotonous and uniform continuity which contains in itself no ground of deviation, and therefore only deviates under the impact of external forces.

And, in fact, the new empiricism is devoid of any originality : all speculative interest has vanished, and there only remains the rigid form of classical empiricism swollen in bulk by external accretions. Its apparent originality is just this process of sedimentation, this extension of its field of action as a result of the introduction of new elements from the natural sciences and from all the different aspects of modern civilization and culture. But its speculative level is unchanged ; and hence arises a certain clumsiness in the hypertrophied mass of material and a kind of incongruity in the farrago of heterogeneous facts which this philosophy has succeeded in amassing. This is where English positivism differs from that of other nations, inasmuch as it has applied more conscientiously the formula of Baconian positivism— first collect facts and then draw inductions—and it has therefore become more clumsy and ponderous. The tastes and traditions of the Latin peoples have seldom if ever permitted such an encyclopædic amassing of information, and their applications of the positivist formula have almost always ended in empty words ; hence the comparative ease with which, in these countries, positivism is being eliminated at the present moment. In England, on the other hand, where the tendency of thought towards minute analytical observation of fact favours the work of compilation on a vast scale, positivism has taken a firmer hold and will not be so quickly eradicated.

Historically, this tendency towards the work of compilation, which so thoroughly arrested the development of the essentially speculative impulse of classical empiricism, originated in the Scottish school at the beginning of the nineteenth century. Here the search for facts became an end in itself : in the psychological museums of Reid and Stewart every trace of mental life disappeared, and philosophy was reduced to a schedule of the senses and the faculties of the mind, drawn up by a process reminiscent of the doctors in Molière. For several decades the Scottish psychology paralysed thought in England and France, suppressing everywhere all speculative interest and handing thought over to the facile revelations of common sense and the pleasant task of applying scissors to the texture of the mind, and cutting it up in as many ways as caprice might dictate. Immediately it ceased to content itself with collecting and attempted to explain, the shallowness of this psychology became apparent. In their theory of knowledge Reid and Stewart opposed the doctrine of ideas, of images, maintaining that reality is known without any intermediation of ideas, just as it is in itself : in other words, that the object of thought is the material thing, the *res*. And this after the *Critique of Pure Reason* had been written in Germany !

The Scottish school set itself up as an opponent of the dominant empiricism, which in ethics took from its greatest representative the title of Benthamism. But in reality both were expressions of the same feeble mentality which in Bentham assumed more repugnant forms, in so far as with him it attempted to achieve a systematic codification of egoism, while in the Scottish psychology it covertly cherished humanitarian tendencies, generally labelled with the title " moral sense."

There have, indeed, been thinkers who attempted to make Reid into a second Kant, by a complete confusion of their true historical positions. Chief among these was Hamilton : but this was because he had observed Kant so exclusively through the spectacles of Scottish psychology as to convert him into another Reid. Nevertheless, we cannot deny the historical importance of Hamilton, and also a certain robustness of thought which enabled him to anticipate the neo-critical theories of modern German philosophy and to infuse a little of the breath of Kantian thought into the spiritless philosophy of the Scottish school. We should be unable to understand recent English empiricism without having first taken a rapid survey of Hamilton's work, although a complete exposition of it would be beyond the scope of this historical outline.

Like the French empiricism, which it anticipated by many years in this respect, Hamilton's philosophy drew from Kant an empiricist inspiration : the negation of the absolute and the affirmation of the reciprocally conditioned character of phenomena. To think is to condition : hence the criticism of the unconditioned, of the infinite which transcends the limits of knowledge and is therefore unthinkable. With this negation Hamilton felt himself able to exorcise the absolute of the post-Kantians, and especially of Schelling, whom he admired more than the other German idealists and placed on a level with Cousin. In his radical empiricism he failed to understand that the absolute he was criticizing was not the absolute of idealism, but simply the shadow of his own phenomenalist position. The contradictions of finite and infinite space, of limited and unlimited time, are the contradictions of the phenomenon itself, of the object fixed in thought which casts its shadow outside thought into an imaginary infinity and eternity. While it appears to consolidate the position of phenomenalism, the criticism of these concepts really damages it irreparably, because it reveals the latent antinomies from which phenomenalism can never escape. The final conclusion of Hamilton's philosophy is therefore an agnosticism—the renunciation of the attempt to explain the contradictions of the real, and the recognition of its mystery—which concentrates into an imaginary entity all the absurdities of the phenomenalist position. We shall encounter this conception again in Spencer, and shall there analyse it at length : but it is highly important that we should point out here that the unknowable of agnosticism does not lie outside the phenomenon, but represents the internal contradiction in the phenomenon itself.

The fallacy of agnosticism lies in its hypostatizing this contradiction and projecting it outside the phenomenon, creating out of the impotence of its own method the God of religion. Thus Mansel developed the irrational element of Hamilton's philosophy into a theological doctrine. He raised the inconceivability of God to a principle, and at the same time tried to acclimatize God—the absurdity of logic, the scandal of thought—in consciousness by means of a doctrine of belief.

The inner reason for this deification of the absurd lies in the very fact that the philosophy of the phenomenon, of the conditioned, finds it impossible to resolve the antinomies inherent in its own position, and yet feels the necessity of recognizing them as belonging to the sphere of the real. The introduction of a double point of view, that of a reality in itself and a reality for us, which is incompatible with the doctrine of the phenomenon, renders it possible for agnosticism in the last resort to provide an excuse for the contradictory conception it has of God, by throwing on God Himself the solution of the antinomies in which we are constrained, owing to the limitation of our faculties, to think His concept. Mansel thus does not scruple to double the dose of incomprehensibility, and even asserts that a God who could be conceived in thought would no longer be a God. He therefore revives without hesitation the formula, *credo quia absurdum*, and concludes his feeble flight of speculation with this Mohammedan ideal of renouncing thought. The strangest thing is that the primacy of the practical reason, which marked for Kant the discovery of the autonomy and creative power of the spirit, is exclusively employed by Mansel and the other neo-Kantians to excuse a vice in their procedure and to assist with a meaningless label the sale of their damaged goods.

The agnostic tendency, like every tendency that offered a comfortable repose from thought and justified speculative indolence, enjoyed great popularity in England during the nineteenth century. Its culminating point was the metaphysics of Spencer ; but the same motive is audible, pitched in a lower key, in the school of Hamilton and Mansel, of which the well-known statesman A. J. Balfour might be considered the last representative.

The contradiction in which agnosticism finds itself involved is, as we have seen, the contradiction inherent in the idea of the phenomenon : the finite and infinite nature of space and time, the regress of the causal series. The antinomy exists, and it is futile to try and conceal it : the merit of Hamilton and Mansel is that they drew attention to it, and their criticism is therefore of value as a negative argument against the position of phenomenalism. If this is true, John Stuart Mill's position in his criticism of Hamilton must be looked upon as a backward step : for he sought to eliminate the antinomy as an illusion, considering the actual infinity of time and space and the causal regress as ideas which are not inconceivable, but merely cannot be imagined.

Mill's alleged solution is closely connected with his nominalist attitude, which we shall shortly have to examine ; and it simply consists in asserting that we can conceive the infinite, the unlimited, so long as by this we merely mean abstracting the quality of finitude or limitation from the finite, and do not demand an imaginative synthesis of the conception of infinity, since this imagination can never be completed. Thus the infinite exists, but only as a name. An admirable solution : but if infinity is only a word, if there is no such thing as *infinitus actu*, why should the antinomy ever have arisen ? In Mill's criticism the problem that in Hamilton was still alive has shrivelled into nothing : no breath of the inspiration of Kant remains, and the atmosphere is one of pure nominalism.

§ 2 JOHN STUART MILL.

Reality in Mill's view is sensation. Everything can be resolved into this primordial element, and every reality is constructed by means of its different combinations. The formula of these combinations is the law of association : from the grouping together of sensations things are formed ; from the associations between the groups, relations of thought.

Mill's constant endeavour was to eliminate every *a priori* element from the domain of experience, and he showed great skill in the pursuit of a series of minute analytical investigations, undertaken in order to demonstrate the merely empirical and *a posteriori* nature of experiences from which it was thought that the *a priori* could not possibly be eliminated. Mill does not recoil from any consequences : even mathematics, which such a radical empiricism as Hume's had left immune from doubt, he explains as merely empirical, a product of the laws of association ; and even the logical principles of identity and contradiction become for him *a posteriori* facts of experience.   Thus by driving empiricism to its extreme limit Mill succeeded better than any criticism in revealing the absurdity of its thesis.

If reality is sensation, what significance can be attached to the principles of the permanence of things and the causality of phenomena ?   We can only understand these principles as equivalent to the stability of the groups of sensations and the empirically ascertainable constancy of the relations of antecedence and consequence between the various groups. So far we have a repetition of Hume : causality is merely the habitual succession of phenomena.   But Mill adds on his own account another element.   While reality is sensation, it is not all actually sensed.   Beyond the immediate present there lies the possibility of the present.   In this way everything which is not at any given moment sensed is resolved into a possibility of sensations, which, in so far as it is constantly being rendered actual by being given in determinate conditions, is a *permanent* possibility of sensations.   Hence our ideas of causation, power, activity, do not become connected in thought with our momentary sensations, except in a small number of cases, but with the permanent possibility of sensations whose existence is guaranteed by the small and variable number of sensations actually present.   " Hence we speedily learn to think of Nature as made up solely of these groups of possibilities, and the active force in Nature as manifested in the modification of some of these by others.   The sensations, though the original foundation of the whole, come to be looked upon as a sort of accident depending on us, and the possibilities as much more real than the actual sensations; nay, as the very realities of which these are only the representations, appearances or effects."[1]   In other words, we succeed in emptying reality and reducing it to the mere shadow of itself.

This doctrine of the possibility of sensations, which is Mill's only original contribution to the theory of knowledge, is the logical complement of modern English empiricism, but at the same time the proof of its great inferiority to classical empiricism. The historical value and importance of this latter lies in its very incompleteness. By denying that reality exists ready-made outside and prior to experience, and by affirming that it is created in and by empirical experience, classical empiricism conclusively refuted scholasticism. The problem of the nature of the world *quâ* not yet experienced, and its relation to the nature of the world *quâ* experienced, is not recognized by the classical empiricists as a real problem at all. Nor could they have dealt with such a problem ; for their conception of the actuality of experience, understood as pure immediacy, was powerless to solve a problem which lies outside it. Empiricism thus left open a vast field to be explored by its philosophical successors, who were wholly occupied in demonstrating the absolute creativeness of experience, and in resolving into the procedure of thought the shadow of the thing-in-itself, projected outside thought into the sphere of the not experienced. The importance of empiricism just consists in this breaking-down of its barriers, which was indeed an example of something like what Hegel called the " cunning of the reason " : for although its methods did not enable it to resolve the fundamental dualism of scholasticism (that of potentiality and actuality, the heritage of Aristotelianism), its very restrictions enabled it to refrain from prejudicing the new point of view. Thus it was careful not to set up a new dualism between possible experience and actual experience ; and still more careful not to elaborate a solution where the problem was only just being formed.

Mill's belated empiricism, on the other hand, is chiefly

[1] John Stuart Mill, *An Examination of Sir William Hamilton's Philosophy*, 1865, p. 195.

preoccupied with the task of closing its own barriers. In the not experienced it sees the possibility of sensations. The result is incalculable. The world is given as a possibility before it is given as actuality ; the creative character of experience is destroyed ; the ancient dualism between the potential and the actual is revived in its entirety ; in a word, Mill's philosophy is just a reversion to the worst type of scholasticism. Its partisans are doubtless ignorant of its inner nature ; for it is a habit with superficial critics to condemn as *a priori* (a term which very frequently means fantastic) any philosophy that does not confine itself to the observation of bald facts, and to praise another as founded on experience simply because the word " experience " is mentioned in it. Mill's philosophy, which is blazoned on the shield of almost every scientist, is simply the negation of science : it is utterly alien to the spirit of Bacon and Galileo : it is scholasticism five centuries out of date, and it has therefore all the defects of scholasticism and none of the great, the inestimable merits.

This makes clear the meaning of our statement at the beginning of the chapter, that modern empiricism cannot be regarded as a continuation of classical empiricism : a fact which will become even more obvious in our examination of empiricist logic.

In order to complete our exposition of Mill's thought, we should say that he himself realized that he had reduced reality to nothing in his empty " possibilities of sensation." And, in fact, according to him not only is external reality resolved into these possibilities, but so is the sentient subject. The belief that my spirit exists when it does not feel or think, and has no consciousness of its own existence, is reduced to the belief in a permanent possibility of these states. Yet here Mill stops short, unwilling to tread forbidden ground. What is really incomprehensible, he says, is that a thing which has ceased to exist, or which has not yet begun to exist, should nevertheless be able to be in some manner present : that a series of feelings of which the greater part lies in the past or the future could be incorporated, so to speak, in a present sensation, accompanied by the belief in its reality. ' I think,' he adds, ' by far the wisest thing we can do, is to accept the inexplicable fact, without any theory of how it takes place.' ¹

Thus the incomprehensible finishes by being the whole of Mill's theory. His sensations are a sort of shadows that do not come to be and do not perish, but only appear together and disappear together in a mysterious manner, independently of any consciousness, and arrange themselves in groups in order to produce consciousness : a process which, as Spaventa pointed out, resembles the naturalistic theory of the production of sensation by means of the movements of matter.

§ 3. The Logic of Empiricism.

On these psychological principles Mill bases his logic. This logic is typical of the whole of empiricist tendency in English thought, and constitutes a fundamental theme repeated with very slight variations by an enormous number of writers. Individually they are all very unimportant, and we shall not deal with them in detail. For an impersonal tendency like this an impersonal exposition is most suitable ; or, better, one personified in the writer who best represents the type.

For Mill, reality is sensation : hence the concept is a compendium of the sensible content, denuded, through abstraction, of its particular elements. In a word, the concept is the name, the empty generality. And since reality is created in sense, the judgment does not create reality, but is simply a relation between concepts which establishes the belief in objectivity—where by objectivity nothing more is meant than mere constancy.

Now, if the concept is merely the result of abstraction from sensible qualities, it is simply what has been conceived, the finished act of intellection, and not the *intelligere*, the act of understanding or thinking. Hence logic has to do, not with the laws of thought as such, but with the laws of the products of thought ; that is to say, logic has nothing to do with thought as such. As the mere product, the concept is not *norma sui*, but something normatively determined by the process of abstraction, which stands outside

¹ *Op. cit.*, p. 242.

it and graduates it to an external scale according to the different degrees of abstractness imposed upon it. Thus the procedure of thought anticipates thought itself, which accordingly finds that before it has started out its road is determined : either from the particular to the general or vice versa, along the rigid line of the grades of abstraction. This is the basis of inductive and deductive logic. Here it is obvious that the empty *schema* of thought, which is really a *posterius* reached by abstraction from completed acts of intellection, is raised to a *prius* of thought, to a pre-ordained standard according to which thought must be modelled. On this fallacy is based the whole of Mill's inductive and deductive logic.

The tendency of this logic is anti-scientific, anti-experimental. The erection of a process of generalization into an end in itself results in the complete mechanization of thought, the negation of any intrinsic originality, and the annihilation of all sense of concrete scientific thinking in a series of empty forms which are imposed on thought *a priori* by the necessities of " Scientific Method." Science is thus reduced to an arbitrary collection of data, held together by an abstract method imposed upon them from without. The empiricism which claimed to have escaped from the idea of a thing-in-itself, a ready-made reality, simply transfers this idea from an external nature to a method, thus turning thought itself into nature : it is still worse off than dogmatism, because it introduces the enemy into its own house. This explains why an acute empiricist like Mach has felt a certain repugnance for the so-called inductive methods, arguing with absolute justice that they only enable us to collect and codify science after it has been created, and do not tell us how science is actually produced. This also explains the continual shifts of opinion which have occurred in Mill's school for and against the various methods ; now one method appearing unfruitful, now another. In reality all are by definition unfruitful, since they are simply abstract *schemata* of the fixed products of thought, and presuppose science as already complete. The apparent fruitfulness of the methods arises from a curious illusion : the method is placed over against the thought which is engaged in invention and discovery, and the method is then said to be a help towards the invention or the discovery.   In other words, a *posterius* is taken for a *prius.*

This logical formalism is also to be found in classical empiricism ; but there it only represents a by-product of a thought that is inwardly alive.   The originality of that movement does not consist in its having thrown into strong relief the inductive method—which is a mere reminiscence of Raymond Lull, and the weakest part of Bacon's work ; but in its having discovered the subjectivity of experience and denied a reality ready-made outside thought.   But these early empiricists did not fully grasp the true import of their discovery ; and this led them to exalt the ceremonial of methods, while in reality they were creating a new universe.

In modern empiricism, on the other hand, ceremonial has become an end in itself : scientific thought exists for no other end than to apply the inductive and deductive methods.   Science exists in order to generalize : we do not generalize in order to produce science.   And it is not a question of a mere misuse of words : the so-called " synthetic " —its true name would be encyclopædic—philosophy, whose greatest representative is Spencer, is wholly the outcome of this error of setting over against thought its own procedure and considering generalization as an end in itself.

But there are even more serious consequences.   The whole of the anti-scientific tendency so conspicuous in recent philosophy is due to this logic of mental mechanism. For thought is confused with the empty *schema* of formalism, and it is then argued that this *schema* is incapable of grasping reality.   But the error of these anti-intellectualist arguments is precisely the same as that of the advocates of formal logic, and consists in identifying science with the mechanized *schemata*, in which nothing is left of science except the *caput mortuum.* We pointed out this error when speaking of the French philosophy of contingence and of the various anti-scientific tendencies that are flourishing to-day.   It is asserted that the principle of identity is unable to establish a single truth, and it is believed that this involves the conclusion that logic, thought, is impotent to attain reality : but this criticism only applies to a false logic which has lost every trace of the concrete nature of thinking.   That curious phenomenon mathematical logic, with which we shall very soon have to deal, is simply a development of this false logic.

In Mill's doctrine and that of his followers the mechanization of thought is complete. These writers are not contented with anticipating thought itself by means of the general *schema* of thought, but in the field of induction and deduction they proceed to more detailed distinctions. They speak of methods of agreement, of difference, of concomitant variations and of residues ; of historical and statistical inductions ; of mathematical and non-mathematical inductions, and so forth. It is a jumble of ill-defined concepts, often of the utmost crudity, reaching its grossest forms in scientific works which are absolutely soaked in the verbalism of the " methods."

The strangest thing is that not only the empiricists but the idealists themselves fall a prey to the illusion of these methods. The celebrated logics of Bradley and Bosanquet do not differ very fundamentally from that of John Stuart Mill : they only differ in the degree to which thought is mechanized. Thus Bosanquet's logic, which is without doubt the best of them all, sets out to be a doctrine of the judgment, which it regards as the creator of truth ; but it then proceeds to lose itself in a wilderness of verbalism among names, mechanical laws of thought, processes of inference and so on. Hence arises the dualism of the double logic ; the logic of being, or metaphysic, and the logic of knowing : [1] a dualism that is in open contradiction with the first principles of the idealistic philosophy.

The only living part of the logic of empiricism is its attempt at a description of the genetic process of knowledge. In so far as it is a theory of the empirical origin of the concept, resolving the problem of validity into that of psychological origin, it is already potentially a genetic logic. This comes out very clearly in Mill, for whom logic simply constitutes a chapter of psychology. Bosanquet, whom we have mentioned above, also inclines towards a similar view, in so far as he conceives the empirical evolution of knowledge

[1] B. Bosanquet, *Logic, or the Morphology of Knowledge*, Oxford, 1888, vol. i. p. 247.

as the emancipation of the individual mind from its accidental limitations. But what eludes empiricism in its inquiry into the genetic process of knowledge is the soul, the inner moving principle of development. Since it regards reality as existing wholly in sensation, the passage of knowledge from one grade to another can only be due to external grounds, which fall outside the developing thought. Such a ground is the concept of psychological association in the philosophy of Mill. Therefore genetic logic can only succeed in grasping the separate stages of thought, and never the movement from one to another : it is reduced to a mere description, more or less external, instead of an explanation of the process of knowledge.

Of late years the completest and richest exposition of genetic logic (so far as its premisses admit of richness) has been given by an American, J. M. Baldwin.

His logic attempts to treat thought as living, and to grasp the different moments of its development. Truth is not made whole in a moment, but is coming into existence through successive stages, and the three fundamental stages are the prelogical, the logical and the supralogical, the latter of which corresponds to the æsthetic and ethical conception of the world.

In this process of thought from the lowest to the highest stages we find a progressive efficiency in the controlling factors through which the indistinct and fluid experience of thought is determined and circumscribed in order to attain to an ever-completer systematization. In the first moments of the process this efficiency in the controlling factors is purely involuntary ; but with the progress of thought it becomes conscious, reflective. The first conscious control through which the content of experience comes to assume a determination is memory. Its mediating work consists in the fact that in the homogeneous tissue of primitive experience, where things are not distinguished from ideas, but with them constitute an undifferentiated psycho-physical state, the memory introduces the first distinction, separating the logical construction of things from the immediate experience of sense.[1] From this point onwards the

[1] J. M. Baldwin, *Thought and Things, or Genetic Logic*, 1906, vol. i. p. 70.

series of mediations and determinations proceeds without a break : in the logical stage, the individuation of objects already started in the prelogical stage grows more and more complete : the laws of identity, of permanence, etc., express just this increasing determination of the content of thought. But— and herein lies the fundamental error of empiricism—this progress is not a genuine progress, because reality is already implicit as ready-made in sensation : in thought it is only given precision and co-ordination. Hence the logical relations do not introduce anything new into reality : they have the same nature as the objects among which they are established. This is exactly the opposite of the view of idealism, for which the objects are resolved into relations. Baldwin's empiricism, just like Schuppe's empiricism, transforms relations into substance, reduces them to facts, to things. Hence what escapes it is just the dynamic character of development : the various phases which thought traverses are regarded by it as so many discrete, static unities.

With his empiricist, descriptive point of view Baldwin can do no more than juxtapose these phases : the mediation, the reflection of thought which he would wish to be the soul of the development, is itself only another external thing set over against the object. Since it is simply a controlling factor, it cannot create anything new ; its only function is to verify the mutual agreement of the facts of experience and the mutual agreement between knowing subjects. It is clearly a problem on a lower level than the transcendental or critical problem of knowledge, because the empirical fact of agreement presupposes the identity of consciousness.

The culminating point of Baldwin's logic is therefore— given the premises—the concept of " syndoxis," of truth as an agreement between ideas, the external identity of opinions.[1]

Here, although Baldwin follows a more strictly scientific procedure, his theory bears a certain resemblance to pragmatism, another offshoot of empiricism which we shall examine separately.

[1] *Op. cit.*, vol. ii. (1908), pp. 60, 61, 63.

§ 4. THE ETHICS OF EMPIRICISM.

With the empiricist psychology, which has an inexhaustible literature, we will not deal here, since it is of no philosophical interest. Like all empiricisms, it does not show any development, but only the superimposition of slightly divergent tendencies. From the psychology of Mill, which remains confined within the immediate reality of sensation, we pass to the naturalism of Spencer and his followers, who wish to base psychology on biology and, applying the Darwinian principle of evolution, attempt to explain Mill's incomprehensible law of association by an appeal to the biological concept of hereditary transmission.

It is more interesting to examine the empiricist ethics, which offers an excellent means of measuring the mental and moral level of the school.

The empiricist ethics starts with a conception of man as an egoistic being differing hardly at all from the brute, and either denies the whole moral aspect of spiritual life, as Bentham did when in a moment of depression he described virtue as an *ens rationis*, or, what is worse, it tries to extract altruism, meaning virtue, out of egoism, by simply playing with the association of ideas.

The least inconsequent of these moralists was Bentham While he did not deny the existence of that sphere of activity which transcends the limits of the individual, he neverthe less refused to see in the tendency towards the advancement of the general wellbeing anything more than a controlled egoism. In his psychological crudity Bentham went in search of a quantitative formula of pleasure, which steered a middle course between the maximum and the minimum ; as though one could weigh human interests in a pair of scales.

Since Bentham the constant aim of the English empiricists has been to include in the empiricist formula that sphere of activity which transcends the limits of the individual and is concentrated, without any egoistic *arrière-pensée*, on the common wellbeing. Here we feel the indirect influence of the Scottish moralists. But in order to explain the trans formation of egoism into altruism, the rise of the moral obligation and its affirmation in consciousness, empiricism has had to resort to all kinds of expedients, amounting some-times to veritable conjuring tricks. And it has revealed a certain philistine narrowness which merits the condemnation passed by Rousseau on Helvetius, that it must be a really abominable philosophy which is embarrassed by the existence of virtuous actions.[1]

Mill substitutes for Bentham's quantitative formula a qualitative formula of pleasure and self-interest. But if in this direction he makes an advance upon his master, in logical rigour he is very much his inferior. For he tries to extract out of the play of these subjective interests something different from them, namely virtue, altruism. Bentham on the other hand, faithful to his principles, had recognized that all the feelings are simply different expressions of one and the same fundamental fact, and that therefore each alike equally manifests the nature and character of that fact. But we must bear in mind that Mill was influenced not only by Bentham, but also by the Scottish philosophers, who, following their usual habit of solving problems by applying labels, had invented[2] a moral sense to explain the existence of virtuous actions. As though morality were the auto-matic product of an appropriate appendage ! In this respect it must be admitted that Mill's theory constitutes an advance, since it is an attempt, however clumsy, to explain morality by means of a process of associations ; it is, in fact, an incipient recognition of the spiritual formation of the moral character, and not the mere turning on of a tap, as it is in the Scottish theory.

Here, as everywhere, the secret of Mill is association Man, who consists exclusively of subjective sensations and subjective interests, finding himself in a society, begins by means of the association of ideas to connect his own well-being with that of others ; it gradually becomes impossible

[1] Guyau, La Morale anglaise contemporaine, Paris, 1885, 2nd ed., p. 20. To this book and Mill's Utilitarianism I owe most of the substance of this section.

[2] The English reader need hardly be reminded that the credit for this invention is due not to the Scottish school but to the so-called " sentimentalist " school of Shaftesbury and Hutcheson a century earlier. See Sir Amherst Selby-Bigge's British Moralists, Oxford, 1897, for bibliography, history and selections from all the chief writers concerned.—TRS.

for him to imagine himself apart from his relations with
others and insensible to the interests of others : and finally,
by reason of his associating his own wellbeing with that
of others, he ends by forgetting his own wellbeing as
his own and by wishing the wellbeing of others as others.
It is at this point that Mill appeals to the famous example
of the miser who desires gold first for the satisfaction which
it obtains for him and afterwards for itself.   Similarly, we
are to suppose, virtue was originally a vice, a form of egoism ;
but with time the ego disappears and virtue remains by
itself.   Frankly, I fail to understand how this piece of
juggling can ever have been taken seriously.   Virtue reduced
to the rank of a habit ! Virtue placed on the same level
as vice, and, indeed, actually containing less than vice, since
it merely consists of vice with one element inadvertently
left out !

We can imagine the consequences of such a doctrine.
Take, for instance, the sentiment of obligation.   Mill suggests
that it is simply the fear of authority transformed into a
new shape.   And Bain—another doughty champion of
empiricism—adds : not only fear but also imitation.   We
feel ourselves under an obligation because we imitate in
ourselves the manner of acting of the externally constituted
authority.   This is all simply monstrous : the inner life of
the conscience, our opposing of ourselves to ourselves in
our most solemn moments, when we impose upon ourselves
a line of conduct involving the sacrifice of a large part of
our very being—all this is reduced to an act of mimicry,
an aping the procedure in a court of law.   It is desirable that
we should be perfectly clear as to the real character of
this theory : it is simply a piece of moral infamy, a literal
outrage on the dignity of our common human nature.   But,
it will be argued, Bain did not intend to do away with our
present idea of obligation in favour of that of imitation,
but only to show that we must look to this latter idea for
the origin of the former.   This is true ; but it is just this
pseudo-historicism which constitutes the most heinous error
of the empiricist ethics.   It makes of morality a natural
product, a sedimentary accumulation of habits ; and it
thus ends by rendering us slaves to our past, irresponsible

products of something that it is no longer in our power to modify. This is what I mean by the pseudo-historicism of the empiricists. The truth is that morality, which includes the whole of the spirit, is continual creation : each moral act is not simply the *résumé* of a past experience, but sums up in itself in its creative originality the whole of the past. When I make a decision, I am not blindly driven on by the impetus of my past life ; on the contrary, I concentrate within myself the whole of my past into my present act of willing, which therefore contains something eternal, and with my decision I profoundly affect my past. Herein lies the originality of the moral consciousness, for which no past is irrevocable. And herein, too, lies the profundity of the religious concept of redemption. It is only that part of the past which is fixed, embodied in fact, that is irrevocable : the part of it which is still living—and that is the deepest part—is within the domain of our will.

The error of pseudo-historicism is aggravated in Spencer, who, by resorting in his treatment of the problems of ethics to biology and heredity, achieved the most complete philosophical failure of the whole school. The clumsy deduction of morality that we find in Mill is at least something which takes place in the lifetime of the individual : the play of associations and obliterations by which morality is formed is something which does depend to a certain extent on him and for which we can assign to him a certain amount of responsibility; but once morality is made dependent on the organic modifications resulting from a gradual sedimentation in the evolution of the species, we return to the " tap " theory of the Scottish school, to the automatic production of morality ; only Spencer makes matters worse because for the childish and really rather attractive simplicity of the Scottish theory he substitutes all the trivialities of a quack science.

In such hands all the concepts of morality, the flower of the serious and profound speculation of centuries, become unrecognizable. Sidgwick believes in duty, yet he says that sanctions are not the consequence of duty, but its necessary condition. This amounts to saying that he does not believe in it after all ; for it is not a question of asserting

the crude fact of duty (if that meant anything) ; to believe
in duty means to believe in the spontaneity of the moral
standard. And finally, with the irresponsibility of a child,
fingering precious things of whose value it has no idea,
Clifford comes along, and, impressed with the hypothetical
character of scientific laws, demands, in order that morality
may be raised to the rank of a science, that its laws
should be hypothetically formulated : If you desire this,
do that. And all this with a kind of puerile air of saying
something new, oblivious or ignorant of the fact that one
of the greatest achievements of thought at the end of the
eighteenth century consisted just in the discovery that
morality is not a hypothetical imperative.

Such, in its main outlines, is the ethics of empiricism :
frivolous and mean ; the work of feeble minds and of
wavering consciences.

§ 5. The Metaphysic of Empiricism : Spencer.

Spencer's metaphysic is the verification *in corpore vili*
of the validity of Mill's logic. The *vile corpus* is science,
subjected as amorphous matter to the logic of induction
and deduction. According to this logic, as we have seen,
thought is the crude fact which conforms to an external
mechanism, to a schematic form which dominates it but does
not interpenetrate it. Upon thought, as upon inert matter,
is superimposed its own procedure : induction and deduction
are considered as two roads, two channels along which
this amorphous matter must pass. Now, in Spencer's metaphysic the amorphous matter consists precisely of the content
of the particular sciences ; induction and deduction are
the *schemata* through which it must filter in order to become
philosophy. Spencer constructs a philosophy for the sake
of employing a method ; such at least is the task which he
sets himself.

It was only this fact that could possibly have enabled
him, before he had developed his system, to decide the number
of the volumes and the order of their composition, and finally
to look for collaborators. His philosophy was already all
potentially contained in the method ; and his facile disposi-

tion, quick to assimilate, not tormented by any philosophical doubt—that doubt which destroys system after system in the mind of any man who really thinks systematically— all this facilitated the completion of the encyclopædic task which he had set before himself.

What truths could such a philosophy reveal to us ? We must reflect that the truth of natural science is not a complete and ready-made truth, but a truth which is in process of creation ; a continual mediation of the crude fact by resolving it into the relations of thought, and an affirmation by this means of the concreteness and actuality of the scientific procedure. For Spencer, on the other hand, natural science is one crude fact, and its truth another : science is simply a moment of that abstract and external procedure of the method : not itself a process, but a mere stage in the process of empirical generalization. Thus philosophy presupposes the truths of science and cannot add anything to them ; nay, since it represents a more abstract stage of generalization, it simply etherealizes these truths which are already given to it and reduces them to a specious play of more or less empty concepts. If anyone replies that a truth, even when thus impoverished and evaporated, still remains a truth, he shows himself to be involved in the very error which we are here criticizing. For he is assuming that truth is found dispersed along the scale of generalizations, while in reality, I repeat, truth is concreteness, process in its actuality.

Spencer's metaphysic is thus shown to be false from the very start. It consists in first assuming two highly general concepts, force and matter, the ultimate residuum of empirical laws and principles, and secondly, in postulating that these first principles move according to a definite rhythm, by which reality passes through phases of evolution and dissolution, of integration and disintegration. The principle once found (and in finding it both deduction and induction are employed) is applied in all the fields of knowledge—astronomy and physics, psychology and sociology. Everywhere reality is accomplishing this Sisyphean labour of making and un-making : all teleology is banned from the process : the life of consciousness and that of humanity do not affect the law in any essential manner ; indeed, they too are resolved into a mere moment of its cycle : into the predominance during a certain temporal period of forces tending to integrate matter.

But how does Spencer justify this first principle : what does he regard as the proof of this law ? To such a question the theorist of the crude fact can find no answer. The pure fact is what it is ; and in face of the understanding that wishes to scrutinize it, it can only refer back to the infinite series of facts which precede it in time, but this does not make it any less impenetrable. In this regress of fact upon fact *ad infinitum*, in this impenetrability of the fact by thought, the acute observer will discern already the affirmation of the unknowable. The unknowable, indeed, lurks within the knowable ; or, more accurately, in the falsity of the procedure with which Spencer attempts to think the knowable. And so, when he is brought to a halt before the mystery of first principles, and seeks to show how the highest laws of science are surrounded by an obscurity which the human intellect cannot penetrate, and in which science and faith, enemies on earth, meet on common ground, reconciled by their common impotence, at bottom he is simply labelling his own irrational procedure with the term " unknowable."

About the Spencerian unknowable a great many inaccurate opinions are current, arising from an ambiguity to which Spencer himself has contributed. It is well known that the part of the *First Principles* which deals with the unknowable was thought out and written after the system was completed. The fundamental idea of the unknowable was in Spencer's mind a very simple one, as we have already shown ; it was simply a question of the inconceivability of the regress *ad infinitum* from fact to fact. But in the meantime a study of Hamilton and Mansel had provided Spencer with the means of treating this argument more fully ; and so, through this acquaintance, at second hand, with Kant's transcendental dialectic, he was able to construct a series of antinomies, showing that thought remains inevitably involved in them when it seeks to understand the inner essence of the concepts of time, space, matter, etc. This has given rise to the erroneous idea that the Spencerian unknowable was something analogous to Kant's thing-in-itself : with the result that many people have taken upon themselves to criticize as illegitimate the positive use which Spencer makes of the concept of the unknowable in the sphere of the knowable ; others have pointed out that the unknowable is at least to a certain extent knowable, in so far as it is spoken of as existing ; and so on. All these criticisms are framed exactly as though they were dealing with Kant, and, indeed, one eminent thinker has gone so far as to say that Spencer is an unsuspecting and unwitting Kantian. These people have coupled together the thing-in-itself and the unknowable because each involves a mystery, when the real question is a distinction between two quite different mysteries ; they have, in fact, shut their eyes exactly when they ought to be opening them wider. Kant's thing-in-itself is indeed fraught with mystery : so much so that out of this mystery, as it gradually revealed itself, there emerged the *Critique of the Practical Reason,* the *Critique of the Judgment,* and the whole of the post-Kantian idealism. The mystery of the unknowable, on the contrary, is the mystery of nothing, the mystery of the person who puts out his eyes and then says that he sees black. If anyone finds anything genuinely mysterious in the unknowable, it is because he is himself refilling the artificial void with his own imaginings. The unknowable is simply the expression of the impotence of the external method of naturalism, which stops in dismay before an infinite regress of fact upon fact, as if that regress contained some strange diabolical power, and fails to realize that it is being scared by its own shadow. For this is what it really is. Solidify that ideal order of laws, which is being given, being produced in experience : consider it as a given, a fact : that is to say, regard that world which is being continually created in experience, and in thought, as a given, complete fact : and you will then see the development of this causal order or world of experience transformed into a uniform, monotonous gyration which perpetually points outside itself to its other, the infinite ; and here you have your unknowable. But do you not see that in doing this you are simply projecting your own shadow eternally behind you, into the night of an empty past ? The illusion of the unknowable arises from the error of desiring to consider reality, which is experience, as a perfect and complete reality, created all at once, and in desiring to apply that order which is valid in reality, which is being created in experience, to that phantom of the imagination, the perfectly complete reality which has existed from an inconceivable and self-contradictory eternity. And so, at bottom this modern philosophy of experience, which claims to derive from Bacon and Hume, conceals an eminently dogmatic and scholastic tendency, essentially hostile to experience.

I repeat it : it is an error to consider this empiricism as the modern restatement of the great empiricism of the past. The new tendency of English empiricism is an altogether modern product, and is completely false : it is a scion of the new naturalism—a tendency, in fact, utterly opposed to science —grafted on the stock of that old empiricism which bore its fruit not in England but in Germany.

The great reputation of the philosopher of the unknowable is not so much due to the positive content of his doctrine, or to any contribution made by him to philosophy, as to the fact that his system is the completest expression of the naturalistic preoccupations and prejudices which dominated the second half of the nineteenth century. With the decay of those preoccupations and prejudices Spencer has been put on one side : his historical function is fulfilled. An indefatigable advocate of an idea which dominates a long period of thought, by his very advocacy he hastens that idea towards its natural death. It is to a large extent as a reply to Spencer that modern idealism has arisen. He will therefore go down to history as an eminently representative figure.

§ 6. THE THEORY OF SCIENCE.

In Spencer's naturalism we have seen the constructive encyclopædic tendency of empiricism find its expression. Parallel with this there was developing in the work of other thinkers a critical negative tendency. These latter are no longer preoccupied with construction ; the task they set themselves is to examine the solidity of the constructions of

the scientist.   We have found the same tendency in Germany
represented by Avenarius and Mach, and in France by
Milhaud and Poincaré ; in England its chief representative
is Clerk Maxwell.   We will only touch upon it very slightly
here, because we are already acquainted with its procedure
and its conclusions.   Simplificatory by nature, it cannot
admit of a great variety of expression : hence it is sufficient
to know a single writer, in order to know all.

For Maxwell the truth of principles lies in their validity,
and this in turn depends on their practical utility.   As
pragmatism would say, ideas are valid in so far as they work ;
thus, for example, the importance of the principle of energy
lies in the fact that it enables us to consider all physical
phenomena as exemplifications, or more specifically as
transformations, of energy.   And since Maxwell, as a pure
empiricist, does not possess any *a priori* criterion for the
determination of the validity of the concept, he is compelled
to resort to the principle of analogy in order to explain how
the concept can " work " in the practice of science.   By
means of analogy the extension of the laws from one domain
of physical reality to another becomes possible ; in the
analogy of physical extension with the laws of number we
have the foundation for the application of mathematics to
the science of nature ; and finally the whole of the mechanical
or atomistic theory depends on the analogy between the
laws regarding the qualitative variations of natural phenomena
and the laws of mechanical movement.   Like Duhem's
principle of the translation of languages, this principle conceals
an unsolved problem while ostensibly advanced as a solution.

We find in Clifford, a writer who has won a great reputation in England and abroad, a compromise between Mill's
sensationalism and Spencer's evolutionism, between the
criticism of science and the cosmogonies of naturalism.
The phrase " mind-stuff," in which he sums up these various
tendencies, concentrates and expresses in a single idea
all the emptiness and poverty of the English empiricist
movement.

Is reality psychical or physical ?   Mill translates physical
reality into psychological terms, Spencer the psychical
world into physical terms : each is equally arbitrary.   To

prove this fact is the sole aim of Clifford's philosophy : physical and psychical correspond with each other point by point, just as a written sentence corresponds with the same sentence read. This means that we are not dealing with two things, but with a single substance which is physical on one side and mental on another ; which accordingly Clifford baptizes with the name of mind-stuff.[1] According to the usual principles of modern empiricism, this mental matter is affirmed as independent of and anterior to consciousness : for it is only when the mind-stuff collects into masses that consciousness arises, and the grade of consciousness depends on the degree of complication in the organization of the material elements.

The gravest charge against Clifford is that he turned thought into matter with his eyes fully open to what he was doing. But it is also a startling indication of the historical and philosophical ignorance of empiricists that he believed that this theory, by revealing the ultimate nature of things, would solve the Kantian problem of the thing-in-itself.

Between Mill and Spencer and Clifford's jumble of the two, the scanty resources of modern empiricism are exhausted. Here its history might be concluded. But we should like to analyse two offshoots of this movement, which have sprung up respectively in America and England : pragmatism and logistic. And finally, we shall examine a doctrine propounded by Hodgson which constitutes the last attempt of empiricism to grapple with the problems of the Kantian philosophy.

§ 7. PRAGMATISM.

Pragmatism was born in America, the country of " business," and is, *par excellence*, the philosophy of the business man.

It was in an article by Peirce, an article which made a great stir and was everywhere translated and commented on, that the first sketch of pragmatism was laid before the world. Its rapid rise to popularity, and still more the fact

---

[1] W. K. Clifford, *Lectures and Essays*, London, 1901, vol. ii. p. 42.

that it retained this popularity for several years, is the most disquieting symptom of the present state of philosophical thought.

Pragmatism is the logical conclusion and therefore the *reductio ad absurdum* of empiricism. If reality is sensation and the concept is merely the arbitrary abbreviation of sensible experience, the sole value of the concept will lie in its character as an arbitrary but convenient fiction. And on the other hand, if the concept is a purely subjective product which does not contain in itself objective reality, its validity can only be determined by its results, by its success when brought to bear on this external objective reality. Hence the demand that ideas should be made to work in order to ascertain their power, their practical efficiency. And as the concept of "working" is purely external, its criterion is likewise external : it is the mere agreement of individuals in the recognition of what it pays to call the truth : thus we arrive at a social concept of truth and falsehood. This is the premiss on which Peirce founds his principle. What constitutes the truth and value of a statement is the result which its truth has for some human interests, and principally for the interest to which it directly refers.

We have already found this doctrine in substance if not in name in the empiricist criticism of science. The difference between that movement and pragmatism is that pragmatism is this same empiricism exalted to a state of complete self-consciousness. The departmental sciences, pragmatism asserts, are not alone in having to devise concepts suitable for working purposes, for pragmatism itself is put forward as a working hypothesis. " We must find a theory that will work," says William James. The pragmatists are therefore quite consistent in replying to the question whether pragmatism is a doctrine of knowledge, a metaphysic, an ethic, or a religion, that it is whatever happens to be convenient. One man hates all metaphysics, another is inclined towards pluralism, another towards monism, and pragmatism can welcome them all ; in her ample bosom every suppliant will find a home.

But with all its frenzy for work, pragmatism in reality does nothing but spin its absolutely empty formula and

rest content with superficial paradoxes and extravagant
fantasies. That ideas should work is all very well, but
in practice they always seem to be other people's ideas :
if it has any of its own it never gives them anything to do.
Philosophy has vanished and we are on the brink of comedy,
if not downright charlatanism.

And here we might end our observations upon pragmatism, had it not swept into its turbid stream, among quantities
of rubbish, fragments of something more solid.   Pragmatism
has, in fact, given expression to one essential part of the
spirit of modern philosophy.   To have affirmed the human
character of truth, to have denied a reality perfect and
ready-made outside thought, to have maintained that truth,
science, is being made, is being created and is not absolutely
given once and for all, is to have struck a blow in the cause
of idealism.   Only in pragmatism these idealistic elements
are deformed, parodied and rendered almost unrecognizable.
The extreme subjectivism natural to a philosophy which is
merely empirical falsifies these truths and gives them the
appearance of fantastic paradoxes.

All the discordant tendencies of the pragmatist thesis
are united in the personality of William James ; a curious
patchwork of good and evil, of seriousness and extravagance.
But the strictly pragmatist basis of his thought represents
a stage of decadence, a sterilization of a personality whose
first appearance was far more complex and robust.

Even in the famous *Principles of Psychology* there were
indications of pragmatist tendencies, but that work contained
much that was of real value.   The acute critic of psycho-
physics, of the doctrine of heredity, of associationism, was
not yet the man who could dedicate his book on pragmatism
to the memory of John Stuart Mill.   But on some points
James had already started on the road towards his final
decadence.   There is something definitely materialistic in
the view of thought expressed in his *Psychology*.   Thought
is for him a stream in which there are moments of rest and
moments of flux : the first consist of sense-material, the
second of thought-relations, and the two are connected in
such a way that the moments of flux are derived from the
moments of rest ; that is to say, thought becomes matter,

fluid, it is true, yet still matter. Here James is not very far separated from Schuppe and Mach.

Having affirmed the undifferentiated psycho-physical state, he too, like Avenarius, criticizes introjection and makes sensible reality impersonal : [1] only in this way can the analogy between thought and the current hold good. In the pure spirit of empiricism he affirms that the sense of personal identity is completely analogous to the identity attributed to any other aggregate. Yet with sudden compunction he adds that the conscious ego cannot itself be an aggregate. He therefore tries to ascertain what it can be : but with his premisses he cannot possibly answer the question, and he becomes entangled in obscurities and confusions,[2] which remind us of the difficulties in which Bergson gets involved when he tries to pass from the empirical conception of matter to the metaphysical theory of memory.

These empiricist principles are already pointing him towards pragmatism. Given reality as an undifferentiated psycho-physical state, the conceptual *schema* becomes " a kind of sieve with which we try to sift the data of the world." A great deal of stuff passes through this sieve : what remains is what is most significant, what most deserves to be fixed. But although James has already set out on the road towards pragmatism, he has not yet reached the point where he becomes sterile. His book on *The Will to Believe* still evinces a lively sense of reality, and expresses a serious preoccupation with the fundamental problems of life. The divorce between will and thought is not yet complete. " The monstrously lop-sided equation of the universe and of its knower," as he says, " which we postulate as the ideal of cognition, is perfectly paralleled by the no less lop-sided equation of the universe and the doer."[3] But he nevertheless affirms that cognition is not complete unless it is " discharged into act," and that the volitional zone of our nature dominates the conceptual as much as it does the sensuous. Yet the will is not reduced to mere egoism : the moral universal still speaks in James's soul strongly enough to make him

[1] W. James, *Principles of Psychology*, vol. i., p. 196.
[2] *Ibid.*, p. 330 *seqq.*, *The Sense of Personal Identity*.
[3] W. James, *The Will to Believe*, p. 84.

criticize the scientific mechanical conception of the world because the order which it gives us cannot reveal any adequate spiritual and moral end.

Just as science cannot disturb moral reality, so it cannot oppose the hope of religious faith. " Belief (as measured by action) not only does and must continually outstrip scientific evidence, but there is a certain class of truths of whose reality belief is a factor as well as a confessor ; and as regards this class of truths, faith is not only licit and pertinent, but essential and indispensable." [1]   In other words, there are cases in which faith creates its own verification.   Here James's view apparently resembles that of the *Critique of Pure Reason*, the creation of the content through the form.   But in reality this is the beginning of the catastrophe of James's thought.   It is not the universality of faith with which he is concerned, but the particular experience ; that verification which faith creates for itself is therefore the first step towards spiritualism and occultism ; a road which becomes for James in his last years a veritable precipice.

Lastly, his book on *Pragmatism* marks the complete decline of his mental faculties, the final impotence of his thought.   Here the pragmatist method is represented as a method of avoiding metaphysical discussions, or, better, of solving every problem by caprice.   Is the world one or many ?   It is one if we look at it in one way, many if we look at it in another.   Let us say, then, that it is at the same time one and many, and let us live in peace.   Must we decide between theism and materialism ?   The past does not tell us anything in favour of either the one or the other.   Let us look within us.   The world of materialism closes in tragedy and gloom : that of theism legitimizes our sublimest hopes.   Is this latter in our interest ?   If so, let us accept it.[2] This is magnificent reasoning ; and the whole book is strewn with similar gems of logic.   Truth is reduced to an economic fact, a form of wealth, a " property " of our ideas ; thought has an exchange value like that of a bank-note which " passes " so long as nobody rejects it ; and so on through a series of ineptitudes that bring disgrace on the name of philosophy.

[1] W. James, *The Will to Believe*, p. 96.
[2] W. James, *Pragmatism*, New York, 1907, pp. 13, 101, 103, 207.

Of the pragmatist school the most serious member is
Dewey, who inclines towards a compromise between pragmatism and the logic of Lotze. He succeeds in grasping
the distinction between the empirical origin of ideas and
their validity ; and realizes the inadequacy of Lotze's view
that logical forms are valid only within the process of thought
and are a mere movement of our minds, observing with
justice that the problem of validity appears as the problem
of the relation between the act of thought and its own
product.[1] But Dewey misconceives the problem of knowledge when he says that it should run, not " How can we
know in general ? " but, " How can we know here and now ? "
He fails to observe that " here and now " is the same thing
as knowing here and now ; that is to say, " here and now "
are just elements in knowledge which his way of putting
the problem would make into the whole of knowledge.

We have a further exposition of pragmatism in Schiller's
humanism. If it is Protagoras' " man " who measures
truth and falsehood, if the merely human interest is the only
one that counts, pragmatism can also be called humanism.
The name is the only novelty here ; under the new name
Schiller develops the same theory of the functional and
instrumental nature of truth, the identification of the true
and the false with the expedient and the inexpedient, and
so on. He also offers us a final vision of reality, which has
an orientation (he says) towards none other than Hegel. If
reality is something which, at any rate for our consciousness,
develops *pari passu* with the construction of truth, and consequently develops in a continual transition from one truth
to another, we have here in a nutshell the scheme of the
phenomenology.[2] Here the caricature of idealism, which
can be traced throughout the whole of Schiller's work, is
complete.

§ 8. Logistic.

Mathematical logic is another offshoot of empiricism.
Like many other semi-philosophies with a dash of science

[1] J. Dewey, *Studies in Logical Theory*, Chicago, 1909, p. 77.
[2] F. C. S. Schiller, *Studies in Humanism*, ch. xix. : *cf.* pp. 422–426.

in them, it has found numerous exponents of late years, of whom the most important is Russell.

In spite of all protests to the contrary, his fundamental principle is the same as that of formal logic, namely that thought is the *schema*, the *caput mortuum* of abstraction. When thought is thus impoverished and reduced to the empty and external form—form as it is understood in formalism—it becomes possible first to associate and finally to identify logic and mathematics,[1] and to express the principles of logic in mathematical terms. But it is clear that the only result is to render logic still more formalistic and empty, since it is deprived of the last remnant of thought and is reduced to the simplest expression of mechanism.

But from this highly abstract starting-point conclusions of far-reaching significance are drawn. Logic and mathematics are not completely identified, but logic is considered as the still more formal *schema* of objects, and mathematics as a mere advancement and specialization of logic. Hence it is claimed that Kant's transcendental æsthetic is confuted ; for, it is maintained, arithmetic and geometry do not require any recourse to intuition and do not rest on synthetic *a priori* principles, but are a series of formal deductions dependent on a definition whose logical consequences develop *ad infinitum*.[2] Thus Kant's great discovery of the synthetic character of mathematics is rejected, and Leibniz, who had founded these sciences on the principle of identity, is reinstated. It is not perceived that the mere analytical principle of identity cannot be the foundation of mathematics because it cannot explain the fundamental datum of mathematics, namely, the definition of quantity, which remains as an arbitrary and inexplicable assertion. Kant's principle had sought to eliminate just this irreducible datum, by resolving it in the creative synthesis of intuition. In fact, the principle of identity only serves to analyse mathematics regarded as already discovered and complete : we can only say that, given certain quantities, relations of equality and of inequality exist between them ; while what remains unexplained and inexplicable is the nature of the presupposition and of the process by which mathematics comes into being.   To explain this, we need much more than the mere principle of identity ; we need the synthetic function of the spirit.

§ 9. HODGSON'S CRITICAL EMPIRICISM.

An attempt to overcome the merely empiricist position and, without abandoning its principles, to satisfy the demands raised by Kant's philosophy was made by Hodgson.   But, as our criticism of neo-Kantianism and of German and French phenomenalism has by this time made clear, this is a road which leads nowhere.   In order to attain to the Kantian point of view we must completely renounce the empiricist position : either 'we penetrate to the heart of Kantianism, or we choose to hover on the surface of the Critical Philosophy and deceive ourselves into thinking that we are Kantians while in reality we are simply empiricists. Hodgson, in fact, is an empiricist, although reminiscences of his study of Kant still cling to him.

Like Renouvier and the other philosophers of his school, with whom we have already dealt, Hodgson reduces reality to the mere presence of the phenomenon to consciousness. His philosophy therefore does not attempt to be, and cannot be, anything else except an analysis of the datum of fact, and is incapable of understanding its genesis.   This incapacity is raised to the rank of a philosophical criterion.   The explanation (he says) of how consciousness is produced, of how sensations are combined with cognitions, is a matter with which metaphysics has no concern : metaphysics must simply accept facts as they are and analyse them into their simplest elements.[1]   Consciousness is treated as if it were a physical fact like motion, and could be subjected to the same kind of analysis.   Following out this line, Hodgson inevitably solidifies consciousness into hard fact : thought and objects are not empirically separate things, but two inseparable aspects of the same complex of phenomena.   He believes that he has got very far beyond naturalism, with its view of thought and reality as distinct elements, not realizing that to substitute for the doctrine of elements

[1] S. H. Hodgson, *Time and Space*, London, 1865, p. 31.

that of aspects is only to displace the error and to revive naturalism in a different form.

Indeed, the naturalism of consciousness is the more dangerous form, because it is harder to eliminate. The thought which transforms its own product, the fact of consciousness, into a substance and sees it as nature, opaque and dead, can never recognize itself in this dead fact. Hence Hodgson denies that any apperception, any reflection, is required in order to constitute the fact of consciousness. And this is quite consistent with his erroneous premiss. It is perfectly true that if you regard thought as that which has been thought, the " I think " is no longer there ; the act is not in the fact.[1] If metaphysics is the science which merely analyses the given, it can only bear witness to the absence of pure thought : while that metaphysic which could reveal the " I think "—and this means the metaphysic of the act, of the producing—has already been dismissed by Hodgson.

Empiricism is the necessary result. Reality is the fact of consciousness within the forms of space and time ; the understanding and the reason are reduced to mere modes of time and of space, applied to perceptions ; the concept, instead of being the creator of reality, is a merely economical presentment of the given, the command issued by action to consciousness to take the shortest way in the representation of relations,[2] and other equally empiricist conclusions. The moral of this result is that the attempt to reach Kant, starting from empiricism, is doomed to failure.

[1] *Time and Space*, p. 73.   [2] *Ibid.*, pp. 296, 308, 309.

CHAPTER II

IDEALISM

§ I. THE NEO-HEGELIAN MOVEMENT.

DURING the period when empiricism and naturalism were
at their height, there arose in English philosophy, in complete
antithesis to them, an idealistic conception of life and thought.
In a very short time this had passed through all the stages
of its development and had placed itself on a level with any
other speculative movement in Europe.

We must frankly confess that we have not satisfactorily
accounted to ourselves for the rise of this new philosophy.
We find a difficulty in understanding how, without an adequate training in Kant, England acquired such a firm grasp
of the new problems, and adapted herself so naturally and
so confidently to a movement of thought which seemed
alien to her type of intellect. It is not a matter of a few
isolated thinkers, but of a whole host ; nor is it a matter of
a simple repetition of foreign ideas, but of an absolutely
original movement which receives its initiative from Hegel,
but transforms his doctrine radically and stamps it unmistakably with the seal of the English intellect.

Still, in its general characteristics we can say that
the new idealism is connected with the spiritual development represented by the names of Coleridge, Wordsworth,
Carlyle, Ruskin and others. Art was conscious of the new
demands of thought before philosophy. But the art of
Coleridge and Carlyle was itself a philosophy with a definite
orientation towards history, rich in elements from Fichte
and Schelling, and particularly sensitive to the dignity and
nobility of life, a fact which marked its profound divergence
from the Philistine utilitarianism of the empiricists.

Moreover, the preoccupation with theological studies—always lively in a religious race like the English, and now stimulated to the point of exasperation by the current agnosticism—supplied another motive towards the development of the new idealism. We shall see idealism in constant conflict with the agnostic thought which makes of God a residual or marginal existence (to use Wallace's happy expression), and constantly striving to realize God in the fullness of reality.

Its religious character is an essential feature of English idealism and the guiding principle of its development. In a religious intuition of the world it finds not only its stimulus but also its whole basis in its acute and insistent attack on empiricism and in the demand for an ever greater concreteness.

Stirling was the first English thinker to attempt a scientific exposition of Idealism as distinct from the imaginative expositions of his predecessors. His chief work bears the suggestive title *The Secret of Hegel*. But the aim of the book is neither to solve a riddle nor to discover a master-key for all the doors of Hegelian speculation. The secret of Hegel is the history of the formation of Hegel's thought ; and since the fundamental point in this history is the Kantian philosophy, the secret of Hegel is Kant. Try really to understand Kant, and you will see that Hegel follows from him as a necessary consequence. A very simple secret, we might think. Yet those Hegelians have failed to grasp it, who occupy themselves solely with the external structure of the system and employ their dialectic upon the rigid concepts of the understanding, without realizing that the " being " from which the logic started was neither lead nor iron, but the pure thought which the three *Critiques* had freed from empirical experience. Neither is it understood by those who, though they move within the Kantian philosophy, oscillate between the poles of empiricism and naturalism and yet marvel that they fail to catch a glimpse of the necessity of Hegel, however much they strain their eyes. For we cannot discover Hegel's secret by merely formulating his Kantian origin ; we must penetrate into and re-live the Kantian life of Hegel. Did Stirling really re-live it ?

He begins with a careful statement of the problem of Hegelianism. Just as Aristotle (with important assistance from Plato) made explicit the abstract universal which was implicit in Socrates, so Hegel, with the less important aid of Fichte and Schelling, made explicit the concrete universal which was implicit in Kant. The Kantian universal is apperception. This expresses my essential and innermost reality, and this not only as regards my subject but as regards my object. The object, in this philosophy, is simply the concrete realization of pure apperception through its forms of space and time and through the categories, and the empirical material is but its contingent " other." All that is permanent and universal in the object is derived from the universality of apperception : this then, together with its empirical " other," constitutes the universe. But according to idealism the " other " of apperception (the thing-in-itself) is itself apperception. Apperception, then, is the universe.[1]

Although it betrays some hesitation, this passage proves that Stirling has really understood Kant, because he has passed beyond Kant's position. To have perceived that the other of apperception is itself apperception is to have perceived in Kant the necessity for Hegel, i.e. the necessity of resolving the whole object into the actuality of thought, of denying the dual logic of being and of thought, of overcoming the Aristotelian dualism between the potential and the actual, which remains the last word of the Kantian philosophy, by demonstrating that the potential (the possible, the " other " of apperception) only exists in and for the actuality of apperception. Kant himself never reached this point : between the universality of thought and the particularity of sense Kant did not succeed in effecting a synthesis, because he did not appreciate at its true value the third term which alone could complete it : the singular, the subject. Hegel's great discovery is the concrete subject, in which the problem of Kant begins to find its solution.[2] Thus with Hegel logic becomes the genetic exposition of the true thing-in-itself, in opposition to the empty thing-in-itself of Kantianism.

[1] J. H. Stirling, *The Secret of Hegel*, Edinburgh, 1898, 2nd ed., p. 98.
[2] *Ibid.*, p. 134.

But Hegel's limit is Stirling's limit too. He gives a sufficiently acute interpretation of the Hegelian philosophy, but he goes no further ; and consequently fails to disclose the profound contradiction latent in the system. How is a philosophy of nature consistent with the principle that the other of apperception is itself apperception ? Yet Hegel, and following him Stirling, attempts to reconcile the two incompatible demands (thus losing the fruit of his discovery) with a realism which, although provisional, betrays nevertheless the dualism it has failed to overcome and the presence of the remnants of the thing-in-itself. Stirling realizes, it is true, the deficiency of the Hegelian construction, but not the radical falsity of the problem, and waits, like the early Hegelians, for someone to renew this construction on a more solid basis.

But the most characteristic part of Stirling's interpretation, and one that is typical of the whole English direction of thought, is to be found in the statement that the sole aim of the inquiries of Kant and Hegel was to restore the belief in God, the immortality of the soul and revealed religion. Hegel's greatness consists for Stirling in having discovered that Christianity is the only true revealed religion, in having rescued it no less from the contingency and externality of history than from the contradictions and discrepancies of the understanding and from the vulgarity of material sensation, and in having restored it to a spiritual reality.[1] This is the germ of a whole theological school of Hegelian exegesis, whose most original and independent exponents end by Platonizing Hegel, and neglecting the gulf which lies between Hegel's dialectic and that of Plato. But we shall see how, from the very womb of theology and from the concrete study of the history of religion, new impulses arise which are far more in accord with the spirit of Hegelianism.

For the moment we have still to speak of some expositors of Hegel, who, less loyal to the external structure of the system, have perhaps succeeded more effectively than Stirling in acclimatizing the main principles of Hegel's speculation to the life of English thought.

Although Stirling confined himself to a commentary on

_____
[1] *Op. cit.*, p. 721.

the *Logic,* he never lost sight of the philosophy of his mother-country, and did not fail to deal his compatriots, the empiricists, and particularly Hamilton, some shrewd blows.   When it is contrasted with empiricism the originality and power of the Hegelian philosophy is thrown into even stronger relief.   Green's introduction to Hume marked the beginning of definite opposition to the empiricist tendency.   And Wallace's *Prolegomena to Hegel* concentrated its critical efforts against the psychological experience in which Mill had found the key to philosophical method.   Wallace realized quite clearly the identity of empiricism and naturalism, which we pointed out when speaking of Mill and Spencer.   The idea or representation, he says, is under psychical form exactly equivalent to the undigested and passively accepted thing to which we give the title of physical or external. It is in the realm of ideas what the thing is in reality : it is, in brief, the crude object, considered not as existing but as a state of consciousness, and constitutes a reduplication in inner space of the thing in outer space.[1]

The fundamental error of empiricism and naturalism consists in isolating from the beginning nature and thought, while neither thought nor the so-called external world are self-subsistent existences.   Thought does not come forth to conquer the world, nor is the world waiting prepared to accept thought.   Thought and the world, the subject and the object, are equally the results of a process.   In proportion as the intellect grows, the limits of the external world extend also.   The difficulty of passing from the world of being to that of thought is a difficulty created by ourselves as a result of analysing mere thought and mere being.   The great merit of Hegel, on the other hand, lies in having demonstrated that the real aim of philosophy is God, the absolute, as a synthetic unity from which the external world and the ego have issued by differentiation and in which they return to unity.[2]

The critical acuteness and at the same time the analytical bent of English idealism are seen very clearly when it con-

[1] W. Wallace, *Prolegomena to the Study of Hegel's Philosophy*, Oxford, 1894, 2nd ed., p. 459.
[2] *Ibid.*, pp. 269, 271.

fronts the facts of which empiricism is so confident, and shows how they resolve themselves into relations. It is here that the neo-Hegelian philosophy attains its maximum of efficiency and demonstrates its absolute superiority over empiricism. But, on the other hand, even here the intellectualist character of this philosophy is revealed. For, by neutralizing the differences of sense in the identity of thought (which, as mere identity, is thought as a product rather than thought as a process), it ends by falling into the opposite error to that of empiricism, and thus fails to attain to that view of the concreteness of knowledge which constitutes Hegel's great discovery.

And at the same time its excessively analytical character is an obstacle in the way of its envisaging a body of problems as a whole. For instance, Wallace's book which we have just mentioned, though rich in acute observations on particular points, presents no synthetic view, and gives the impression of being fragmentary and disconnected.

Caird's small volume on Hegel, on the other hand, is far more organic. He sketches with admirable truth and clearness the respective positions of Kant and Hegel, and shows the necessity for the transition from the logic of essence, the furthest point reached by the Kantian analytic, to the logic of the concept. This latter reveals the profounder significance of the categories, which in Kant had become opaque to themselves, and for the first time places Kant's " Copernican revolution " in its true light.

The most attractive thing about Caird is his lively sense of the problems which he is discussing ; and if he does not succeed in assuming a very definite attitude towards the Hegelian logic, yet the intimate correlation in which he conceives the problems of logic and ethics shows that he has overcome the abstract logic of the first Hegelians and is on the road towards absolute spiritualism. As we shall see later on, Caird only assumes a more definite position in his studies in the history of religion.

So far, English idealism is still in its infancy ; but already, in its sustained effort to grasp Hegel, English thought has begun to grasp itself and to assume an attitude of its own. Within the Hegelian movement itself two opposing schools spring up, each of which confers upon Hegel its own special point of view. One school takes its inspiration from the doctrine of the absolute spirit, which it detaches from its context in the system and, led on by theological interests, finally interprets Hegelianism as a kind of Platonism. The other, more in conformity with the spirit of the Hegelian philosophy, discovers the living sources of the system in the *Phenomenology*. The first, confining itself more and more within the motionless and eternal idea, makes the dialectic merely a transitional process of thought in the pursuit of that idea, and thereby transforms it into a series of necessary errors which thought must overcome in order to attain the truth. Following this course, it ends by losing sight of the essential principle of the Hegelian philosophy. The second, taking its cue from the *Phenomenology*, displays a much more lively appreciation of the dialectic, and understands that the absoluteness of the idea is not an end outside the process of the spirit but inheres in the process itself. Among the interpreters of Hegel, the first school is represented by MacTaggart, the second by Baillie. The latter is also the author of a doctrine inspired by the Hegelian *Phenomenology*, and we shall refer to him in due course ; for the moment we will turn our attention to MacTaggart.

MacTaggart puts forward a Platonistic interpretation of Hegel which is very closely connected with Green's philosophy. Yet, if only in order to understand Green clearly, we must anticipate him with an exposition of MacTaggart's doctrine. In this case the usual order is reversed : the son must explain the father's personality. This is because the published works of Green bear on the face of them no relation to Hegel ; but yet, although we have no documentary evidence for it, we can argue with confidence from his actual conclusions that there must have taken place in Green's mind a complete process of dissolution of Hegelianism.[1] Now MacTaggart's doctrine is inspired by that of Green, and represents exactly this process of the dissolution of Hegelianism. Consequently, although it is later in point of time, it can serve to indicate

[1] The author's hypothesis is confirmed by the testimony of Sidgwick in his essay on *The Philosophy of T. H. Green* in *Mind*, N.S. 37.—TRS.

the passage from Hegel to Green.   There is therefore nothing arbitrary in our anticipation.

According to MacTaggart, the dialectic does not represent adequately the nature of pure thought, but only the inevitable course which our minds are constrained to take when they aim at pure thought.   The ultimate reality of things cannot therefore be considered as a process : it is an eternal motionless state to which we attain by means of a process in which we are gradually freed from the imperfections of empirical experience.   It will be seen that this is a return to Plato ; and once this premiss is established every fresh development of it is merely a further step towards Plato.   First and foremost, how can the eternity of the idea be reconciled with the process of the mind ?   Only in one way.   If the process is viewed not as constructive but as reconstructive, i.e. as reproducing in the subject this reality which is given *ab æterno* in the eternally realized idea.[1]   Here MacTaggart, to be logical, ought to have asked himself what exactly is the nature of the idea in itself, and where it is to be found realized ; but he is unconscious of his Platonism and believes that he is sailing in Hegelian waters.

Now, assuming that the universe is eternally realized and perfect, and that there is no process except in our minds, the problem necessarily arises, how can thought ever reach reality, if reality is outside and above thought ?   What is it which impels thought to pass from one stage to another through a series of errors, which are just errors and no more, to absolute truth.   To say that the impetus comes from the very contradictions inherent in empirical experience is to say nothing ; or if it is to be given a meaning, this meaning is in direct opposition to MacTaggart's assumption ; for the contradiction can only be recognized as such, and therefore overcome, in so far as thought is always thought of the truth.   But where there is no immanent spirit of truth, where truth is conceived as outside the process of thought, the contradiction remains simply a bare contradiction, and all attempts to surmount it only render it more inexplicable.

But there is a further objection.   Once the dialectic is considered simply as the subjective process which the mind

[1] J. M. E. MacTaggart, *Studies in the Hegelian Dialectic*, Cambridge, 1896.

goes through in its search for truth, it forgoes all spontaneity, all its self-creative character, and requires a " given " on which to work. Thus MacTaggart is compelled to admit the existence of the given, the crude fact which thought must elaborate and rationalize. What this " given " is, how it can be resolved in thought if it is not thought— these are problems which date back to a period considerably antecedent to Hegel.

With such premisses, what possible significance can be attached to MacTaggart's statement that the one reality is the spirit, and that in the concreteness of the spirit the abstractness of logic is resolved ?[1] Apart from the actuality of thought, that is to say apart from the dialectic, the subjectivity of the spirit vanishes and only the Platonic idea remains. Starting from Hegel, but lacking a real grasp of his doctrine, MacTaggart ends unknowingly with Plato.

§ 2. THE HEGELIAN RIGHT : GREEN.

This same process of dissolution took place in the mind of Green. But Green is a thinker of greater stability, who does not so easily fall foul of history. His criticism of Hume, whose inadequacy he has really perceived, saves him from MacTaggart's pitfall. Nevertheless, his tendency is always the same as MacTaggart's. The fundamental idea of Green's philosophy, which he reiterated in every key, is as follows : Experience or knowledge is a process, a changing ; but this necessitates, as a condition of its being such, the existence, throughout the various phases of that which changes, of a consciousness which does not itself change, but remains one and the same. For example, we notice that things change in time, and we are accustomed to consider this change as something intelligible in itself alone : but if there were not a changeless consciousness present equally in every phase, all change would be inconceivable. Time, therefore, presupposes something timeless : and in general, all nature presupposes a principle which, just because it renders nature possible, is not itself nature.

This is simply the Kantian theory of pure apperception :

[1] *Op. cit.*, pp. 29, 75.

without synthetic apperceptive unity, no variety is possible. But what is this synthetic unity ?   On this point Kant did not see clearly : the categories, which were for him the very transparency of reality, became opaque to themselves, and the *a priori* synthesis remained the ultimate limit of his speculation rather than the fruitful principle of a new development. Green is in the same position. He understands that it is consciousness which renders nature possible, but he never explains consciousness itself. Bolder than Kant, he maintains that this identical and eternal consciousness is the spirit, is God ; but he does not develop this idea, and he ultimately ends by crystallizing the spirit into something immobile and abstractly eternal, something, that is to say, which does not create itself but is realized *ab æterno*. The origin of this error is as follows : After explaining that succession in time is impossible without a consciousness which is identical throughout the various moments, he predicates of this consciousness exactly the opposite quality to that of succession, namely eternal presence to itself ; after explaining that movement presupposes a principle of unity, he predicates of this principle the quality of immobility.   And he does not understand that he is thus committing the very error which he is criticizing. For immobility is a natural fact belonging to the same category as movement ; and in the same way identity at different times is merely correlative to change in time.   This fallacy is even more evident in MacTaggart than in Green : both of them crystallize thought while they think that they are freeing it from the contingency of natural facts.   But in this way the relation between thought and its object becomes inconceivable ; for how can the motionless produce movement and the eternal produce time ?   The reason for this inconceivability is more simple than might be supposed : it is that thought itself is reduced to the position of its own object, hardened into a product : how then can it produce anything when it is no longer conceived in its actuality ?   Bradley's scepticism takes its initiative, as we shall see, from this point.

It was Green's illusion that he could remain in Kant's half-way house to idealism and at the same time succeed where Kant failed, in defining the nature of the common

principle. All he did in reality was to change the signs
of the determinations of empirical fact and apply them to
thought, to the spirit. The spirit accordingly, in spite of
its apparent richness, remains a mere formal identity
which does not explain reality; or rather, which explains the regress from the conditioned to the condition,
from diversity to unity, but does not explain the progress,
the differentiation of the unity; it resolves, in short, but
does not create. And it does not create because it is already
rendered motionless and transformed into nature, divine
indeed, but still nature.

This becomes still clearer when we ask how Green conceives the relation between thought and sensation. The
simple sensation, he rightly says, is a fiction, like the atom
of physics. No sooner do we attempt to isolate this sensation than it eludes us, or rather loses its character as a
sensation and is resolved into a thought-relation. Sensation and thought are therefore indistinguishable. It is the
same world of experience which considered as a manifold
object may be called feeling, and considered as the subject
presenting such an object to itself may be called thought.[1]
This is pure intellectualism. Sensation has disappeared in
logical thought; and the distinction between sensation and
thought is no longer inherent in the unique act of thought,
which is unity differentiating itself, but in the abstract points
of view which fall outside the act of thought and are therefore
doubly inconceivable.

And so, with the denial of the creative process of knowledge
and the solidification of reality in the eternally realized
spirit, with the negation of the world in the empty identity
of thought, Hegelianism is dissipated and we stand on the
edge of neo-Kantianism.

Green's ethical theory is merely a replica of his logic
with the terms changed. Just as consciousness is distinct
from impression, so it is distinct from impulses : and just
as pure sensation is impossible, so the crude animal impulse
is impossible. The agent is not impelled *a tergo* by his
impulse, but in so far as he acts from the consciousness of
it he transforms it into a motive, a desire, i.e. into a spiritual

[1] T. H. Green, *Prolegomena to Ethics*, Oxford, 1884, 2nd ed., pp. 48, 51.

fact. Action consequently is not a natural fact, but implies the presence of a principle which is not nature ; the consciousness, the moral nature, of the agent.

Just as nature points to that which transcends it and is the condition of its being, so impulses, instincts, passions, point to a moral good. This is present to the eternal consciousness, and human development aims at the realization of the idea. In considering this process we must bear in mind the fact that the human capacities which are realized in time are realized eternally in the consciousness of the eternal mind, and that the goal of the evolutionary process must be an actual fulfilment of the capacities presupposed by the process. Now this cannot be an infinite process, a process without completion or conclusion ; it must have an end, which represents a state of existence not itself temporal, but comprised in the eternal mind. Yet such a state must not be held to imply the extinction of self-conscious personality : on the contrary, it must represent its complete integration. The solution of the problem is that this state can only be realized in society and still more fully in humanity, where the individual personality is integrated without being extinguished.

This brings out more clearly than ever the Platonistic character of Green's argument, and accentuates the discrepancy between the moral development of man and the eternal realization of the good in the divine mind. These two demands cannot be reconciled, because if the good is, in Platonic fashion, given *ab æterno*, all human development becomes impossible, once that which ought to be its stimulus is made to fall completely outside it.

§ 3. Bradley.

Green's philosophy conceals but does not resolve the antinomy between the absolute and the contingent, the spirit and nature. Confined within the empty identity of mind, it destroys, swallows up and neutralizes the variety of time and of sensible experience : but no sooner do we wish to pass from the regress to progress than it becomes inconceivable how movement can be produced from the motionless or time from the timeless. The concept of relation which ought to represent the unity of thought and of feeling only effects a further separation. Thought, instead of realizing the truth of feeling, destroys it, and leaves more incomprehensible than ever the manner of the passage from the identity and eternity of the spirit to the variety and contingency of the sensible world.

This antinomy reappears in an aggravated form in Bradley, as a dualism between reality and appearance. With Green he maintains that the true reality is the spirit, one and self-identical ; but he perceives at the same time that this conception does not provide any means of passing to the world of experience. This therefore becomes for him a world of illusion, of appearance. Between the eternal and the temporal, the absolute and the contingent, mediation is impossible : the concept of relation which was intended by Green to hold together the two terms is rejected by Bradley, since a relation between heterogeneous terms appears to him inconceivable. Bradley, indeed, concentrates the forces of his criticism upon the concept of relation ; and so it comes about that Hegel's philosophy, which is *par excellence* the philosophy of relation, is transformed in the Hegelian school into a philosophy of the unrelated. The criterion of truth is transformed into the criterion of error.

What does Bradley mean by appearance ? We can only understand it as the antithesis to reality. We think of reality as a totality complete in itself and thus individual, in which existence and content are identical. Appearance, on the other hand, is disagreement between existence and content. Now all that we experience is really appearance. We believe that we individualize an object fully by saying, it is. But we are mistaken, because when we wish to indicate the content of this " being," the " what " of this " is," we have to admit that this content transcends this particular " being " : so far from individualizing it, it resolves it into another. We believed we had grasped our object, and lo ! it vanishes before our eyes. Our experience is experience of finite things : now every finite thing presents the contradiction that it is not only finite, confined within itself, but also a relation to another. Its " is " is found in contradiction with its "what." Hence no object of experience is self-determined and self-contained, every one is infected with externality, relation : every finite is self-transcendent, alienated from itself and passing away from itself towards another existence. The finite as such cannot, then, be reality ; it is mere appearance.[1]

In this criticism of the concept of relation Bradley displays his immense dialectical penetration, but as the principle on which he develops the dialectic is false, it borders on sophistry. And in fact, what Bradley considers a sign of demerit in experience, is on the contrary a sign of merit. To have demonstrated the inconsistency of the pure finite and to have shown how this resolves itself into its opposite is the beginning of the dialectic, that is to say of the recognition that reality is to be found in the very process of the finite. But Bradley has already created for himself an absolute in the manner of the scholastics, eternal, motionless, and he therefore sees in the movement of pure thought through which the finite is negated as such, the mark of appearance.

But appearance is the appearance of something, which is not itself appearance, that is to say of an absolute : and lo ! after having rejected " relation," Bradley is constrained to readmit it. But since by now he has burnt his boats, the readmission does not save the situation ; it only leads to absurdities. The absolute is motionless, yet movement is an appearance of the absolute ; the absolute has no history, yet it contains in itself infinite histories ; experience is imperfect, yet it is an appearance of the perfect. At times one almost feels as if Bradley were wilfully blind. He goes so far as to recognize that unless it " appeared " the absolute would be nothing ; but, as he has denied the concept of relation, he fails to see that the true absolute is not this phantom of a reality in itself, motionless and perfect (for if it requires to appear it is not already perfect), but is appearance itself, in so far as it is the absolute process of appearing, the phenomenalization of the absolute. In short, Bradley has created for himself two abstractions, a mere appearance and a mere absolute. He sees the inconsistency of both, in that each necessitates the other :

[1] F. H. Bradley, *Appearance and Reality*, London, 1902, 3rd ed., p. 486.

yet he cannot overcome the double abstraction, because by denying the reality of relations he has thrown away his only hope of doing so.

Like Green's Spirit and MacTaggart's Idea, Bradley's Absolute is the old naturalistic abstraction transported into the field of thought and with the signs changed. True, it is the immutable as opposed to the mutable, but it has the same characteristics. This idealism is an idealism cut in half. It does not discover any new categories, but only criticizes the old ; and owing to the inadequacy of its criticism finishes by reintroducing them with a change of sign. Bradley's absolute is an absolute which explains nothing, but needs itself to be explained by the appearance, the phenomenon ; it is intended to be the *individuum omnimodo determinatum*, and yet it is indetermination itself ; it is in fact an absolute of straw.

But the strangest thing is that after having denied the concreteness of relation and reduced this to a mere appearance, Bradley finds himself compelled to affirm that if the absolute is to mean anything, it must stand in relation to appearance ; and he ends by admitting that empirical reality (appearance) has grades in which it reveals its ever closer unity with the absolute. But this is a very strange unity : one which is both relation and not relation : it expresses all the in-determinateness characteristic of the Bradleian conception. And midway between an absolute which by itself is powerless and an appearance which is inconceivable if it is not the appearance of something, the unity of the two, which ought in Bradley's conception to constitute the true centre of the world, only sums up in itself the double void and the double inconsistency.

§ 4. THE HISTORY OF RELIGIONS.

In the school of T. H. Green, Hegelianism is displaced in favour of a Platonistic point of view. This leads to a combination of two contradictory conceptions which finally issues in Bradley's veiled scepticism. But there are certain other thinkers in whom Hegelianism is preserved in a much purer form. For although they derive their inspiration from theology, yet their studies in the history of religion have served to nourish and stimulate their lively sense of spiritual reality ; and their grasp on the principle of development in religious life has saved them, if not altogether, at any rate in part, from lapsing into Platonism. As among the most notable representatives of this school we may mention Wallace and Caird.

But before them the idea of the development of religion was formulated with great clearness by a writer who has no apparent connection with the Hegelian philosophy, a writer whom the recent history of modernism has thrown into great prominence : namely, Cardinal Newman. The points of affinity between the Hegelian school and Newman are of very great significance to us, all the more since the former stands for Anglicanism and the latter for Catholicism. They mark the point at which the divergencies of creed have become so slight as almost to be merged in the unity of philosophical thought.

Newman's autobiography sets before us the stormy history of his conversion from Anglicanism to the Catholic faith. The impetus to conversion came from the idea of the development of religion, which forced itself upon him with increasing clearness and depth, and is incompatible with the principles of Anglicanism.

Anglicanism shares with the other forms of Protestantism a contempt for history and an abstract way of conceiving the relations between man and the Deity. The Protestant theology of England in the nineteenth century is completely summed up in the agnosticism of the school of Hamilton and Mansel, which reduces the Deity to an incomprehensible principle outside human reality, and in the dualism of Martineau and his school, which, inspired by neo-Kantianism, moves between the two poles of phenomenal and noumenal reality and attempts to combat agnosticism by finding in the principle of causation a passage from the one extreme to the other : a historical curiosity, like a hundred other theories which fill the museums of Kantianism.

Newman's historicism is the direct opposite of the Anglican attitude. For him the truth of religion cannot be separated from its history : the central idea of Christianity cannot be understood apart from its development. In the age-long effort to illuminate and focus the different aspects of its idea, the great truth of Christianity, whose centre is the Incarnation, achieves its own germination and grows by degrees to maturity. But this process is a real development ; for all the different aspects whose union determines the final shape of the idea really belong to the idea : they are not accretions from without, but expansions from within. Those who believe that Christianity was purer and greater at its beginning are deceived. " It is indeed sometimes said that the stream is clearest near the spring. Whatever use may fairly be made of this image, it does not apply to the history of a philosophy or a sect, which on the contrary is more equable and purer and stronger when its bed has become deep and broad and full." In early times religion wavers in uncertainty : at length it strikes out in one definite direction and enters upon strange territory : " points of controversy alter its bearing ; parties rise and fall about it ; dangers and hopes appear in new relations, and old principles reappear under new forms ; it changes with them in order to remain the same. In a higher world it is otherwise ; but here below, to live is to change, and to be perfect is to have changed often." [1]

But, as we have already seen in the modernists, so in their spiritual father Newman, side by side with this genuinely immanentist tendency there persists a Platonistic strain which falsifies or at least attenuates the idea of development. Thus Newman said that development in time is necessary for the comprehension of great ideas only because the finite understandings of men cannot succeed in comprehending them all at once and exhausting their fruitfulness. Here inexhaustibility is no longer a quality of the idea regarded as development, but of the idea existing once for all ; a principle which is in open contradiction with that of development, because it affirms in the same breath that reality is ready-made and that it is in the making.

And, at bottom, the final ambiguity of this position is expressed by a passage in which Brémond summarizes Newman's thought. " The image of an idea," he says, " changes

[1] Newman, *The Development of Christian Doctrine*, 1878, 3rd ed., pp. 38, 40.

without this idea necessarily changing with it. And thus the perseverance of type is a guarantee which is more secure, in proportion as this perseverance is maintained in the midst of a greater number of variations." One cannot help asking, what is it which remains truly identical amid variety ? Is it the human spirit or the idea which it conceives of God ? According to the doctrine of development, the identity which persists in difference is the spirit : the motionless idea of God does not explain the variety ; on the contrary, it suppresses it. Newman and the modernists play on this ambiguity, and by arbitrarily displacing the subject at a certain point believe that they can elude the absolute immanentism from which they started.

The view of dogma which Newman expressed is in many ways an anticipation of that which we have already seen developed by French modernism. In both an attempt is made to fuse the letter and the spirit and to revivify the one by means of the other. The contradiction between the divine and the human is repugnant to the concrete vision of modernism. This characteristic reappears in Tyrrel, who distinguishes between a purely external religion consisting of formulæ and ritual and a purely internal religion which refuses to have any connection with the concrete manifestations of life, and proceeds to point out that each is an abstraction which the true religion tries to avoid. " Just as man's soul fashions to itself a body to complete its otherwise imperfect spiritual nature, so man's thoughts and theories and abstract ideas must always fix and embody themselves in some concrete form that appeals to the imagination and the senses, in some story or myth or symbol or picture ; or at least in some form of words, by which the ideas may be caught and tied down to earth before they vanish into thin air." Hence the double character to be observed in all positive religions, the external and the internal, the visible and the invisible. The extremer forms of Protestantism, which demand a purely philosophical and spiritual religion discarding all external and imaginative expression, are violently unnatural and foredoomed to failure.

But the outward and visible expression ought to let itself be governed by the inward truth, not perverting or

obscuring it, " but suffering it to shine through without
distortion, as light through pure crystal." Now, the religion
of the Incarnation is before all else an external religion,
approaching the soul from without : but this externality
cannot have any other aim or purpose than the development
of the internal religion of Christ. Such is the relation between
the Church visible and invisible : the religious individualism
which would deny all externality is false, for it is only in
association with others and by recognizing ourselves as part
of a living organism that we can really develop our own
nature aright. Such is the great principle embodied and
symbolized in the doctrine of the visible Church.[1]

This unity of the divine and the human, of the external
and the internal in concrete religion, which is a very different thing from theology, is also recognized by the Hegelian
school of Caird and Wallace : indeed, Tyrrel (like Loisy and
the other modernists) owes much to this school. According
to Edward Caird the living principle of religion is not to be
sought for in any one religious form, but in all religions,
considered as stages of a single process ; or better, in the
transitions of thought whereby one religion develops out of
another or asserts itself in conflict with it. But the search for
the animating principle ought to be conducted in the highest
religions rather than in the lowest. To find the quality
of the seed we must look at the tree. The development of
religion is not a mechanical process but a real development.
We must consider each stage not as the cause of that which
follows it, but as the imperfect expression of a principle
more completely manifested in the succeeding stage. In
the more elementary phenomena of life there is a unity which
is not exhausted in them, a unity which grows by a progressive
subordination of its environment to itself, and maintains its
own self-identity while enlarging its sphere of manifestation.

Now, the history of religion is a dialectical process. And
as religion involves the whole of conscious life, the actualiza-
tion of religion can only emphasize the moments already
present in consciousness, namely objectivity, subjectivity,
and the unity of both in the synthesis in which they find

[1] G. Tyrrel, *External Religion ; Its Use and Abuse*, London, 1899, pp. 24,
25, 27, 41, 65, 72, 73, 103.

their truth. Neither Spencer nor Max Müller understood
the idea of this cycle. They conceived the infinite as a mere
" beyond " of the finite, a mere negation of limit : that is
to say, the false infinite criticized by Hegel. Yet Descartes
had long ago remarked, in the *Meditations*, that we do not
think the infinite as a mere negation of the finite : that the
infinite in fact contains a more positive reality than the finite.
In conceiving the false infinite, on the other hand, we simply
hypostatize a moment in the dialectic of consciousness,
forgetting that the synthesis, the concrete God, is not a
posterius over against the various moments, but a *prius* :
that is to say the presupposition and at the same time the
end of the process. God or the Infinite is the presupposition
of all our rational life, and yet the knowledge of God is the
final end at which it aims.[1]

Here, in the attempt to justify his theism, Caird really
misrepresents the significance of the dialectic. A close examination will show that the terms of the dialectic are no
longer three but have become four. The presupposition and
the end of the process are both called by the name " God,"
but they are in reality not identical : one is the *ratio essendi*,
the other the *ratio cognoscendi*. This equivocation, in fact,
upsets the whole of Caird's procedure, because unless the
beginning and end of the movement are identical the cycle
does not close and there is no process : if the third term is
ambiguous, the unity without which there can be no variety
does not exist. It is a note out of tune in the dialectical
scale, which a trained ear can hardly fail to notice—significant of the conflict between the spirit of the dialectic and the
demands of orthodox theism.

But this *quaternio terminorum* is no more than a note out
of tune, which does not affect Caird's system as a whole
His grasp on the triple character of the dialectical process
is really quite secure ; and it is this that enables him to give
a very penetrating interpretation of positive religion. To
the assertion of the object, of the subject, and of the synthesis
correspond three forms of religion. The first, the lowest, is
the religion of the object. God is here represented as the

---

[1] E. Caird, *The Evolution of Religion*, Glasgow, 1899, 3rd ed., vol. i.
pp. 48, 65, 100, 146.

external object of perception. Such a religion is essentially polytheistic ; its logical conclusion is pantheism, which at the same time marks the point at which it dissolves through its very abstractness. The second stage is the religion of subjectivity, represented by the Jewish religion. Here the mind, no longer entirely absorbed in the object, returns upon itself and discovers in itself the principle which at once underlies and transcends all objective experience. But the supreme integration of the two moments is the religion of the spirit, the Christian religion : this carries the consciousness of God to its true form, as the consciousness of a unity which persists throughout difference, and resists the temptation of regarding God as a universality that simply abolishes difference. It brings the consciousness of the finite to a perfect unity with the consciousness of the infinite, and reconciles the Judaic idea of the transcendence of God with the pantheistic idea of His immanence. The idea of the distinction between man and God is not abolished, but the distinction does not annul the unity of the terms. God, conceived as the divine spirit, is above the distinction of subject and object and all other qualities ; and is the presupposition and the goal, the beginning and the end, of our finite existences. The error and illusion of our ordinary consciousness is that of taking the finite for the true infinite, and therefore of considering the world as a collection of independent existences which do not realize the unity presupposed in them all—the unity of all finite objects with one another, and their unity with the mind which knows them.[1]

The concrete unity of the world in the religion of the spirit : this is the centre of the neo-Hegelian speculation. For Wallace, too, the great fact which emerges from the life of Christ is the unification of God and of man, the discovery that the supernatural is in the natural, the spiritual life in the physical. The incarnation of Christ is thus understood not as a mere temporal fact, but as the eternal truth of human life and history,[2] an idea which we find repeated in French modernism.

[1] *Op. cit.*, vol. ii. pp. 54, 85, 160, 161.
[2] W. Wallace, *Lectures and Essays on Natural Theology and Ethics*, Oxford, 1898, p. 91.

The development of this principle leads to an ever increasing emphasis on the reciprocity of the divine and the human. If it is true that God creates man in His image, it is no less true that man re-creates God in his own.   But does Wallace attain to the conception that this re-creation is itself a creation, and that there is not a double act of creation, but one alone ? He sees it, but he does not clearly grasp it : theism and idealism are once more at cross-purposes, and he oscillates in perplexity first in the one direction and then in the other, unable to make up his mind which position to adopt.   In general, we may say that the tenor of his mind is theistic, with a certain leaning towards mysticism.   For no sooner has he asserted the concept of reciprocity, in which the transcendence of the divine was on the point of being resolved, than he feels it necessary to say that God transcends this reciprocity, is a more than personal reality : here the categories of thought are thrust aside, and we enter into the arbitrary domain of mysticism.

Yet on the whole, with its strong orientation towards history, this tendency of thought stands out in sufficiently broad contrast with that of Green : although they both show theistic proclivities, yet here the theism is only the residuum of the procedure ; it serves only to indicate the failure to drive the dialectical method home ; while in Green, who has definitely rejected the dialectic, it forms the centre of the system.

It is important also to observe how the movements of Catholicism and Hegelianism in England as in France travel along converging lines ; though in England the convergence takes place not in the field of confessional religion but in that of philosophical reflection upon religion ; that is to say, in the field of philosophy itself.

§ 5. The Hegelian Left.

The immanentist and dialectical tendency is developed further by a school which I have referred to as the Hegelian Left, not because it has any connection with the German school called by that name, but because it constitutes a decisive contrast to the Platonism of Green and MacTaggart, and is very much more in harmony with the spirit of the Hegelian philosophy.

We have already remarked on this schism in the Hegelian movement. The one school solidifies the idea into a motionless, crystallized entity ; the other emphasizes the dialectic, the phenomenology, and conceives the idea in the actuality of its process. The chief representatives of this latter movement are in England Baillie, in America Royce. The latter, who has no connection with Baillie and is the more original thinker, is the most important figure in modern Anglo-American philosophy.

Baillie, like Green, would conceive experience in its universality ; but unlike Green he regards the universal not as something *per se*, apart from the process of history, but as in this process ; or, more precisely, he regards this process as the way in which it appears. Thus in contrast with Green's emphasis on the eternal absolute mind, Baillie emphasizes the concept of concrete individuality. Just as we have already found Weber doing in France, so Baillie attempts to formulate a doctrine of absolute experience which eliminates the transcendence of the object. In so far as it is universality, it must be the experience of a conscious life ; in so far as it is unity, it must be the experience of a subject, of an absolute individuality. There is no experience which is not individualized. But at the same time it must be acknowledged that the mere historical individual, as such, is a pure *ens rationis*, the creation of abstract thinking, and a creation of exactly the same kind as that of a universal experience *per se*. The truth of the two extremes is universal experience individualizing itself and individuality universalizing itself.[1]

All types and forms of experience contain these two moments : every form of experience is neither more nor less than a form of individualization. The history of experience is the history of self-conscious individuality, the history of the spirit. Everything which is experienced is individuality, but not all individuality of the same kind : the individuality of the perceptual life is one thing, that of the reflective

[1] J. B. Baillie, *An Outline of the Idealistic Construction of Experience*, London, 1906, pp. 25, 33, 34.

activity is another, and so on ; and the processes of individualization in the several cases differ accordingly.   In perception, it consists in bringing sensible qualities to a focus,
which is called a " thing " ; in reflection it consists in bringing the idea to a focus called " judgment."   Here we see
how Baillie's theory resembles that of the *Phenomenology*,
but his advance upon it consists in the fact that according
to him the whole of reality is included in this mental process
(in so far as the object is not the thing already created, but
the dialectical negative moment of the process, dissolving
at every moment and changing with every change of the
subject) : phenomenology is thus the whole of philosophy.

The development of the real thus becomes identical with
the development of the forms of knowledge : the mainspring
of the development is the ideality of knowledge, an ideality
not abstract, but actual in each form, implicit in the lowest,
explicit in the highest ; or rather, conceived as an impulse towards progressive explication.   Sense, understanding, reason are the phases of this process.   In reason the
synthesis of subject and object is completed, and thus is
eliminated the conflict between finite individuality and universal experience, between subjective reflection and objective experience, which are the abstract assertions of inferior
stages.   The distinction of the object in itself and the
object for us is a creation of the understanding : in reason,
on the other hand, the object is transparent to itself and this
self is at one with the world.   We no longer find any antithesis between the observing mind and the object observed :
we are in immediate contact with the object, and the object
itself forms the content of our life.   In the descriptive phases
of the reason we describe what the object is, not in the terms
of our individual life, but as it really is : the " in itself "
is identical with the " for us."   But this descriptive moment
is superseded by the explicative moment of reason : the
moment of laws.   These are operations of the active unity
of reason ; they do not regulate objects, they constitute
objects ; for they are phases of the world of reason, inside
the unity of which its objects fall.   They are not the
forms of reason, but its substance, and they are therefore
not forms of the object, but its reality.   And finally, in their

ultimate signification they do not represent what the reason finds or discovers, but they are expressions and developments of the content of the reason itself.

This is a principle of the utmost importance. We have found it in France in Lachelier and still more clearly in Weber. It means that the content is brought to the same degree of concreteness as the form : in absolute knowledge every relic of transcendence in the object disappears, and thought, science, reflecting on its own incessant quest of an apparently external reality, discovers the true reality in itself.

Yet although Baillie shows himself so far advanced towards the attainment of a doctrine of absolute immanence, or as Weber expresses it of absolute positivism, he nevertheless fails to escape entirely from these remnants of the abstract point of view which still linger in the Hegelian phenomenology. What, after all, is meant by this process of the grades of reality? It can hardly be supposed that the creative work of the spirit really takes a definite number of days for its completion, or that it moves from the abstract to the concrete. The spirit is always absolute concreteness : and its process can only be completed in and by the act of thought. In so far as I think, I create this process : in so far as I will to individualize by my thought the simplest object, the whole of reality must become the life of my life. It must be destroyed as sense, as perception, as understanding, in order to be rediscovered only in the intimacy of my act, and to regain there all the wealth which it seemed to have lost. But these moments in their succession are simply the analysis of this synthesis, the subsequent analysis of a primary synthesis : the act of my thought does not traverse them, in order to emerge from the process enriched, but creates them ; and it can only conceive them in their eternal succession, in their development out of one another, in so far as it creates them and does not find them already created. Reality is indeed that Bacchic orgy of which Hegel speaks, it is that daily death of which the Apostle tells us ; but this death is enacted in life and through life, this tumultuous orgy is nothing else than the translucent calm of thought itself, in so far as it only exists for the simple and indivisible act by which I think.

It is a noteworthy fact that the rise of theism in the neo-Hegelian philosophy is due to the failure to grasp the reality of the dialectical process as it exists in actual thinking. As soon as this happens, the successive moments of the process lose their cohesion and fall apart ; their internal unity is destroyed and they have to be held together by an external bond, a unity which falls outside them. This is what happens to Baillie and to other writers as well who, having lost their hold on a central unifying principle, have lapsed from idealism into monadism. Ward is one of these. He adopts a pluralistic view of the universe and then believes that he can qualify pluralism by means of theism ; failing to realize that if the unity is not there at the beginning it is no use attempting to introduce it by way of an afterthought. So far from filling the gap, theism simply conceals the lack of internal organization in the system.[1]

Even in Royce the same embarrassment recurs, but on a very much higher plane of thought.

§ 6. AMERICAN HEGELIANISM : ROYCE.

Baillie's attempt to construct a philosophy of absolute immanence was anticipated by Royce, who pierced into the heart of the Kantian philosophy and threw into sharp relief its fundamental weakness. The Kantian philosophy, as Royce explains it, is an arrested idealism. It attempts to substitute the concept of actual knowing for that of possible experience, but it does not entirely succeed ; and therefore it fails to individualize reality completely. It thus offers us an indeterminate conception of reality, a conception with which we cannot rest content. For reality, viewed as truth, must be something definite and determinate, something inclusive, no doubt, but exclusive too. But the abstract universal leaves its own content undifferentiated, and therefore does not penetrate the whole of reality : hence the necessity, in order to embrace the whole of reality, for individualizing the universal in such a way that the idea reveals itself as embodied in a content adequate to it, for which no

[1] J. Ward, *The Realm of Ends, or Pluralism and Theism*, Cambridge, 1911, pp. 131, 437.

other content could be substituted or need be sub-stituted.[1]

More specifically, the abstractness of the Kantian concept of a possible experience lies in the fact that this concept only determines the "what" of such an experience and not the "that," the actual existence. It determines the concept of the definite—of an object of thought distinct from thought—but not its being. Now, Royce's great merit consists in having grasped that the "that" of a possible experience is explained in the act of knowledge, in so far as this act expresses, as he says, the attempt of thought to concentrate the whole of reality into actuality. If we are asked to explain the existence of ideas and objects and the relation between them, we shall reply that to treat these concepts in this way is to move in a world of abstractions. We ought rather to maintain that being, truth, is a living concrete thing, a complete design, the empirical expression of a purpose, an individual whole which attains its end. To be such a life is to be real. Now, when I think of an object my idea is at once a fragment of this life, and—so far as it, relatively at least, achieves its end—a general type of it. As a fragment my idea seeks the other of itself, its complement; but, since it is one with its object, my idea in seeking for its other only seeks for the expression of its own will in an empirical and conscious life.[2]

In other words, reality is not Kant's merely possible experience, which leaves its object indeterminate, or at most determines the "what" and not the "that." Reality is the living individual act of knowledge in the widest sense, which also includes volition. This act is an incomplete, imperfect attempt to resolve and include in itself the whole of reality, to concentrate it, so to speak, into its own centre of action ; thus the possibility of experience is displaced by the absolute actuality of the spirit, conceived in its attempt to fulfil its own end and to express from its isolated and fragmentary point of view the life of the whole.

Of exactly *what* my object is, Royce continues, my idea

[1] J. Royce, *The World and the Individual*, New York, 1901, vol. i., pp. 260, 290, 296, 336, 337.
[2] *Ibid.*, pp. 357, 387.

only gives an incomplete definition ; *that* my object exists, is true in so far as the whole " what " of my object is empirically expressed in an individual life, which is my real world. Thus it is the " that " of true existence (that is, of the act of thought) which determines the " what " of experience, in so far as experience, being the expression of the fulfilment of my effort, is conceived in the same terms as my effort, as a conscious and individual totality.

This is a very important point. If for the " that " and the " what " we use the classical terms of existence and essence, it runs as follows : the essence of the object of thought is not the mere possibility of experience, it is the existential act of thought itself, in so far as this act summarizes from its individual point of view the whole of reality ; and conversely the existence of my object depends on the essence of the object itself in so far as this essence is expressed in my individual act of knowledge.

But Royce is unable to maintain this speculative level for long. He does succeed in grasping the supremely concrete character of the act of knowledge, as individuality which concentrates in itself the universality of experience ; but he fails to see the full significance of this relation, which if logically developed would eliminate all abstract universality. As a matter of fact, this concept annihilates the empirical idea of the world as a plurality of beings who from different points of view complete the same synthesis. This idea is a relic of the abstract universal ; for plurality only exists in and for the single act of thought, which is no mere fragmentary view of reality but the whole of reality, a whole which leaves nothing outside itself, no residuum. But Royce stops short at this abstract plurality, and thus misses the supreme absoluteness of the synthesis. His conception of the world is a conception of diverse processes, of multiple individualities, which complete each one its own design ; and he therefore feels the necessity of a new principle to unify this diversity. This principle is the abstract God of theism ; and it is in vain that Royce seeks to repeat the process of individuation in order to escape from the position of transcendence : once the many is affirmed as many, in vain do we hope to extract from it the one, The assertion of a plurality of points of

view, a plurality of selves, is really equivalent to asserting
the totality of the world as a pre-existent world of beings
over against experience ; the concreteness of the act of
knowing has disappeared, and in its place we find a totality
already given and lying outside it.

From this point onwards Royce's profoundly speculative
vein is exhausted, and he sees the world as a rationally
connected system of beings, each fulfilling its own purpose,
and all finding their unity in the individual of individuals,
in the absolutely absolute being. But there is no such
thing as individuality or absoluteness raised to the second
degree. The attempt to raise absoluteness to a higher
power is really to reduce it to impotence ; for the attempt
betrays the residuum of the abstract universal, which Royce
is trying to eliminate by the mechanical reduplication of
the original process.

Here, in spite of all protests to the contrary, a vein of
Leibnizian monadism insinuates itself into Royce's metaphysic when he least suspects it. He would say that for
him the spirit is not a monad but a life individuated by its
scheme of the world, that is to say by the unique view of
reality which is brought into focus by its experience. His
whole theory, he would say, presupposes that individuals
can be included in other individuals ; that a life can form
part of a larger life, and that the ties which connect the
different finite individuals are simply indications of the unity
of all the individuals in the Individual Absolute [1] : but it is
exactly in this affirmation of the plurality outside the unity
of the single act that he reveals his monadism. And so
it is futile to speak of trying to discover the act of the
act in which the plurality is resolved : once the plurality
is asserted as such it can never be overcome. Thus
Royce's great truth, that the ego is the unique expression of the divine purpose, is lost when he affirms the
existence of other isolated expressions alongside of and
outside this expression.

In short, the error lies in asserting a pre-existent totality,
a world of being, over against thought (and that in a metaphysic of thought, which ought to have absorbed the whole

[1] *Op. cit.*, vol. ii. (1904), p. 238.

19

metaphysic of being), and then proceeding to grapple with the problem of unifying the disconnected diversity without realizing that the unification is already effected in the single act of thought, and that the other attempted unification is a relic of naturalism.

But although he has stopped half-way, Royce has discovered a truth ; he is one of the very few thinkers who open out new roads to thought.

§ 7. SUMMARY.

Anglo-American philosophy develops in an extremely simple manner along two divergent lines. As regards the first of these, we have pointed out that between the empiricism of Mill and the naturalism of Spencer there is no advance, but only a progressive polarization of one and the same attitude into an undifferentiated opposition—an opposition, that is to say, in which the terms are convertible with one another : for crude sensation is simply an equivalent, in psychological terms, of the crude thing. In Mill's permanent possibility of sensations there is already implied the whole of the clumsy construction of the Spencerian naturalism. And the absence of any real difference between the opposites is signalized by Clifford, when he converts mind into matter and *vice versa* in his hybrid concept of " mind-stuff."

The *schema* of this philosophy is that empiricist logic which transforms thought into nature, into a kind of amorphous substance capable of being poured into the ready-made moulds of concept and generalization. And just as the association of ideas in Mill's psychology is an inexplicable law acting upon the play of sensations from without, the *Deus ex machina* of this decadent drama ; just as Spencer's law of evolution falls outside natural reality and vanishes, on inspection, into the void of the unknowable ; so, in logic, the laws of thought fall outside thought and consist of a *schema*, arbitrarily superimposed upon thought, which in reality is the shadow of thought itself, as the unknowable was the shadow of the knowable. The philosophy of fact is never able to straighten itself out ; it is always bent double and biting its own tail. It is a truth that ought never to be forgotten, that a fact is at once itself and its own shadow.

Empiricism offers as the complement of its metaphysic a moral philosophy which reflects both its vulgarity and its congenital feebleness. Incoherent from the very beginning, it seeks to construct life, with all its richness and variety, out of the imaginary fragments which it calls sensations ; and its claim to reproduce in this species of patchwork the most impressive masterpieces of moral reality results, with Mill, in a grotesque caricature of the ethics of Kant. The culminating point of this empiricism is the theory of the automatic production of the good, which is outlined in Mill's principle of association and perfected in Spencer's biological principle.

English idealism arises in sharp contradiction to this movement. In its first phase it carries out its work of preparation by an accurate study of Hegel ; but no sooner has it left its support and begun to walk alone than it separates into two schools. One school converts the Hegelian idea into the Platonic idea. MacTaggart effects this completely, Green still continues to cling to Kant ; but each, so far as he resolves the diversity of the world in the unity of the idea, destroys the diversity instead of explaining it. This leads to the conflict between the idea and experienced reality, culminating in the negation of the latter in Bradley's scepticism, which attacks just that concept of relation which still held the two worlds united. But the criticism of the concept of relation only reveals the profound reality of this concept, whose very negation creates a new and imperative demand for its reaffirmation.

A clearer insight into the truths for which Hegel stands is shown by the historians of religion. This school never loses touch with the reality of human experience, and in its development finds the progressive realization of the Deity. Here Catholicism and Anglicanism, enemies on earth, join hands in the Olympus of philosophy, which, Olympus though it be, is yet the native earth of true humanity and the temple in which the human truth of all religions is enshrined.

A second Hegelian school takes its inspiration from the Phenomenology, but attempts to include in this the Logic

and the Philosophy of the Spirit : it culminates with Baillie
in the view that in the highest moment of spiritual development the content and form of thought are one, and that so-
called natural reality, pursued but not recognized in inferior
stages, is nothing but this same content of reason, conceived
in its development.   This unity of the self and its other in
the absolute act of the spirit had already some time before
been the goal of Royce's speculation.   He attains his goal
in the conception of thought as a process of individuation
into whose unity the universe is focused : but he loses it
again by dispersing the unity of the act into a plurality,
and then vainly struggles to reconstruct it by driving his
own method over the problem again by mere force of inertia.
This new unity, which Royce deludes himself into thinking he
has discovered, is merely the shadow, projected in advance,
of the procedure itself : where the plurality is affirmed outside the act of thought, its unification can only be the
abstract God of theism.

But the failures ought not to blind us to the successes.
The speculative level reached by English idealism is very
high ; the school can well bear comparison with its contem-
poraries in France, and towers head and shoulders above
anything produced by modern Germany.

PART IV

ITALIAN PHILOSOPHY

CHAPTER I

FROM MACHIAVELLI TO GIOBERTI

§ 1. THE NEGLECT OF ITALIAN PHILOSOPHY.

IT is our intention to trace the history of Italian philosophy farther back than we have done in the case of other schools. If there is any country that can boast of an original development of thought from the Renaissance up to the present day, that country is Italy. And at the same time it would seem that no country can complain with greater justice than Italy of the way in which her intellectual life has been completely overlooked.

With Renaissance Italy everyone is familiar ; but after that period Italy lost touch with the general currents of European thought. Vico is a dead letter in foreign countries ; and the nineteenth century offers the anomaly that while second-rate thinkers like Hamilton, Cousin, and later Lotze, won European reputations, three philosophers of genius like Rosmini, Gioberti and Spaventa were entirely ignored : yet these were keeping alive the speculative tradition of European thought just at the time when it seemed to have been submerged in the apparent collapse of German idealism.

I am not going to waste time here in a ridiculous attack on foreigners for neglecting us. If they forgot our past, it was only because we had forgotten it ourselves, and failed to live up to it ; and indeed the condition of civil and political affairs in Italy during the nineteenth century contributed only too largely to their attitude of scornful neglect. For thought to-day does not circulate in the same way as it did in the time of the Renaissance. Then, even though politically we were slaves, we could dictate to foreigners the laws of culture. The dominating idea of thought was precisely that abstract naturalistic universal which neutralized differences of historical circumstance : it was expressed in Bruno's concept of substance, the undifferentiated unity of opposites. The nineteenth century, on the other hand, has witnessed the inception of a profound movement towards individuality : it is the period of historicism. Thought no longer lives in abstraction from its life-history ; outside the political, moral and social individuality of a people it is nothing, a *flatus vocis*. Thus the German, the French and the English cultures, being those of established nations, have left their impress : ours has not. We had in the early nineteenth century two great thinkers, Rosmini and Gioberti, but they lived before their time ; Italy was not yet a nation. We did not begin to honour them until we desired to make our history : their thought blazed forth with a brilliant light in 1848 ; but it was dead by 1849. And the Italy that took shape in 1860 was neither Rosminian nor Giobertian. Why ? The decadence, mental and moral, of this new Italy is only too well known : she spoke not with the rich voice of Gioberti, but in the soft effeminate tones of Mamiani and the rough accents of Ferrari.

In 1861, in a course of lectures which will always be memorable in the history of Italian philosophy, the third of the great Italian thinkers, Bertrando Spaventa, recalled the glories of our past and maintained the originality of Italian thought in its relation to European thought before an audience to whom such an idea was entirely new. In the new light thrown by Spaventa upon our philosophy, Bruno and Campanella took their place in the history of thought as precursors of Descartes, Spinoza, and Locke ; Vico as the genius who heralded Kant ; and finally Galluppi, Rosmini and Gioberti represented the gradual completion of Kantianism, as Fichte and Hegel did in Germany. But Spaventa pointed out that it was characteristic of the Italian genius throughout to be a precursor ; that Italy had always foreseen new truths, but been unable to develop them, and had ended by misinterpreting and falsifying them. Spaventa nevertheless hoped that with the renewal of interest in history, and now that Italy had risen again to political unity, she could resume in full consciousness her ancient

and proper position in culture.   And he himself led the
way with his persistent effort throughout the whole of his
lifetime to obtain a complete grasp of the historical movement, restraining all original impulses of his own thought
in order to achieve the closest sympathy with the thought
of others : putting himself perpetually back to school in
order to become the true teacher of Italy.

But the Italy to which he spoke had not arrived at the
stage at which it could understand him : it was the same
Italy which had perverted Giobertianism to a flaccid and
lifeless speculation, the philosophy of the Brahmins, as
Spaventa himself called it.   Hence the inspired Hegelian
appeared to some a mystic, to others a subverter of the
scholastic philosophy ; no one saw him as he really was.
One-sided nationalists objected to his Hegelianism, bigoted
Hegelians objected to his nationalism ; while actually each
was objecting to the other's errors and he was immune from
both charges.   The feeling of his philosophy belonged to
Italy, its thought to the universe.

And so the teaching of Spaventa, like that of his great
fellow-countryman, De Sanctis, was at first unfruitful :
people's minds were not prepared to receive it.   It is not
so to-day ; we are becoming more conscious of the unity of
Italy and beginning to live in communion with our past,
knowing that our speculative life can only develop by means
of a firmer continuity with historical tradition.   Modern
Italy was not created once for all in 1860 ; she is taking
shape to-day.   In her political life she has outgrown the
specious abstractions of socialism, and in her speculative life
she is equally passing beyond the desolating void of positivism : socialism and positivism in Italy stand or fall
together.   And with the revival of our culture the fame of
our great men, Francesco de Sanctis and Bertrando Spaventa,
is also reviving, and through them we are linking ourselves
to our past.   I will describe briefly the manner in which
they (and also those who have carried on their work and
have contributed with them to the present reawakening) are
indebted to this past.

§ 2. The Renaissance and Machiavelli.

The dawnings of modern thought are first visible in humanism. In its philology we can already detect a glimpse of the principle and direction of the new philosophy : it already indicates that return to the ancient which is really a creation of the new. Beneath the blows dealt by humanism, scholasticism was beginning to crumble. This process was continued still more rapidly in the revival of civil and political life and of the speculative thought in which it found expression. What do we mean by scholasticism ? It is the marriage of Christianity and Aristotelianism ; the God that became man in Christ becomes nature in the Aristotelian logic ; he is enclosed within the walls of the syllogism and converted into being, the object. Anselm's ontological proof is the crowning achievement of scholasticism. It is naturalism, but it is a great advance on any previous naturalism : it is not the physical naturalism of the pre-Socratics, nor the ideal naturalism of the Platonists, but divine naturalism. It furnished the basis for the development of the Christian paradox which affirms at once the humanity and the divinity of God. And the new naturalism of the Renaissance, which asserted itself as the negation of the scholastic naturalism, really conceals the same paradox in its single affirmation of the divinity and humanity of nature. With this phase the truly human age of philosophy begins.

As regards its speculative procedure, the whole of scholasticism is contained in the principles of syllogistic logic. Its ethical vision of the world is asceticism and mysticism : the Messianic hope implies the denial of all value to actual reality and life. The Renaissance is the antithesis of both these tendencies. It exaggerates the value of life (a tendency fostered and intensified by communal liberty, commercial activities and political relations) ; and at the same time it is a new attitude of speculative thought, no longer concerned with a ready-made reality standing over against it, to be treated by syllogistic methods, but creating its own reality, by observation, proof and induction. Thus arise two sciences, political and physical, as parallel applications of the same tendency to humanize the relations of civil life and natural reality. But neither science understands the other, or regards it in any light except that of a rival : from this mutual ignorance is derived that phantom of the transcendent, the residuum of scholasticism, which saps the force of the new speculation : the double projection of the unknown, from either region to the other. Italy never attained the conception of a universal science, which constituted the finest achievement of philosophers like Spinoza or Leibniz. Machiavelli and Galileo remained strangers to one another.

Thus in Italy we have on one side the politicians, on the other the natural scientists : the philosophers never succeed in focusing the two points of view into a single clear vision. Their vision is still blurred : the new movement has not yet reached the maturity of reflection. The new reality which is taking form in the mind of Machiavelli and Galileo is not yet clearly expressed in the speculation of Bruno or of Campanella.

The thinker who best represents the modern spirit in its formation is Machiavelli. In him scholasticism is already virtually superseded. In the place of the ascetic life of the Middle Ages we find the active life of political society : in the place of the art of syllogizing, observation of human reality in the causal sequences of history. In him we already find in a concentrated form all the tendencies of the new humanity. As a humanist he reverts to the past in order to escape the barbarous language of scholasticism ; just as Bruno later harked back to the philosophy of Pythagoras and of the Eleatics in order to overcome the same barbarisms in philosophy, so Machiavelli sought to obtain from the great historians of antiquity the means whereby to liberate man from historical contingencies such as the forms and institutions of mediæval life, supported by the authority of an irrational tradition.[1] This tendency inevitably leads to the annihilation of historical divergences, to the conception of humanity as a mighty force controlled by implacable and inexorable laws, by an internal logic that destroys all individual freedom. Humanity is conceived not as mind—a comparatively modern conception—but as sub-

[1] G. Gentile, *B. Telesio*, Bari, 1911, p. 30..

stance : Machiavelli anticipates in politics the position of
Bruno and Spinoza. It is true that in the *Prince* he em-
phatically affirms human individuality, but only in the manner
in which Bruno affirmed the monad in his naturalistic
philosophy : not as Leibniz conceived it, the beginning and
premonition of spiritual life, but merely as the atomic point
in which the nature of substance finds a condensed and concentrated expression. Thus Machiavelli's ideal type, the
Prince, does not exalt humanity to a free spiritual life, to a
true individuality, but on the contrary embodies and enshrines
the most rigid type of naturalism.

But this is quite a new naturalism, the antithesis to that
of scholasticism. It sweeps away the old transcendence
and explains man in his actual reality, according to the
forces and laws of his own nature : it is the first affirmation
of human autonomy and the immanence of the historical
process : it is modern thought acquiring consciousness of
itself as the author of its own history. But, as naturalism,
it has the defect of all naturalism : that of creating a new
transcendence in the very heart of the immanent. Machiavelli's concept of the state, as De Sanctis remarks, is too
like the old transcendent God, and absorbs in itself religion,
morality and individuality. His state is not content with
being autonomous itself, but deprives of autonomy everything else. The state has rights : the individual has none.
We are in fact dealing with the undifferentiated unity of
substance.

§ 3. BRUNO AND CAMPANELLA.

The speculation of the whole of the sixteenth and seven-
teenth centuries never succeeds in going beyond this conception and does nothing more than develop it ; indeed,
owing to the inherent speculative difficulty of the position,
it is not always able to keep to such a height, and often
falls back into the easier alternative of pure scholasticism. Telesio, Bruno and Campanella are the exponents
of the new naturalism. With them begins the deliberate and
conscious destruction of the Aristotelian philosophy, or of
that part of it, at least, which forms the basis of scholasti-

cism. The dualism between matter and form, potentiality and actuality, on which the mediæval view of the world rested, is vigorously attacked. Telesio already regards nature, matter, not as mere privation but as a positive reality that has not to seek its sufficient reason outside itself, but is explained *juxta propria principia*. And Bruno in his dialogues pours scorn on the dualism : if matter is pure potentiality, he asks, how can it ever attain actuality ? This alleged potentiality would be more truly described as an impotence. Bruno's new conception is that matter is the source of actuality, and that form is not external to it ; indeed, when we state the cause of decomposition we do not say that the form escapes or leaves the matter, but rather that the matter rejects one form to assume another. Thus matter, as Bruno conceived it, is not the mere matter of physics, but the matter which is consubstantial with its own form, that is to say, the speculative concept of substance.

This is typical of Bruno's whole attitude. He wishes, he says, to enter into the deep discussions of the natural philosophers, and to leave the logicians to their imaginings. This contempt for logic marks the discovery of the new logic, the logic of the mind in correlation with nature. The scale according to which nature descends in the production of things is the same as that by which the mind ascends in the cognition of them ; both proceed from unity to unity, passing through the multiplicity of middle terms. It is the logic of substance, of pure immediate identity : no longer the empty identity of the syllogistic logic, but the identity of the scale, or of the causal order, as Spinoza put it more explicitly.

Bruno maintains the unity of substance with a truly magnificent trenchancy and enthusiasm. The deep discussions of the natural philosophers prove to him that all numerical difference has its root in pure accident, a mere question of the shapes or complex arrangements assumed by substance. All production, of whatever kind, is an alteration, the substance always remaining the same ; for there is only one substance ; one divine, immortal being. It alone is stable and eternal : every appearance, every aspect, every thing other than it, is vanity and as nothing ; everything except the one substance is a nonentity. Spinoza himself did not speak with greater trenchancy ; but, unlike Bruno, once he had reached this position he never retreated a single step. The Italian philosopher, like Telesio before him and Campanella after him, mingles the new with the old : more vehement than Spinoza, he is far less coherent, and he allows the old God to continue side by side with the new.

Campanella is still more vacillating than Bruno, although he represents a new demand of speculative thought. The difficulty about the concept of substance is that thought thus conceived becomes a natural object and cannot explain itself. How is it possible that substance should be known and not know itself ? How can man, a mere mode or accident, apprehend substance and rise to the knowledge of God, if he is no more than an effect ? How can the effect recoil upon the cause ? [1] The problem of knowledge is the new problem which the concept of substance introduces into philosophy, and to which the friar of Stilo seeks an answer.

Campanella is, confusedly, both the Descartes and the Locke of Italian philosophy. He starts with sceptical doubt and finds certainty in the consciousness of self, through the *sensus abditus*, but on the other hand he bases the knowledge of nature on the mere *sensus additus*. He does not reconcile these two demands : nor indeed shall we find them reconciled by any philosopher before Kant. Hence the certainty of external things appeared to Campanella now an advance, now a decline; now an addition to consciousness, now a limitation of it. In metaphysics, the general trend of his thought is rationalism—the doctrine of the primacy of reason based on the *sensus abditus* ; in the theory of knowledge, empiricism—the mere certainty of the senses, and the conception of the understanding simply as a less vivid sensation.

But if in this direction he makes a great advance on Bruno, he still remains far behind him in the conviction and faith in the infinite presence of God in the Universe. In a kind of way, and as it were unconsciously, Campanella is what Spaventa called him, the philosopher of the Catholic

[1] B. Spaventa, *Saggi di Critica*, Naples, 1886, 2nd ed., p. 112.

revival ; his rationalism removes the shackles from science only in order that science should reimpose them on itself and offer a voluntary submission. To find the real counterpart of Bruno's enthusiasm we must turn to the indomitable perseverance of Galileo. In the philosophy of the Renaissance scholasticism was only virtually superseded ; with Galileo it was overthrown for all time. Naturalism is no longer merely extolled as a new tendency of the spirit, it is grasped as its new achievement ; in the new science Nature is so thoroughly humanized as to be no longer the mere negative entity of the schoolmen, or the still transcendent Deity of the new philosophy, but science itself, the affirmation of the concrete human character of the world—of a world not external to us but immanent in us, whose life is our own life of continual search and discovery.

§ 4. Vico.

The intellectual outlook of Vico is separated from that of Machiavelli by two centuries of development. There is this resemblance between them, that the eyes of both are fixed on the past as a source of inspiration ; but the point of view from which they regard it has undergone a profound change. Machiavelli sees in the past a means whereby he may liberate the present from historical accidents and penetrate in thought to the inmost substance of human nature, the passions : he thus lays the foundations of political philosophy. With Vico the human naturalism of the Renaissance is already superseded ; to him the study of history suggests no longer the distinction between substance and accident, but the new idea of the development, the unfolding of the human mind : Vico lays the foundations of history.

The two attitudes of thought are fundamentally different. The tradition of political philosophy is carried on by Guiccardini, Paruta and Sarpi, and finds a belated representative in the eighteenth century in the Abbot Galiani. He, like Vico, criticizes his own century and the growth of Jacobinism, but his criticism does not anticipate the following century ; it is the criticism of the old politician who is incapable of understanding the new aspirations of the younger generation and uses his experience to point out its puerilities and to laugh at its illusions.[1]

Vico's criticism is, on the contrary, a really new departure. It attacks the whole of eighteenth-century thought, Cartesianism and sensationalism alike. To the abstract universality of the former, which fails to explain science because it attempts to establish it on the immediate revelation of self-evidence, Vico opposes the genetic intuition of things, which explains them in their origin and development : thus foreshadowing the historicism of the nineteenth century. And while sensationalism bases a wholly materialistic type of philosophy upon sense-experience, Vico constructs upon the same foundation the imaginative universal, poetry and language, in their spiritual creativeness, thus foreshadowing romanticism. These two brilliant intuitions are combined and focussed in the single conception of the human mind, which in the course of its development presents itself as scattered in sense and imagination and as concentrated and reflected in thought. Vico thus has a glimpse of a metaphysic of the mind, an ideal eternal history through which run the histories of individual nations : the modifications of the mind are for him identical with the moments of historical development. Herein lies Vico's great originality. Machiavelli treated humanity as nature, as substance ; and thus its development was rigidly determined by its own inner logic. Vico introduces the true concept of mind when he expounds his doctrine of the providence immanent in the development of nations. Machiavelli still retains—in spite of all appearances—the theological view of the world and the melancholy of a Messianic expectation. Man is alienated from himself, and his true humanity is not immanent but transcendent. All this is changed with Vico : history as he conceives it is the complete expression of human nature in its entirety. Yet that same Vico, who realized his new idea so magnificently in his study of Roman history, left intact the superstition of the arbitrary election of the Hebrews. The application of his idea to Roman history at once crowned and exhausted the effort of his thought, and he had not

[1] An acute observation of Croce's ; cf. *Il pensiero del Abate Galiani,* in *La Critica,* 1909, p. 404.

the strength to pursue the application of it to the history of the Hebrews, as Croce observes in his brilliant monograph on Vico. Was it cowardice or prejudice ? Perhaps the truer view is that it was an inherent defect of his system. Vico was unable to escape from the narrow particularism of his national units : he lacked the concept of the universality of the particular, of the humanity of the nation, which was to be the work of the century following him. And thus the transition from the Romans to the Hebrews, which seems to us to-day so easy, was not possible even for his genius.

Vico never won the recognition that was his due, either in Italy or abroad, either in his lifetime or after his death. In our century, as we shall see, the positivists have laid claim to his doctrine and have grotesquely misinterpreted his well-known formula of the equivalence of the true and the created. The vindication of his memory and the continuation of his thought have been the work of Spaventa, De Sanctis and, still more, Croce. To these scholars we are indebted for the filling of an important gap in the history of Italian thought. Machiavelli and Vico are the greatest figures in that history from the Renaissance down to the commencement of the nineteenth century.

§ 5. ROSMINI AND GIOBERTI.

Vico's intuition of a metaphysic of the human mind was a presentiment of the critical philosophy developed in the following century by Galluppi, Rosmini and Gioberti. The historical position of these thinkers was generally misunderstood, and not least by themselves, until Bertrando Spaventa's criticism freed their philosophy from its accidental wrappings and revealed its near kinship with German philosophy.

A consideration of the environment in which the new theories arose and were developed will explain this misunderstanding. At the beginning of the nineteenth century Italy was overrun by the French sensationalism of the preceding century ; the only elements of Kantianism were those which were imported along with the psychology of the

Scottish eclectics, and the highly original and valuable Kantian concept of subjectivity was entirely unknown. The revival of Catholicism which was beginning at this time threatened to undermine the foundations of sensationalism, but not in the name of Kant. Sensationalism ultimately leads to scepticism ; it is an empty play of subjective elements which can never form a foundation for objectivity or knowledge. But (it is asked) is not Kant also enclosed in the subjectivity of the forms of sensation and of the understanding ? And does not Kant also end in scepticism ? With this criticism, it is claimed, we can dismiss Kant and pursue our search for an objective basis of knowledge in a diametrically opposite direction. But the motive of this procedure is precisely Kant's motive ; and the only difference is that Kant with his clearer vision avoids the danger of frequent lapses into positions of thought that ought to have been left behind for good. This is the objectivism of Rosmini and Gioberti.[1]

The same critical attitude can be detected even in the philosophy of Galluppi, which at first sight is pure empiricism. In so far as it distinguishes sensation from the consciousness of sensation, and makes the latter the basis of the former, it is virtually Kantianism. But Galluppi does not understand the value of the distinction, and therefore does not consistently maintain it. In other words, he does not understand that the consciousness of sensation is not another sensation but thought, and thus fails to attain the conception of the *a priori* synthesis. Rosmini, on the other hand, does attain it with his concept of intellective perception. This is the synthesis of the particular of sense and of the universal of the understanding, which is effected in the idea of being. This idea informs the contingent and changeable sense-content and confers on it the universality and objectivity of knowledge.

Rosmini, like Kant, holds that to think is to judge : in the fundamental and primary act of judgment the synthesis of sense and of intellect is consummated. But what is the nature of the intellectual idea of being, apart from the judgment ? It is not an empirical reality, not a sensation,

[1] See the penetrating remarks of Gentile in his book *Rosmini e Gioberti*, Pisa, 1898.

because it is objective : it is not a transcendent reality, because it is ideal : it is a transcendental conception. Rosmini does not actually state this, but it is implied in all his reasoning. His complementary idea therefore, that being is the object of intuition, must be regarded as a useless addition. If reality lies not outside the act of judgment but within it, the introduction of an object of intuition can only be due to the anxiety to save reality at all costs from mere subjectivity, and the failure to realize that it is already saved. And so the doctrine of intuition drives objectivity, which was secure in port, out once more into the open sea.

Being for Rosmini, like the category for Kant, is, however, the mere universal that is never individualized. It is possible being, the basis of a possible experience : the possibility is not yet absolute actuality. This possible experience in fact still contains the residuum of dogmatism : for what will make this possibility actual ? Alike for Kant and Rosmini the act of judgment, of intellective perception, is inadequate to resolve the whole object : there remains outside it the thing-in-itself, the unknown term in sensation, the invisible coefficient of actual thinking. Thus the category does not resolve all presuppositions and therefore fails truly to interpenetrate the sense world, but is fitted on to it, so to speak, from the outside.

Now, unless Rosminianism is to degenerate into a mere psychological analysis, it must resolve the whole object : a theory of knowledge which leaves its presuppositions intact is a mere psychology. We must, in fact, solve the ontological problem as well as the psychological, and conceive a transcendent psychology which is at the same time the true ontology. This is what Gioberti accomplished. To put the problem in other words, we must give an individual content to Rosmini's universal and unite the " that " of experience with its " what."

Gioberti finds the solution in the concept of creation, of absolute relation which establishes at once being and existence, the idea and the reality. Only in the act of creation is absolute potentiality identified with absolute actuality : to confer individuality upon the real can only mean to create it. To create, in fact, is to render concrete ; it is,

Vico would say, to equate the true with the created. In the first phase of Gioberti's philosophy the concept of creation still has a transcendent significance : the absolute *a priori* character of the creative relation is not yet affirmed, and thought is simply the intuition, the vision of the act of creation. But in the later phase this abstractness is overcome. Gioberti now criticizes intuition : its perspective, he says, unlike that of reflection, has no distances, no relief : it has length and breadth, but no third dimension—no depth. It is visible but not tangible. Intuition sees the creative act, but does not participate in it.

In this new phase the organ of philosophy becomes reflection, the dialectic. Only in reflection does the human act rise to the level of the divine and become truly creative : creation is the peculiar and essential function of thought. Our spirit creates continually : creation is synonymous with thinking and thinking with creation. Being and thought are the two opposite poles of the mind, which are reunited and neutralized in pure activity, i.e. in creation. This act is the true concrete union of opposites : it is the absolute relation, more substantial than its terms : it is the root of the dialectic. Thus, for instance, man is not soul *plus* body, but the relation of the one with the other. Man is that indivisible point in which the physical and the moral neutralize each other. He is before all a unity : the duality comes afterwards. We must not ask, then, in what way the soul enters into relation with the body, that is to say, how the duality is united, but rather how the unity becomes a duality.

In Gioberti's latest period, this idea of creation flared up into a perfect blaze of vivid and striking thoughts. In few philosophers are we vouchsafed such a wonderful richness of thought ; indeed, one can say of Gioberti's genius what he said of genius in general, that it resembles God when He said *Fiat lux*. But at the same time he recalls to our minds Quintilian's criticism of Ovid : if only he had curbed his genius instead of giving it a free rein ! He lacked the scientific instinct for deliberate constructive research ; like Schelling, he had an explosive temperament.

But through him the Italian philosophy of the first half

of the nineteenth century attained to the height of the German. As Spaventa was the first to observe, we have in Gioberti the Fichte, the Schelling and the Hegel of our philosophy, but without the gradual transition from the one to the other ; they are combined confusedly and the transition is effected by leaps. After Gioberti, the task imposed on our philosophy was to build up the scientific sense that we lacked and to kindle in us the consciousness of our position in the history of European thought. This was effected by Bertrando Spaventa, who was thus the successor of the great Turinese and developed his thought to its logical conclusion.

But before speaking of this writer, who was for us what Lachelier was for the French and Stirling for the English, we must make some mention of the various movements of thought that flourished in the second half of the nineteenth century. Spaventa's work was indeed going on during the same period ; but it remained comparatively without influence till, largely thanks to Gentile and Croce, it was revived at the beginning of the twentieth century.

CHAPTER II

THE CLOSE OF THE NINETEENTH CENTURY

§ I. Scepticism.

AFTER the unfortunate ending of the war of 1848–9 and Gioberti's exile, Italian philosophy seems to have been overcome by an invincible somnolence. Whoever, out of mere curiosity, glances through some of the many volumes published between 1850 and 1860 cannot help being impressed by the atmosphere of sleep that weighs upon them. One can no longer distinguish one tendency from another or pick out any single doctrine : such is the mediocrity and poverty of all alike, that all relief and variety has disappeared. The arch-mediocrity of the period is Terenzio Mamiani. I am simply unable to say what his philosophy was, and I do not think that he knew either. He attacked Rosmini and received an unforgettable cudgelling at the hands of the " saint of Rovereto," as he himself admitted with delightful frankness. He did not understand Gioberti at all, or hardly at all ; he showed himself so far a fervent empiricist as to assert a physical interaction between consciousness and objects ; so far a pure Platonist as to maintain that reality existed ready-made, outside and independent of thought, and that therefore truth was a transcendent ideal with which thought must try to bring itself into conformity ; so far a complete sceptic as to deny that the mind could probe the ultimate essence of things. He was all this and he was nothing ; in reality the admirers of his nerveless and languid style simply took it as a mental opiate.

But the almost universal popularity enjoyed by Mamiani for a certain time in Italy must not mislead us into assigning to him the whole cause of the decadence of our philosophy. He was at once its cause and its effect : in the domain of thought the principle of reciprocity is universally valid. He thus became the recognized exponent of Italian thought, and his philosophy of mediocrity finally found a historian in Luigi Ferri, who explained it as the centre of convergence of nineteenth-century philosophy. Ferri's book is the only document on Italian philosophy which foreigners possess : on the basis of it they have erected Rosmini, Gioberti and Mamiani into a triad, and have been misled into extending to the first two the contemptuous opinion they have formed of the third.

But Ferri does show more inclination than Mamiani to take up a definite position. This consists in the dualism of thought and being, and the attempt to conceive a third term which shall constitute the unity of the real. This third term, however, does not exist, even in the imagination of Ferri ; it is simply postulated, as it were, as a witness to the futility of his method. With these premises his philosophy must inevitably terminate in eclecticism, the conception of truth as the conformity of thought both to its own laws and to those of being, or in other words the mere cloaking of the mystery. We shall find this dualism of thought and being, revived and brought up to date, in the work of Bonatelli and several other writers ; but its main defect, that of postulating a double logic, remains unaltered.

The fallacy is due to forgetfulness of the lessons of history : of that history which overthrew the old conception of being and, for the doctrine of thought as the vision of a ready-made reality, substituted the doctrine of thought as the production and creation of reality. When Rosmini and Gioberti introduced an imaginary intuitive faculty they revived, though with some important modifications, the old Platonistic point of view ; and even if their own conception of knowledge was not substantially impaired by it, because it constituted simply the superficial integument of their theory, it was a source of very real danger for less practised minds. Among these was Bertini, the author of a book on the *Philosophy of Life*. According to him, thought is simple vision, severed from all action or passion on the part of the seer ; as such it presupposes being, reality, as already formed and completed. Hence the inquiry initiated by Bertini with regard to that reality lay within the field of the old metaphysic. Yet, in spite of its dogmatic character, his philosophy has a vein of something more modern in it, derived from Jacobi. That direct immediate intuition of reality, which reaches beyond the finite to the infinite, to God, resembles Jacobi's conception ; and on the other hand the firm conviction that every judgment about nature, about the value and purpose of life, implies a solution of the problem of reality as a whole, lends to his thought a certain emotional and religious colouring.[1]

In spite of these merits Bertini's philosophy shows already a great falling off from that of Rosmini and Gioberti, to which it is so near in point of time. But if we wish to see the completest expression of this decadence we must look for it in another thinker.

Ferrari's *Philosophy of Revolution* is the philosophy of a bankrupt revolution, the philosophy of Novara. It is the new obscurantist scepticism which thrusts itself forward with its blatant negations of God, of religion, of thought, and prepares the way for the positivist Babel. Ferrari heaps antinomy upon antinomy in the most fantastic order and with the most comic anachronisms ; but the motive behind all this display of erudition in the science of antinomies is bald enough—to show how futile is the claim of thought to dominate nature. These contradictions can only be solved by the opposite method, by which thought submits to nature and bows before her revelations. There are, Ferrari says, two kinds of criticism, " the one negative, the other positive. The first throws us into a state of continual irresolution, the second forces us continually to come to a decision ; with the first we can do nothing but destroy ; the second constructs at the same time as it destroys. The result of the negative criticism is that nature confesses herself to be contradictory ; the result of the positive criticism is that nature accuses us of contradiction. There are two things, doubt and science : negative and positive criticism : universal contradiction and physical contradiction. We shall avoid

[1] S. M. Bertini, *Idea di una filosofia della vita*, Turin, 1850, vol. i., p. 9.

the illusion of metaphysics if we distinguish between the two kinds of antinomy, and examine whether the contradiction lies in nature or the intellect, whether it is begotten by the logic that dominates nature or by the nature that dominates logic. Appearance alone can decide, because every phenomenon is explained by itself."[1] And so we cease to think and abandon ourselves to the revelations of nature. But what are these revelations that Ferrari foists upon us in the name of nature ? There is nothing very new about them : the blind assertion of the phenomenon, the negation of metaphysics, and especially the elimination of God. Faith in God is described as the most primitive and natural error of the human race : the ignorance that creates religion is that of the man who knows the positive side of phenomena and does not suspect the critical side. But the nature that is explored by physics cannot be the field of Christian revelation ; all progress is therefore a struggle against the God of Christianity.[2] And so on, in the vein of the atheistical tub-thumper.

Thus clamorously Italian positivism announced its entry on the stage.

§ 2. Positivism.

But to tell the truth, Italian positivism, when once it fairly arrived, was not so very boisterous ; indeed, it showed the becoming modesty of one who knows that he has no great revelations to make. Its first advocates were scientists, historians, economists, people, in fact, who did not trouble much about subtlety and to whom positivism was rather a programme of work than a conception of reality. This renders it, up to a certain point, attractive, and invests it with a more serious aspect than it has had in other countries ; and really, when we reflect on the miserable condition to which metaphysics in Italy was reduced—a watered Platonism on the one hand and an inconclusive semi-scepticism on the other, with here and there sporadic revivals of Thomism, laborious and artificial creations at best, and in no sense

[1] G. Ferrari, *Filosofia della rivoluzione*, London, 1851, vol. i., pp. 250, 251.
[2] *Ibid.*, vol. ii., pp. 252, 279.

growing naturally out of the previous state of culture—we cannot help regarding even positivism as an advance. It did at any rate come forward as a criticism of futile ideologies and bring people's minds back to the study of facts. This demand for a return to facts was almost always exaggerated, but it is only to us, who live in a more refined mental atmosphere, that it appears so ; at that time the exaggeration was a useful reaction against intellectual futility.

Cattaneo, a diligent student of the social sciences, was one of the first positivists. A man of a really positive turn of mind, he attacks metaphysics as a futile science that serves no useful purpose. " It would be something if it gave even a counterfeit assistance to morality ! But the doctrine of being is always a contemplation of mere possibility, and does not establish any principle of human society, nor any rule of family and customary life." [1] What we require is facts, observations and experiments. " The word ' phenomenon ' has never been made to express the whole meaning of the word ' fact.' To the ancients and to their successors up to Kant, Schelling and Leroux, phenomenon means appearance as opposed to reality. To them reality and meaning lie in the idea ; phenomenon only contains appearance and inanity. But to the active sciences and to us phenomenon means the manifestation of force ; it is active force, force in so far as it is force." [2] The demand is a just one ; yet how many exaggerations, philosophical and historical, are contained in these few sentences ! But to continue, how does Cattaneo establish his facts on a much more solid basis than Kant did his phenomena ? The phenomenon, he says, is not illusory but real, because we feel its action on our consciousness : in the efforts which we make, our consciousness feels and measures the living forces that besiege it on every side. This statement is enough to show us that we are dealing with the empirical psychology which Maine de Biran bequeathed to the spiritualist and dualist metaphysicians of the school of Cousin ; that is to say, the very subjectivism which Kant and Rosmini had rejected for the excellent reason that it does not succeed in establishing the

---

[1] C. Cattaneo, *Opere edite e inedite*, Florence, 1892, vol. vi., p. 120.
[2] *Ibid.*, p. 248.

objectivity of knowledge. Kant and Rosmini, then, were better positivists than the worthy Cattaneo.

This is just one instance of the many positivist *naïvetés* that were subsequently to increase in frequency and were aggravated by a total ignorance of the history of thought. Cattaneo has still at any rate a smattering of this history. His positivism is personified by three names : Bacon for the study of nature, Locke for the study of consciousness, and Vico for the study of humanity.[1] Fortunately he does not ever attempt to combine the three thinkers, and he confines himself to the study of humanity under the guidance of his Vico. But from Vico he was unable to extract anything better than the idea of a psychology of associated minds—a mixture of the psychology of the individual and the so-called social psychology—where for lack of any philosophical criterion the social organization of thought was understood as a mere reflection of the organization of things outside the mind.

We have dealt with Cattaneo rather fully, partly because he is the most intelligent of the early Italian positivists, partly because the exposition we have given of his doctrine saves us the trouble of speaking in detail of other writers. At bottom they are all alike : Villari, Gabelli, Angiulli, to mention the most important. They are usually specialists who wish to avoid the bugbear of metaphysics, which is frequently the creature of their own imagination. Villari argues as follows : " If Kant's system is true, then the whole of Condillac's speculation is a mass of absurd propositions ; if Rosmini's system is true, then Hegel's is absurd, and *vice versa*. You perceive, in fact, that the philosophers of the various schools do not dispute about subordinate truths ; they deny one another even the name of philosophers, because their differences turn on the very nature and essence of their most general and fundamental doctrines." [2] So he turns from metaphysics to the study of facts looked at in the light of ideas. " Since in history you have only sought for facts and from the human spirit you have only been able to produce speculations, you have on the one side a pure

[1] *Op. cit.*, vol. vii., p. 262.
[2] P. Villari, *Arte, storia e filosofia*, Florence, 1884, p. 442.

empiricism and on the other a scholastic philosophy. But now that Vico has discovered that the laws of the world of nations are the laws of the human spirit itself, which has created this world of society, you can have on the one hand historical science, and on the other the proved and demonstrated science of man. In fact, if history stands to you as an external world on which you can experiment and verify the inductions of your psychology, psychology in its turn becomes a torch that illumines history. The laws of the one, if they are true, ought to find a counterpart in those of the other, and *vice versa."* [1]

These appeals to Vico that occur in the works of the positivists are very quaint : they are to be found in Gabelli and Angiulli as well as Cattaneo and Villari. Vico is made a precursor of positivism, his formula of the convertibility of the true with the created (*verum et factum convertuntur ;* the identity of thought and being, as mind or development) is most frequently understood to mean that truth lies in fact and not in the mind. Yet these reminiscences of Vico at any rate prevented the first positivists from lapsing into a materialistic metaphysic. They are all very non-committal, even if only because they have nothing to say. Angiulli is perhaps the most enterprising ; he has a more philosophical disposition than the others ; yet his positivist manifesto published in 1869 does not contain a single new idea.

And when in the logical course of its development positivism degenerated everywhere into materialism, our Italian positivists straightway disclaimed the conclusions of these new doctrines, of which they disapproved. Villari enters into a controversy with the French materialists ; Gabelli distinguishes between an old and a new positivism and declares his aversion to the latter. There is a certain *naïveté* about these misgivings, characteristic of the person who embraces a doctrine without understanding its import ; and the French materialists were more consistent than the Italian positivists in their denial of the vague idealism which the latter still allowed to hover over their facts. But if in this respect they were worse philosophers, yet in their reservation our positivists showed the better sense ; for after all

[1] *Op. cit.,* pp. 479–80.

their exertions to free themselves from a pseudo-idealistic metaphysic they were reluctant to become entangled in another metaphysic with materialistic tendencies.

The triviality of this metaphysic very soon became evident. It was a product of the alliance between philosophy and biology ; it was called monism, a name which tells us even more about it than the arguments on which it relied for support. Its advocates were doctors, naturalists, botanists, physicists, and so on. Their work would undoubtedly have been dispersed and lost if Enrico Morselli had not had the happy idea of collecting it together and disciplining it in a *Review of Scientific Philosophy*. Although this review lasted only a few years it will remain as a precious memorial of the condition of Italian thought towards the close of the nineteenth century.

But the most extravagant exaggerations of materialistic positivism are to be seen in the school of anthropology founded by Cesare Lombroso, the famous author of a series of books in which genius and crime are coupled together in a happy *coincidentia oppositorum*. We need not discuss these doctrines, which have become the common property of every lawyer and sully the squalid assembly-rooms of our Courts of Assizes. We merely indicate them as an offshoot of Italian positivism which has become incorporated in the propaganda of our socialist demagogues, particularly through the labours of Enrico Ferri ; and we would recommend that Ferri's preface to an ungrammatical translation of Engels' *Antidühring* should be read as a splendid example of the cultural level of Italian socialism.

But in spite of all this activity on the part of Italian positivism we should only have had a few scattered and fragmentary records of it, if it had not been systematized and, so to speak, condensed into a single doctrine by Roberto Ardigò. We will therefore deal with him at somewhat greater length.

Ardigò's philosophy displays exactly the same naturalistic tendency which we have observed in English positivism. It is an undifferentiated fusion of sensationalism and materialism, but without the logical rigour of Mill and the wide outlook—for wide it is, however superficial—of Spencer.

English empiricism is genuinely monistic in the sense that it asserts sensation as a natural fact and looks upon the distinction between subject and object as derivative from and posterior to it. Ardigò, on the other hand, betrays from the very beginning his dualistic bias, typical of a naïve realism. Thus he states as fundamental the distinction between an internal and an external sense, between " auto-synthesis " and " heterosynthesis," that is to say, on one side the association of stable psychical data which constitute the ego and on the other the association of accidental psychical states which constitute the non-ego. This is a proof of the inferiority of Ardigò's doctrine to the other forms of positivism, since the distinction simply adumbrates that between matter and sensation, and justifies that illusory reduplication of the world in knowledge which empiricists like Avenarius and Mach condemn as a veritable monstrosity. Any common term, such as " mind-stuff," which is intended to apply in both regions, the internal sense and the external sense, is really a mere name, and precisely equivalent to the " un-differentiated," which Ardigò makes the foundation of reality.

Ardigò is said to have criticized Spencer's unknowable ; and there actually is an essay of his on this subject ; but we should rather say that he went in search of the mote in his friend's eye and did not perceive the beam in his own. Poor Spencer could at least cherish the illusion that he saw God in his unknowable, while in the case of the undifferentiated it is no longer possible to imagine even this. With this concept in his hand Ardigò made a clean sweep of the unknowable, the unconscious, and other similar products of the specious eclecticisms of to-day ; he only retained the harmless satisfaction of saying One, when, in spite of the positivist, things appeared to wish to say Two.

Ardigò's undifferentiated, therefore, no longer contains any trace of God. The idea of God is absolutely banished from the pages of his philosophy, and in its place there is introduced the new concept of the infinite or of the permanent possibility of experience. Like Mill's concept of the possibility of sensations, this shows the immanentist preoccupation of positivism, and therefore its initial psychological motive is praiseworthy. But the actual theory is most inadequate. It still labours under the old Aristotelian dualism, and conceals with its apparent plausibility its failure to solve the problem and its ignorance of the magnificent achievements of twenty centuries of speculation in which this dualism has been gradually overcome.

This outline of the fundamental tendency of Ardigò's work will suffice as an indication of his thought. The development of his doctrine proceeds according to the general rules of empiricism, and consists in the attempt to group together in various forms and guises the plastic material of sensation, a field of research which English empiricism had long ago exhausted and which in Ardigò was rather a fruit out of season.

§ 3. FROM DUALISM TO MONISM.

In the polluted atmosphere of materialistic theories many modest voices were stifled, which in a kindlier environment might perhaps have exercised more influence. As it was, at a time when materialism, with its bigger display, dominated social life, their influence on Italian thought was very small indeed. They succeeded, however, in finding at the universities a more restricted audience, at the same time one that was more in keeping with their temper. And just as in France the eclectic spiritualism which had already been overshadowed by the new movements was preserved in university circles, so in the positivist and materialistic Italy of the second half of last century, a philosophy with spiritualistic tendencies was still being taught in the universities.

We have already mentioned the Platonic type of dualism which was taking form in the works of Mamiani, Ferri and Bertini. It attempted to keep an even balance between the two mutually exclusive spheres of thought and of being, but came to grief in its account of the mediation between the two, namely knowledge. It was unable therefore to claim any advance over the positivism which laboured under the same difficulty, and it simply tried to conceal the difficulty by means of unproved statements. Nor had the same dualism any better chance of success in the new form given to it by Bonatelli and Cantoni, although it was improved and brought up to date ; for at bottom it still contained the same difficulty, which was at most removed a step farther back.

Throughout a life of untiring study and research, Bonatelli never succeeded in bettering the initial position of his thought, which we know from the essay entitled *Thought and Knowledge*, written in 1864. Here, taking his inspiration from Lotze, he starts from the theory of the empirical subjectivity of consciousness and vainly struggles to establish the objectivity of knowledge. He reduces thought simply to the finished product of thought, the mere form indifferent to all content, like the form of the Aristotelian logic ; and he has thus from the very beginning cut himself off from the possibility of understanding the relation between thought and being. It is true that he asserts the identity of thought and judgment, but he does not grasp the value and import of this great Kantian truth, which is neutralized by the fundamentally Platonistic standpoint of his theory.

Hence, if thought is mere thought, then the certainty which we have of the real is merely inference, an analogy, by which we interpret things external to us in terms of our subjective experience. But what is reality in itself ? It is at one moment something similar to the reals of Lotze, at another moment it is thought itself, understood as the ideal norm according to which we attempt to model the particular instances of knowledge.[1] This is obviously a feeble solution, for while the principle of analogy leads us to believe we are passing beyond mere subjectivity, we are actually not passing a single step beyond it ; and on the other hand the ideal norm set up outside actual thought is mere objectivity, deprived of any means of transition to the subject. The result is pure and simple objectivity and pure and simple subjectivity : and the solution really does nothing more than restate the problem.

The Platonism of the first essay is unmodified in the later ones ; at most it is clarified. In the short study *Perception and Thought* it is laid down that the object acts on the subject, impressing on it the image of itself, an image

[1] F. Bonatelli, *Pensiero e conoscenza*, Bologna, 1864, pp. 5, 29, 34, 35.

in no way disfigured and deformed by the passivity of the knower, for the change which takes place in him only means that he knows what he did not know previously.[1] Knowledge becomes in this way more and more relieved of the Copernican task which Kant had tried to impose upon it, and is therefore reduced to a mere inexplicable reduplication of a ready-made reality. Following this course, Bonatelli's speculation ends in the complete reversal of the Kantian thesis : the form no longer belongs to the subject, but to the object as a thing-in-itself ; and to the subject is attributed merely the sense-modification, or in other words the matter.[2] Unless I am mistaken this is simply an attempt to reduce the dualistic thesis to an absurdity.

Cantoni, in spite of his extensive though superficial Kantian scholarship, is another dualist with a leaning towards the philosophy of Lotze. In his praiseworthy attempt to acclimatize Kantianism in Italy, he raised the famous problem concerning the psychological origin of the *a priori* element in knowledge, which had a great vogue in Germany in the latter part of the century and was for many years the rock on which one neo-Kantian after another suffered shipwreck. Cantoni meant this problem to preserve the Critical Philosophy from the pure subjectivity in which he thought Kant had confined it : the recognition of the psychological formation of the *a priori* element was intended to indicate the point at which the action of thought converged with that of reality. But the law of the heterogenesis of ends, the fertility of which is amazing, vitiated Cantoni's inquiry with precisely the very subjectivism which he believed he was attacking. For how can we speak of the psychological formation of the *a priori* element unless this is understood as the mere *a priori* of the empirical consciousness, and not of consciousness regarded as identical with reality ? Such language presupposes on the one hand a consciousness, on the other a ready-made reality ; and then explains that in appropriating this reality this consciousness proceeds by stages : it is at first a mere *a posteriori*, and it gradually

[1] F. Bonatelli, *Percezione e pensiero* (*Atti del R. Instituto Veneto di Scienze, lettere ed arti*, vol. iii., series vii., 1892), p. 1536.
[2] *Ibid.*, p. 1605.

renders itself *a priori* by stripping reality of its sensible content and conceiving the abstract form of things which thought can master (conceive universally, necessarily) just because it is devoid of content.[1]   But this is the false analytical *a priori* from which Kant had freed himself in his *Critique*, and which Lotze, by a real anachronism, had tried to revive. It has no power unless thought is placed on one side and reality on the other, and thought is made to play a game with itself in its empty subjectivity.   And this is exactly what Cantoni does ; for once off the right track, he talks of the " application " of the categories to the real and of a " correspondence " between them,[2] completely reversing all the fundamental principles of Kantianism.

Francesco Acri is a scholarly writer with an interesting mystical tendency : his personality is very characteristic of modern Italian philosophy.   In a period of great spiritual crudity, when materialism reigned unopposed, Acri had the courage to shake off the yoke of the tyrant and meet the enemy face to face.   He turned upon the naturalists with the words :   " You believe that with your cells you can explain the whole of conscious life, and in reality you do not explain anything ; the cell contains nothing which throws light upon the identity of consciousness, or its unity, or its formative or speculative or volitional faculties ; nothing which throws light upon the humblest of its operations." [3] And in order to point out the impossibility of combining the one with the many he made use of the delightful illustration of the eagle in Dante which appeared a single being but was really a collection of beings, and gave the impression from a distance that it was saying " I, I," while in reality, when heard from near at hand, it said " We, we."

But Acri's Platonism reproduces the same difficulty on a higher plane, and ultimately the illustration of the eagle recoils on his own head.   Assert the Platonic ideas, and thought can no longer be explained ; assert the immediate intuition of ideal truth, and the reflection of self-consciousness becomes inexplicable.   Hence it is in vain that Acri tries to

---

[1] C. Cantoni, *E. Kant*, Milan, 1879, vol. i., pp. 209, 213, 219.
[2] *Ibid.*, pp. 330, 334.
[3] F. Acri, *Videmus in ænigmate*, Bologna, 1907, p. 55.

sketch by means of poetical imagery the principle of reflection which in reality his philosophy lacks. He appeals to the example of the twinkling of the stars, but this example reveals the exact difficulty of Platonism : the twinkling of the star is merely the appearance of the reflection of the light, it is the subjective illusion of our vision. The doctrine of consciousness is thus the afterthought in Acri's conception : these compromises between Plato and Kant, separated as they are by so many centuries, always have something fictitious about them.

The dualistic tendency of the Italian philosophy of the latter part of the nineteenth century is epitomized in the names of Bonatelli, Cantoni and Acri. More recently it has had another follower in De' Sarlo, the founder of the review *La Cultura filosofica*. Rising in antithesis to positivism and agnosticism, and reviving some of Lotze's ideas, this review attempts to develop and restore the old dualism by bringing it into contact with contemporary European philosophy, and particularly with new epistemological doctrines and with the researches of experimental psychology.

And finally at this point we should not fail to mention a thinker who in the last ten years has made a notable attempt to attain an idealistic view of reality : we refer to Varisco. In his book *Science and Opinion*, published in 1901, he was still moving in the sphere of dogmatic metaphysics. He understood the world as " a collection of primary elements or monads that act upon one another. There are two kinds of reciprocal interaction between the monads. They determine (1) a variation *in* each monad, and (2) a variation *between* the monads, so that their arrangement (their spatial distribution) is modified. The facts of the first kind are psychical, those of the second physical." [1] This is the dualism of dogmatic metaphysics, and consists in the theory that the relations of the physical world are absolutely outside the monad. On the other hand, it is repugnant to monadology to assert the existence of inter-

---

[1] B. Varisco, *The Great Problems*, transl. by R. C. Lodge (Library of Philosophy), London, 1914, p. 291 foll., where the earlier doctrine is summarized. Cf. further *Scienza e opinioni*, Rome, 1901, pp. 247, 256, 261, 271, 307, 321.

monadic actions (the monads have no windows), seeing that
once they *are* asserted, knowledge of these external relations
becomes inconceivable, because if they are outside the
monad it is impossible to say where they are.

But by deepening the concept of monadology Varisco
has overcome the dualism of dogmatic metaphysics. In
his volume *The Great Problems* the dualism between the
physical and the psychical assumes an epistemological signification, in the sense that that distinction is no longer between
two realities extraneous to each other, but is a distinction
within the domain of knowledge itself. The physical reality
of *Science and Opinion* becomes a psychical reality, a complex
of sensibilia ; the subject (the psychical reality of the older
doctrine) becomes the unity of the multiplicity of sensation. On this basic duality Varisco builds his theory. On
the one side there exists the reality of sensibilia, constituted
according to its own special laws : on the other the reality
of the subject, constituted according to the principle of the
unity of consciousness. Thus the dualism is not resolved.
It is not resolved because Varisco has not developed the
concept of the unity of consciousness to its logical conclusion, by eliminating the residuum of Aristotelianism,
which consists in setting over against consciousness a world
of sensibilia which are not sensed, potentialities that are
waiting to be made actual. In fact, the shade of dogmatism,
of the priority of these sensibilia to the act of self-consciousness, remains with him still. Varisco has not really resolved
the physical reality of *Science and Opinion* ; it reappears in
psychological attire.

In order to overcome the dualism he has recourse to a
concept of Rosmini's, namely universal being, but he absolutely alters the significance of it, which is in his view no
longer transcendental but empirical, and expresses the mere
identity of thought as a product—the undifferentiated state
of subject and object ; in other words, that elementary
psychical reality on which the dualism between the physical
and the psychical must be based. Varisco makes a notable
attempt to show how through an inner necessity this undifferentiated state becomes differentiated, and thus shows
that he is quite familiar with the difficulties of idealism ;

but he does not seem to me to succeed in solving his problem, because he does not recognize the subject as the principle of differentiation. For he still regards this differentiation from the point of view of the metaphysic of being and not of knowing ; he considers it, that is to say, as the basis of a monadology and not of a phenomenology. In order to attain to this latter we must put aside altogether the prejudice of a ready-made reality, whether described as nature or as the potentiality of thought, and guard against anticipating in any way whatsoever the concrete act of thought by pre-supposing the world.

But in the doctrine of personality outlined by Varisco there are already indications of an incipient penetration of the true conception of subjectivity. I quote the following passage : " When that which I judge is myself, my action is no longer merely reconstructive ; it is truly constructive. The ego in the true sense of the word, that is to say the unity of self-consciousness—a very different thing from the pure unity of consciousness of the animal subject—only exists in so far as it affirms itself." [1] Good ; but once it is understood that in the world of consciousness, of reality *in fieri*, reproduction is production, then we must advance further, deepen the concept of creative reflection, the pivot of modern philosophy, and disclose all the treasures that it contains ; then and only then shall we see in the transparency of consciousness a complete vision of reality in its entirety. But Varisco stops half-way ; he glimpses, but does not develop, the all-significant principle of idealism.

§ 4. THE NEO-KANTIANS.

Italian neo-Kantianism has in many respects earned our gratitude for having given a great impetus to historical scholarship, in which we were very deficient. We must remember that even the two profoundest Italian thinkers of the nineteenth century, Rosmini and Gioberti, distorted in the most deplorable manner the history of thought, which led them to take a false view of their own historical position with regard to modern speculation. And in the field of the history of philosophy, Fiorentino, Tocco, Masci, Tarantino

[1] Varisco, *I massimi problemi cit.*, p. 129. *Cf.* Eng. tr. pp. 126–8.

and Chiappelli, among others, have attained genuine distinction. But in its theoretical attitude neo-Kantianism is closely connected with the tendency of which we have just spoken.

The special development of the system takes place within the boundaries of Kant's Transcendental Analytic. Hence its speculative impetus is kept within the limits laid down by the antinomies and paralogisms of the Transcendental Dialectic; a limit, however, which it attempts to surpass by demonstrating the vanity of all metaphysics. But neo-Kantianism is compelled in spite of itself to take account of metaphysics when it tries to explain the *a priori* element in knowledge, which it accepts from Kant. No sooner does it get beyond the simple distinction between the problem of the empirical formation of knowledge and that of its validity, and attempt to explain the how and the why of the latter, than it finds itself face to face with metaphysics. As we have already pointed out, value is a neutral concept oscillating between thought and being; for this reason the explanation of value forms the metaphysical problem of the relation between thought and being. How are we to solve it? Since neo-Kantianism is unable to see in the categories anything else except this simple fact of value, it has already exhausted its source, and cannot go back to Kant once more for this further explanation; it therefore searches for it in psychology and biology, and ends by finding itself in a position on which its own starting-point was a considerable advance.

This difficulty of neo-Kantianism is typically exemplified in the trajectory described by its first Italian representative, Fiorentino. Failing to maintain his initial position, and yielding to the pressure of the new biological investigations, to which German neo-Kantianism had already succumbed, he ends by entirely misrepresenting the significance of the Kantian *a priori* knowledge and contaminating it with evolutionary naturalism.

Masci is more faithful to the spirit of neo-Kantianism, and can be considered as its greatest living representative. His negative arguments against the misinterpretation of the fundamental principles of Kant's philosophy are sound, but the positive foundation of these same principles gives rise to the difficulties to which we have already called attention when dealing with neo-Kantianism in general. Masci defends with great justice the *a priori* character of space and time as spiritual functions, against the psychological theory which deludes itself into thinking it has satisfied the requirements of the Transcendental Æsthetic with the mere construction of the representation of space and time, and believes that with its mosaic of sensations it is constituting their form, while in fact presupposing it at every step. Nor do the biological researches on the problem of *a priori* knowledge offer any better substitute for Kant's deduction. They absolutely fail to take account of the nature of the problem with which they are dealing.

Another error which is often committed in the interpretation of Kant is that of reducing reality to mere representation. Thus, Masci observes, the real is dissipated, since according to the principles of Kantianism the psychical series has no greater claim to recognition than the physical. But do the physical and the psychical exist as two realities in themselves? This is the problem. At one moment it looks as though Masci were on the road towards a solution consonant with absolute idealism, by recognizing the emptiness of the thought which seeks to fall back upon a reality outside the act of self-consciousness.[1] Yet he fails to realize that beyond this act there is not a reality that is debarred to us because of the poverty of our mental faculties, but nothing at all except the projection of our own shadow. Once he has lost hold of the criterion of concrete unity, the physical and the psychical remain confronting him as two distinct facts, which he nevertheless feels the need of unifying. He reaches his monistic conclusion thus : " It is not a question of knowing how matter generates thought, nor how this generates material actions. To state the problem in this way is to render it insoluble, because the ideas of matter and spirit are one-sided generalizations, abstractions of our own, operating in opposite directions, from what is really a single process." [2] He accordingly tries to transfer

[1] F. Masci, *Il materialismo psicofisico*, Naples, 1901, vol. ii., p. 93.
[2] *Ibid.*, vol. iii., pp. 18–19.

this unity to a past in which the psychical and the physical were undifferentiated. " When psychical reality is referred back to a state which we can think of as prior to the existence of a differentiated nervous system, and thus prior to the existence of nervous structures in unicellular animals and in amorphous protoplasm, the difficulty of conceiving the unity of nature and of spirit becomes reduced to a minimum ; for psychical existence can be traced back to the inner dynamism of reality, to the qualificative, determinative and directive principles which we cannot deny without rendering unintelligible the mechanical phenomenon itself. The unity is seen better at the beginning than at the end, in the seed than in the fruit, in the initial stages of the development than in the ultimate products of the progressive differentiation of which the development consists. Similarly, proceeding in this direction, the reduction becomes by degrees more intelligible until the opposites, as it were, merge into and interpenetrate each other in the concepts of the atom and of the monad, which tend to be identified." [1] The unity of the real is thus transferred to an obscure past ; it is no longer the unity which is being created in the luminous transparency of consciousness, according to the new metaphysic of knowledge founded by Kant, but that which existed already created between the two heterogeneous realities of the old metaphysic of being.

Masci's thought seems to me to be torn between two conflicting claims, a monadology on the one hand and the new principle of self-consciousness on the other. Martinetti, an able young writer, falls a victim to the same difficulty, and remains entangled in it in spite of a great effort to escape, in which he attempts to fuse the metaphysic of being with the metaphysic of knowing. Like Boirac, he conceives the real as a plurality of monads, or (to remove the possibility of a historical misrepresentation) of conscious centres or synthetic subjective-objective unities.[2] But this plurality, realistically understood, is incompatible with a monadology. For the affirmation of the monad or at least of the subject-object relation deprives the other

[1] F. Masci, Il materialismo psicofisico, Naples, 1901, vol. iii., pp. 35, 36.
[2] P. Martinetti, Introduzione alla metafisica, Turin, 1904, pp. 410, 413.

monads of reality (in the realistic sense), since their existence is only possible as ideal creations in the monad.   The development of idealism consists in the deepening of this new concept of ideal creations, in which the true and concrete reality is realized : thus the old concept of the world as a natural totality has been abolished and the new concept of the world as absolute experience has taken its place.   Martinetti, on the other hand, still holds firmly to the idea of the world as a natural whole : he disperses throughout it his conscious centres, and does not perceive that this is incompatible with the new concept of ideal creations which he has ostensibly adopted.   Hence despite all his efforts he remains a realist, and as such he is seen to be involved in an insoluble difficulty when he attempts to fuse the plurality of conscious centres into a higher unity.   Once the plurality of consciousnesses is dogmatically affirmed, their unity will either be an empty name or a transcendent principle, because, I repeat, plurality as such is external to the act of consciousness.

This residuum of dogmatism renders it impossible for Martinetti really to overcome the metaphysic of being.   He only succeeds in effecting an apparent reconciliation between it and the new metaphysic of knowledge by demonstrating that the inherent instability of conscious centres, through which they are developed and advanced to ever higher syntheses, is presented in the field of knowledge as a progress of knowledge from the simplest undifferentiated forms of sensation to the highest synthesis of the understanding and of reason.   Here he is simply reproducing that same plurality over again.   Just as the unity of the reals fell outside them, so the principle of the organization of the forms of knowledge is external to all particular forms, and the passage from the one to the other is simply the Herbartian dialectic, that is to say the principle of contradiction applied to the progressive organization of the sense-data.

Certainly Martinetti's work is not lacking in indications of a very much more profound dialectical conception, but at bottom he only accounts empirically for the dialectical development : he simply supplies an empirical genesis of the forms of knowledge and is impotent to resolve the given element in sensation.   The flaw in his theory lies in the unmediated affirmation of the discrete unity of consciousness, and this is repeated in his epistemology in the equally unmediated affirmation of sense reality : any further development of thought can only be a mere elaboration, a purification of the given, and will never succeed in explaining its creation. The realistic presupposition of his metaphysic is echoed in his theory of knowledge : the assertion of the ascending scale of monads involves the correlative assertions of the grades of knowledge, understood realistically and not, as with Hegel, transcendentally. An acute observer will perceive that this doctrine of grades of knowledge cannot hold good unless we presuppose a ready-made reality to which knowledge must conform. And so Martinetti's attempt to fuse the two metaphysics, that of being and that of knowing, seems to me to have failed, because by continuing to assert the existence of a " given," even though he insists that the " given " is spiritual and not natural, he has removed all possibility of resolving being into knowledge ; in a word, this " given " will always end by pointing to something outside knowledge, that is to say to a being, even though, as in Martinetti's conception, it is a spiritual being. Yet, in spite of the difficulty which I have pointed out, his conception seems to me to be one of the most notable achievements of Italian thought in late years.

CHAPTER III

ABSOLUTE IDEALISM

§ 1. Vera and Spaventa.

In a previous chapter we stated that with Vincenzo Gioberti the Italian speculative thought of the nineteenth century attained to the height of the German. But Gioberti misunderstood his own historical position, and it was only in later years that he began to recognize the Fichtian and Hegelian elements in his system ; and even then he continued to criticize the alleged German pantheism and to believe that his own dialectic was that of Plato, while in fact it was the dialectic of absolute thought, that is to say of the spirit.

Bertrando Spaventa was the first to envisage clearly the position in history of Italian thought : he therefore represents this movement of thought coming to a clear consciousness of itself. He also developed Gioberti's brilliant intuitions into a scientific system.

For many years Spaventa taught in the University of Naples ; among his colleagues was a Hegelian of European fame, Augusto Vera. But neither paid the slightest attention to the other ; their points of view were too divergent. On the one hand, the young Hegelian, whose fresh and ardent spirit was infusing new life into Hegel's thought ; on the other, the old Hegelian, the relic of a glorious past, full of mystic adoration for his Hegel—the Christ of philosophy, as he called him—and able to regard the life of a whole century as meaningless or as a series of errors to be avoided. Here we are still among the " epigoni " ; there we can detect the birth of a new philosophy.

He is a curious type, this old Hegelian, who cannot move without stumbling and is so blinded by the mists that he does not see the precipice at his feet. We find him in embarrassment from the very first moment of his entrance into the sanctuary of philosophy, and lost in a maze of reasonings in order to discover the best way of entering. " How is it possible," he asks himself, " to teach the Hegelian philosophy ? " He knows from experience that the people before whom he ventures to speak of Hegel habitually laugh at him behind his back ; and so he concludes that " Hegelianism can only be demonstrated to an Hegelian." [1] And then there rises the further and more serious problem : " How does one become an Hegelian ? " The situation is growing rather complicated, seeing that one cannot become an Hegelian unless one is already an Hegelian. Here is an antinomy to be solved ; and the only possible way to solve it is to assert that Hegelians are born and not made. This idea comes to Vera as a genuine revelation, and he ends by convincing himself that he is an Hegelian by divine right. From the height of this conviction he can afford a glance of pity to the non-elect, accept with resignation the weakness of his pupils, and abandon himself, without any desire to be understood or comprehended, to his contemplation.

Vera's philosophy is simply the contemplation of the priest of Brahma. The goal at which he is aiming is the idea in its empty universality without any connection with the world of life. In order to reach it we must rise above the sphere of feeling, renounce our own individual consciousness and purge ourselves of all our human contingency. Exactly what Vera believed he would attain by such a method it is difficult to say ; certainly not the concrete universal of Hegel. And it is indeed amazing to see how the pages of the *Phenomenology* and the *Logic*, which are so full of life, in which the whole world of history is fused into a magnificent epic, are supplanted in the work of this somnolent Hegelian by a watered Platonism that takes the ideas for entities and for mere representations of things, and works on them with its dialectic till they vanish from our sight among the clouds. Thus Hegelianism is distorted into a new metaphysic of being, far worse than the old, because it crystallized the ideas into things and then deduced these things from one another—

[1] A. Vera, *Introduction à la Philosophie de Hegel*, Paris, 1864, 2nd ed., p. xvi.

deducing horses from donkeys, so to speak—substituting a
scale of empirically generated things for the scale of ideas
deduced each from the last in progressive stages of perfection.
Compared with such a metaphysic even the amateurish efforts
of a Schopenhauer were to be welcomed ; and yet Vera
thought it necessary to protest against Schopenhauer's
views.

Bertrando Spaventa's conception of Hegelianism was a
very different thing. Gioberti had asserted, just as Hegel
did, that to think is to create. The idea of thought as creation
is the new idea of the Kantian philosophy ; Descartes and
Spinoza did not go farther ,than the concept of thought as
causation. But Gioberti had arrived at the new principle
all at once, in a sudden burst ; he had intuited but not proved
creation ; for him it was a fact which admitted neither of
deduction nor of demonstration. Yet he himself, in an
exceedingly important passage of his posthumous work, had
completed the formula that to think is to create by adding
this other, that to prove is to create.[1]   Thought proves the
creative act by reproducing and re-creating it within itself ;
but to reproduce is to produce, to re-create is to create.   This
is the important new concept of the mind, as increasing not
by the sedimentation and reproduction of its products but
by the creation of a new reality.   The product itself only
exists in this new production, the creative act only in this
act which re-creates it. Gioberti failed to arrive at this
conclusion ; indeed, from the idea that to prove is to create,
he tried to infer that creation is indemonstrable.   But since
proof is the essential character of mental activity (by this
the mind is distinguished from substance, which only admits
of definition), the problem which Gioberti's philosophy set
before its successors was this : to prove the reality of creation.
And this is just Spaventa's problem.   " Gioberti says :
to be is to create, to think is to create, to create is to think.
This identity must be proved.

" To create is Being in its concreteness," Spaventa adds ;
" it is to make, to realize, to individualize, to substantiate,
to ' entate,' to make exist ; it is reality, absolute reality.
It is absolute reality because, for Gioberti, God Himself is

[1] V. Gioberti, *Nuova protologia*, ed. Gentile, Bari, 1912, vol. ii., p. 211.

the act of creation, the creation of Himself. Remove the act of creation and you have nothing. Yet one never has nothing, for to remove means here to think; the thought remains, and is always with us. This amounts to saying : the act of creation when removed remains ; because to remove is itself an act of creation : that is to say as mere removing— negation—it is a moment of creation. Now how can reality, creation, be proved ?

" Thought *is* ; it cannot not be. Thought proves itself ; to deny thought is to think. Thought is Certainty, absolute Certainty. Thought is a dialectical act, a world, a totality, a system. In thinking, simply thinking, I—simply as thought—make, construct, create this world, this world of mine, which is Thought itself. This world, created by Thought, is absolutely certain as Thought, it is Thought itself. (The pure mode of Thought is just logic.)" [1]

It is clear that Spaventa's problem is the Cartesian problem developed to its full significance. Descartes starts with the dogmatic affirmation and negates it by doubting ; but this doubt is itself a thought, and the being which is destroyed in the doubt rises again as the new being, the being of thought, no longer the old being, the mere arbitrary assertion, but the new being, as dialectical process, as the being which destroys itself in order to rise again through the very act of self-destruction, that is to say as understanding, as an absolute process, self-mediated, which is affirmation because it is negation, certainty because it is victory over doubt, truth because it is the overcoming of error, creation because it is all this at once : originative act of thought which does not stop short at the given, but recognizes it by assimilating it ; productivity of thought, rising perpetually from its own ashes ; creativity of thought, arising out of itself and nothing but itself, since life and death, affirmation and negation, faith and doubt are alike its own work.

These are the treasures of the Cartesian *Cogito*, that *Cogito* of which Descartes himself did not understand the value and which remained in his hands a lifeless fragment. The great value of the Hegelian logic consists in the fact that

---

[1] B. Spaventa, *La filosofia Italiana nelle sue relazione con la filosofia europeo*, Bari, 1909. Appendix, *Schizzo d'una storia della logica*, p. 254.

it developed this new concept and realized its inexhaustible possibilities. Hegel's *Logic* explains the spontaneous creative process in which thought by creating its own determinations creates itself ; it is the ideal eternal history of thought envisaged as a scientific system. This is the meaning of Spaventa's statement that the explanation of creation is logic.

This logic, the framework of which Spaventa takes from Hegel, is developed by him in its profoundest aspect, since he regards it from the historical (Cartesian) point of view. His interpretation of the first three categories, being, not-being, and becoming, constitutes in itself alone the strongest proof of Spaventa's great originality. He understands being as the immediate assertion of thought, in the sense of the product of thought. It is the absolute abstract, thought extinguished in being. But I think of being : and in so far as I think of it, being is no longer the mere abstract, but my act of abstracting, my act of thought. And so in virtue of thought itself the self-extinction of thought in being is in truth a self-distinction, an assertion of itself as something other than mere being.

The argument is so important that I will repeat it in the actual words of the author. " In defining being," he says, " I do not *distinguish* myself, as thought, *from* being : I *extinguish* myself, as thought, *in* being ; I *am* being. Now this extinction of thought in being is the contradiction of being ; and this contradiction is the first ray of the dialectic. Being contradicts itself because this extinction of thought in being (and only thus is being possible) is really a negation of extinction : it is distinction, it is life. To think of not thinking, to make an abstraction from thought, that is to say to define being, is to think ; it is abstraction, that is to say, thought." This contradiction of thought as extinguishing itself in Being, and, in this very act, thinking and therefore distinguishing itself and rising again, is *becoming*, understood as thinking.

" Being and not-being, as they exist after being validated in the category of becoming, are no longer the same as before they were so validated ; each is now that same unity in difference which is becoming ; and in so far as it is such a unity

it is truly, that is to say actually, distinct.   In so far as they
are truly one and distinct, they can be said to be really
validated, that is to say, they are moments of becoming.

"Being, as a moment, is a being that becomes ; it is beginning, birth (distinction) ; not-being, as a moment, is a not-
being that becomes ; it is cessation, perishing (extinction).

"Thus becoming is itself a beginning that ceases, and a
cessation that begins ; a birth that dies and a death that is
born (distinction that is extinguished, and extinction that is
distinguished).   Eternal death, eternal birth.   This eternal
death that is eternal birth, this eternal birth that is eternal
death, is thought.   I think, that is to say, I am born as
thought ; but I cannot comprehend myself as thought, but
only as past thoughts, and therefore I perish as thought.
But in perishing as thought, I think : and therefore I am
born again as thought.   And so on for ever." [1]

I have introduced this long quotation because it gives
a very profound insight into the *Logic* of Hegel and is at the
same time a complete refutation of the system of his *Encyclo-
pædia*.   Into the dialectic of being and not-being Spaventa
introduces a factor which Hegel, faithful to the systematic
partition of his philosophy, kept rather in the shade : it is
Descartes' *Cogito* and Kant's *I think*.   What this amounts
to is that the dialectical process of Hegel's logic is not to be
conceived as a mere system of science, as a pure development
of the notion in itself, but as an immanent activity of consciousness.   The identity of thought and being, the resolution
of being in thought, is a process that takes place in the light
of my consciousness, and is just as much psychological as
logical and historical.   Here phylogeny is no longer merely
recapitulated by ontogeny, it is itself ontogeny : thought
does not arise as a mere psychical reality confronted by an
objective world of nature or of science, but it is itself the
reality of that world ; and it does not reproduce in its psychological genesis the historical genesis, but it is itself this historical genesis.   It is said that we exist in virtue of our past ;
it might be added that our past exists in virtue of us, of our
thought : the true meaning of this reciprocity is the eternity

[1] B. Spaventa, *Le prime categorie della Logica di Hegel* (in *Scritti filosofici,*
ed. Gentile, Napoli, 1901, pp. 196–200).

of thought, the divine eternity of the act in which present and past are one and in which reproduction is not distinct from production.

This implies the complete fusion of phenomenology, logic, philosophy of nature and philosophy of the spirit in a single science of psychology or phenomenology, whichever term is preferred, which is at the same time an ideal eternal history of the spirit in its development. This absolute psychology or absolute empiricism seems to us to be the logical conclusion of the whole of the post-Kantian philosophy.

But Spaventa failed to draw any conclusion from his premises, and continued to distinguish phenomenology from logic and both from the philosophy of nature and of the spirit. Hence he was involved in the difficulty of having to distinguish two beginnings, one of consciousness, the other of science (logic). From this arose the problem : What is the *primum* of science ? This led to the antinomy : " A proved *primum* is a contradiction ; for if it is proved, it is not a *primum*. We must conclude that it cannot be proved. But, on the other hand, it cannot be asserted in this arbitrary manner, asserted just because it is asserted ; it must be proved ; otherwise it would be a *primum* indeed, but not the *primum* of science." [1] And he attempted to solve the antinomy by reconnecting logic with phenomenology, which by purging thought of empirical elements should prepare the way for that pure thought, that being, which should form the starting-point of logic. But this problem which so troubled Spaventa is really meaningless. It is rather like the attempt to derive thought from something other than thought ; though perhaps no one ever perceived more clearly than Spaventa that thought can only be derived from itself. Thought is deduced from itself ; its deduction is a production ; to prove the *primum* of thought is still to think. The regress is here merely apparent. It is in reality a progress ; hence the argument which refers back the proof to an antecedent stage of thought is fallacious. Equally fallacious is the idea of attempting to search for a *primum* of science. The essential character of thought is that in every act it forms its own

[1] B. Spaventa, *La filosofia Italiana cit.*, p. 258.

22

primum, at every moment it constitutes its own centre ; and thus the search for a determinate *primum* is meaningless, because where all is *primum* there is no *primum* ; and the absolute *primum* is concrete thought.

But once embarked on this course, Spaventa was led on insensibly to aggravate the error ; the distinction laid down between a phenomenology and a logic, a propædeutic and a science, involved as a consequence another distinction ; that between truth in itself and truth for us, a μέθεξις and a μίμησις, in the phraseology of Gioberti. " This propædeutic," said Spaventa, alluding to the phenomenology, " which is science and proves the *primum* of science, only exists in so far as we exist, finite consciousness or spirit ; we ought to rise to the level of science, but we are not immediately science. The true science, on the other hand, exists absolutely in itself ; it is not only human but divine ; while the other is only human, not divine. It is divine as a moment of genuine science, not as a propædeutic ; God has no need of a pro-pædeutic." [1] What a number of fallacies in order to conceal one false step ! At bottom Spaventa shows himself here a dogmatist of the first water, a Platonist distinguishing between a truth in itself and a truth for us, a distinction which is totally repugnant to the new idealism. The reason for his error is that Spaventa entirely lacks a phenomenology of error ; hence he fails to develop the new concept of truth as development, as a process, although it belongs to the spirit of his philosophy ; and ends by unconsciously objecti-fying truth into something created and complete, into a reality in itself. Here we still have a remnant of the outlook of the older type of Hegelian, who while he asserts the reality of progress, movement and the like, is yet induced by his overpowering loyalty to the letter to deny all these things when he arrives at the climax of his speculation.

But it is not on this side that the great vitality of Spaventa's thought is manifested. The same Spaventa who affirmed the abstractly divine character of science maintained with far greater truth that the *a priori* is itself the new power of nature, *the human power*, which results and is concentrated and individualized from the whole of

[1] *La filosofia Italiana cit.*, p. 265.

the scattered antecedent actuality, and is therefore at the same time an absolute *a posteriori*.[1] Here we have a glimpse of the true Spaventa, the thinker who has understood better than anyone else the truly human character of the absolute, that absolute which is not foreign to us, but most intimate, and is not outside our contingency, but is this same contingency *sub specie æterni*. He says : " All those who level against Hegel two opposite charges, of relativism and absolutism, are the prey to an optical illusion peculiar to the position which they occupy ; each party attacks that side of the Hegelian absolute which particularly offends it : the semi-subjectivists, experience (the phenomenon, the mani-festation, becoming) ; the objectivists, thought. Neither of them have sufficiently powerful minds to realize it as it really is, that is to say as *absolute reason*, outside, beyond and above which there is nothing ; to realize that the relative and the so-called absolute are simply abstract entities, limbs torn from the living organic unity. On the one side relation is confused with the relative (as opposed to the absolute), and on the other absoluteness with the absolute (as opposed to the relative). To the first I say : The process from the first thinkable (from pure being) to the absolute thinkable (to the absolute subjectivity of the world, as unity of knowledge and will, of truth and goodness), and from this, as first existence, homogeneous and undifferentiated externality or space, to internality or corporeal subject, to the animal, to sense, as human or spiritual sense, to the spirit or absolute subject—this process is not an empty play of thought with itself in my understanding alone, or a pallid reflection of a distant and invisible object, but, as infinite act, as the thought which is self-determined, embodied in its own determinations, epitomized and concentrated and articulated and asserted as absolute thought, it is the act of the absolute, its understanding, its presence, itself. To the second I say : This process, just because it is the production and critical observation of thought by thought—a process which simply is thought and nothing but thought—is the beginning and substance and end of that which is commonly called experience ; it does not go on outside and apart from it, as it were, in thin

[1] *Scritti filos. cit.*, p. 313 (*Paolottismo, positivismo, razionalismo*).

air ; the process is not only empirical, it is the true and absolute empirical, and always has greater value than any disconnected fragment and article to which that name is attached." [1]

Here, with a few reminiscences of the old Hegelian schematism, we have the new thought which concentrates all the vitality of Hegelianism. The concept of absolute relation, which is this same concept of the phenomenalization of reality in human thought, banishes all question of a dualism between thought in itself and thought for us, between a process of consciousness and a process of science ; and inasmuch as reality is neither the mere contingent nor the mere absolute, but the absolute process of the contingent, it is not merely a solution, nor a ready-made reality presented to our eyes in advance of any problem that may be raised, nor something that is always sought for and never attained, an eternal problem that is never a solution ; but it is an eternal problem which is at the same time an eternal solution, an absolute possibility which is also absolute actuality. The development of this concept means the satisfaction of the thousand-years-old demand, first made by Aristotle, for the unification of potentiality and actuality ; a satisfaction which can only be found in the absolute identity of each with the other. Pascal made the profound remark that we could not seek unless we had already found ; to this we can now add Spaventa's equally profound saying that the spirit is an eternal problem which is an eternal solution, a saying that may well stand as the motto of our whole speculative life.

§ 2. F. De Sanctis : The History of Literature.

Spaventa's teaching did not at first exercise any great influence. A few faithful pupils, among whom should be mentioned De Meis, Jaia and Maturi, collected and jealously preserved their master's thoughts ; but just as he had been unable to reap the fruit of his brilliant intuitions and define his exact position with regard to Hegel, so his pupils in their turn failed to realize what a radical transformation of Hegel-

[1] B. Spaventa, *Principii di etica*, Naples, 1904, pp. 22-3.

ianism was taking place under their eyes : indeed, they increasingly tended to emphasize the Platonistic and contemplative aspect of Spaventa's philosophy, which became for them a veritable religion, a creed to be carefully preserved intact. And so they were unresponsive to the claims of a new age with new needs : their mystical and religious temperaments converted the speculative value of a philosophy into the mystical value of a faith, and finally reduced the life of thought to a life of stagnation. This was not in the spirit of Spaventa : his thought was continually re-forming itself under the shock of new ideas, and he had thus brought out an element of Hegelianism that had never yet been properly recognized : the sense of the positive character, the absolute concreteness of thought. He thus demonstrated the value of positivism ; at any rate its negative, dialectical value.

The same dissolution of Hegelianism which was being unconsciously effected in Spaventa's thought was taking place in a different manner in the work of his great fellow-countryman, Francesco de Sanctis. His history of Italian literature, a work unique in the history of European thought, traces the development of the Italian spirit from its first dawnings right through the ages up to the formation of the modern mind.

Art is for De Sanctis identical with mind regarded as individualized in sense and rendered transparent to itself ; it is the content of life brought to the same degree of clearness as the form. The history of art is therefore the process by which mind individualizes itself ; it is the unity of thought and sense, a unity which is a development. Remove from the work of art its individual character, and you get abstract science ; which is valid for an empty eternity, but has for that very reason nothing spiritual in it, because the spirit is life, variety of attitudes and forms. Remove the transparence of the idea, of the universal immanent in sensation, and sensation itself grows dim ; it is no longer the luminosity of the imagination, but the opacity of the mere fancy, an empty play of psychological mechanism. In this reciprocal relation of universal and individual lies the secret of art, which is neither the caprice of the individual nor the mere imaginary reflection of life, but life itself, which in its development attains its own intuitive clearness. Herein lies, if I am not mistaken, the significance of that correspondence which De Sanctis is always trying to find between art and the content of the life out of which it grows ; a correspondence which is not that of the mere representation to that which it represents (because then art would merely be a copy of reality), but rather the correspondence of reality with itself, so to speak ; that is, the equilibrium or the lack of equilibrium between the various moments of the formation of the spirit.

If this is true, then the relation of the content of life—religion, morality, science and so forth—to art is not the mere relation of content to form, but just the process of historical individualization by which content attains the clearness of form. What falsifies art is the arbitrary forcing of an inert content into a spurious form ; it is the demand that Machiavelli should do the cooking and Ariosto gird on the sword. Thus an ethical view of life would come as a discord in Machiavelli, because the clear atmosphere of the Renaissance world is entirely due to its human naturalism and the absence of any suggestion of spiritual life ; but in Manzoni it has a concrete æsthetic value, because the cycle of historical progress has by now developed the full force of the new concept of humanity. Science, again, whose expression in literature up to the time of Dante was always an artistic failure, because its content was conceived as transcendent and external to the spirit, acquires real æsthetic value in Bruno and Galileo, because with the recognition of the human character of knowledge all conflict is overcome.

This does not imply that art is measured by an external standard or subjected to the contingency of time ; it is eternal, but its eternity is contingency itself, regarded as concentrating and individualizing the universality of the spirit. Dante, Machiavelli, Manzoni are outside history just because—it may seem paradoxical—they are so profoundly rooted in history. Here, as everywhere else, the absolute is not outside the contingent ; it is its very inmost life.

With a few names, to mark the culminating moments of the development of the spirit, and with many digressions and transitional passages, De Sanctis constructs his history of literature. Its central idea is the formation of the world of Dante as the completest expression of the Middle Ages, and its dissolution in the following centuries right up to its total negation in the prescient scepticism of modern times and the fresh formation of an entirely human world in complete antithesis to the ancient transcendence. " In the Middle Ages," he says, " Man and Nature look for their foundation beyond themselves, to the other world : their motive forces are personified under the names of universals endowed with a separate existence. This concept of life gives birth to the *Divine Comedy*. The controlling power of history lies outside history, and is called Providence. In the world of Boccaccio this controlling power is Chance, Fortune. The notion of Providence is dead ; the notion of Science is as yet unborn. The marvellous is no longer called a miracle, nay, the miraculous is ridiculed ; it is called a puzzle, a problem, an extraordinary accident. Passions, characters, ideas are not the forces which rule the world, subordinated as they are to this new fate, the volatile and capricious Fortune. Machiavelli rejects both Fortune and Providence, and seeks in man himself for the forces and laws which shape his destiny. His idea is that the world is what we make it, and that each man is to himself his own providence and his own fortune. This idea cannot but have profoundly transformed art "

With the new science there rises the new literature. The old transcendence is negated, and man acquires consciousness of his own subjectivity. The new poetry, like the new science, is human. It announces its arrival in Tasso's malady, the malady of the modern man. The human character of this art is best expressed in the one word " lyricism." De Sanctis perhaps does not throw into strong enough relief this lyrical aspect of art ; to develop this notion has been the work of Croce. In our opinion it ought to be interpreted more definitely in terms of history : but from a purely ideal point of view it figures largely in the general plan of Croce's philosophy, with which we shall very shortly seek acquaintance.

De Sanctis's great merit consists in having actualized in its most concrete form the Hegelian idea of the spirit as

development, and in having attained a new concept of
art as a dynamic element of life itself, a concept free from all
arbitrary schematism. His work, like Spaventa's, was not
understood in Italy and attracted no followers. The merely
learned refused it the title of history, and more favourable
critics chose to describe it as a collection of essays. Such
blindness amazes us to-day ; but our amazement ceases
when we reflect how difficult it must be for those who do
not move to understand movement.

§ 3. MARXIANISM.

Antonio Labriola's theory of historical materialism is an
offshoot of Bertrando Spaventa's teaching, grafted on the
stock of positivism. A lively and clever writer, yet without
any great depth or genuine speculative bent, he has succeeded
in investing his Marxianism with a character all his own.
And while in Germany Marxianism has degenerated into an
empty dualistic ideology, he has interpreted it into a really
monistic theory of history. "History," he says,[1] "does
not depend on the difference between true and false, or just
and unjust, still less on the more abstract antithesis of possible
and real ; as though things stood on one side and ideas, their
shadows and phantoms, on the other. It is always all of a
piece, and depends entirely on the process of formation and
transformation of society, which is to be understood in an
absolutely objective sense and independently of any satisfaction or dissatisfaction on our part." But this objectivism
of Labriola's, which is a reminiscence of Vico and Engels,
is not a denial of the human value of history, but only of
human caprice. Hence he can say that " by successively
producing different social environments, that is to say, the
successive artificial territories, man has produced himself ;
and herein lies the real kernel, the concrete reason, the
positive foundation of the reality which ideologues, through
different imaginative combinations and with different logical
structures, misinterpret as the progress of the human spirit." [2]

[1] A. Labriola, *Saggi intorno alla concezione materialistica della storia :*
I. *In memoria del manifesto dei comunisti,* Roma, 1895, 2nd ed., p. 15.
[2] *Ibid.,* III. *Discorrendo di socialismo e filosofia,* Rome, 1902, 2nd ed.,
pp. 80, 104.

This is pure idealism ; and just for this reason Labriola ought to be very reluctant to insist on the distinction between the economic structure and the political and social super-structure of society, as indeed appears from his acute criticism of the doctrine of " factors " in history. Hence the more strictly socialistic part of Marx's theory is rather out of place in Labriola's philosophy of history, and often results in a pure travesty of Hegelian ideas. Thus he asserts that, for historical materialism, becoming or evolution is real —indeed, it is reality itself, just as the work of self-creation by which man ascends from the immediacy of animal life to perfect liberty (that is, communism) is real. And further, there is not an unknowable, or any kind of limit whatsoever to knowledge, for in the endless process of work which con-stitutes experience men know all that they need, all that it is useful for them to know. The travesty here, even though it is the work of a man of talent, is still a travesty, and very closely resembles that of pragmatism.

But apart from these reminiscences the substance of Labriola's work consists just in this, that the concept of history, if it is deepened, is found to contain the implicit refutation of historical materialism. With the negation of all dualism, of every theory of " factors " in history and of every simplificatory interpretation of human development, very little justification remains for any distinction in history between the economic foundation and the social super-structure, or for the theory which makes the former the basis of the latter. When it is considered in its most concrete expression and purged of that compound of history and naturalism which gave it a special significance in the works of Marx and Engels, historical materialism no longer has any *raison d'être* as a philosophy of history.

This fact, the collapse of historical materialism as a philosophy, has been pointed out by Croce in a review of Labriola's work. In Croce's view it remains a mere canon for the interpretation of history, or rather " a collection of new data, of new observations that come within the con-sciousness of the historian." But it seems to me that the most conclusive criticism of the doctrine has been provided by Croce himself in an article entitled " The End of Socialism," which, while refraining from any theoretical comment, simply gives a historical sketch of the origin and development of Marxianism. The facts so summarized demonstrate vividly the merely contingent and transitory value of historical materialism, whose communistic Utopia was a hasty generalization (and one belied by the event) from the historical data relative to the growth of capitalism.

Thus the historical materialism which in Germany and in France struck out along different roads towards the realm of Utopia, has arrived in Italy in time to read its own epitaph. It has been rejected as a philosophy of history; but at the same time it has provided an effective stimulus to the formation of our own theories of historical science.

§ 4. B. Croce : The Philosophy of the Spirit.

The different tendencies visible in the previous history of Italian idealism are gathered up and brought into a single brilliant focus by the philosophy of Croce. The general character and outlook of his thought, with its peculiar dual bent towards the theory of history and the theory of art, was stamped upon it from the first by the influence of Vico's historical and æsthetic speculations and De Sanctis's large views of literary criticism. The more strictly philosophical interest of his doctrines only emerged later, when they were already almost complete ; and its effect has been not so much to transform them, still less to destroy their equilibrium, as to weld them more firmly into a systematic whole. This explains why Croce has been able so clearly to determine his own position with regard to Hegel, and to perform the hitherto unattempted task of distinguishing the living parts of the Hegelian system from the dead, while all Hegel's followers have become entangled more or less irremediably in the meshes of that system. It is because Croce has never been an Hegelian in the strict sense of the word ; he never became a really close and earnest student of the philosopher of Stuttgart till after he had already found himself. What attracted him particularly in Hegel was his lively feeling for the problems, a temperamental aversion to all vague sentimentalism and morbid mysticism, and finally that serious and robust outlook on life which comes from persistent work and not from the facile revelations of intuition or feeling; qualities possessed in an eminent degree by Croce himself.

But alongside of this Hegelian aspect of Croce's character and in antithesis to it there is another which, to continue the historical analogy, I would call Herbartian. Just as we find in Herbart a speculative faculty of the highest order, developed to a degree nowhere equalled except in Hegel, but then suddenly coming to a standstill, the dialectic strangled and the unity of the real shattered; so in Croce we can remark in the apparent uniformity of his thought a profound hiatus, an unreconciled contradiction between an intensely living and dynamic mentality and a taste for distinctions and classifications by which all vitality is either killed outright or at least banished to another sphere. Whoever reads those brilliant passages on the dialectic of the opposites in Croce's book on Hegel, or again in the *Philosophy of Practice*, the book which marks the culminating point of his thought, is very soon convinced that he has before him no reminiscence of Hegel or of any one else, but an entirely fresh and original mind whose whole thought is controlled by a firm grasp of the actuality of the problems with which it is dealing. Yet if one reads on, one sees the vitality of the thought beginning to disappear, the speculative impulse to evaporate, between the meshes of a network of distinctions; the system has no place for the intimate nature of reality and a lively sense of history, and these tend more and more to vanish from the system and to take refuge in the personality of the philosopher who dominates it. It seems to me that Croce is still the centre of two conflicting cultures. On the one hand, the insistent and decisive criticism of naturalism in all its forms, whether in literature, in logic, or in ethics, has left in his thought traces of this same naturalism, leading him to combat the amorphous philosophy of the last fifty years by setting up a series of sharp and clear distinctions which frequently, as we shall see, break up the unity of the spirit; while on the other hand, his living and concrete method of visualizing philosophical problems, in which nothing is second-hand and nothing is laboured, but every-

thing springs from life and returns to life, has given rise to a
series of new and profound ideas—indeed, to a wholly fresh
mentality to which immanence is no mere word, but an act,
and which invests its problems with that character of actuality of which only genuine thinkers know the secret.   Croce
has thus infused new life and interest into philosophical
problems that had become dormant ; and whatever the nature
of the solutions he has advanced, whether they are accepted
or rejected, there always remains for him the merit of having
effected a revival of Italian culture.

The advance made by Croce on the speculation of the
nineteenth century consists in this, that he has set on foot
the dissolution of the Hegelian system, which by its mere
weight was suffocating the living problems that were stirring
in Hegel's own thought.   If the dialectic is thought in becoming, the negation of fact and its conversion into thought, the
work of dissolution of the huge mass of the Hegelian system
is in the spirit of Hegelianism itself.   The two points which
Croce's criticism has effectively established are the definite
negation of any philosophy of nature and of any distinction
between a phenomenology and a philosophical system.   In
Hegel's own philosophy this distinction is of historical value
only, corresponding as it does with successive phases in the
growth of his thought ; a logical value it can never have in
an idealistic philosophy, which denies that there is a ready-
made reality to which thought must conform and identifies
reality with thought itself, that is to say, with the process
through which thought itself passes in the attainment of
truth.   And as for the idea of a speculative elaboration of
the concept of nature, it is a contradiction in terms, for it
amounts to nothing less than endowing an arbitrary construction of thought with an independent reality ; it is, in short,
we should say, a relic of the old metaphysic of being.   To
think of nature as nature is an absurdity ; in so far as it is
thought about, nature is already spirit ; hence no philosophy
is possible except the philosophy of the spirit.

Having disposed of Hegel's errors, we are in a position
better to appreciate his truths. And the fundamental
truth of the Hegelian philosophy is the discovery of the
concrete concept, the synthesis of opposites. Thought is

not empty identity nor mere opposition, but the profound
unity of opposition. " The opposites are not an illusion,
and the unity is not an illusion. The opposites are opposed
to one another, but they are not opposed to the unity : for
the true and concrete unity is nothing but the unity or
synthesis of opposites : it is not immobility, but movement ;
it is not a static state, but a development. The philosophical
concept is the concrete universal ; and therefore it is the
thinking of reality as at the same time united and divided."
Without the dialectical process there is no development.
Whoever speaks of a pure identity of thought with itself,
speaks of a truth that is not the overcoming of error ; a good
that is not a triumph over evil ; a beauty that is not a victory
over ugliness ; and therefore, far from conceiving spiritual
reality in its concreteness, he is grasping an empty and abstract
schema.

In Croce's view the dialectical conception of Hegelianism
is completely summed up in the first triad of the logic :
being ; nothing ; becoming. " What is being without
nothing ? What is pure, indeterminate, unqualified, ineffable
being, i.e. being in general, not this or that particular being ?
How can it be distinguished from nothing ? And, on the
other hand, what is nothing without being, i.e. nothing
conceived in itself, without determination or qualification,
nothing in general, not the nothing of this or that particular
thing. In what way is this distinguished from being ? To
take one of the two terms by itself is the same as though
you had taken the other alone ; for the one has meaning
only in and through the other. Thus to take the true
without the false, or the good without the evil, is to make of
the true something not thought—because thought is struggle
against the false—and therefore something that is not true.
And similarly it is to make of the good something not willed
(because to will the good is to negate evil) and therefore
something that is not good. Outside the synthesis, the two
terms taken abstractly pass into one another and change
sides. Truth is found only in the third ; that is to say, in
the case of the first triad, in becoming ; which, therefore,
is, as Hegel says, the first concrete concept." [1]

[1] B. Croce, *What is living and what is dead of the Philosophy of Hegel*,
tr. Douglas Ainslie, 1915, p. 23.

Hegel's permanent achievement lies then, according to Croce, in the discovery of the dialectic of opposites : his mistake consists in having abused this concept and wrongfully extended the dialectic of opposites to " distincts," that is to say, to the " forms " of the spirit. True and false, good and bad, are really opposed to one another, and hence for them the Hegelian principle is valid, that the positive term only exists as a triumph over the negative. But the same thing cannot be said of the concepts of the beautiful and the true, or of the true and the good ; these latter couples differ from the former in that each term does not cancel the other, but can be harmonized with it. " The true is not in the same relation to the false as it is to the good ; nor is the beautiful to the ugly in the same relation as it is to philosophical truth. Life without death and death without life are two opposed falsities whose truth is the life which is a nexus of life and death, of itself and of its opposite. But truth without goodness and goodness without truth are not two falsities which are annulled in a third term ; they are false conceptions which resolve themselves in a series of grades in which truth and goodness are at once distinct and united." [1]

This distinction in unity is the dialectic of distincts, or more precisely the doctrine of " grades of the spirit." If the beautiful and the true are not subject to the same dialectic as the true and the false, and on the other hand cannot be considered eclectically as the species of a genus, the solution of the problem of their relation can only lie (according to Croce) in the conception of them as two moments of the cognitive activity of the spirit : a primary grade, the imaginative : and a secondary, the logical : the first conceivable logically without the second, but not *vice versa*. The imaginative or intuitive activity does not presuppose the logical activity and is the primary, ingenuous form of the spirit ; while, on the other hand, the idea, the concept, only lives in so far as it is intuited and expressed, and therefore it implies the first grade of spiritual activity. Thus for the empirical doctrine of the *classification* of the forms of the spirit is substituted the philosophical doctrine of the *implication* of the various forms, which does not destroy the universality of each, but

[1] *Op. cit.*, p. 92.

gives it full recognition ; and at the same time determines the ideal order of all, understood as a process by which spiritual reality is raised successively to higher and higher powers.

Developing this theory of grades, Croce distinguishes two fundamental forms of the spirit, the theoretical and the practical, and within each of these, two subordinate classes : intuition and the concept in the first, and corresponding to these in the second, economic action and moral action, conceived in the same relation of implication. The transition from the one to the other constitutes the life of the spirit ; but, unlike the dialectic of opposites, it does not involve the destruction of the superseded forms, because the spiritual process is circular, and therefore each can return *ad infinitum*. And on the other hand the transition does not take place because of contradictions inherent in each form, but by reason of the contradiction inherent in reality itself, which is becoming ; otherwise either all return would be rendered impossible or an inconceivable regress would be implied.

Such, in its broad outlines, is Croce's doctrine of the grades of the spirit or of the dialectic of distincts. We shall see in the sequel how hard he has struggled to reconcile it with the dialectic of opposites ; but his endeavour seems to us foredoomed to failure, because so far from being capable of reconciliation the two dialectics are mutually destructive.

Let us approach the question from the point of view of history. The whole advance made by Hegel upon Kant consists in his having converted the *a priori* synthesis, which for Kant was a synthesis of distincts, into a synthesis of opposites. It was only thus that the *a priori* synthesis, which in Kant was still an inert principle, could be developed in all the richness of its content. On the fundamental opposition of sensation and understanding, which leads inevitably to the antinomies, is built up the mediating activity of the reason, which solves the antinomies as they arise, and is thus conceived as an eternal rhythmic development. But for Croce the unity of sense and of intellect is not a unity of opposites, but of distincts, and hence the two terms cannot pass over into one another and give rise to contradictions and antinomies ; consequently the *a priori* synthesis—a synthesis

of distincts—contains the mere static unity of these determinations, while the spiritual development eludes it : the life
of the spirit falls to a certain extent outside the spirit. Croce
maintains, it is true, that life does give rise to contradictions,
antitheses (which are the leaven of the development), although
they do not exist as between the various forms of the spirit ;
but he does not realize that he is thus making life fall absolutely outside these forms, which ought to comprise it bodily
in themselves, leaving nothing outside. The fact is that he
combines two opposed, unreconciled demands of thought :
on the one hand, in so far as he affirms development, he
implicitly denies the static determinations of the forms of
the spirit ; on the other hand, in so far as he affirms these
forms, he denies development. We shall see how the conflict of these two ends finishes by paralysing and neutralizing some of his acutest conceptions.

The first theoretical form of the spirit is art, intuitive
knowledge. In this field, to have identified intuition and
expression ; to have understood that art is not merely representative, but subjective, lyrical and emotional ; to
have founded literary criticism on a scientific basis ; to have
identified æsthetic and the science of language ; to have
criticized conclusively the doctrine of literary classes and of
all the old apparatus of rhetoric which prevented critics from
understanding the real and intrinsic value of a work of art—
I can do no more than refer to a few of the main points—
these are among the great and undeniable merits of Croce's
work, and connect it with that of De Sanctis, of which it is
the scientific and systematized development.

These principles render possible the appreciation of the
work of art in its inner individual character. But as regards
the relation between the work of art and the development
of life in general, Croce affirms, indeed, that the change of
spiritual attitude which takes place in the course of history
involves a parallel change in art, and thus in a certain sense
he affirms its historical character ; but the exaggeratedly
monadistic character which he attributes to a work of art
prevents him from effecting a real fusion between art and
history ; and the result is that the idea of development,
though he feels the need of it, is external to, rather than

immanent in, the concept of artistic activity. But this difficulty attaching to the Crocian conception is seen more clearly in the treatment of the problems of logic : in the field of æsthetic it is less evident, because Croce himself resolves it in his actual literary criticism, where his lively sense of spiritual reality takes the upper hand.

From art or intuitive knowledge, the first ideal moment of the theoretical spirit, we pass in Croce's system to the second moment, which is constituted by logical thought or the concept. Just as art is apprehension of the individual, so the concept is the thought of the universal, that is to say, the self-conscious reflection of thought ; and through the principle of implication, or the dialectic of distincts, logical thought is the unity of the two moments, universal and individual, concept and intuition. As such it is judgment, at once scientific and historical : scientific, that is, synthetic *a priori*, so far as it predicates the categories of the individual, intuitive subject ; historical, in so far as in virtue of this same character it creates reality. The judgment so conceived is sharply distinguished from the classificatory judgment, which is simply the abbreviated and schematic formula of a reality assumed as pre-existing.

But we must repeat, with regard to Croce's manner of understanding the synthetic *a priori* judgment, the objection that we have already raised when speaking of the dialectic of distincts in general. As the unity of distinct and not opposite determinations, it is not truly the identification of its terms with each other, and therefore not the activity of judging (which involves identity as development), but the discrete unity of its moments : a static unity of static determinations. It lacks the dialectical character. Now, although the conception of dialectic has left a deep mark upon Croce's *Logic*, yet the conception itself is more or less suffocated by the doctrine of distincts. In proof of this statement we would refer to the phenomenology of error.

In an idealist logic the theory of error claims a central place ; because if a reality ready-made outside thought is denied, truth cannot be a finished product corresponding to an external standard or model, but must on the contrary be understood as an effort, a search, a process, and hence as

23

an internal criterion for the overcoming of error. To Croce is due the credit of having called attention to this important problem ; a problem generally passed over by modern philosophy, which still for the most part cherishes the superstition that truth is in the object regarded as a physical or ideal whole, and therefore makes error something merely distinct from truth. But it is surely obvious that thought cannot think truth and falsehood indifferently ; a thought which thinks the false is an absurdity, a contradiction in terms. Now, Croce's merit consists in having shown that the false is not the distinct, but the opposite of the truth ; and as such it is not-being, the simple dialectical negation. Thought is thought of the truth, and therefore the continual overcoming of error, and therefore a dialectical process, a development. But here, at the crucial moment, Croce throws away the fruits of his discovery. If error is mere not-being, he asks himself, how can we explain its apparently positive character ? How, for example, is it possible to attribute error to others ? To answer this question he falls back on the dialectic of distincts. The positive reality which we found in error is not really error, because it is not an act of thought ; it is a practical economic fact, a volitional fact. A man who makes a mistake does not think—because if he really thought he would overcome the mistake—but he wills : he wills to attain an end of his own, he wills to hasten a conclusion, he wills to mystify his neighbour. Hence the practical character of the so-called theoretical error.

Here we can actually see the two dialectics, the dialectic of opposites and the dialectic of distincts, at blows. We shall attempt to show that reconciliation is impossible, that the battle is bound to end fatally for both parties. And really, once the principle of distincts is admitted, once granted that the false can be defined as a practical fact and allowed, so defined, to coexist with the true, we fail to understand what further *raison d'être* there can be for the principle of opposites ; for in spite of the change of terms we now find ourselves confronted by the false as false on the one hand and the true as true on the other. Truth thus increases by itself alone, and so does error ; and since truth always remains exactly what it was at the beginning, it can increase, but cannot develop. But the dialectic of opposites means nothing, unless it means that the true and the false are not static determinations of thought, but are both comprised in a single spiritual process, which is at once phenomenological and historical, and for which error is truly the leaven of development. In short, the two principles are conceived as mutually exclusive.

But once they are asserted as coexisting, there is within logic itself a reference to the practical activity : knowledge refers us on to action, in order to integrate the spiritual unity. The Crocian doctrine of the empirical sciences as based on the classificatory judgment and therefore not instances of knowledge but practical *schemata*, points the same way. The inspiration of this theory is derived from the empirico-critical philosophies, with their view of science as an economy of thought ; but Croce's doctrine is no merely derivative idea, for when subordinated to the speculative principle of distincts, scientific pragmatism takes on an absolutely different significance. For Croce, natural science is not the mere abstract, a thing which in idealist philosophy would be the same as nothing ; in so far as it is a spiritual moment, it is concrete : it is abstract if it is invested with a theoretical value which does not belong to it, but it is concrete as a practical spiritual act. What, then, is its relation to history, which is the concreteness of the theoretical life ? Here, just as throughout the whole system, the principle of the development of science falls outside science. But we have only to consider that the moment of schematism, of law, which epitomizes for Croce the arbitrary character of science as compared with thought, is itself an abstract moment of the scientific procedure, transcended by science in the course of its own development—we have only to realize this in order to raise empirical science to a level with history and philosophy, not as knowledge of an alleged natural reality, but as a reality in its own right, historical, actual.

The antithesis which we have hitherto been considering between the two opposite demands of thought recurs in the *Philosophy of Practice* : a book which displays a greater wealth of vitality and depth of passion than any that has yet come from Croce's pen. Here the strictly philosophical theme is the doctrine of the practical judgment and the dialectic of good and evil. Croce must be credited with having, in my opinion conclusively, criticized the theory of the judgment of value, the worst stumbling-block which intellectualism has ever placed in the way of the free development of spiritual activity. Once abolished the idea of a valuation of activity which anticipates the activity itself, once destroyed the network of *schemata* with which abstract thought claimed to preordain the path of the spirit and thus to reduce it to a mere mechanism, the concept of creative freedom springs up in its full concreteness and the road is opened for the conception of the dialectical dynamism of the spirit. In the dialectic of good and evil this new idea is powerfully developed. Evil is regarded as not-being, not in the Platonic sense but in the Hegelian, that is to say, the perennial leaven of the life of the spirit, which is a struggle and a triumph over evil, a progressive attainment of the good. In this conception of life as a struggle and persistent effort, not as an easy and empty wooing of ideals and Utopias, in this necessity for the stimulus of evil and passion in order that the good may be created, lies all the seriousness of the modern vision of life ; a life that turns away from all mysticism, all asceticism, all virginity of the moral feelings, and does not fear to sully its ideals through contact with the wickedness of the world. Here, in this dialectical process, is realized that transformation, sought by Vico, of the Republic of Plato into the "dregs of Romulus." But once more the dialectical process is suffocated by the principle of distincts ; which, in order to explain the apparently positive character of evil, creates two forms, economic action and ethical, and makes the good something created from eternity and, though the terms are changed, finishes by making evil something merely distinct from good. Here, in short, we have a repetition of the same phenomenon which we have already pointed out when speaking of the dialectic of truth and error.

Any further discussion of Croce's work would be beyond the limits of this historical outline. In conclusion, we will only say that in our opinion Croce's work is the greatest achievement of recent Italian philosophy and one which raises it to a level with European thought. Since Croce—

or rather, since the Philosophy of the Spirit ; for Croce is an indefatigable thinker, and in the development of his thought may yet surpass that position—the task before philosophy is, in our view, to fuse into a fresh unity the distinctions of the Crocian system, without, however, ignoring the just demands which these distinctions are designed to satisfy. Above all, it is necessary to deepen the concept of reality as spiritual actuality, that is to say concreteness, or to use an expression of Gentile's, of reality as philosophy. Thus art is philosophy not in the sense that it thinks out philosophical problems or is resolved into a higher form of knowledge, but in so far as it is spiritual reality, that is to say historical development. The contradiction of art—a motionless monad balanced in the movement of things—is thus resolved by art itself conceived as part of the very development of reality. Science is philosophy, not as the knowledge of a reality external to thought, but as the spiritual reality itself which affirms and resolves the empty and motionless eternity of natural law. Similarly, the practical activity is conceived as belonging to the same historical process of individualization which is the spirit ; for in so far as it is not mere caprice, but self-reflective and self-conscious activity, it is spiritual activity, pure thought. In this profound spiritual identity which does not destroy, but recognizes and validates the different activities of the spirit, philosophy emerges from the restricted specialism of the schools and is historical reality itself in the fullness of its manifestations ; it is the reflective consciousness of the human reality of the world, the invisible God manifested in the visible world. This is the new conception of reality that emerges from the very heart of the Crocian philosophy, developing all that is dynamical and vital in it.

5. G. Gentile : Absolute Idealism.

This is the road which Gentile has travelled after passing through many recantations and reconstructions of his thought ; and the same is true, *si parva licet componere magnis*, of the present writer.[1]

[1] See an essay by G. de Ruggiero entitled, *La scienza come esperienza assoluta*, Palermo and Bari, 1912.

In his essay on the relations between philosophy and the history of philosophy, Gentile showed that he had already grasped the necessity of conceiving the real in its profoundest unity. He developed in this essay an original thesis on the identity of philosophy with its own history, understood not as a static motionless identity but as development, in the sense that philosophy, in creating its own history, creates itself. Hence an absolute immanence of philosophical truth in the historical process, which is at the same time the phenomenological process of the spirit. According to this principle, the search for truth is also an ideal history of error : for error is nothing but the dialectical negative moment of the spirit, the necessary coefficient of development.

The foundations of this identification were laid by Hegel and Spaventa : but so far from being developed by them it was suffocated in the external structure of their systems. In it modern thought is attaining to a clear consciousness of itself and of its own work. Modern philosophy is the negation of reality as object, as given, and its affirmation as subject, as creation, as history. To assert the historical character of philosophy therefore means asserting the identity of being (as modern philosophy understands being) and the consciousness of being, of reality and of reflection upon reality : and this leads, as we shall shortly see, to a transformation of the concept of philosophy.

In his theory of the absolute forms of the spirit, Gentile starts from the concept of self-consciousness as the synthesis of subject and object, and hence deduces three forms of the spirit, corresponding to the essential moments of self-consciousness : affirmation of the subject, of the object, and of their synthesis. These moments are only logically distinguishable, since the synthesis is primary, a priori, and therefore cannot be transcended in re ; but they can be called, in the language of Kant, transcendental.[1] They sum up the whole of spiritual reality : outside them there is nothing, except the imaginary projection of the content of consciousness itself.

To the three moments correspond three absolute forms

of the spirit, namely art, religion and philosophy: distinct from one another, and bound together by the same relations as the said moments. Art is consciousness of the subject, religion consciousness of the object, and philosophy consciousness of the synthesis of subject and object. Hence the corollary, that art is by itself contradictory and has need of being integrated in religion. This, too, is by itself contradictory and needs to be integrated in art: an integration that comes to be the simultaneous integration of both in philosophy. True philosophy is the final form in which the others are resolved: and it represents the truth, the complete actuality of the spirit.[1]

The criticism of this concept is evolved in the course of the development of Gentile's own thought. To say that true concreteness is the synthesis of subject and object, that is to say, philosophy, is to say that art, in so far as it is concrete, is philosophy; and similarly with religion. Thus the process from subjectivity to objectivity is not something initiated in art and completed elsewhere, for this would imply a transcendence; it is completed in art itself, in so far as the moment of subjectivity is the mere abstract over against the concrete concept of art: hence art is not resolved into philosophy, but is itself philosophy in so far as it is reality and concreteness. Similarly, to make religion the mere moment of objectivity means to stop at an abstraction, to place the essence of religion in mysticism, which has on the contrary only a negative value as the leaven of religious development and is therefore both affirmed and resolved in religious experience itself. And so religion is philosophy, not as a system of philosophical concepts and theories as to the ultimate reality of things, in which case it would be a false philosophy, but in the sense that it is the concreteness of religious experience, spiritual development; and as such it continually resolves the transcendent which, by an internal necessity, it affirms.

From this point of view the concept of philosophy is invested with a quite new significance. It no longer expresses a particular form of the spirit, but the very fullness of the life of the spirit in all its forms; it is the consciousness of the creative freedom of the spirit in its history.

[1] *Op. cit.*, p. 235.

This is the goal towards which, if I am not mistaken, Gentile seems to be moving. His last essay, *The Act of Thinking as Pure Act*, contains in this respect a complete programme. Here the philosophy of abstraction is finally eliminated and the doctrine of art and religion as thesis and antithesis, with philosophy as synthesis, is implicitly rejected. " We must," he says, " enter into the concrete, the eternal process of thought. And here being moves in a circular orbit, returning upon itself and thus annihilating itself as being. Here lies the life, the genesis of being ; which is thought. Being (thesis) in its abstractness is nothing ; that is to say, the absence of thought (for thought is the true being). But thought is eternal, and is therefore never preceded by its own absence. Nay, this absence, this nothing, is affirmed by thought itself, and—because it is a nothing of thought—is the thought of nothing : and therefore thought, and therefore everything. The synthesis does not presuppose the thesis ; on the contrary, it alone renders possible the thesis, creating both it and its antithesis, and so creating itself. Thus the Pure Act is the act of self-creation." [1]

We can see from this that Gentile is reviving and developing the concept of the dialectic outlined by Spaventa in his essay on the first categories of Hegel's logic : it is the dialectic of being and of thought, which alone seems to us to be at all fruitful and to correspond to the spirit of the post-Hegelian idealism. The absolutely *a priori* character of the synthesis, in this dialectical process, is the absolute immanence of thought, as Pure Act or concrete thinking. As such, it is our thinking : outside this actuality lies not thought, but the product of past thought, namely nature, matter. And the dialectical rhythm of thought is just the conversion of thought into the product of thought, of act into fact, in order to rise again eternally from itself.

Such is Gentile's theory of absolute immanence. The true concreteness, according to this theory, is actual thought. It explicitly rejects all anticipation of the actuality of thought by means of a reality conceived as potentiality of thought ; and it rejects with equal emphasis the old concept

[1] G. Gentile, *L'Atto del pensare come atto puro* (vol. i. of the *Annuario della Biblioteca filosofica di Palermo*, 1912, p. 41).

of the world as an imaginary totality. So far, Gentile has given us the bare outline of the new philosophy, sketched in a few pages. Any further discussion with regard to it is premature : we must first know it in its completely developed form.

§ 6. SUMMARY.

In the foregoing pages we have followed the development of modern Italian thought from its origins right up to the present day. This development does not show any sharp breach of continuity, as has been mistakenly alleged. The naturalism of the Renaissance precedes and foreshadows the Cartesian movement in the same way in which the dissolution of that naturalism which was effected in Germany by Kant and his successors was anticipated in Italy by Vico and continued a century later by Rosmini and Gioberti, working unconsciously to carry out the programme of the new metaphysic of mind.

In the second half of the nineteenth century, Italian speculative thought, like European thought in general, enters upon a period of decadence : the surviving threads of metaphysical speculation are tenuous and without consistency, like the shadows in Plato's cave. In Italy, as elsewhere, positivism rises with the sound programme of refusing to anticipate reality by thought, but it fails to live up to its promises, and declines into a hybrid eclecticism with an ill-concealed tendency towards materialism. Its first expressions are the work of specialists like Cattaneo, Gabelli and Villari. They have little to boast of in the way of philosophical outlook or speculative ability, but within their narrow limits they are at least accurate. The later developments show a leaning towards natural science, and particularly biology. Roberto Ardigò is the best representative of this school. His work was by no means original ; but its earnest and persevering character lifted Italian positivism almost to a level with the other great positivistic schools.

The revival of speculative thought is heralded by a deepening of the dualism between thought and being. This was already indicated in the works of Mamiani and Ferri, and the same influence causes the transition from Bona-telli's dogmatic dualism to Varisco's epistemological dualism. Neo-Kantianism, unable to develop the new concept of *a priori* knowledge, labours under the same problem. It never really transcends the old metaphysic of being, and ends by falling back into it, thus destroying the new concept of the spirit which it inherited from Kant. And finally, hovering in an uncertain position between the two metaphysics, but yet an interesting and original thinker, Martinetti marks the point in which the mentality of the neo-criticism begins to develop in the direction of Absolute Idealism.

But the classical direction of Italian thought is resumed by Spaventa, who develops the tendencies of the Giobertian philosophy with a clearer consciousness of its true bearing, due to the new Hegelian culture. With him is implicitly begun that dissolution of the Hegelian philosophy which is at the same time the construction of a new metaphysic, whose ideal is the full expression of reality in terms of the human spirit, the ideal of the Kantian *a priori* knowledge, to be attained by a resolute denial of all transcendence.

This is the road whose first stages have been marked out by Croce and Gentile. Their work indicates the beginning of that convergence of which we spoke at the close of the Introduction. In them we find Italian philosophy, like the other European philosophies, moving towards a metaphysic of absolute immanence which can be indifferently described as absolute idealism and as the true and absolute positivism.

CONCLUSION

CONCLUSION

WE have endeavoured to trace the progress of modern thought along each independent line of its development. The reader has doubtless been able to detect, behind the different tendencies and directions, that profound spiritual identity which overrides the seeming independence of the various schools and converts the several histories of a number of contemporary movements into the single history of modern thought in the various moments of its life-history.

And we are now confronted with the questions : To what goal is it tending ? Is all this ferment of thought dissipating itself in a purposeless game, in a procession of theories each nourished for its moment of life by the death of another, and each awaiting in turn the sound of its own death-knell ? Or is this death itself a moment of life ? and if so, what is the purpose of this life ? The agnostic, with his specious wisdom, would content himself with renouncing the attempt to grasp the inner nature of thought, calling it a vain pretence on the part of us mere atoms lost in the immensity of thought to attempt to set ourselves up as its judges : for how can a transitory element raise itself to a level with the whole ? But to us this " learned ignorance " is repugnant. We know that thought it not a terrifying abyss stretching out beyond us ; it is our own thought, it is the intimacy of our own self-communion. There is nothing terrifying in its immensity, because it does not lie extended before us, but is built up within us in the continuous process of research through which we advance from one position of thought to another. The history of the thought of the world is simply the psychological history of each one of us who lives in himself the moments of this universal thought.

There is great comfort in this conviction. In the history of our own inner life we remember a thousand defeats and a thousand victories ; we remember the procession of theories which seemed only to be born in order to perish. And yet this memory evokes no pessimistic reflections ; for the steady consciousness of our actual thinking is the consciousness of strength, of life and not of death, and we can even praise death itself, because we feel that out of the triumph over death our own life is built up. And so it is with all history.

The epitaph of many theories which we have written here is no other than the epitaph of the past phases of our own life. And with the same confidence we can take up the task of interpreting the new life which focusses and individualizes the various currents of modern thought, because we feel that it is the actual life which is stirring within ourselves and is giving us strength to master the moments of the life we have left behind us.

History is no source of pessimism, nor is it a source of easy optimism, but of strength, of tenacity, of work. To-day positivism is dead, Kantianism is at its last gasp, and the philosophical improvisations which at one time appeared to be the first expressions of a new philosophy raise but a smile. They were the cries of our infancy in which we can no longer recognize our own voices. To some we may perhaps seem over-confident. Are you certain, they will say, that you are not the belated survivors of a long dead movement of thought, shadows and not living beings at all ? This is a question for history to answer ; and then it will be seen whether we—I speak in the name of the new idealism, not merely Italian but also European—who are starting to renew the ancient philosophy, are, as Bruno said, in the dawn which ends the night or in the twilight which ends the day.

Modern idealism has completed the criticism of that Kantian movement which culminated in Hegel. But the modern criticism of this movement, far from being destructive, as its ill-informed advocates have believed it to be, is genuinely constructive ; it has begun to bridge the gulf between Kant and Hegel and to develop the new features of their philosophy. The Kantian philosophy, with its concept of the thing-in-itself, opened the door to the various forms of transcendence, which can all be epitomized as representing the unresolved dualism between being and thought. With his denial of this dualism and his identification of the logics of being and of knowing, Hegel virtually suppressed the idea of transcendence ; but in actual fact he reintroduced it into the very heart of his newly grasped immanence. For science and consciousness, the notion and nature, nature and spirit, are simply the old forms of this dualism under a new guise.

All Hegel's greatest inspirations seemed to have suffered hopeless shipwreck in the decadence and discredit which fell upon the idealistic philosophy after his death. Naturalism and positivism proclaimed the bankruptcy of metaphysics and exalted facts, experience. But this new movement, childish and incoherent as it was, was yet the expression of the demand emphasized by Hegelianism for the negation of the transcendent, for absolute immanence. We find this immanentist theme frequently recurring in the history of philosophy : in the reaction of Aristotle against the theory of ideas, of Bruno and Spinoza against scholasticism. But this continual recurrence forms a continual progress. The immanence which made its appearance in the nineteenth century is no longer a purely ideal or a purely divine, but a strictly human immanence.

From this point of view, considered as the expressions of new demands, naturalism and positivism are of great historical importance : but the same cannot be said of the manner in which they have attempted to carry out their own principles. Thus, while in the course of our exposition we have emphasized the theoretical importance of these doctrines, we have carefully refrained from giving a full account of them, simply because their authors are too ignorant to know in what the originality of their own position consists, with the consequence that they revive all manner of old superseded arguments, which they mix together into the most extraordinary hybrid compounds. But the philosophical significance of the naturalism which springs from the biological sciences consists in this : that the attempt to transform thought into a vague and nebulous entity descending in some mysterious way to illumine the world of matter is futile : if we would provide a true and proper explanation of thought we must inquire into its genesis. And the significance of positivism consists in its negation of all empty ideologies which try to depreciate the importance of facts and by some means or other to anticipate them by thought. We have, in short, an instance of that eternal movement towards immanence with which the culture of the nineteenth century has completed the criticism of the eighteenth.

But naturalism and positivism are of philosophical significance only because of the new problems they involve, not because of their solutions. For in its attempt to discover the biological genesis of thought naturalism returned to the pre-Cartesian period of history, in other words to the doctrine of the physical interaction between soul and body. And on the other hand, with its appeal to fact as the absolute reality, positivism relapsed into the transcendent view which it had implicitly denied. The idea of fact carries with it a double affirmation of transcendence. On the one side, regarded as something fixed and permanent, fact is asserted as transcendent over against thought ; on the other, as a complex of finite determinations it is already transcended in so far as it represents a past moment of thought. Hence the relations between natural reality and thought are doubly incongruous and their significance for one another doubly inexplicable. As expressions of problems, naturalism and positivism preserve a real value : as solutions, the first concludes with the deification of itself (and what was impressive in a Bruno is ridiculous in a philosopher of to-day), the second ends in agnosticism, that is to say, in a confession of sterility and impotence.

Positivism is self-contradictory in the discrepancy between its promise and its performance. It comes forward in the name of immanence, and yet it always clings to transcendence, whether in the form of agnosticism or of materialism. It is the desire to solve this contradiction that has caused the appearance of new philosophies, which all wish to be regarded as continuing the work of positivism. It is a remarkable fact that every thinker who has attained to a concrete and intimate vision of his problems has deemed it necessary to baptize his philosophy as the genuine positivism—all going to show that the really vital element in positivism is not that which is dissipated and destroyed in the positivist schools, but rather that element which in all our spiritual development spurs us on towards a vision of life in its actuality.

But the first theory of immanence which arises to express the positive spirit pervading the thinkers of the second half of the nineteenth century is the poorest form of this theory, being the immanence of sense and of immediate consciousness. This is the most frequently recurring theme of the period, and is indeed typical of the whole half-century.

Whether it takes the form of empiricism as in thinkers like Mill, Mach or Schuppe, or of phenomenalism as in the whole neo-Kantian school, or of intuitionism as in the philosophy of Bergson and many others, the fundamental theme is identical throughout ; it is merely repeated, so to speak, in different keys. We have observed how the principle of immediate experience brings about its own destruction, and how, so far from being an expression of complete immanence, it is fatally impelled towards a doctrine of transcendence in which the transcendent ousts the principle of immediate experience and becomes the whole of thought, in so far as it constitutes a " beyond " of thought, albeit denied and distorted into a thousand disguises. The philosophy of immediate experience breaks out into transcendence in several directions. At one time, inasmuch as the unexplored regions of scientific thought tend to solidify into an opaque " nature " lying beyond knowledge, we are faced by a recrudescence of naturalism ; at another time, of religious mysticism ; at another again, of an immediate romantic vision of those ultimate problems which the logic of immediate experience is impotent to solve ; at another, of a projection of social ideals into a sphere outside the process of history. These are as much absolute refutations of this principle as they are at the same time its inevitable goal.

It must not be imagined that this is merely a matter of a superficial inconsistency of theory. In our opinion, the inconsistency infects the whole of modern life. A passionate intuitionism in philosophy has its counterpart in the sensualism of everyday life. And just as at first sight we seem to find in the philosophies of immediate experience a wonderful exuberance of explosive energy which would burst the bonds of any dry logical schematism, so modern life appears to present a dazzling wealth of aspects, forms and tendencies that would seem to brook no restraint. But the fullness of life represented in these philosophies is mere appearance : the wealth of sense is an illusory wealth, wholly superficial, which cloaks and conceals the direst inner poverty. Its pretended strength is in reality weakness and disease. Whoever tries to probe to the bottom of this false type of immanence, conceived as a powerful explosive force that breaks down all barriers, will perceive that it is devoid of inwardness and that the life which appears to be focussed, concentrated, ready to explode, is on the contrary a life that is already dissipated. The philosophy of Bergson particularly gives us this feeling of emptiness in the midst of the most dazzling wealth.

In the same way the apparent exuberance of modern life is a mere cloak for a profound underlying sterility. There seem to be no longer any limits to the expansion of this life ; the man of our time seems to live in a dizzy whirl of energy which is always seeking new fields for its expression. But it is the dizziness of hunger ; a strength which dissipates itself—an energy spasmodic because devoid of any direction. It is feebleness, not strength ; anæmia, not exuberance ; it is in fact the life of the senses, totally bereft of all inner spiritual significance. And just as in philosophy sensationalism finds its crowning expression in the working success of the concept, and by a kind of logical opportunism which makes thought simply play its own hand against a reality it can never conquer, so sensationalism in everyday life is expressed in a similar opportunism which induces the spirit, in face of a real world of events over which it has no control, to abandon itself to caprice and swim with the tide. The individual labours under the illusion that in this abandonment he is living in complete harmony with the whole, he is making himself the mouthpiece and in fact the master of the universe, while actually this life of dilettantism means the most complete dissipation of spiritual strength, the surrender of the individual to the caprice of events, not their master but their slave.

This opportunism poisons our art, our science, our religion. Our art is darkened by sensualism, full of an empty music which tries to create a fictitious spiritual intimacy by subtle elaborations of meaning and lives hysterically on its own disease. Our scientific opportunism is still worse, because it is not cleansed in the pure waters of art. The intellectual attitude of the modern scientist combines the most niggardly specialism with the grossest form of empiricism which denies everything that does not enter into its narrow purview. And finally there is a total lack of any true religious spirit : there is only an appearance of religion, consisting of an illusory communion with God through the senses, and of subjective revelations : we have given up worshipping humility in order to worship pride, and even though history warns us that obedience is a constitutive element of religion, our modern religion is rebellious to the core.

Such is the culture which is now drawing to its end. But we feel that, although we are antipathetic to it, we have originated from it. We feel that its unfruitfulness is rather due to immaturity than to decrepitude and exhaustion ; that, after all, it was pregnant with a new culture. From this point of view this very dissipation of strength, this life of the senses, is the expression of something which even for us is important : it is, as it were, a struggle to create a new conception of life which is still lacking, a striving after something which it does not succeed in defining and which therefore provokes the spasm of impotence. Far above the rank and file of this opportunist culture, there stand out serious thinkers in whom the discrepancy between what is desired and what is actually attained becomes a profound crisis. In the course of our exposition we have become acquainted with several instances of this kind of temperament : in them we see, as on a higher plane, the fermentation of the highest products of the new culture.

Here, in response to the demand for a deeper inwardness, the false subjectivism and individualism of this culture, for which thought means the success of the concept and life is a game of chance, gives way to a worship of the transcendent, and a mysticism which in certain thinkers assumes a note of genuine exaltation. But mysticism does not further the logical definition of the problems : it rather represents the moment at which some thought, till now developed within the limits of determinate premisses, makes new claims which render these premisses inadequate and expresses the need for reconstruction.

And so this immanentist view of life, which was one of the convictions of the thought of the nineteenth century and failed to find a satisfactory formulation in positivism, fails also to find expression in the philosophy of immediate experience, which itself passes into transcendence.

The historical experience of ages has shown that the realization of the principle of immanence depends upon the solution of two problems which at bottom can be reduced to a single problem : the problem of the expression in terms of human life of history and of the material world. The philosophy which we have been considering was incapable of solving either of these problems.

Positivism reduced the development of history to a mechanism by introducing a type of naturalism, and therefore of transcendence, into the very heart of humanity ; in the shape of its concept of the blind, helpless, common herd of men ; and even the new intuitionist and empirical philosophy was unable to appreciate the value of history : for the consciousness of the historical character of reality is in direct antithesis to the conception of life as immediacy.

Moreover, the recognition of the human character of the so-called material world could not have come from either of these two philosophies : for positivism did not even realize that there was a problem, and the philosophy of the immediate betrayed its dualistic character from the very start, and represented external reality, whether as the physical world or as natural science, as something transcendent. Yet even in this ground the seeds of a renaissance were germinating. The criticism of the sciences was actually beginning to effect, in the very heart of the empirical philosophy, a dissolution of that naturalism which had solidified the concepts of the empirical sciences and transformed them from the creatures of thought into a kind of opaque matter set over against thought. We have criticized this tendency and shown that ideally it does not represent any advance upon Kant's solution of the problem of science. It simply stands midway between pure dogmatism and Kant, a fact which renders its whole position equivocal and some of its assumptions contradictory ; whereas if they had been fully worked out they would have contained profound truths. But the historical value of this criticism of the sciences is very great, if we reflect that it had to combat not Kant, but the naturalism and positivism which had rendered science impervious to thought. Thus, to have rediscovered the immanent action of the spirit in a field which had been held to be entirely alien to it ; to have demonstrated that the world of science— which is the world of nature—enters once more within the province of human freedom ; and to have thereby abolished the rigidly mechanical conception of the world which not only the positivists, but (incredible to relate) even the Kantians had finally adopted : these are the truly great merits of this huge movement of criticism of the sciences which sprang up in the latter part of the nineteenth and the beginning of the twentieth century.

Thus the conception of the world as a solidified reality set over against thought is slowly dissolving, and an ever clearer understanding is being attained of the actual immanent value of experience, which is no mere reproduction of a thing-in-itself, but a production of reality and of human values. But the most effective contribution to this process has been made by students of the history of science : this, far more than the simplificatory theory of scientific pragmatism, has succeeded in demolishing that figment of intellectualism, the system of natural laws regarded as a reality created *ab æterno*. The history of science teaches unmistakably that the true centre of natural reality is not natural law but human thought, which in the course of its evolution affirms it and negates it : and so the most fundamental claim of Kant's philosophy is revived by the very doctrines which seemed to all appearance to have rejected it.

Under the stimulus of these new ideas, the study of Kant is also reviving. For a long time Kant was represented as aiming simply at the firm establishment of sheer naturalism : but now his thought is being revealed in an entirely new light, and the rediscovery of his *a priori* synthesis (a rediscovery as yet by no means complete) is shifting the centre of the problems of science by including them in the dynamism of the spirit. Inspired by their study of Kant, Lachelier, Weber, Royce, Baillie and many others are interpreting in a new way the philosophy of science : they aim at eschewing all transcendence such as results from anticipating thought by physical reality and establishing the unity of the subject and object in the absolute actuality of scientific research. This is a theme which may prove very fruitful : it is a question of overcoming two abstractions, on the one hand that of the pure empiricism represented by the criticism of the sciences, which only knows the merely arbitrary act of the scientist and to which science is a problem without a solution ; and on the other hand that of naturalism, which regards natural reality as created *ab æterno* in the form of natural law, and to which science is a solution without a problem. We must conceive the unity of both in the concept of mental activity as an eternal problem which is an eternal solution and an eternal solution which is an eternal problem.

The fruitful principle of the new philosophy is Kant's immortal discovery, the *a priori* synthesis.

Yet it was not Kant but Hegel who developed this principle to its greatest fullness : he explained the real nature of this synthesis, the deeper significance of which Kant had failed to understand. Hegel, once proscribed, has returned to favour, and occupies the position of honour with the young idealistic philosophy. In France, in England, in Italy, neo-Hegelianism stands for the highest expression of national culture. We have seen that the living element of Hegel's problem consists in its search for immanence, the negation of all dualism, the concrete vision of reality. For Lachelier this means the inclusion of the genesis of the whole in the self-creative process of thought : for Weber, the attainment of a concrete view of science as an " absolute positivism " : for Blondel, the solution of the problem of life by the dialectic of life itself : for Royce, the supersession of the Kantian abstraction of a " possible experience " and the individualization of reality in actual thought : for Baillie, the unification of the form and the content of experience : for Croce, the denial of the double abstraction of an infinite and a finite process in reality, and the establishment of a conception of history in which both exigencies find their truth : for Gentile, the final abolition of the Aristotelian dualism between potentiality and act by the resolution of the whole of potentiality in the act of thought, understood as our own thought. In these doctrines we see the gradual realization of the aspiration of contemporary culture for a theory of absolute immanence which denies the empty thing-in-itself, and refrains from anticipating the world by thought or thought by the world—the respective fallacies of ideology and naturalism. This new philosophy does not shut reality in a leaden shroud by presenting a solution which denies the necessity of the problem, but on the contrary it contends that in every form of human activity solutions give birth to new problems and that this movement from the one to the other is not a purposeless game but a spiritual development.

Thus the Hegel who is honoured to-day is not the Hegel of the old Hegelians, who had spoken the last word in philosophy, but simply the Hegel who gave a new significance to the Kantian *a priori* synthesis and opened out a new intellectual horizon, although nevertheless his imperfect apprehension of his own discovery caused him to shut out this horizon from his own view. The renaissance of Hegelianism—or, to speak more correctly, of the idealism which has, consciously or unconsciously, been occupied with the same problem as Hegel—has completely established the Copernican conception of the world, which in Kant was still entangled with the Ptolemean. In the sphere of logic the attack is directed against the thing-in-itself, in that of action against the heteronomy of the " ought to be " and of all abstract ideals. The world of thought is actuality, concreteness, search and achievement, aspiration and attainment ; this new conception of the world as the world of our struggle and labour must supplant the old conception of the world as a natural whole which is simply the creation of our imagination, arising from the accumulation of our past experiences and the expectation of new experiences. Past and future, huddled together into this inert, senseless mass, form a mere nothing, a double void ; and are only endowed with a true and profound meaning in this new world of thought, where the past is our own past experience living on through our present experience, and the future is not a limitless void before us, but the new problem itself which rises from the present condition of our thought. The present thought which looks forward to find itself in the new problem is science, as the creation of new experiences, of new life : the past which is focussed in this same present is history, as the creation of ourselves by ourselves, as the creation of a present humanity out of a past humanity, and the re-creation of past humanity out of present humanity. This is the meaning of the eternal element in history.

And history is held in honour by the new culture : for history forms its whole substance. Naturalism made history a purposeless play of the unconscious masses of mankind ; we were the playthings of history, not its masters. But idealism has endowed it with an entirely new significance : we are beginning to understand the true meaning of human continuity throughout the course of history, and in possessing our past we are learning to possess ourselves. This movement of culture is hardly begun. The neo-Kantian schools, indeed, have already shown a disposition to adopt a historical attitude, in which the neo-Kantian movement is overcoming its own limitations ; but, as we have seen, they lack the idea of development, of the *a priori* synthesis. They can produce a methodology of history, but not a theory of science. But the neo-Hegelian culture is beginning to produce in this field results of far greater significance. The conviction of the profound identity of philosophy with its own history is giving a tremendous impetus to the study of the great philosophies of the past, and little by little we are freeing ourselves from the tangled thought of the nineteenth century, which was a hybrid blend of the most disparate concepts, confusing Kant with Aristotle and Hegel with Plato. To-day the idea of the development of philosophical thought is beginning to take a hold upon people's minds, and is inducing them to determine more precisely the exact position occupied by those corner-stones of philosophy which are inscribed with the names of Aristotle, Spinoza, Kant, Hegel—names which are genuine categories of philosophical thought.

But we still have no real civil and political history. We

have got rid of the cruder sociologies, but we have not succeeded in rising to the level of history. And it is vital for us that we should do so, because it is only by a thorough study of history that we can obtain a definite standpoint for our life and our thought. Only thus can we overcome in our social life the dominating abstract formulas, which, still imbued with the conceptions of the French Revolution, are more than a century behind the culture of to-day : only thus can we deepen, in our speculative thought, our conception of the unity of reality, seeing it as a human unity, spiritual and dynamic. The history of the human mind will reveal itself as universal history, as soon as the new conception of the spirit is established and natural, physical reality is included in the spiritual process : for it is not something extraneous to us, it is our science itself : it is our research and our achievement. Vico and Kant will thus be harmonized : and this will be the crowning point of the renaissance of history.

This recognition of history is doubly conducive to effort ; in the first place, because we can only become acquainted with the history of the past through laborious study and not through spontaneous revelations, and secondly, because history teaches us that the conception of the human reality of the world removes all justification for laziness and fatalism and comfortable reliance upon a kindly providence, and that we must depend upon ourselves for strength, because we are what we make ourselves, and our reality is our own work. But at the same time, although it deprives us of all hope in the aid of a providence consisting of external forces, the recognition of history is a source of comfort and fresh inspiration. It tells us that we are not alone and lost in the world, but that the whole of our past is focussed and individualized in us, and that what we seem to be doing as individuals, we are really doing as servants of the whole ; the contingency of our action is not outside the eternal, it is the act of the eternal itself.

This reflection brings with it a sense both of our moral dignity and of our freedom. This past which is focussed and individualized in us does not react on us by a kind of irresistible impetus or mechanical impact making us the unconscious instrument of a power outside ourselves ; it is

not, in short, simply a fatherhood for which we are not respon-
sible, it is at the same time a sonhood voluntarily accepted,
inasmuch as it lives in us to the extent that we make it live,
and thus, so far from infringing our freedom, it consolidates it
since the freedom with which we will our spiritual development is the same freedom which makes our past live in us
and determines the spiritual continuity of our history.

The departmental sciences are one of the most fruitful
fields for historical culture. It perhaps lies with historicism
to overcome the apparent disconnection of the empirical
sciences and to build up a more solid unity throughout.
The problem of the sciences only arose in the nineteenth
century. In the Hegelian philosophy there are no sciences,
there is only science ; and this is why Hegel's philosophy was
so ready to devour its own offspring and so anxious to absorb
and include everything in itself. The ramification of scientific
activity in a thousand different directions, the rise of the
special sciences, each developing independently of the rest,
constituted the progress of the nineteenth century. Hence
a new problem was imposed on philosophy in the task of co-
ordinating all this scattered knowledge into the unity of the
spirit. Positivism made the first attempt at a rough classification of the sciences ; but this was vitiated by a formalism
which anticipated scientific research by means of a pre-
ordained method, and arranged the sciences according to a
scale of generality, as if an abstraction was something like a
fungus, growing by degrees larger and more tasteless. In order
to solve the philosophical problem of the sciences we must
definitely get rid of formalism, and realize the elementary
philosophical truth that the abstract as such does not exist ;
a fact which, moreover, physical science itself indicates :
for in its actual procedure it is always concrete, even when
it apparently moves among the emptiest abstractions. The
abstract as such is a *posterius* placed over against the process
of thought ; it is simply the product of thought projected,
by an optical illusion, in advance of the process of thinking.
Accordingly, in the actuality of its life and creation, science
continually negates it.

This view of the concreteness of scientific knowledge is
a complete refutation of the futile positivist systems which

lose sight of the actual procedure of research in their attempt to integrate the abstractions of science in the abstractions of philosophy : they destroy science, without achieving philosophy. In this attempt, at least, positivism at its starting-point came nearer than it believed to the philosophy of Hegel, who considered philosophical knowledge to be the only autonomous knowledge, and inferred that the lower grades, such as art and religion, ought therefore to be resolved in it. But the experience of the nineteenth century has shown that the sciences are wholly justified in vindicating their complete autonomy. The theory of the division of labour, mechanically understood, between the sciences is another naturalistic superstition ; it amounts to assuming the existence, outside scientific thought, of a ready-made reality which can be cut in pieces and then reconstructed, each of the sciences contributing by patching together its share. Every science, in so far as it is actuality of thought, concentrates in itself the whole of reality, which is no longer something outside it, but its own internal life. In this field the experience of history can give many fruitful lessons.

And it would seem that in order to meet the new demand of thought for immanence, the attitude of philosophy towards the sciences must be radically transformed : it must proclaim their freedom and autonomy and no longer try to absorb them. Thus, so far from being hostile to philosophical thought, the sciences are shown to be themselves philosophy, in the sense that their life is actuality, concrete thought—in other words, absolute immanence.

And so from the very heart of the Hegelian culture, of that culture which seemed at one time to be the farthest removed from everyday life, there have sprung up along divergent lines these new and profound movements in which philosophy is brought back again to life and identified with it. The conception of the absolute actuality of thought in which this new metaphysic culminates is at bottom the expression, purged of all transcendence, of the intimacy and concreteness of life. But before Philosophy could reach this culminating point, it was and is necessary for her to describe a long circuit in the domain of transcendence, of metaphysics in the depreciatory sense of the word. This circuit is necessary because only so can the conception of spirit as the living and actual reality be purged of all tendencies to abstractness and rendered proof against the assaults of problems which in the intervening stages remain unsolved and continue to urge their unsatisfied claims. And if we cannot dispense with this long preliminary circuit, neither can we arrest it half-way : those who would do so can expect nothing but to be swept off their feet by the dialectic of thought itself.

BIBLIOGRAPHY

BIBLIOGRAPHY

ONLY those books are mentioned here which have a special bearing on the text. For a more exhaustive bibliography, reference should be made to F. Ueberweg's Grundriss der Geschichte der Philosophie (vol. iv, Die Phil. seit Beginn des neunzehnten Jahrhunderts), 10th ed., edited by M. Heinze. Berlin, 1906.

INTRODUCTION.

On modern philosophy in general, extensive notices will be found in reviews such as La Critica, Rivista di Filosofia, Cultura Filosofica, Mind, Revue de Métaphysique et de Morale, Zeitschrift für Philosophie und philosophische Kritik. See also W. WINDELBAND, A History of Philosophy, Eng. tr. by J. H. Tufts. 1893. H. HÖFFDING, Modern Philosophers, Eng. tr. by Alfred C. Mason. 1915. P. MARTINETTI, Introduzione alla metafisica. Turin, 1904. F. DE SARLO, Studi sulla filosofia contemporanea. Rome, 1900. GUIDO VILLA, Contemporary Psychology, Eng. tr. by H. Manacorda. Library of Philosophy, 1903. L'Idealismo Moderno. Turin, 1905. A. ALIOTTA, The Idealistic Reaction against Science, Eng. tr. by Agnes McCaskill, 1914, on which see the criticism by de Ruggiero in La Critica, 1912, No. 1.

PART I : GERMAN PHILOSOPHY

O. KUELPE, The Philosophy of the Present in Germany.

CHAPTER I

The Break up of Hegelianism : J. H. ERDMANN, Grundriss der Geschichte der Philosophie. Berlin, 1896. **On the Tübingen School :** F. C. BAUR, Die Tübinger Schule und ihre Stellung zur Gegenwart. Tübingen, 1859. E. ZELLER, C. Baur et l'Ecole de Tubingue, Fr. tr. 1883. F. STRAUSS, The Life of Jesus, Eng. tr. by George Eliot. 1898. The Old Faith and the New, Eng. tr. by M. Blind. 1873. For the comparison of Strauss and Renan see E. ZELLER, Strauss and Renan, Eng. tr. 1866. **Historical Materialism :** see CARL MARX, A Critical Analysis of Capitalist Production, Eng. tr. by S. Moore and E. Curling. 2 vols., 1887. The Poverty of Philosophy, Eng. tr. by H. Guelch. 1900. F. ENGELS, Herrn Eugen Dührings

Umwalzung der Wissenschaft. Stuttgart, 1894. A. LABRIOLA, Saggi intorno alla concezione materialistica della storia. 3 vols., Rome, 1895–1902. G. GENTILE, La filosofia di Marx. Pisa, 1899. BENEDETTO CROCE : Historical Materialism and the Economics of Karl Marx, Eng. tr. by C. M. Meredith. 1914. The Psychology of Peoples : Zeitschrift für Völkerpsychologie und Sprachwissenschaft, edited by M. LAZARUS and H. STEINTHAL, 1860–90. Naturalism : F. C. C. L. BÜCHNER, Force and Matter, Eng. tr. by J. F. Collingwood. 1864. E. DU BOIS-REYMOND, Die Sieben Welträthsel. Leipzig, 1903 (3rd ed.). These are the most important works ; other works are : E. DÜHRING, Kursus der Philosophie, 1875 and 1894. Logik und Wissenschaftstheorie, 1878. TH. FECHNER, Zend Avesta. Leipzig, 1851. EDWARD VON HARTMANN, Philosophy of the Unconscious, Eng. tr. by W. C. Coupland. 3 vols., 1884. Kategorienlehre. Leipzig, 1897. A. DREWS, Das Ich als Grundproblem der Metaphysik. Freiburg, 1897. On Naturalism in General, see A. LANGE, History of Materialism, Eng. tr. 3 vols., 1881. For works by HERMANN LOTZE, see Microcosmus, Eng. tr. by Eliz. Hamilton and E. E. C. Jones. 1885. Logic, Eng. tr. by B. Bosanquet. 1884. Metaphysik. Leipzig, 1879. On Lotze : G. CASPARI, Hermann Lotze in seiner Stellung zur deutschen Philosophie, 1883. H. SCHOEN, La Métaphysique de Hermann Lotze. Paris, 1902. W. WALLACE, Lectures and Essays. Oxford, 1898. (Appendix, pp. 481–510.) G. DE RUGGIERO, La filosofia dei valori in Germania. Trani, 1911 (first published in La Critica).

CHAPTER II

E. LAAS, Idealismus und Positivismus. Berlin, in 3 vols. (i. 1879, ii. 1882, iii. 1884). W. SCHUPPE, Erkenntnisstheoretische Logik. Bonn, 1878. Grundriss der Erkenntnisstheorie und Logik. Berlin, 1910 (2nd ed.). J. REHMKE, Lehrbuch der allgemeinen Psychologie. Leipzig, 1905 (2nd ed.). Philosophie als Grundwissenschaft. Leipzig, 1910. The so-called Philosophy of the Given has its official organ in the Zeitschrift für immanente Philosophie, which was founded in 1895. For the theory of objects, see the articles by A. MEINONG in the Zeitschrift für Phil. und phil. Kritik, particularly the one entitled Ueber die Stellung der Gegenstandtheorie im system der Wissenschaften (1906–7). See also Untersuchungen zur Gegenstandtheorie und Psychologie, edited also by MEINONG. For the general orientation of the theory, see the address given by HOFLER to the International Congress of Psychology, Rome, 1905. Sind wir Psychologisten ? Critical Empiricism : see R. AVENARIUS, Philosophie als Denken der Weltgemäss dem Prinzip des kleinsten Kraftmasses, Prolegomena zu einer Kritik der reinen Erfahrung. Berlin, 1903 (3rd ed.). Kritik der reinen Erfahrung. 2 vols., Berlin, 1888–90. Der Menschliche Weltbegriff. Leipzig, 1905 (2nd ed.). For works on AVENARIUS, see Wundt's essay in Philosophische Studien (13) 1896 ; a lucid article by A. DELACROIX in Revue de Métaphysique et de Morale, 1897 (pp. 764–79), 1898 (pp. 61–102). J. PETZOLDT, Einführung in die Philosophie der reinen Erfahrung. 2 vols., Leipzig, 1900–4. E. MACH, The Science of Mechanics, Eng. tr. by Ph. E. B. Jourdain, 1915. Die Prinzipien der Wärmlehre historisch-kritisch entwickelt. Leipzig, 1904 (2nd ed.). Die Analyse der Empfindungen. Jena, 1906 (5th ed.). Erkenntniss und Irrtum. Leipzig, 1905. H. CORNELIUS, Einleitung in die Philosophie. Leipzig, 1903. Besides Helmholtz and Kirchoff, H. HERTZ also shows a similar tendency : see the interesting introduction to his Prinzipien der Mechanik. Leipzig, 1894. **On the Philosophy of Illusion :** A. SPIR, Denken und Wirklichkeit. Leipzig, 1873. Esquisses de Philosophie critique. Paris, 1887. H. VAIHINGER, Die Philosophie des Als Ob. Berlin, 1911.

CHAPTER III

F. ALBERT LANGE, History of Materialism, Eng. tr. 3 vols., 1881. G. LIEBMANN, Kant und die Epigonen. Stuttgart, 1865 (2nd ed.). Analysis der Wirklichkeit. Strassburg, 1900 (3rd ed.). A. RIEHL, Der Philosophische Kriticismus und seine Bedeutung für die positive Wissenschaft. 3 vols., Leipzig, 1876–87. (The second volume has been translated into English by Dr. H. Fairbanks under the title, The Principles of the Critical Philosophy.) For Mathematical and Platonic tendencies in Kantianism, see H. COHEN, Kants Theorie der Erfahrung. Berlin, 1883 (2nd ed.). System der Philosophie : 1st Part, Logik der reinen Erkenntnisse. Berlin, 1902. 2nd Part, Ethik des reinen Willens. Berlin, 1904. Æsthetik des reinen Gefühls. Berlin, 1912. For works on Cohen see the various numbers of Kant-studien, 1912. P. NATORP, Platos Ideenlehre. Leipzig, 1903. Die logischen Grundlagen der exakten Naturwissenschaften. Leipzig, 1910. E. CASSIRER, Substanzbegriff und Funktionsbegriff. Berlin, 1910. For the Philosophy of Value, in addition to the works of Lotze already mentioned, see C. SIGWART, Logik. Tübingen, 1873–8. F. BERG-MANN, Reine Logik. Berlin, 1879. W. WINDELBAND, Beiträge zur lehre vom negativen Urteil (Strassburger Abhandlungen zu E. Zellers 70 Geburtstag, 1884). Präludien, Aufsätze und Reden zur Einleitung in die Philosophie. Freiburg i.-Br., 1911 (4th ed.). Vom System der Kategorien (Philosoph. Abhandl., C. Sigwart zu seinem 70 Geburtstage gewidmet. Tübingen, 1900). Ueber Willensfreiheit. Tübingen, 1905. Zum Begriff des Gesetzes (Bericht über den III Intern. Congress für Phil., Heidelberg, 1908). H. RICKERT, Der Gegenstand der Erkenntniss, ein Beitrag zum Problem der Philos. Transcendenz. Tübingen, 1904 (2nd ed.). Zwei Wege der Erkenntnisstheorie. 1910. In this connection see the essay by De Ruggiero already cited, La filosofia dei valori in Germania. For Historicism, besides the essays by Windelband, see W. DILTEY, Einleitung in die Geistwissenschaften. Leipzig, 1883. P. BARTH, Die Philosophie der Geschichte als Socio-logie. Leipzig, 1897. G. SIMMEL, Die Probleme der Geschichts-philosophie. Leipzig, 1905 (2nd ed.). H. RICKERT, Die Grenzen der

Naturwissenschaftlichen Begriffsbildung. Eine logische Einleitung in die historischen Wissenschaften. Freiburg i.-Br., 1896–1902. S. HESSEN, Individuelle Kausalität. Berlin, 1909. On the social sciences : C. BOUGLÉ, Les Sciences sociales en Allemagne. Paris, 1896. G. SIMMEL, Einleitung in die Moralwissenschaften. 2 vols., Berlin, 1892–3. Philosophie des Geldes. 1900. R. STAMMLER, Wirtschaft und Recht nach der Materialistichen Geschichtsauffassung. Leipzig, 1906 (2nd ed.). Die Lehre von dem richtigen Rechte. Berlin, 1902. On the theological movement : A. RITSCHL, Die Christliche Lehre von der Rechtifertigung und Versöhnung. 3 vols., Bonn, 1895 (4th ed.). The Christian Doctrine of Justification and Reconciliation, Eng. tr. by H. P. Mackintosh and A. B. Macaulay. 3 vols. W. HERMANN, Die Religion in Verhältnis zum Welterkennen und zur Sittlichkeit. Halle, 1879. On Ritschl and his school, see BOUTROUX's important observations in Science and Religion. Paris, 1908. A. HARNACK, What is Christianity ? Eng. tr. For Neo-Kantianism generally, see the review Kantstudien, which was started in 1896 under the editorship of Vaihinger and is now edited by Bauch.

CHAPTER IV

Psycho-physics : see TH. RIBOT's German Psychology of To-day, The Empirical School, Eng. tr. by J. M. Baldwin. Philadelphia. **Psychologism :** see HUSSERL, Logische Untersuchungen. 2 vols., Halle, 1900–1. F. BRENTANO, Psychologie vom empirischen Standpunkte. Vol. i., 1874 (the second volume announced in 1874 has not yet been published). TH. LIPPS, Grundthatsachen des Seelenlebens. Bonn, 1889. Leitfaden der Psychologie. Leipzig, 1903. A. MEINONG, Psychologisch-ethische Untersuchungen. Götz, 1894. CH. EHRENFELS, System der Werttheorie, vol. i. Allgemeine Werttheorie. Psychologie des Begehrens, vol. ii. Grundzüge einer Ethik. Leipzig, 1897. Concerning this latter theory, see F. ORESTANO, Valori umani. Turin, 1907.

CHAPTER V

W. WUNDT, System der Philosophie. Leipzig, 1897 (2nd ed.). Einleitung in die Philosophie. Leipzig, 1904 (3rd ed.). F. PAULSEN, Einleitung in die Philosophie. Berlin, 1905 (12th ed.). System der Ethik. Berlin, 1903 (6th ed.). J. BERGMANN, System des objectiven Idealismus. Marburg, 1903. For **Naturalism :** E. HAECKEL, The History of Creation, Eng. tr. by E. Ray Lankester. The Riddle of the Universe, Eng. tr. by Joseph McCabe. W. OSTWALD, Vorlesungen über Naturphilosophie. Leipzig, 1905 (3rd ed.). L. BUSSE, Geist und Körper, Seele und Leib. Leipzig, 1903. F. NIETZSCHE, The Birth of Tragedy ; Thus spake Zarathustra ; Beyond Good and Evil (Complete Works: Eng. tr. edited by Oscar E. Levy). See also Berthelot's essay on Nietzsche published in Evolutionnisme et Platonisme,

Paris, 1908. For the metaphysic of the transcendent, R. EUCKEN, Main Currents of Modern Thought, Eng. tr. by Meyrick Booth. The Problem of Life as viewed by the Great Thinkers from Plato to the Present Time, Eng. tr. by W. S. Hough and W. R. Boyce Gibson. J. VOLKELT, Erfahrung und Denken. Hamburg and Leipzig, 1886. T. LIPPS, Naturphilosophie (in Die Philosophie im Beginn des Zwanzigsten Jahrhundert, edited by Windelband, Heidelberg, 1907, 2nd ed.; it is not included in the 1st ed.). J. COHN, Allgemeine Æsthetik. Leipzig, 1901. Voraussetzungen und Ziele des Erkennens. Leipzig, 1908. H. MÜNSTERBERG, Philosophie der Werte. Leipzig, 1908.

PART II : FRENCH PHILOSOPHY

P. H. DAMIRON, Essai sur la Philosophie en France au XIXᵉ Siècle. Paris, 1834 (3rd ed.). I. TAINE, Les Philosophes français du XIXᵉ Siècle. Paris, 1895 (7th ed.). F. RAVAISSON, La Philosophie en France au XIXᵉ Siècle. Paris, 1904 (5th ed.). E. BOUTROUX, La Philosophie en France depuis 1867 (3rd International Congress of Philosophy, Heidelberg). See also L'Année philosophique, edited by PILLON, and the Revue de Métaphysique et Morale, edited by LÉON.

CHAPTER I

Eclecticism : V. COUSIN, Fragments philosophiques. Paris, 1866 (4th ed.). JOUFFROY's most important and representative work is his Préface à la Traduction des Esquisses de Phil. morale de Dugald Stewart. Paris, 1826. AD. GARNIER, Traité des Facultés de l'Ame. 3 vols., Paris, 1852. CH. DE REMUSAT, Essai de Philosophie. 2 vols. The biological doctrines of the eclectic school were dealt with comprehensively in an article by SAISSET, L'Ame et le Corps, in Revue des Deux Mondes, August 15, 1862. For eclecticism generally, see the note by DE RUGGIERO, L'eclettismo francese, in Rivista di filosofia, 1910, No. 2. **Positivism** : A. COMTE, System of Positive Philosophy, Eng. tr. by J. H. Bridges, F. Harrison, E. S. Beesly and others. 4 vols., 1875–9. E. LITTRÉ, A. Comte et J. S. Mill. Paris, 1866. La Science au Point de Vue philosophique. Paris, 1873. A. COURNOT, Essai sur les Fondements de nos Connaissances. 2 vols., Paris, 1851. Traité de l'Enchaînement des Idées fondamentales dans les Sciences et dans l'Histoire, new edition edited by L. Lévy-Bruhl. Paris, 1911. H. TAINE, On Intelligence, Eng. tr. by T. D. Haye. 1871. For the Metaphysic of Positivism, see E. VACHEROT, La Métaphysique et la Science. 2 vols., Paris, 1858. **The New Spiritualism** : F. RAVAISSON, La Philosophie en France, as above. JANET, Final Causes, Eng. tr. by W. Affleck. Edinburgh, 1883. Principes de Métaphysique et de Psychologie. 2 vols., Paris, 1897 (a collection of University lectures which will be of assistance in understanding the significance of this tendency). E. VACHEROT, Le nouveau Spiritualisme. Paris.

1888. See in this connection De Ruggiero's article, Il nuovo spiritual-
ismo francese (Rivista di filosofia, 1910, No. 111). **The Philosophy
of Freedom :** CH. SÉCRETAN, La Philosophie de la Liberté. 2 vols.,
Paris, 1849. Janet's article on Sécretan, referred to in the text,
was published in the Revue des Deux Mondes, April 15, 1877, and
reprinted with an article by Sécretan in Janet's volume, Principes
de Métaphysique et de Psychologie, cited above.

CHAPTER II

Phenomenalism : CH. RENOUVIER, Essais de Critique générale.
I : Logique. 3 vols., Paris, 1875 (2nd ed.). II : Psychologie rationelle.
3 vols., Paris, 1875 (2nd ed.). III : Principes de la Nature. 1892
(2nd ed.). IV : Introduction à la Philosophie analytique de l'His-.
toire. 1896 (2nd ed.). La nouvelle Monadologie (in collaboration
with L. Pratt). Paris, 1899. Le Personnalisme. Paris, 1912. See
also L'Année philosophique, edited by Pillon, in which many articles
by Renouvier and his school have been published. H. GOURD, Le
Phénomène. Paris 1888. Les Trois Dialectiques (Revue de Mét. et
de Mor., 1897, pp. 1–34, 129–61, 285–319). Philosophie de la
Religion. Paris, 1911. E. BOIRAC, L'Idée du Phénomène. Paris, 1894.

CHAPTER III

J. LACHELIER, Du Fondement de l'Induction, Thèse de Doctorat.
Paris, 1871. Psychologie et Métaphysique, in Rev. philos., 1885.
This essay has been reprinted in the appendix to the 2nd ed. of Du
Fondement de l'Induction (1902). On Lachelier, see NOEL's article
La Philosophie de Lachelier, in Revue de Métaphysique et de Morale,
1898. For the French Hegelian studies : G. NOEL, La Logique de
Hegel. Paris, 1897 (previously published in separate sections in the
Revue de Mét. et de Mor.). In BERTHELOT's Evolutionism and
Platonism a paper is printed on Hegel, together with an interesting
discussion to which it gave rise. For the Kantian Studies : L. LIARD,
La Science positive et la Métaphysique. Paris, 1879. F. EVELLIN,
La Raison pure et les Antinomies. Paris, 1907. Evellin's book L'Infini
is also noteworthy. L. BRUNSCHVICG, Spinoza. Paris, 1906 (2nd ed.).
La Modalité du Jugement. Paris, 1897. L. WEBER, Vers le Posi-
tivisme absolu par l'Idéalisme. Paris, 1903.

CHAPTER IV

The Philosophy of Contingency : E. BOUTROUX, The Contingency
of the Laws of Nature, Eng. tr. by Fred. Rothwell. 1916. Natural Law
in Science and Philosophy, Eng. tr., do. 1914. G. MILHAUD, Essai
sur les Conditions et les Limites de la Certitude logique. Paris, 1898
(2nd ed.). Le Rationel. Paris, 1898. A. HANNEQUIN, Essai critique
sur l'Hypothèse des Atomes. Paris, 1899 (2nd ed.). J. PAYOT, La

Croyance. Paris, 1896. H. Poincaré, Science and Hypothesis, Eng. tr. by W. J. G. 1905. La Valeur de la Science. Paris, 1909. P. Duhem, La Théorie physique. Paris, 1906. **Intuitionism :** H. Bergson, Time and Free Will, Eng. tr. by F. L. Pogson. 1910. Matter and Memory, Eng. tr. by Nancy Margaret Paul and W. Scott Palmer. 1890. Laughter, an Essay on the Meaning of the Comic, Eng. tr. by Cloudesley Brereton and F. Rothwell. 1911. Introduction to Metaphysics, Eng. tr. by T. E. Hulme. 1913. Creative Evolution, Eng. tr. by Arthur Mitchell. 1911. On Bergson : See De Ruggiero's essay, Lo svolgimento della filosofia di H. Bergson, in Cultura (February 15, 1912). Le Roy, Science et Philosophie (Rev. de Mét., 1899, pp. 375–425, 503–62, 708–31 ; 1900, 37–72) ; Un nouveau positivisme (Rev. du Mét., 1901). Rémacle, La Valeur positive de la Psychologie (Rev. de Mét., 1894).

CHAPTER V

The Social Sciences : A. Espinas, Les Sociétés animales. Paris, 1878 (2nd ed.). G. Tarde, Les Lois de l'Imitation. Paris, 1904 (4th ed.). E. Durkheim, Editor of Année sociologique, La Division du Travail social. Paris, 1901 (2nd ed.). Le Règles de la Méthode sociologique. Paris, 1904 (3rd ed.). **History :** P. Lacombe, De l'Histoire considerée comme Science. Paris, 1894. A. D. Xénopol, Les Principes fondamentaux de l'Histoire. Paris, 1899, reprinted with important additions in 1905 under the title, La Théorie de l'Histoire. **Platonizing Positivism :** A. Fouilée, L'Avenir de la Métaphysique fondée sur l'Expérience. Paris, 1895 (2nd ed.). Le Mouvement idéaliste et la Réaction contre la Science positive. Paris, 1904 (2nd ed.). R. Berthelot, Evolutionisme et Platonisme cit. Ch. Dunan, Les Deux Idéalismes. Paris, 1911. **The Ethics of Platonism :** A. Fouilée, Critique des Systèmes de Morale contemporaine. Paris, 1894 (4th ed.). J. M. Guyau, A Sketch of Morality Independent of Obligation or Sanction, Eng. tr. by G. Kapteyn. 1898. L' Irreligion de l'Avenir. Paris, 1904 (7th ed.).

CHAPTER VI

The work of Gratry referred to in the text is : De la Connaissance de l'Ame. 2 vols., Paris, 1898 (5th ed.). L. Ollé-Laprune, De la Certitude morale. Paris, 1881. Le Prix de la Vie. Paris, 1895 (2nd ed.). La Raison et la Rationalisme. Paris, 1906 (posthumous). V. Brochard, De l'Erreur. Paris, 1897. M. Blondel, L'Action ; Essai d'une Critique de la Vie et d'une Science de la Pratique. Paris, 1893. See also Blondel's important paper read to the 2nd International Congress of Philosophy held at Paris, La Logique de l'Action, and the articles published under the pseudonym of " Testis " in the Annales de Philosophie chrétienne. **Modernism :** L. Laberthonnière, Le Réalisme chrétien et l'Idéalisme grec. Paris, 1904

(3rd ed.). Essais de Philosophie religieuse. Paris, 1903 (2nd ed.).
LE ROY, Dogme et Critique. Paris, 1907. A. LOISY, The Gospel
and the Church, Eng. tr. by Christopher Home. 1908. Autour d'un
Petit Livre. Paris, 1903. G. FONSEGRIVE, Morale et Société. Paris,
1907. E. BOUTROUX, Science et Philosophie. Paris, 1908. G. GENTILE
has written a searching criticism of Modernism in his book Il modernismo e i rapporti tra religione e filosofia. Bari, 1909. PREZZOLINI
provides a good bibliography in his volume Il cattolismo Rosso.
Naples, 1918. For SOREL, see Les Illusions du Progrès. Paris, 1908.
Reflections on Violence, Eng. tr. by T. E. Hulme. 1916.

PART III : ANGLO-AMERICAN PHILOSOPHY

CH. RENOUVIER, De l'Espirit de la Philosophie anglaise contemporaine (in La Critique philosophique, 1872). F. BRENTANO, Les
Sophistes grecs et les Sophistes contemporains. Paris, 1879.

CHAPTER I

Scotch Philosophy : H. SIDGWICK, The Philosophy of Common
Sense (Mind, vol. iv. 1895). W. HAMILTON, Lectures on Metaphysics
and Logic, edited by Mansel and Veitch. 4 vols., London, 1859–60.
H. L. MANSEL, The Limits of Religious Thought. Bampton
Lectures. London, 1867 (3rd ed.). J. S. MILL, Examination of
Sir William Hamilton's Philosophy. 1865. **Logic :** J. S. MILL,
A System of Logic, Ratiocinative and Inductive, being a Connected
View of the Principles and the Methods of Scientific Investigation.
2 vols., 1875 (9th ed.). Essays on Some Unsettled Questions of Poli-
tical Economy. 1874 (2nd ed.). (This volume includes an important
essay dealing with the theory of definition.) F. H. BRADLEY, The
Principles of Logic. 1883. B. BOSANQUET, Logic, or the Morphology
of Knowledge. 2 vols., Oxford, 1888. J. M. BALDWIN, Thought and
Things (A Study of the Development and Meaning of Thought or
Genetic Logic). 2 vols., London and New York (i. 1906 ; ii. 1908).
On the Psychology of Empiricism : TH. RIBOT, English Psychology,
Eng. tr. 1873. The Ethics of Empiricism. J. S. MILL, Utilitarianism.
1863. HERBERT SPENCER, Data of Ethics. 1879. See also G. M. GUYAU,
La Morale anglaise contemporaine. Paris, 1885 (2nd ed.). HERBERT
SPENCER, First Principles. 1862. On Spencer, see O. GAUPP, Herbert
Spencer. Stuttgart, 1897. **On the Theory of Science :** J. C. MAXWELL,
Discourse on Molecules (in Scientific Papers, edited by Niven, 1890).
Matter and Motion. London, 1872. W. K. CLIFFORD, Lectures and
Essays. 2 vols., London, 1902. **Pragmatism :** C. S. PEIRCE, How
to Make our Ideas Clear (the Popular Science Monthly, January,
1878). W. JAMES, Principles of Psychology. 2 vols., Boston, 1890.
The Will to Believe. New York, 1897. The Varieties of Religious
Experience. New York and London, 1902. Pragmatism, a New

Name for Some Old Ways of Thinking. New York, 1907. J. DEWEY, Studies in Logical Theory. Chicago, 1909. For literature on Pragmatism see the Journal of Philosophy, Psychology and Scientific Methods, edited by F. J. E. Woodbridge. **Humanism :** see F. C. S. SCHILLER, Studies in Humanism. **Logistic :** BERTRAND RUSSELL, The Principles of Mathematics. Cambridge, 1903. L. COUTURAT, Les Principes des Mathématiques. Paris, 1905. S. H. HODGSON, Time and Space, 1865. See also F. DE SARLO, La metafisica dell' esperienza dell' Hodgson, in Rivista filosofica, 1900 ; and an article by L. DAURIAC in L'Année philosophique, 1901.

CHAPTER II

English Hegelianism : J. H. STIRLING, The Secret of Hegel. Edinburgh, 1898 (2nd ed.). W. WALLACE, Introduction to the Study of Hegel's Philosophy. Oxford, 1894 (2nd ed.). E. CAIRD, Hegel (Blackwood's Phil. Classics). 1888. J. B. BAILLIE, The Origin and Significance of Hegel's Logic. 1901. J. MacTAGGART, Studies in the Hegelian Cosmology. Cambridge, 1904. T. H. GREEN, Introduction to Hume's Treatise on Human Nature (Hume's Works, edited by T. H. Green and Grose). 1874–75. Prolegomena to Ethics (edited by A. C. Bradley). Oxford, 1884 (2nd ed.). On Green : D. PARODI, L'Idéalisme de T. H. Green in Rev. de Mét. et de Mor., 1896. F. H. BRADLEY, Appearance and Reality, a Metaphysical Essay. 1902 (3rd ed.). **The Philosophy of Religion :** J. H. NEWMAN, Grammar of Assent. 1870. The Development of Christian Doctrine. 1878 (3rd ed.). Autobiography. G. TYRRELL, External Religion : Its Use and Abuse. 1899. E. CAIRD, The Evolution of Religion. 2 vols., 1899 (3rd ed.). W. WALLACE, Lectures and Essays on Natural Theology and Ethics (posthumous, edited by Caird with a biographical sketch). Oxford, 1898. **The Hegelian Left :** J. B. BAILLIE, An Idealistic Construction of Experience. 1906. J. WARD, Naturalism and Agnosticism. 2 vols., 1903 (2nd ed.). The Realm of Ends, or Pluralism and Theism. Cambridge, 1911. **American Hegelianism :** J. ROYCE, The Spirit of Modern Philosophy. Boston, 1892. The World and the Individual. 2 vols., New York, 1902.

PART IV : ITALIAN PHILOSOPHY

B. SPAVENTA, La filosofia Italiana nelle sue relazioni con la filosofia Europea. Bari, 1909. F. FIORENTINO, La filosofia contemporanea in Italia. Naples, 1876. G. GENTILE, La filosofia in Italia dopo 1850 (published in La Critica, 1903). A great deal of valuable material in the form of critical and other essays, documents, etc., is to be found in La Critica, Rivista di Letteratura, Storia e Filosofia, which was started in 1903 under the editorship of Benedetto Croce.

CHAPTER I

On the Renaissance : B. SPAVENTA, Saggi di critica. Naples, 1886 (2nd ed.). G. GENTILE, B. Telesio. Bari, 1912, and Storia della filosofia Italiana. V. FAZIO ALLMAYER, Galileo Galilei (in the series published by Sandron : I grandi pensatori, Palermo, 1912). For an estimate of **Machiavelli's** position, that given by De Sanctis in his History of Italian Literature still holds the field. On **Bruno**, see B. SPAVENTA, Saggi di critica *cit.* ; also La filosof. Ital. nelle sue relaz., etc. ; and G. GENTILE, Giordano Bruno nella storia della cultura. Palermo, 1907. On Campanella, see SPAVENTA's two works cited above and AMABILE, La congiura, il processo e la follia di T. Campanella (Naples, 1883), and Campanella nei castelli di Napoli, in Roma e in Parigi. Naples, 1887. The firm of publishers Laterza (Bari) are bringing out in their Scrittori d'Italia a new complete edition of Vico's works ; an edition of the Scienza Nuova has been published in Classici della filosofia moderna, edited by F. Nicolini, with a full commentary and an important preface. On **Vico**, see B. SPAVENTA, La filos. Ital. *cit.* ; F. DE SANCTIS, St. della lett. It. *cit.* ; B. CROCE, The Philosophy of Giambattista Vico, Eng. tr. by R. G. Collingwood. 1913. G. GENTILE, La prima fase della filosofia di Vico (in the Miscellanea di studi in onore di F. Torraca). Naples, 1912. **Nineteenth Century :** of GALLUPPI's work, see Saggio filosofico sulla critica della conoscenza. Naples, 1819–32. Several references to Galluppi are to be found in SPAVENTA's works ; see also G. GENTILE, Dal Genovesi al Galluppi. Naples, 1903. A. ROSMINI-SERBATI, The Origin of Ideas, Eng. tr., 1883. On Rosmini, see B. SPAVENTA, Scritti filosofici, edited by Gentile. Naples, 1900. G. GENTILE, Rosmini e Gioberti. Pisa, 1898. Of GIOBERTI's work see also La nuova protologia, edited by Gentile. Bari, 1912 (in the Collana di Classici della filos., etc.). On Gioberti, see B. SPAVENTA, La filosofia di Gioberti. Naples, 1863 ; La filos. Ital. *cit.* ; and GENTILE's essay Rosmini e Gioberti *cit.*

CHAPTER II

T. MAMIANI, Del rinnovamento della filosofia in Italia. Paris, 1834. Confessioni di un metafisico. 2 vols., Florence, 1865. L. FERRI, Essai sur l'Histoire de la Philosophie en Italie au XIXe Siècle. 2 vols., Paris, 1869. Il fenomeno sensibile e la percezione esteriore, ossia i fondamenti del realismo (Acc. dei Lincei, 1877–88). G. M. BERTINI, Idea di una filosofia della vita. 2 vols., Turin, 1850. F. FERRARI, La filosofia della rivoluzione. 2 vols., London, 1851. **Positivism :** C. CATTANEO, Opere edite e inedite. Florence, 1892. P. VILLARI, Arte, storia, filosofia. Firenze, 1884. A. GABELLI, L' uomo e le scienze morali. Milan, 1869. A. ANGIULLI, La filosofia e la ricerca positiva. Naples, 1868. La filosofia e la scuola. Naples, 1880. R. ARDIGÒ, Opere filosofiche (hitherto eleven vols. have been published). On Ardigò, see G. MARCHESINI, La vita e il pensiero di R. Ardigò. Milan, 1907. From 1881 to 1891 the Rivista di filosofia scientifica, edited by E. Morselli, was the official organ of positivism. See also the Rivista di filosofia e scienze affini, edited by a pupil of Ardigò's, Marchesini. (From 1909 this review has been amalgamated with Cantoni's Rivista filosofica under the title Rivista di filosofia, and has assumed an eclectic standpoint). **Dualistic Philosophy :** F. BONATELLI, Pensiero e conoscenza. Bologna, 1864. Percezione e pensiero (Atti del R. Istituto veneto di scienze, letture ed arti, vol. iii. ser. iii., 1892). C. CANTONI, E. Kant : vol. i., La filosofia teoretica ; vol. ii. La filosofia pratica : vol. iii. La filosofia religiosa, la critica del guidizio e le dottrine minori. Milan, 1879–84. F. ACRI, Videmus in ænigmate. Bologna, 1907. F. DE SARLO, Studi sulla filosofia contemporanea. Roma, 1901. I dati dell' esperienza psichica. Florence, 1903. Also numerous articles published by him in Cultura filosofica, of which he is editor. B. VARISCO, Scienza e Opinioni. Rome, 1901. The Great Problems, Eng. tr. by R. C. Lodge, 1914. Know Thyself, Eng. tr. by G. Salvadore. 1915. (This latter volume appeared when this chapter was already in the press.) **Neo-Kantianism :** F. FIORENTINO, Elementi di filosofia (for use as a text-book), edited by Gentile. Naples, 1909. F. MASCI, Una polemica su Kant, l'estetica trascendentale e le antinomie. Naples, 1872. Le forme dell' intuizione. Chieti, 1881. Il materialismo psicofisico e la dottrina del parallelismo in psicologia. Naples, 1901. P. MARTINETTI, Introduzione alla metafisica. Turin, 1904.

CHAPTER III

Hegelianism : A. VERA, Introduction à la Philosophie de Hegel. Paris, 1864 (2nd ed.). La Logique de Hegel. Paris, 1859. B. SPAVENTA, La filosofia di Gioberti. Naples, 1863. Saggi di critica filosifica, politica, religiosa. Vol. i., Naples, 1883 (2nd ed.). Esperienza e metafisica, a posthumous work edited by D. Jaia. Turin, Rome, 1888. Scritti filosofici, edited with notes and a biographical and critical sketch by G. Gentile. Principii di etica, edited by G. Gentile. Naples, 1904. Da Socrate a Hegel, new essays, edited by Gentile. Bari, 1905. La filosofia Italiana nelle sue relazioni con la filosofia Europea, edited by Gentile. Bari, 1911. A new edition of DE SANCTIS, Storia della letteratura Italiana, edited by B. Croce, has been published by Laterza in the series Scrittori d'Italia. **Marxianism :** A. LABRIOLA, Saggi intorno alla concezione materialistica della storia : i. In memoria del manifesto dei communisti. Rome, 1902 (3rd ed.) ; ii. Del materialismo storico. Dilucidazione preliminare. Rome, 1896 ; iii. Discorrendo di socialismo e di filosofia. Rome, 1902 (2nd ed.). BENEDETTO CROCE, Historical Materialism and the Economics of Karl Marx, Eng. tr. by C. M. Meredith. 1914. **Absolute Idealism :** B. CROCE's works : The Philosophy of the Spirit : i. Æsthetic as Science of Expression and General Linguistic ; ii. Philosophy of the Practical ; iii. Logic as Science of the Pure Concept, Eng. tr. by Douglas Ainslie.

1909, 1913 and 1915. What is Living and What is Dead in the Philosophy of Hegel, Eng. tr. by D. Ainslie, 1915 ; Saggi filosofici : i. Problemi di estetica e contributi alla storia dell' estetica Italiana ; ii. The Philosophy of Giambattista Vico ; Eng. tr. by R. G. Collingwood, 1913. See also his writings in La Critica. G. GENTILE, besides the articles published in La Critica, Rosmini e Gioberti. Pisa, 1898. Il concetto scientifico della pedagogia. Rome, 1900. Dal Genovesi al Galluppi. Naples, 1903. Il concetto della storia della filosofia. Pavia, 1908 (from Rivista filosofica). Il modernismo e i rapporti tra religione e filosofia. Bari, 1909. L'atto del pensare come atto puro. Palermo, 1912 (Annuario della Biblioteca filosofica, vol. i.).

NOTE TO ENGLISH EDITION.—Important additions to the bibliography of Italian idealism since 1912 are : CROCE, Teoria e storia della storiografia. Bari, 1917. GENTILE, Pedagogia come scienza filosofica : vol. i. Pedagogia generale ; vol. ii. Didattica. Bari, 1913–14. Teoria generale dello spirito come atto puro. Pisa, 1916.

INDEX

395